JOHN

Writings on

JOHN LOCKE

Writings on Religion

Edited by

Victor Nuovo

*To Jennifer —
dear friend & fonzof neighbor.
Oxford. Dec. 2003

Victor*

CLARENDON PRESS · OXFORD

OXFORD
UNIVERSITY PRESS

Great Clarendon Street, Oxford OX2 6DP

Oxford University Press is a department of the University of Oxford.
It furthers the University's aim of excellence in research, scholarship,
and education by publishing worldwide in

Oxford New York

Auckland Bangkok Buenos Aires Cape Town Chennai
Dar es Salaam Delhi Hong Kong Istanbul Karachi Kolkata
Kuala Lumpur Madrid Melbourne Mexico City Mumbai Nairobi
São Paulo Shanghai Singapore Taipei Tokyo Toronto
with an associated company in Berlin

Oxford is a registered trade mark of Oxford University Press
in the UK and in certain other countries

Published in the United States
by Oxford University Press Inc., New York

© This edition Oxford University Press 2002
Introduction and other editorial matter,
© Victor Nuovo 2002

The moral rights of the author have been asserted
Database right Oxford University Press (maker)

First published 2002

All rights reserved. No part of this publication may be reproduced,
stored in a retrieval system, or transmitted, in any form or by any means,
without the prior permission in writing of Oxford University Press,
or as expressly permitted by law, or under terms agreed with the appropriate
reprographics rights organizations. Enquiries concerning reproduction
outside the scope of the above should be sent to the Rights Department,
Oxford University Press, at the address above

You must not circulate this book in any other binding or cover
and you must impose the same condition on any acquirer

British Library Cataloguing in Publication Data

Data available

Library of Congress Cataloging in Publication Data

Locke, John, 1632–1704.
[Selections. 2002]
John Locke : writings on religion / edited by Victor Nuovo.
p. cm.
Includes bibliographical references and index.
1. Religion. I. Nuovo, Victor, 1931– II. Title.
B1255.N86 2002 230–dc21 2001055482

ISBN 0-19-924341-7
ISBN 0-19-924342-5 (Pbk.)

1 3 5 7 9 10 8 6 4 2

Typeset in Galliard
by Joshua Associates Ltd., Oxford
Printed in Great Britain
on acid-free paper by
Biddles Ltd
www.biddles.co.uk

To Maurice Wiles
Friend and Mentor

Preface

This volume offers a selection of Locke's writings on religion. I have as much as possible relied on existing critical editions. Where none exist, I have made transcriptions from Locke's manuscripts. Locke's spelling and punctuation have been maintained. However, some silent changes have been incorporated in the texts. For example 'y^t' and 'y^e' and 'w^ch' have been changed to 'that' and 'the' and 'which'; 'X^t' and 'L^d' have been expanded to 'Christ' and 'Lord'. Very rarely, punctuation has been added where sense seems to require it. I have kept the ampersand in Locke's manuscripts, and have restored it to some transcriptions that I have borrowed from elsewhere to give at least some sense that Locke left them as working manuscripts and not as fair copies. There are a few editorial insertions of what seem to be missing words. These are enclosed within angle brackets, ⟨ . . . ⟩. A pair of angle brackets enclosing sublinear dots signifies an indecipherable word in a manuscript, ⟨ . . . ⟩. In several instances, where it seemed that some words or lines deleted by Locke would be of interest to the reader, I have included them. They are distinguished in the text by means of ~~a strikethrough~~. Other than these, no critical apparatus is provided.

Except for the few exceptions noted above, there are no editorial markings in the texts, no superscript numbers, and no footnotes. Line numbers have been provided in the margins to facilitate reference to editorial notes, which have been gathered below on pp. 257–64. Information concerning the occasion and circumstances of each of the selections is given in the Introduction. The catalogue listings of the manuscripts included in this collection are given in the bibliography. The bibliography also signifies abbreviations used in the notes.

I am grateful to the Bodleian Library and to the Keeper of Western Manuscripts, Mrs Mary Clapinson, for permission to include the following texts in this collection: 'Ethica 92', 'Of Ethick in General', 'Adversaria Theologica', 'Immediate Inspiration', 'Scriptura Sacra', 'Critical Notes Upon Edward Stillingfleet's *Mischief* and *Unreasonableness of Separation*', 'Homo ante et post lapsum', 'Ecclesia', 'On the Priesthood of Christ'; and to Paul Schuurman, for permission to use

viii PREFACE

his critical text of Locke's *Of the Conduct of the Understanding*. Three items included here ('Sacerdos', 'Peccatum originale', and 'Error') have been transcribed from a microfilm copy of Locke's 1661 commonplace book which is deposited in the Bodleian Library. This commonplace book is in private possession.

I should also like to acknowledge the assistance and support I have received from other institutions besides the Bodleian Library: the Egbert Starr Library of Middlebury College and members of its staff, especially Fleur Laslocky, Joanne Schneider, Bob Buckeye, and Michael Knapp; the Center of Theological Inquiry and its former director, Daniel Hardy, whose wise advice given almost a decade ago is still bearing fruit; Middlebury College, for financial support from its Emeritus Enrichment Fund; the Principal and Fellows of Harris Manchester College for their hospitality and for the honour of electing me a Senior Research Fellow; the Public Records Office and the Pierpont Morgan Library for providing me with photocopies of manuscripts.

I have also received help in a variety of ways from friends and colleagues: Don Adams, Richard Arthur, Michael Ayers, Jane Chaplin, Eric Eve, Mark Goldie, Douglas Hedley, John Price, Paul Schuurman, John Stephens, Sandy Stewart, and John Walsh. Peter Momtchiloff of Oxford University Press has given encouragement and support from beginning to end. So has my wife, the Honorable Betty Nuovo, although in different ways. I am indebted to Charlotte Jenkins and Nigel Hope who used their considerable skills to see this book through the press. To Maurice Wiles I owe a very great debt. He has been a critic, a friend, and above all an example of scholarly excellence.

Victor Nuovo

Middlebury, Vermont, and Oxford
Autumn 2001

Contents

Chronology	xi
Introduction	xv

1. Theology, its Sources, and the Pragmatics of Assent   1

2. Morality and Religion   7
   'Of Ethick in General'   9
   'Ethica'   15
   'Sacerdos'   17

3. 'Adversaria Theologica <u>94</u>'   19

4. Inspiration, Revelation, Scripture, and Faith   35
   'Immediate Inspiration'   37
   'Scriptura Sacra'   42
   A Discourse of Miracles   44
   'An Essay for the Understanding of St Paul's Epistles by
       Consulting St Paul himself'   51

5. The Nature and Authority of the Church   67
   'Infallibility'   69
   'Critical Notes upon Edward Stillingfleet's *Mischief* and
       Unreasonableness of Separation' — Extracts   73
   'Ecclesia'   80
   'Error'   81

6. The Reasonableness of Christianity   85
   The Reasonableness of Christianity, as delivered in the Scriptures   91
   A Vindication of the Reasonableness of Christianity, &c.   211

CONTENTS

7. Fall and Redemption   227

'Peccatum originale'   229
'Homo ante et post lapsum'   231
'Resurrectio et quae sequuntur'   232
'On the Priesthood of Christ: Analysis of Hebrews'   238
'Christianae Religionis synopsis' *or* 'Christianae Religionis brevis delineatio'   242

APPENDIX A list of theological places in *An Essay concerning Human Understanding*   245

Notes   257
Bibliography   275
Index   285

Chronology

1545–63 Council of Trent
1564 Death of Calvin
1618–19 Synod of Dort
1625 Death of James I. Accession of his son, Charles I
1626 Death of Francis Bacon
1632 29 August, Locke born at Wrington, Somerset
1633 William Laud becomes Archbishop of Canterbury
1642–6 First English Civil War
1643 Westminster Assembly of Divines convened
1645 Laud executed
1647 Locke admitted to Westminster School
1648 End of Thirty Years War. Parliament adopts the Westminster Confession
1648 Second English Civil War
1649 Trial and Execution of Charles I
1652 Locke elected to studentship at Christ Church, Oxford
1653 Cromwell becomes Lord Protector
1656 Locke graduates BA
1658 Graduates MA. Cromwell dies
1660 The Restoration. Founding of the Royal Society. Locke becomes acquainted with Robert Boyle and becomes a member of Boyle's circle in Oxford. Writes his first *Tract on Government*
1661 11 December, Locke's father dies. Locke elected lecturer in Greek at Christ Church
1662 Writes second *Tract on Government*
1663–4 Censor of Moral Philosophy at Christ Church. Writes *Essays on the Law of Nature*. December 1664, delivers *Censor's Valedictory Speech*
1665 November until February 1666 in Cleves as secretary to Sir Walter Vane during his embassy to the Elector of Brandenburg
1666 Receives a dispensation to retain his studentship at Christ Church without taking holy orders

CHRONOLOGY

1667 Joins Lord Ashley's household in London. Writes *An Essay on Toleration*. Meets Sydenham and begins collaboration with him in medical research

1668 Elected fellow of the Royal Society

1671 Composes first drafts of *An Essay concerning Human Understanding*. Appointed secretary to the Lords Proprietors of Carolina, a position he holds until 1675

1672 Lord Ashley is created Earl of Shaftesbury and is appointed Lord Chancellor by Charles II

1673–4 Locke appointed Secretary to the Council of Trade and Foreign Plantations

1675 Locke returns to Oxford to study medicine. On 6 February, graduates as Bachelor of Medicine. On 12 November, travels to France where he will remain until 1679

1676 Translates three of Nicole's *Essais de Morales*

1677 Meets Nicholas Toinard in Paris and forms a lasting friendship. The following year Toinard presents Locke with a set of printed sheets of his harmony of the Gospels and Acts

1679 30 November, returns to London

1679–81 The Exclusion Crisis: Shaftesbury forms the Whig party in an attempt to exclude James II from succession to the throne

1681 Locke meets Damaris Cudworth in London

1682 Shaftesbury accused of treason and acquitted

1683 January: Shaftesbury dies, while in exile in Holland. September: Locke goes into exile. In Amsterdam meets Philip van Limborch and forms a lasting friendship with him. In succeeding years, Locke moves his residence from Amsterdam, Leiden, Rotterdam, Utrecht, and back to Rotterdam

1685 Death of Charles II. Accession of James II. The Duke of Monmouth's rebellion fails. Revocation of the Edict of Nantes by Louis XIV

1687 February: resides at the home of Benjamin Furly in Rotterdam until February 1689, when he returns to London

1688 Glorious Revolution

1689 Accession of William and Mary. Locke returns to London. Publishes *An Essay concerning Human Understanding*, *Two Treatises on Government*, and *A Letter concerning Toleration*. Appointed Commissioner of Excise Appeals. Meets Isaac Newton in London

1690 Publishes *A Second Letter concerning Toleration*. Invited to

CHRONOLOGY

Oates, the home of Sir Francis Masham and Lady Damaris Cudworth Masham; he establishes a permanent residence there

1692 Publishes *Some Considerations of the Consequences of the Lowering of Interest, and Raising the Value of Money* (2nd corrected edn. 1696), and *A Third Letter concerning Toleration*

1693 Publishes *Some Thoughts concerning Education*

1695 Publishes *The Reasonableness of Christianity, A Vindication of the Reasonableness of Christianity*; also *Short Observations on a Printed Paper, Intituled, For encouraging the Coining of Silver Money in England &c.*, and *Further Considerations concerning Raising the Value of Money*

1696–1700 Member of Board of Trade and Plantations

1697 Stillingfleet publishes *A Discourse in Vindication of the Doctrine of the Trinity*, with critical comments on Locke's *Essay*. Locke publishes a reply, *A Letter to the Bishop of Worcester*. Also publishes *A Second Vindication of the Reasonableness of Christianity*

1698 Publication of *A Second Letter to the Bishop of Worcester*

1702 Death of William III. Accession of Queen Anne

1704 28 October, dies at Oates. Buried in the churchyard at High Laver. A marble tablet was placed above his grave (it has since been removed to the interior of the church) with the following epitaph (in Latin) that had been composed by Locke:

Stay traveller. Near this place lies John Locke. If you wonder what kind of man he was, the answer is that he was one contented with his modest lot. A scholar by training, he devoted his studies wholly to the pursuit of truth. Such you may learn from his writings, which will also tell you whatever else there is to be said about him more faithfully than the dubious eulogies of an epitaph. His virtues, if he had any, were too slight to serve either to his own credit or as an example to you. Let his vices be interred with him. An example of virtue, you have already in the Gospels; and example of vice is something one could wish did not exist; an example of mortality (and may you learn from it) you have assuredly here and everywhere. That he was born on August 29, 1632, and died on October 28, 1704, this tablet, which itself will quickly perish, is a record. (trans. Maurice Cranston, *John Locke: A Biography* (New York, 1957), 482)

Introduction

This book makes available to scholars and students a broad selection of John Locke's writings on religion. It is the first comprehensive collection of this sort ever produced. Locke lived and worked during an age, the last in western European history, when religion pervaded every aspect of human life. This is true of much of what he wrote. Religion is the principal theme of some of his works, but most of his other writings, when properly contextualized, also bear upon it. His contemporary readers, whether friendly or hostile, were sure of this. His friends and admirers and Locke himself believed that his writings would benefit true religion.[1] His critics and defamers feared that they would lead many astray into heresy and impiety, and he was forced to defend himself against them in long and often acrimonious discourses.[2] Today, many of the themes treated in his works would not be considered religious: e.g. the nature of knowledge and belief, the origin of ideas, the nature of language, metaphysical questions concerning substance, personal identity, the relation of mind and body, the foundation of morality,

---

[1] Locke's principal friends and defenders were Samuel Bold, John Le Clerc, Catherine Trotter Cockburn, Philippus van Limborch, Damaris Cudworth, William Molyneux, Stephen Nye, and James Tyrrell. In addition to those cited in the next footnote, notable among his critics were Henry Lee, John Milner, John Norris, John Sergeant, and Daniel Whitby. For further details see the bibliography.

[2] The controversies in which Locke became embroiled all directly or indirectly concern religion. The earliest, with Jonas Proast, was over the *Letter concerning Toleration*. It began in 1690 and seemed to end in 1692, only to be resumed again in 1704 by Proast. Locke's last response, his *Fourth Letter concerning Toleration*, was left unfinished. The second controversy involved Locke with John Edwards and was over *The Reasonableness of Christianity*. It began in 1695. Locke turned away from it in 1697, after he published his second *Vindication*. A less acrimonious exchange occurred between Locke and Richard Willis over the *Reasonableness*. Locke answered Willis also in the second *Vindication*. In 1697 Locke's *Essay* became the object of public controversy. In that year, the Bishop of Worcester, Edward Stillingfleet, published a defence of the Trinity, and in this connection he raised questions about the theological implications of the theories of certainty and substance presented in the *Essay*. Concerns about the moral and religious consequences of its doctrines were also expressed by Thomas Burnet. Locke's response to Stillingfleet was voluminous. His reply to Burnet consisted of a brief appendix to his first *Reply* to Stillingfleet. However, Locke's annotated copies of Burnet's pamphlets survive. Details of these writings may be found in the bibliography.

xvi INTRODUCTION

free will, the origin of civil society. Even religious toleration is today more a secular than a religious issue. But neither Locke, nor his friends, nor his enemies ever doubted that these themes rightly fit within a particular religious frame which the writings collected here should help to define.

If we are to understand Locke aright we must view all of his opinions within this frame. One advantage that we now have, which Locke's contemporaries lacked, is access to his manuscripts, a copious selection of which will be found here.[3] The availability of these unpublished writings, many of which have been critically edited and published in the volumes of the Clarendon Locke, with more still to come, has caused a new era in Locke studies.[4] An assuredly irreversible conclusion of these studies is the deep and pervasive influence of religion on Locke's thought. The pursuits of political philosophers and historians have been very well served by anthologies of Locke's political writings that include extensive manuscript sources.[5] One may reasonably hope that they along with philosophers, theologians, and intellectual historians will be equally well served by a selection of his writings on religion.

Religion, the practice of reverence towards God, and theology, the enquiry into doctrines and rules that inform, justify, and explain this practice, converge in Locke's writings.[6] They are grounded in an

---

[3] These manuscripts together with about one-third of Locke's library now reside in the Locke Room of the Bodleian Library, Oxford. For an account of the books and manuscripts contained in this collection see John Harrison and Peter Laslett, *The Library of John Locke*, 2nd edn. (Oxford, 1972); P. Long, *A Summary Catalogue of the Lovelace Collection of the Papers of John Locke in the Bodleian Library* (Oxford, 1959); and W. Von Leyden, *John Locke: Essays on the Law of Nature* (Oxford, 1954).

[4] Among the major recent studies that draw extensively on Locke's manuscripts are Ian Harris, *The Mind of John Locke* (Cambridge, 1994; 2nd edn. 1998); John Marshall, *John Locke: Resistance, Religion and Responsibility* (Cambridge, 1994); G. A. J. Rogers, *Locke's Enlightenment* (Hildesheim, 1998). See also G. A. J. Rogers (ed.), *Locke's Philosophy* (Oxford, 1994), esp. the articles by J. R. Milton and Ian Harris; and M. A. Stewart (ed.), *English Philosophy in the Age of Locke* (Oxford, 2000), articles by John Marshall, M. A. Stewart, and myself. For the volumes of the Clarendon Locke, see the bibliography.

[5] Two collections of Locke's political writings that are especially valuable for anyone with an interest in Locke's religious thought are David Wootton, *Political Writings of John Locke* (London and New York, 1993) and Mark Goldie, *Locke: Political Essays* (Cambridge, 1997). Goldie's volume provides the full text of three early works that should be counted among Locke's religious and theological writings, but which, because of length, could not be included here. They are the first and second *Tracts on Government* (1660 and 1662) and *Essays on the Law of Nature* (1663-4). Locke's manuscript entitled 'Infallibility', which is included here, belongs biographically to this group of writings.

[6] The distinction between religion and theology is clearly made by John Wilkins in his *Ecclesiastes*, 8th edn. (London, 1704), 143: '*Religion* may be described to be, That general habit of reverence towards the Divine Nature, whereby we are enabled and inclined to

INTRODUCTION

xvii

ultimate concern, mankind's highest interest to live happily forever in a transfigured state. This is a benefit which only God can provide, and which he offers to all who honour and obey him. For Locke, religion converges with theology because theological enquiry is a religious duty suitable to the rational nature of human beings. For such beings, the practice of religion requires belief that God exists and is infinitely perfect, that he is the creator of the world and everything in it and thereby has a right to impose a law on those of his creatures endowed with reason and the ability to follow a rule, and to reward, punish, and forgive them. This belief follows when rational beings attend to the evidence of divine wisdom, power, and goodness in nature. Locke believed that religion is the only way to perfect happiness and that Christianity was the only *sure* way to it. Being a Christian involves first of all believing that Jesus is the Messiah, the divinely appointed king of the universe. But this primary faith, which makes one a Christian, entails the duty of regular study of divine revelation, which is recorded in Scripture and vouchsafed by evidence that reason must certify.

Likewise, theology converges with religion, for according to Locke, theology is the supreme practical science that involves 'the comprehension of all other knowledg [theoretical and practical] directed to its true end i.e. the honour and veneration of the Creator and the happynesse of man kinde'.[7] In an era that required removing the 'rubbish' of Aristotelianism to make way for the new science, there are noticeable remnants of Aristotelianism present in Locke's description of theology. In Aristotle's *Nicomachean Ethics* politics is the supreme science.[8] But in the *Metaphysics* Aristotle attributes this dignity to theology.[9] Both Aristotle and Locke identify happiness as the supreme practical goal of mankind, and both make provision for worldly and transcendent enjoyment in their respective conceptions of it. As Locke conceived it, theology lends its wisdom to other human pursuits, enlarging the human mind and setting it free from arrogant partialities that cause it to miscarry, putting an end to factions and their destructive conflicts brought on by a zealous conformity to unedifying sorts of religion emanating from Rome or Geneva.

worship and serve God after such a manner as we conceive most agreeable to his will, so as to procure his favour and blessing. The *Doctrine* which delivers the Rules of this, is stiled THEOLOGY, or Divinity.'

[7] See below, p. 3.
[8] Bk. A (I), §§ 1, 2 ($1094^a1-1094^b11$).
[9] Bk. L (XII), ch. 7 ($1072^a19-1072^b30$).

xviii INTRODUCTION

These practical purposes are all that our species is supposed to pursue in its present state and so all that our cognitive capacities are fit for, but in the world to come all this is supposed to change and we shall receive the cognitive power of angels, perceiving things as they are in their real nature, and not only things but God himself, so that here too theology and religion converge.[10] The convergence of religion and theology in Locke's thinking permits treating the terms as virtual synonyms. I shall often use them singly, with one standing for both, choosing which one as the context requires.

Locke's theology is not an idiosyncratic moment in the history of Christianity that can be safely ignored by all but Locke specialists. He represents an enlightened and universalistic version of the Christian religion that in the West has been overshadowed by the dark clouds of Augustinianism and Calvinism, but never completely obscured by them. It reaches back to such figures as Clement of Alexandria, his successor Origen, and the Cappadocians, in particular, Gregory of Nyssa, to Chrysostom, Pelagius, and John Cassian. In the modern era, its leading representatives include Sebastian Castellio, Erasmus, Hugo Grotius, the Remonstrants (James Arminius, Simon Episcopius, and his nephew Phillip van Limborch, who was Locke's friend and confidant), and the Cabbalists, most notably Locke's acquaintance and house guest, Francis Mercury van Helmont. Socinians belong to this tradition also: Laelius and Faustus Socinus, the Crellii, father and son, and others, whose works were well known to Locke. In England, the members of the Tew Circle and the Cambridge Platonists carried on this tradition, and also John Tillotson, Latitudinarian divine, Archbishop of Canterbury, Locke's friend and counsellor. This line of the Christian tradition may be characterized as Christian humanism. Viewed diachronically, this unofficial yet formative tradition is the product of the incorporation of Greek *paideia* into Christianity.[11] This process is already apparent in the

---

[10] For Locke's conjectures concerning the cognitive powers of angels see *Essay* II. x. 10; II. xxiii. 13; and II. xi. 23. In his Paraphrase of 1 Cor. 13: 12 he writes, after St Paul, that we shall have an 'intuitive comprehensive knowledg' of things. This idea of intuitive or contemplative cognition contrasts with intuitive cognition in this life, which is a knowledge only of the agreement or disagreement of ideas that are present to the mind. Cf. *Essay* IV. ii. 1.

[11] See Werner Jaeger, *Early Christianity and Greek Paideia* (Cambridge, Mass., 1961). Hellenism was not, however, merely a way of advancing Greek culture, which is the way Jaeger represents it, but also, as I note, an instrument for appropriating alien wisdoms. See Arnaldo Momigliano, *Alien Wisdom, the Limits of Hellenization* (Cambridge, 1975). The term *paideia*, transliterated from the Greek, signifies the education and training of youths. In his great work, *Paideia: The Ideals of Greek Culture* (Oxford, 1954), Jaeger

INTRODUCTION xix

New Testament, in the style and method of instruction exemplified in the epistles of St Paul, and in the very important episode in the apostolic narrative that portrays him preaching to the Gentiles on the Areopagus about an unknown god, borrowing lines from pagan poets to make his point. Here we see the appropriation by the apostle to the Gentiles of the method of popular moral instruction, which itself had become a vehicle of importing alien wisdoms into the Hellenistic world.

Doctrinally, the characteristic differences of this liberal theological tradition from its overbearing rival in the West concern the consequences of Adam's sin for his posterity, the punishment of the damned, and the competence and duty of mankind to fulfil the moral conditions of salvation. Locke takes his place alongside the representatives of this tender-hearted tradition by restricting the consequences of Adam's sin to mere mortality, by rejecting the Augustinian doctrine of original sin which leaves mankind utterly dependent upon grace, by rejecting also the notion that the damned would suffer endless torment, and by presenting Christianity as an essentially moral religion.[12] Unlike his antique forerunners, however, Locke was no ascetic. Otherwordly expectations are confirmed and supplemented by worldly convenience, for the very design of this world evokes admiration, and the benefits that it yields, which include health and prosperity and other happy prospects, are constant reminders of the power, wisdom, and goodness of God. Thus, Locke could affirm that even a mere mortal life is better than none at all, although it is not the best. This tradition of Christian humanism is also unequivocally and most seriously Christian. The Christian revelation is unqualifiedly affirmed by its bearers. All human knowledge of God and ourselves is framed within a sacred history of real events that begins with creation and ends with the Last Judgment. While dogmatism as an attitude is eschewed, faith as an assent to doctrine is taken as a fundamental condition of membership in the Church, as is repentance and the maintenance of a moral life in conformity to a universal divine law.

Locke himself was not self-conscious about his historical antecedents nor did he concern himself about the continuity of a tradition other than

---

writes that this programme of education provides the key for understanding the genius of Greek culture and helps to explain its influence on the shaping of Western civilization.

[12] On tender-hearted Christians who reject the prospect of eternal punishment, see Augustine, *City of God*, XXI. xvii. Although he denied the doctrine of eternal punishment, Locke himself was not tender-hearted. He concluded, on biblical grounds, that the damned would be annihilated after undergoing a horrible ordeal of suffering. See below, pp. 234–7.

XX INTRODUCTION

one of pure Christianity. He was by conviction a Protestant, whose primary concern was Scripture and its interpretation, a concern that did not cut him off from the past, but which made it possible for him to pursue theological enquiries without worrying about what his predecessors might have thought beyond what it could be fairly said that they learned from this source. The writings presented here are those of a Protestant philosopher who, although nurtured in a Puritan home and educated by Presbyterian divines, became a rational theologian and Latitudinarian. The meaning of these terms, although somewhat vague in concept and for the most part coextensive, can be made clear enough for our purposes. A rational theologian is someone who assigns reason a decisive role in the method of theology. This role is especially evident in defining and demonstrating the general principles of natural religion upon which any revealed religion is based: the existence and attributes of God, his work as Creator, the duties owed him by mankind, and the expectation of reward and punishment. A rational theologian may accept the possibility of a revelation, and, in Locke's case, argue the necessity of it. Yet here also, reason is instrumental. It is the only reliable means of authenticating a revelation and of interpreting its meaning, and although the content of a revelation properly consists of things above reason, that is, matters of fact that are not discoverable by rational enquiry and great mysteries about things to come, a presumed revelation that is obviously contrary to reason should be rejected (*Essay*, IV. xvii. 23).

'Latitudinarian' is a label that applies to an influential party of clergy within the Church of England that flourished more or less from the Restoration through 'the long eighteenth century'.[13] Locke, although a layman, was connected with them in significant ways. The themes of his earliest writings, composed just after the Restoration, show that he participated in their programme: viz. the utility of ecclesiastical authority backed by secular power, the moral nature of Christianity, its continuity with natural religion, a rejection of enthusiasm, and a reliance on reason, along with Scripture itself, as the proper interpreter of Scripture. Through his mature work he gave Latitudinarianism a solid intellectual footing. His reputation as a religious thinker waxed and waned with the rise and fall of the Latitudinarian clergy. He did not, however, choose to join in their defence of orthodoxy, and although he shared their preference for a broad comprehensive Church, he later repudiated the idea of a national Church that was maintained in part by secular

---

[13] The term is used by historians to denote the period from 1688 to 1832.

INTRODUCTION

authority, although he himself remained a communicating member of the Church of England.[14]

I

The writings collected here are arranged topically rather than chronologically. However, the time and circumstances of composition of each text are discussed below. Where several pieces are gathered under a single head, they are arranged chronologically. By this method, the reader can identify the theological issues and themes that interested Locke and observe the development of his thought about them. The topical arrangement also serves to show the scope of Locke's theology. Although Locke did not choose to write a system of theology, he did consider more than once what such a system might involve and how it might be arranged. The several 'Adversaria', including the 'Adversaria Theologica 94' which is included in this collection, give ample evidence of this.[15] It makes perfectly good sense, therefore, to view Locke's theology as a whole. This section of the introduction is devoted to a discussion of the writings that are the parts of this whole, to the times and circumstances of their composition, and to their main concepts and arguments. The numbered subsections correspond to the division of the collection of texts. Section II will offer concluding remarks about the character of Locke's theological work and its historical significance.

1. Theology, its Sources, and the Pragmatics of Assent

Locke believed that there are two sources of theology: nature and revelation; and two complementary forms of religion corresponding to them. God is the author and the object of both. There is nothing startling about this. Natural religion and revelation have been joined together in the Christian tradition at least since St Paul's sermon on the Areopagus.[16] What concerned Locke and many of his contemporaries, was to find a safe way to appropriate the knowledge that these sources are supposed to deliver. This task was especially critical during the seventeenth century, when the advocates of the new science succeeded

[14] The best introduction to Latitudinarianism is in Isabel Rivers, *Reason, Grace, and Sentiment*, i (Cambridge, 1991), ch. 2. Rivers's whole work (vol. ii, Cambridge, 2000) offers an informative and reliable account of the context of Locke and his successors.

[15] The term 'Adversaria' means a set of topics for commonplacing. For more discussion of Locke's use of the term, see below, p. xxix.

[16] Acts 17: 18–32.

xxii INTRODUCTION

in supplanting Aristotelianism, only to find themselves fenced in by their own expertise, and when Protestant divines endeavouring to replace ecclesiastical tradition with pure doctrine founded solely on Scripture became embroiled in fractious doctrinal disputes and ended up with a hopelessly divided Church. Locke proposed two remedies. One is architectonic. Theology had to be restored to its proper place as a first science above all the rest, if the myopia among natural philosophers was to be corrected. This was not an idle remark, for Locke believed that theology had a scientific prospect that was as good if not better than most other natural disciplines. The other remedy is methodological. Locke, who was the first modern philosopher of language, was well aware of the ill effects of partisan discourse in politics and religion. Fundamental to both remedies is Locke's realism. He maintained that it was possible to look through the conflict of discourses to things themselves, whether natural or supernatural, nature or revelation, and that these realities, rather than some a priori conceptual scheme that we bring to them, determine how we represent them. A striking expression of this realism occurs in *Of the Conduct of the Understanding*:

It is a certain truth that res nolunt male administrari [things are unwilling to be badly managed]. tis noe less certain res nolunt male intelligi [things are unwilling to be badly understood]. Things them selves are to be considerd as they are in them selves and they will shew us in what way they are to be understood. For to have right conceptions about them we must bring our understanding to the inflexible nature and unalterable relations of things and not endeavour to bring things to any præconceived notions of our own.[17]

The first two pieces in this section are taken from the *Conduct*. They were composed in 1697 or later. The third is an extract from the *Essay concerning Human Understanding*. It appears in all of its editions and, therefore, must have been composed before 1689, when the first edition was published.

The idea of the *Conduct* occurred to Locke early in 1697. He thought he might make it a chapter in a new edition of the *Essay*. Its purpose is complementary to the task that Locke assigned to himself as an 'Under-Labourer' in the 'Commonwealth of Learning' to remove 'some of the Rubbish, that lies in the way to Knowledge'.[18] He worked on it intermittently over the years, but never completed it to his satisfaction.[19]

---

[17] *Of the Conduct of the Understanding*, ed. Paul Schuurman (Keele, 2000), 194.
[18] *Essay, Epistle to the Reader*, 10.
[19] Locke to William Molyneux, 10 Apr. 1697, *Correspondence*, vol. vi, no. 2243. The 3rd edn. of the *Essay* appeared in 1695, the 4th in 1700.

INTRODUCTION   xxiii

He conceived of it as a practical guide, not a set of rules of thinking, but a collection of remedies for vexatious 'miscarriages' of the mind to keep it on a path to truth, a pragmatics of assent. In his last letter to Peter King he listed it together with some other manuscripts that might be published posthumously, thus abandoning the hope of making it a part of the *Essay*.[20]

The theme of § 23 (para. 49) of the *Conduct* is identified by a marginal notation as 'theologie'.[21] It is placed in the middle of a discussion of partiality. Locke distinguishes between two sorts: partiality of opinion and partiality of study, that is, the partiality that one has towards one's own area of specialization. It is the latter that concerns him here. He remarks that men tend 'to value and extol' those sciences in which they have expertise and to look with contempt upon others of which they know nothing. The consequence of this arrogance of expertise is to put blinkers on the mind to prevent it 'from lookeing abroad into other provinces of the intellectual world more beautyfull possibly and more fruitfull than that which it had till then labourd in, wherein it might finde besides new knowledg ways or hints whereby it might be inabled the better to cultivate its owne' (§ 22 (para. 48)). The study of theology can become a remedy for this disorder, because it accommodates all other subjects of study and because, especially with the addition of revelation, it is truly mind-expanding. This remedial property belongs only to those theologies that are the outcome of free enquiry, however.[22] This idea of theology fits well with Locke's belief that it is a duty to be practised by the individual Christian, one that cannot be fulfilled by another.

Indifferency, the theme of § 34 (para. 68) of the *Conduct*, is Locke's recommended antidote to prejudice or prejudgement. It is the discipline of withholding assent until one has sufficient justifying evidence. The two examples that Locke gives to illustrate the utility of indifference are taken from the study of medicine, or 'Physick' as it was then called. In the second example, Locke fancies an infallible book containing the whole art of medicine. The allusion to the Bible is obvious. Surely he intended that his readers make the connection and reflect that there is one science, theology, where the possibility of an infallible textbook has been

---

[20] Locke to Peter King, 25 Oct. 1704, *Correspondence*, vol. viii, no. 3647.

[21] On the sectional designations of the *Conduct* adopted here, see p. 1 below.

[22] This interpretation is not unproblematic, for § 23 (para. 49) seems to be an insert placed in the middle of a discussion of partiality that has not yet been worked into its context. One cannot be certain why Locke put it there. Hence, the interpretation given above must be taken as a hypothesis on how it might fit.

xxiv INTRODUCTION

realized, one that contains a complete system of moral religion infallibly conveyed. The infallibility of the Bible derives from its author, God, who can neither deceive nor be deceived, but the advantage from this infallible source of truth is not to be gained unless the mind is 'unprepossess'd' of dogmatic presuppositions, unless it become an open mind.

Essay III. ix, from which the third selection has been extracted, treats the imperfections of words. According to Locke, words are conventional signifiers. They are imperfect when their meaning is either doubtful or unclear. These imperfections apply equally to the words of Scripture, notwithstanding their infallible author. Locke extends this application even to the incarnate son, a figurative word made flesh, who is nonetheless the perfect bearer of divine revelation. Curiously, he contrasts the unclarity of revelation with the 'legible Characters of [God's] Works and Providence' and the sufficiency of human reason to read them. He also contrasts the disunity and disagreement among interpreters of Scripture with the general agreement concerning the precepts of natural religion. It would be reading too much into this to suggest that Locke is advocating Deism by suggesting that the evidence of natural religion is more reliable than its revealed counterpart. What he advocates is a dual task for the theologian: a 'careful and diligent' observation of the evidence of nature, and a 'less magisterial, positive, and imperious' method of reading Scripture.

Since most of Locke's mature writings on religion deal with Christianity, it might be thought that this strong endorsement of natural theology is an anomaly and may be disregarded. This would be a grave error. Any shortage of natural theology in Locke's other writings is more than made up for by him in the *Essay*. The Appendix to this collection provides a list of religious and theological places in the *Essay*. It shows that Locke's principal work contains not only some but a large amount of theological discourse on a variety of topics, most of which belongs to natural theology and religion. As the reader will discover who makes use of this directory, Locke repeatedly reminds his readers of the wisdom, power, and goodness of God evident in nature, and of our proper religious response to this, viz. that God should receive our grateful praise. He reflects on the metaphysical attributes of God: immutability, immensity, and eternity. He affirms the discoverability of the principles of natural religion, viz. the existence of God, the duties owed to him, and the posthumous consequences that will befall those who do them and those who do not. He asserts the capacity of human beings to discover the divine law of nature and to obey it. He represents

INTRODUCTION   XXV

the human person as a responsible being, competent to be judged. He accepts that the universe is a plenitude of beings, hierarchically arranged, which is further evidence of divine wisdom and goodness.

The mere occurrence of these remarks and affirmations by itself does not make the *Essay* a theological work. It has been claimed that Locke did not really mean them.[23] But their frequent occurrence in the *Essay*, and the manner in which Locke worked them into it, favour the contrary position. Although the main theme of the book is the human understanding and not God, Locke develops his theme within a theological framework and gives it religious meaning. This may not have been his original intention. Drafts A and B contain some theological matter, but there is no theological motive expressed in them.[24] It is only when we come to Draft C, and to the successive editions of the *Essay*, that a deliberate theological design becomes apparent.[25] The theological frame is divine providence, the wisdom and goodness of the Creator in fitting us out with all the capacities that are needed to satisfy our interests in our well-being here in this world during this life, and most importantly in the life to come. Moreover, because our capacities are such that we cannot know the whole of being or even an appreciable part of it, divine providence must be recognized in spite of our limitations. Locke's programmatic statements and the admonitions that accompany them are significant here.[26] It is as though he is advocating a sort of passive obedience of the mind. This may have been his intention in adding the motto from Ecclesiastes 11: 5 to the title page of the fourth

---

[23] This is the opinion of Leo Strauss and his school. See his *Natural Right and History* (Chicago, 1954), 165–6, 202–51, most especially Strauss's interpretation of Locke's 'caution', pp. 206 ff. Locke is depicted here as a cautious man of affairs (in contrast to a cautious scholar) who 'would try to enlist all respectable prejudices [in particular, Christianity] in the service of a good [worldly] cause'. In the Introduction to a new edition of Locke's *Essays on the Law of Nature* (Robert Horvitz, Jenny Strauss Clay, and Diskin Clay (eds.), *John Locke Questions concerning the Law of Nature* (Ithaca, 1990)), Robert Horvitz denies that the *Essays/Questions* (neither title is Locke's) express a Christian theistic viewpoint; and in the Translator's Introduction, Diskin Clay remarks on the two main 'voices' in the text: that of a Christian theist, and a 'more sustained' pagan voice. See the review of this new edition by M. A. Stewart in *The Locke Newsletter*, 23 (1992), 145–65. For another Straussian view of Locke, see Thomas L. Pangle, *The Spirit of Modern Republicanism* (Chicago, 1988), 198–230.

[24] Peter H. Nidditch and G. A. J. Rogers (eds.), *John Locke, Drafts for the Essay concerning Human Understanding*, i, *Drafts A and B* (Oxford, 1990), 10, 41, 43, 65–6, 71, 82, 119, 121, 127, 269.

[25] Draft C (The Pierpont Morgan Library, MS 998) consists of a version of Bks. I and II of the *Essay*. It is dated 1685. A critical edition of it will appear in vol. ii of *Drafts*.

[26] See *Essay* I. i. 3–5; I. ii. 1; but compare with I. iv. 25.

INTRODUCTION

edition. Revisions of chapters and additions, in particular the chapters on Power (II. xxi) and Identity and Diversity (II. xxvii), also suggest that Locke was progressively working the *Essay* up into a work of natural theology.[27] Space allows only the introduction of this claim and not a justification of it. There is, in any case, sufficient evidence in the Appendix to convince any reader that the *Essay* contains a good deal of theological writing.

The expression 'the pragmatics of assent' used in the title of this section requires comment. It is meant to be reminiscent of another expression that has gained currency today and has been employed by some of Locke's interpreters and critics, viz. 'the ethics of belief'.[28] I prefer the former to the latter, because I think that it more correctly describes Locke's programme, which is to assist the mind on the pathway to truth.[29] 'Ethics of belief' is misleading if it is taken to mean that we have a moral obligation to accept or reject certain propositions as true according to the weight of evidence available to us; that, therefore, assent must be voluntary, since it is an obligation; and, accordingly, that the giving of assent is subject to moral praise or blame. As Locke represents it, the pursuit of truth is more a matter of interest than of obligation, one that is better served by removing obstacles on the way to truth than by moralizing about its outcomes. These obstacles inhibit enquiry and handicap judgement. So long as they remain, to enquire whether assent is voluntary is idle; once they are removed, Locke supposes that, human frailties notwithstanding, judgement and the other rational faculties will take care of themselves. They may be relied upon just because they have been contrived by God to discover truth. One of the tasks of natural theology is to confirm our spontaneous confidence in our natural faculties and make us content to live within their limitations. There are sufficient places in the *Essay* that address this task to warrant the conclusion that Locke was sure that it could be accomplished.

---

[27] For an insightful account of Locke's intellectual progress from the *Drafts* to the *Essay* see Ian Harris, *The Mind of John Locke*, 1st edn. (Cambridge, 1994), 127–59, 252–79.

[28] See J. A. Passmore, 'Locke and the Ethics of Belief', in Vere Chapell (ed.), *Locke* (Oxford, 1998), 279–99; also Nicholas Wolterstorff, *John Locke and the Ethics of Belief* (Cambridge, 1996), esp. 218–26.

[29] I also prefer the term 'assent' to 'belief'. First, because, as Passmore has observed, it is more Locke's word than is 'belief'; secondly, because its sense is more circumscribed, signifying only the act of taking a proposition to be true or false; and thirdly, because it keeps one free of the ambiguity of the term 'belief' in contemporary analytic philosophical discourse.

INTRODUCTION   xxvii

2. Morality and Religion

'Of Ethick in General' appears to be a preliminary draft for a chapter of
the *Essay*. The numbers at the top of the page indicate that Locke meant it
to be the final chapter. Von Leyden estimates that it was composed
towards the end of Locke's exile in Holland, *c.* 1687, although almost a
whole paragraph of it appears to have been taken from Draft B of the
Essay. Hence a part of it must have been written as early as 1671.[30]
'Ethica' and 'Sacerdos' bear the notations 92 and 98 respectively,
signifying, according to Locke's practice, 1692 and 1698.

'Of Ethick in General' is primarily concerned with the foundations of
morality, but it includes other interesting content as well: the
eudaimonistic principle that the main business of human life is the pursuit
of happiness and the avoidance of misery; the hedonistic principle, that
happiness and misery are a function of pleasure and pain, which are also the
basis on which we distinguish good from evil; the cultural pluralist
principle, that while there seems to be no society without a morality, nor
any that lacks distinctions between good and bad, virtue and vice, yet the
meanings of these terms are just as various as are human pursuits of
happiness; and the idea of morality as conformity of an action to a rule or as
following a rule. Also interesting is Locke's use of his doctrine of complex
ideas, or mixed modes, to explain this relativity of moral discourse.

Locke's expression of surprise that in antiquity morality should have
been treated as a separate discipline, distinct from theology, leads to the
question of foundations. Morality in antiquity was the province of
philosophers. They failed to carry out their task, because they made no
attempt to ground their doctrine on the principles of natural religion,
viz. that the moral law is a divine law with sanctions to follow in the life
to come. Rather they were guided by the values implied in cultivated
moral discourse and by the sanctions of social reputation and disgrace.
Had they attempted what was needed, they would have become divines,
for morality is properly the business of divines. Of course, they would
have been natural divines.

Locke's decision to abandon this chapter has been taken as evidence of
his disillusionment with this natural theological project.[31] The chapter

---

[30] See Von Leyden, *John Locke: Essays on the Law of Nature*, 69–72; also Goldie, *Locke: Political Essays*, 298, and 300 n. 67. Section 10 of 'Of Ethick in General', which treats a law of nature, is taken from Draft B, Nidditch and Rogers, *John Locke, Drafts*, 269–70.

[31] John C. Higgins-Biddle, Introduction to *The Reasonableness of Christianity*, pp. xcvii–cviii; Marshall, *John Locke*, 385 ff.; Harris, *The Mind of John Locke*, 268–89, 290–317.

xxviii INTRODUCTION

breaks off just where the demonstration should begin. His petulant response to those who pressed him to complete it is taken as evidence that he came to believe the project impossible.[32] It is further supposed that in *The Reasonableness of Christianity* he attempted to compensate for this, by appealing to revelation to provide what natural theology could not. The difficulty with this hypothesis is that it overlooks that at least the possibility of a natural theological founding of morality, if not the albeit imperfect actuality of it, is fundamental to the case for Christianity made in the *Reasonableness*. More will be said about this later. Here I shall offer another, more modest, hypothesis. Locke abandoned this chapter not because of disillusionment with the natural theology project, but because of his dissatisfaction with what he had written here about it. It is not hard to imagine what he found wrong with the chapter, especially when one compares it with the two succeeding pieces. The account that it gives of morality is problematic, because it makes the law of nature depend on the mere will of a lawmaker. It thereby loses any real distinction between natural and positive law.

'Ethica 92' elaborates Locke's thoughts about the eudaimonistic and hedonistic principles. What Locke attempts to do in this piece is to forge a link between pleasurable pursuits and the practice of morality. The good that attracts the rational agent is not the base pleasure of the moment. There is an ascent of the mind, from the momentary sensual to the contemplative to universal love. This is a mere sketch, not a system with demonstrations, but at least we perceive a tendency of thought to discover a more satisfying and universally acceptable moral content on mere rational grounds.

'Sacerdos 98' provides a record of Locke's occasional thoughts concerning paganism, morality, and Christianity. The occasion of these thoughts seems to have been his reading in Pierre Bayle's *Pensées diverses de la comète*, which he cites in an appended note.[33] Mark Goldie's description of 'Sacerdos' as a commentary on § 127 of Bayle's book is, I think, a misrepresentation of it, for in 'Sacerdos' Locke's thoughts follow

---

[32] See Locke, *Correspondence*, vol. iv, nos. 1307, 1309, 1312. See also Locke's response to Burnet, *An Answer to Remarks upon An Essay concerning Human Understanding, &c.* It was originally published in a Postscript to Locke, *Reply to the Bishop of Worcester* (London, 1697). Reprinted with Burnet's text and replies in *Remarks Upon an Essay concerning Humane Understanding* (New York, 1984).

[33] The first edition of this work, a copy of which Locke owned, was entitled *Lettre à M. L. A. D. C., docteur de Sorbonne, Où il est prouvé par plusiers raisons tirées de la philosophie, & de la theologie, qui les comits ne sont point le presage d'aucun malheur*, and was published in Cologne in 1682 (LL no. 237ᵃ).

INTRODUCTION   xxix

a different course from the one pursued by Bayle.[34] Bayle uses the
example of paganism to illustrate a contradiction among Roman
Catholic philosophers and literati who, although they are attentive to
reason and accept the rational criticism of Roman traditions privately,
nevertheless continue to adhere to them publicly. Locke, on the other
hand, cites the division in pagan society between religion and morality in
order to contrast it with the excellence of the Christian revelation which
unites them. A *sacerdos* or priest is a mediator between gods and men,
whose expertise is in 'the arts of propitiation and atonement'. These arts
are the means by which priests in pagan antiquity were supposed to win
the favour of the gods for their human clients. Philosophers, on the other
hand, were teachers of useful arts and of morality. In antiquity,
philosophers and priests observed a strict division of labour and kept
their domains separate and distinct. Christ, who brought true religion
from heaven, abolished this division and united the two offices in his
own person, thereby also uniting the domains of revelation and reason.
He abolished the need for priestcraft and refounded religion on morality.
As the divine teacher of a moral religion, he may be styled as the new
archetype of the philosophical divine whose principal concern is moral
religion.

3. 'Adversaria Theologica 94'

The title 'Adversaria Theologica 94' belongs to a notebook in Locke's
library. The Latin word 'adversaria' means an account book or
notebook.[35] Locke used the word in three senses: to signify either the
practice of note-taking, or its results, viz. extracts arranged in a notebook
under general heads, or a list of topics of commonplaces. Successful
commonplacing requires not only an adequate set of topics but also an
efficient way to facilitate retrieval. Locke wrote a small work describing a
method of commonplacing that is more or less followed in this
notebook.[36]

The date in the title indicates that Locke set up the notebook sometime

[34] Goldie, *Locke: Political Essays*, 344. It should be noted that Locke's citation of Bayle
is incidental. He cites the *Pensées diverses*, § 127 only as the source of a text from Cicero
that he quotes in a note to 'Sacerdos'. In the light of this, it might be more accurate to
regard 'Sacerdos' as an elaboration of some lines from Cicero on the separation of religion
and moral philosophy in pagan Rome that Locke read in Bayle.

[35] *Oxford Latin Dictionary* (Oxford, 1968).

[36] *A New Method of a Common-Place-Book, Posthumous Works* (London, 1706), 311–
36. For other lists of commonplaces, see Goldie, *Locke: Political Essays*, 215, 265–7, 288–
9. See also BOD MS Locke f. 15, p. 120.

xxx INTRODUCTION

in 1694. In a letter to Limborch dated 11 December 1694, he wrote of his plan to devote himself to the study of theology.[37] It seems most likely that by the end of 1694 Locke had the notebook ready for use. What is remarkable about the 'Adversaria' is its comprehensiveness. It can be used as a checklist of all the topics of enquiry and dispute that engaged European scholars in the seventeenth century. It portrays the intellectual world in which Locke lived. Almost everything that he wrote about falls under one or more of its heads. What is most noteworthy is that all of these topics are subsumed under the general heading of *theology*. Thus, it appears that at this time Locke began to construct a theological map and historical gazetteer of the world. His reason for doing this is unknown. In his letter to Limborch, he suggests that it was the availability of leisure, but this applies to the opportunity and not the motive.

The world described by this list of topics is one full of beings, a plenitude, with God, who is possibly three, but most certainly one, above all, *Deus Optimus Maximus*, God the best and greatest of beings. Beneath him and because of him in decreasing order of excellence, we find the invisible realm of spirits, mankind, animals, and lifeless matter. The last three inhabit the visible world, which consists of planetary systems. This is no eternal world, but one in between whose beginning and end a sacred history unfolds from the fall of angels to the final consummation.

Some of the topics listed may strike the reader as curious for Locke. One may well wonder why under the heading 'Anima humana', the human soul, he listed the pre-existence and revolution of the soul. The notes entered under these heads in the text treat the materiality of the human soul, its mortality and corruptibility, a position that Locke, following St Paul, seems to favour in his comments. Hence, while it can be safely concluded that Locke accepted neither the pre-existence of the human soul prior to a particular life (although, as will be observed shortly, he did come to accept the pre-existence of the rational nature of the Messiah), nor the Platonic doctrine of the revolution of souls, he did not at this time wish to close his mind to them. The nature and origin of spiritual beings are part of Christian sacred history. His curiosity about their faculties may have been aroused by his expectation that the redeemed would exist in a spiritual state and possess the angelic

---

[37] *Correspondence*, v. 1826. For a more detailed account of the 'Adversaria' see my paper, 'Locke's Theology 1694–1704', in Stewart (ed.), *English Philosophy in the Age of Locke*, 184–94.

INTRODUCTION

faculties.[38] The set of topics under 'Ethics or the Duty of Man' is curious. One wonders why Locke considered it necessary to make such a detailed list of beings to whom duties are owed instead keeping to the standard three: God, others, and oneself. What sort of duties did he think we have towards evil spirits?

Locke made two sorts of entries in his notebooks: extracts from his reading and his own thoughts on various subjects. In the latter case, he most often but not always appended his initials, 'JL'. Some entries are combinations of both. Some of the initialled entries, especially those that found their way into his books, represent considered opinions, others are more conjectural, while still others may have had only a passing interest for him. None of them record idle thoughts. One can hardly doubt that all of the entries, whether initialled or not, are about topics that interested Locke, but just what was the nature of that interest and where it led him is not immediately evident and has to be decided in each particular case.

Although the approximate time when Locke began this notebook seems assured, the date of the particular entries remains uncertain. He did not, as he prescribes in his *New Method of a Common-Place-Book*, fill the pages in sequence. There is a gap of several pages between the list of topics and the first entries, and further page gaps between successive entries. Hence we cannot be sure that the temporal order of his inscriptions on these pages follows the order in which they are found in the book. Two of the entries, *Lex Operum* and *Lex Fidei*, the law of works and the law of faith, anticipate a central theme of *The Reasonableness of Christianity*. They are written on the later pages. If we assume that Locke did write the comments in something like the order in which they make their appearance, then it would follow that all the entries were written in a period that begins around December 1694 and ends when Locke became engaged in writing the *Reasonableness*. In sum, these may be notes taken by Locke during a period of about one to three months. There is at least one reason to take exception to this dating and the supposition that in the 'Adversaria' Locke filled the pages in temporal order. Locke's note on 1 Cor. 15: 44 in his *Paraphrase and Notes on the Epistles of St. Paul*, which was probably not composed before 1699, contains some lines that are almost identical to ones found in the 'Adversaria' under the head, *anima humana immaterialis/materialis*.[39] This entry occurs several pages prior to the pages containing notes on *Lex*

---

[38] See above, p. xviii, n. 10. [39] See *Paraphrase and Notes*, i. 254.

xxxii INTRODUCTION

Operum/Lex Fidei, which conforms to remarks on this theme in the *Reasonableness*. However, it remains plausible that Locke wrote these notes on 1 Corinthians earlier, in 1694, and later, in 1699, incorporated them in his *Paraphrase and Notes*.

The notes fall mostly into two groups: some concerning the Trinity, including the divinity of Christ and of the Holy Spirit; and others concerning the human soul. The former consist mostly of extracts or summaries drawn from the works of others. The signed entries preponderate in the second group. For his notes on the Trinity, Locke extracted from writings by the English Unitarian divine John Biddle (Bidle).[40] Extracts from the 'Adversaria Theologica 94' published in Peter King's biography are selected only from these. They are presented in a way that gives the impression that Locke was leaning towards Unitarianism.[41] However, King leaves out one set of notes in which the writings of Biddle are quoted extensively. These notes present evidence for and against the mere humanity of Christ. Those in favour preponderate, and they all come from Biddle. On the other side, under the heading 'Christ is not a mere man', there is a single argument. This one, however, is signed with Locke's initials. Locke cites 1 Peter 1: 11, and remarks that Christ could not be a mere man because his spirit inspired the Old Testament prophets.

In between the first set of trinitarian entries are two brief notes whose brevity should not be taken as reason for their unimportance. They are set on successive pages, and entitled 'Cultus' and 'Propitio Placamen'. The first concerns the act of worship: at the command of the King the whole congregation worships God who is Lord and King. The second concerns access to the means of atonement by which one is restored to favour with God and is an admonition that God must disapprove of any attempt to limit access to the means of grace. Oddly enough, Locke uses a quotation from Cicero to make the point. Together they represent the idea of the worshipping church, whose ruler is Christ the divine King, and which excludes no one from the means of grace offered in public worship.

The longest initialized entry in the 'Adversaria'—it is initialled in four places—appears among a set of arguments gathered on facing pages for

---

[40] For bibliographical details, see the notes on the text.

[41] King, *The Life of John Locke, with extracts from his correspondence, journals and common-place books* (new edn. London, 1830; repr. Bristol, 1991), ii. 186–94. King includes Locke's notes under 'Trinitas/Non-Trinitas' and 'Christus Deus Supremus/ Christus non Deus Supremus'.

INTRODUCTION   xxxiii

and against the materiality of the human soul. It is a striking example of Locke relying on Scripture to resolve what to us must seem a purely philosophical problem. This entry, numbered '2', consists of a smaller set of arguments or evidences, mostly biblical citations. It is located on the side favouring immateriality. However, it does double duty, for when he comes to the corresponding place on the materialist side, Locke cites this very set of arguments in support of materialism.[42] Needless to say, it must be read carefully. Briefly, Locke appears to affirm the identity of every redeemed man, whose body, although not numerically the same, is mortal before the resurrection and immortal after it. However, he makes it clear that it is not just the body that is resurrected but the whole man who, before this, was altogether mortal. Thus he seems to be affirming the doctrine of mortalism, that the whole man, body and soul, is mortal, while denying the resurrection of the same body.[43] In this same long note, Locke also admits the possibility, following St Paul, that matter may be capable of animality and spirituality, that is, of life and thought. This is a much bolder affirmation than the remark made in *Essay* IV. iii. 6 that God might 'superadd to matter a Faculty of Thinking'.[44] If the dating of this entry were to be set at winter 1694–5, then it would have come not long after Locke had completed writing the chapter on personal identity (II. xxvii), which was added to the second edition of the *Essay*. What is interesting is that Locke considers some of the same topics that he did in that chapter, but here almost wholly in the context of biblical revelation.

4. Inspiration, Revelation, Scripture, and Faith

The writings gathered in this section treat a miscellany of topics, all of them related to receiving and appropriating revelation.

Locke's manuscript entitled 'Immediate Inspiration' offers a summary

---

[42] See below, 30.24.

[43] Locke affirmed the doctrine of mortalism in the *Reasonableness* in his account of the consequences of Adam's Fall. See below, p. 92. The question of the resurrection of the same body was an issue that Locke debated with Bishop Stillingfleet; see his *Mr. Locke's Second Reply to the Right Reverend the Lord Bishop of Worcester's Answer to his Second Letter* (London, 1699), 165 ff. The part of the *Reply* relevant to this issue is appended as a long note to *Essay*, at the end of *Essay* II. xxvii, 5th edn.

[44] See John W. Yolton, *Thinking Matter* (Minneapolis, 1983), ch. 1. The remark on thinking matter is present in the 1st edn. of the *Essay*. In the 4th edn. it is modified in a way that makes it more explicitly materialist. See Nidditch's critical apparatus to p. 541, lines 1–3 of his edition. This modification would roughly coincide with Locke's note in the 'Adversaria'.

xxxiv INTRODUCTION

of his religious epistemology written when the first edition of the *Essay* was very nearly complete. It is dated December 1687. At that time, Locke was staying in Amsterdam, where he had gone to see through the press a French-language abridgement of the *Essay*.[45] Since February 1687, his principal residence was in Rotterdam, in the house of Benjamin Furly, an expatriate Englishman, who after emigrating to Holland had engaged in business ventures and prospered. Furly possessed a large library, and his home was an important meeting place for scholars, a centre for the 'commonwealth of letters'. Furly was a Quaker, which may begin to explain the origin of this manuscript, for Locke connects the doctrine of immediate inspiration with the belief of Quakers. A number of Locke's unpublished papers consist of questions and critical comments on manuscripts of various authors, and this may be an instance of this sort, viz. comments on a manuscript entitled 'Immediate Inspiration' by an unnamed author.[46]

From Locke's manuscript, it may be inferred that the author of 'Immediate Inspiration' claimed that an immediate inward revelation is the cause of divine or saving faith, and that this supernatural cause and its consequence, a strong and, to the believer at least, unmistakable persuasion, distinguish divine faith from ordinary belief. The author is an innatist. Therefore, immediate inspiration does not signify a state of unmediated conviction. There are ideas latent in the mind that are 'excited' and brought into play by an inward revelation.

Locke's purpose in writing this manuscript is to refute the author's claim. His argument, which is both philosophical and biblical, is rich, complex, and disconnected, but clear enough when sufficient care is taken to identify its main lines. He contends that there are no criteria by which to distinguish a purely inward revelation from illusion, and that even if there were some psychological difference, this internal perception would be objectively unverifiable. Some external criteria must be provided by reason or revelation. For an original revelation, a miracle will most often do the job. 'Thus god spoke to Moses not by a bare influence on his minde, but out of a bush all on fire . . .'[47] In instances where faith is not the outcome of an original revelation but is mediated by traditional revelation, Scripture and reason are sufficient to produce

---

[45] Maurice Cranston, *John Locke: A Biography* (New York, 1957), 290.

[46] See 40.2, where Locke refers to 'the author'; but see also 37.7 and 39.8, where Locke addresses the author directly in the second person. See also Locke's letters to Furly, *Correspondence*, vol. 3, nos. 986 and 989.

[47] 40.29–30.

INTRODUCTION   XXXV

it.[48] Locke alludes to the schools of the prophets set up to propagate revelation once received.

He suggests that the author's mistaken doctrine of saving faith may be a consequence of a failure to understand the idiom of biblical language. He observes that Scripture often represents events of decisive or existential import as the consequences of direct divine action rather than, as they most often were, the effects of a general providence, which operates through the system of nature.

Locke was concerned, however, not only about the epistemological errors of the doctrine of immediate revelation, but also about its danger to religion. It makes way for an 'extravagant boundlesse' and unregulated enthusiasm and it 'takes away all reasoning about religion', which also has its biblical precedents.[49]

'Scriptura Sacra' (holy scripture) consists of a set of notes on a book entitled *A Vindication of the Divine Authority of the Old and New Testaments* (London, 1692). Its author, William Lowth (1660–1732), was a well-connected Latitudinarian divine. His *Vindication* was written against Jean Le Clerc, a friend of Locke, who two years earlier had published a work on the inspiration of Scripture, entitled appropriately, *Five Letters on the Inspiration of the Holy Scriptures*.[50] Locke doesn't seem to have read very far into Lowth's book. He commented on lines excerpted only from the first twelve pages. His comments, in the form of queries, do not appear to favour one side or the other. Indeed, the difference between Le Clerc and Lowth is not great. Lowth accepts Le Clerc's claim that not all biblical books are equally inspired and that the inspiration of the biblical authors is proportional to their capacity to receive a particular revelation. He finds fault with Le Clerc because the latter ignored 'that these Writings were design'd by God for the Perpetual Use and Instruction of the church and to be a Rule of Christian Faith to all Ages'.[51] Locke's concern is more for clarification than disputation. He questions the notion of equal inspiration. He asks, rhetorically, whether for something to be a rule, it must not be 'very plain' and 'infallibly intelligible' to whomever it is supposed to apply. He wonders whether every inspired writing must have been intended by God 'for the perpetuall use of the church?' If Matthew

---

[48] On the distinction between original and traditional revelation, see *Essay* IV. xviii. 3.

[49] Enthusiasm is the doctrine of non-rational belief, that is, of belief established directly by divine inspiration without the mediation of reasons or evidence.

[50] Locke received a copy of Lowth's book from the publisher, Churchill, whom Locke directed to send a copy to Le Clerc. See *Correspondence*, iv. 501 n. 3.

[51] Lowth, *A Vindication*, 2 f.

xxxvi INTRODUCTION

wrote his Gospel for Jewish Christians, does it follow, since he was inspired, that he also 'had thoughts that it should be an universal rule?' Is having such thoughts essential to being inspired?

Answers to some of these questions are to be found in later work. Fitness for a revelation is relative to the divine plan for propagating a revelation, rather than proportional to the faculties or learning of those who are to be its vessels. It is just because the first apostles were not 'men of parts' that they were selected to be instructed by the Messiah and to be the first to preach his gospel.[52] Those parts of Scripture that apply everywhere and always as rules of faith and practice must be plain and infallibly intelligible.[53] Some of the writings, for example the apostolic letters, may be inspired but apply to the particular circumstances of the early churches and do not easily fit other circumstances.[54]

The date of composition of *A Discourse of Miracles* cannot be fixed precisely. It was among the manuscripts that Locke wrote to Peter King might be published after his death.[55] It first appeared in 1706, in *Posthumous Works*. The date 1701/2 is written at the end of the text and most likely was transcribed from the original manuscript. In a postscript, which appears to have been written by him, Locke remarks that the occasion of his thoughts on this subject was his reading of two short works: William Fleetwood's *An Essay on Miracles* (1701) and Benjamin Hoadly's *A Letter to Mr. Fleetwood* (1702), written in response to it.[56] At issue was the definition of miracles. Locke considered Fleetwood's definition too strict, and he was bothered that Hoadly failed to provide one.[57]

Fleetwood insisted that events, no matter how 'new, strange, prodigious, and astonishing' they may appear, do not count as miracles unless it is known that they violate 'an established law of nature'.[58]

---

[52] *Reasonableness*, below, 152.8–39. However, see Locke's remarks about St Paul's fitness for his special ministry, *An Essay for the Understanding of St Paul's Epistles*, below, p. 60.

[53] *Reasonableness*, 201.   [54] Ibid. 206.   [55] See n. 20 above.

[56] Fleetwood (1656–1712), later Bishop of Ely, was a fellow at Eton when he wrote the *Essay on Miracles*. It was written as a sort of compensation for his failure to give the Boyle lectures when invited to do so some years earlier. Hoadly (1676–1761), ultimately Bishop of Winchester, was rector at St Peter-le-Poor, London, when he published *A Letter to Mr. Fleetwood &c*, in 1702. Hoadly's *Letter* was published anonymously, and Locke does not mention him by name in the Postscript to the text.

[57] Hoadly does provide an extensional definition of miracles on p. 3 of his *Letter*, which may be sufficient for his purposes.

[58] William Fleetwood, *A Compleat Collection of the Sermons, Tracts, and Pieces of all Kinds* (London, 1737), 127.

INTRODUCTION   xxxvii

Locke prefers a less strict definition, one that disregards the metaphysics of miracles and attends only to their context. For Locke, a miracle is any event, or 'sensible Operation', that is believed by an observer of it to be contrary to nature and, hence, supernatural. The remainder of the *Discourse* is a defence of this definition against obvious objections: first, that, on this definition, what is taken to be a miracle by one person may not be by another; secondly, that, under this definition, events that are neither truly extraordinary nor supernatural in the sense of being against the laws of nature may be counted as miracles. Locke concedes both, but he denies that these concessions would deprive miracles of their evidential force.[59] The conclusion of Locke's defence is that miracles, so defined, are infallible indicators of divine revelation.

This is a very strong claim, but the degree of the claim is complemented by the limitations of its application. Both Locke and Fleetwood assert that miracles are not meant to prove the being of God but only his power, and, its corollary, that miracles have evidentiary force only for theists. In the light of this, Locke's assertion that miracles are supernatural and serve as credentials of a divine messenger if and only if they are employed to verify the one true religion whose principles are already accepted avoids circularity. To theists, who know or believe that God exists, and that he is almighty, wise, and good, the occurrence of an apparently supernatural event would be explicable by their pre-existing knowledge or faith. Moreover, theists would accept only those extraordinary events as authentic miracles that vouchsafe a revelation that is consistent with their theism.[60] Locke's other claim, that miracles are authenticating if and only if they manifest the superior power of God over all worldly powers, and its corollary that the one true God would never let himself be defeated in a contest of the sort that Moses and Elijah engaged in, seems, however, to beg the question.

The last item in this section, *An Essay for the Understanding of St Paul's Epistles by Consulting St Paul himself*, was written as a preface to Locke's

[59] Locke's theory of miracles allows that one may accept the revelatory truth of a biblical testimony and yet conclude on later reflection that the miracle that gave it credibility was neither extraordinary nor contrary to nature.

[60] Locke distinguishes between two kinds of miracles: those that vouch for a revelation and those that do not. The latter are wonders performed by the 'God of this World' (45.18). Any extraordinary event that vouches for a revelation is necessarily from God, whether or not it is such that only a supernatural agency could have caused it. Although Locke nowhere mentions Lord Herbert, his account of pagan religion in the *Discourse* could be taken as a direct response to Herbert's interpretation and evaluation of it. Cf. *De religione gentilium*, English trans., *Pagan Religion*, ed. John Anthony Butler (Ottawa, 1996), ch. 1.

xxxviii INTRODUCTION

Paraphrase and Notes on the Epistles of St Paul and first published with them in 1707. I shall refer to it as the *Preface*. In his last letter to Peter King, Locke mentions that there exists only one 'first and foul' copy of it and advises care that it not be lost.[61] From an internal remark, it appears that Locke wrote it after he had completed his paraphrase and notes on Galatians, 1 and 2 Corinthians, Romans, and Ephesians, hence, very near the end of his life.

Although the *Preface* was intended as an introduction to reading St Paul's letters, its directives are meant to apply to the whole of Scripture. It gives a lesson in how to appropriate revealed truth from the Bible. Locke's remark, that before he began the studies that produced the *Paraphrase and Notes* he did not understand them, or at least their 'doctrinal or discursive parts', although he was conversant with them, may be taken more as an indicator of the intensity of these last studies than as evidence of a deficiency in his understanding of St Paul, for, as will be seen shortly, *The Reasonableness of Christianity* is framed in Pauline theology, and there is a great deal of the same in the 'Adversaria Theologica 94'.

Consistent with his empirical realism, Locke proposes not a theory but a practice of reading St Paul, one that includes hermeneutical but not dogmatic or confessional presuppositions.[62] Its hermeneutics is not theory-laden or a priori but emerges from a reading of the text in its proper context. If anything is presupposed it is the assurance that beneath the various voices and personae of St Paul there is a thinking self, a mind crowded with thoughts, cultivated but prolific, and faced with opportunities and demands to express them. A mind and circumstances much like Locke's own, but in Locke's judgement more divine.

Locke's first prescription is to read the whole text through repeatedly until the tenor and purpose of the author who wrote it become known. The only frame that should surround a biblical text is what can be constructed out of elements of the thing itself: genre, the circumstances of writing, language and idiom, the author's styles and personae. This is all very much in keeping with Locke's philosophical insights on knowledge and belief and the function of language. But it also sheds light on Locke as a historian and his understanding of the role of

[61] Locke to Peter King, 25 Oct. 1704. *Correspondence*, vol. VIII, # 3647.

[62] See also *Conduct*, § 20 (45), ed. Schuurman, p. 189, and *Some Thoughts concerning Reading and Study for a Gentleman, The Works of John Locke*, 8th edn. (London, 1777), iv. 600–5.

INTRODUCTION   xxxix

historical understanding in theology. Whatever the merits of the claim
that Locke, in his political writings, was indifferent to historical
explanation in political argument, the same cannot be truly said of his
method of theological interpretation and argument.[63] His understanding of St Paul is thoroughly historical, and, as his preface makes
evident, he uses this understanding to make political as well as theological
points. His description of the apostle's intellectual character and varieties
of expression is unsurpassed. Moreover, he seems to have discovered the
practice of contextualization long before it became fashionable.

In the concluding paragraph to the preface, Locke's rather solemn
admonition that his readers should not follow his interpretation of
Scripture beyond the evidence of the text, is reminiscent of his advice to
readers of the *Essay*.[64] Finally, the entire paragraph illustrates the
convergence of religion and theology. Biblical study, even as sophisticated
as the sort that Locke prescribes here, is above all 'the Study of the way to
Salvation'.

5. *The Constitution and Authority of the Church*

The full title of 'Infallibility' is a question and answer in scholastic mode:
'Whether it is necessary to grant that there be an Infallible Interpreter of
Most Holy Scripture in the Church? Denied.' Locke composed it in
Latin in 1661. It belongs to a set of writings similar in form, written
while he was at Oxford.[65] All of these Oxford writings address
theological issues. Locke chose to publish none of them, perhaps
because he considered them youthful works that did not fully represent
his mature opinions.

The particular occasion and motivation of 'Infallibility' is unknown.
The general context, however, is evident. The multiplication of sects
since the Protestant Reformation, each one claiming that its particular
doctrine is soundly biblical, left little doubt that, although Scripture itself
may be infallible, human interpreters of it are not. But, without the
assurance that one's faith is truly founded in Scripture, there is no safe
way to salvation, or so it seemed. The Roman Catholic Church was an
attractive refuge to serious Christians, because it claimed to be an
infallible guide. It attracted William Chillingworth, who spent a brief

---

[63] J. G. A. Pocock, *Politics, Language & Time* (Chicago, 1989), 8.

[64] *Essay, Epistle to the Reader*, Nidditch, p. 7.

[65] The 'Two Tracts on Government' (1661, and 1662) and 'Essays on the Law of
Nature' (1663-4). See bibliography.

xl INTRODUCTION

time during his youth under the tutelage of Rome.[66] The fallibility of the sects, made more evident during the interregnum, the possibility, shortly after the Restoration, that Roman Catholics might be permitted to practise their religion in England, and the threat that this posed to the English Church and society, gave new life to the issue.[67]

Locke presents two arguments against the necessity of an infallible interpreter. The first is an argument from providence. If there were a need for an infallible interpreter, then God would have provided one. But there has been none 'since the time of the Apostles'. This argument begs the question, and requires a supplement. The second argument is based upon the premiss that what cannot be usefully employed cannot be needed. The utility of an infallible interpreter depends upon his possession of infallible credentials.[68] The very disagreement among the churches on this issue is, Locke supposes, sufficient to prove that this is not the case. The supplement has problems also.

More interesting than these arguments is Locke's alternative to an infallible interpreter. It is a distinctly Protestant one. Scripture must be its own interpreter. However, Locke does not use this Protestant principle baldly and naively. The clear and perspicuous character of Scripture's teaching of fundamentals, those things necessary to be believed and to be done for salvation, shows the sufficiency of Scripture. But Locke acknowledges that there are obscure and difficult parts of it also. His point, that it is not the inadequacy of language that is the problem but limited human understanding, fits with his realist principles of looking to things themselves. Interpretations are discourses. What is needed for the understanding of these hard places of Scripture is not 'facility of speech' but new faculties of the mind and 'a new understanding' whereby divine things may be perceived and understood. Since Locke explicitly disallows enthusiasm, it must be supposed that he

[66] 'I RECONCILED myself to the church OF ROME, because I thought myself to have sufficient reason to believe, that there was and must be always in the world some church that could not err; and consequently, seeing all other churches disclaimed this privilege of not being subject to error, the church of Rome must be that Church which cannot err' (*An Account of what moved the Author to turn Papist* . . . in *The Works of William Chillingworth, M.A.* (Oxford, 1838), iii. 386). John C. Biddle (who has since changed his surname to Higgins-Biddle) identifies Jeremy Taylor and William Chillingworth as possible sources of Locke's discourse. However likely that may be, Locke's arguments, when compared to theirs, appear to be his own.

[67] For a detailed account of the context and sources of 'Infallibility' see John C. Biddle, 'John Locke's Essay on Infallibility: Introduction, Text, and Translation', *Journal of Church and State*, 19 (1997), 301–27.

[68] See *A Discourse of Miracles*, 44 below.

INTRODUCTION   xli

regards this as a state that must await another life. For those ambiguous parts of Scripture that concern matters of indifference, ones that do not pertain to salvation, but to order and decorum in the Church, Locke prescribes another sort of infallible interpreter, who gives pastoral directions that can be safely followed, even if they are mistaken, and which, when followed by all, ensure unity and peace in the Church.[69] Here by 'infallibility' Locke means not an impossibility of error, but an impossibility of erring dangerously.

Locke's genial commendation of pastoral wisdom and his representation of it as benign, at least for the laity, is in striking contrast to the strident tones in which he portrays, in the next three selections, the efforts of Roman Catholic priests or orthodox Protestant divines to dictate belief and the greater danger of submitting to them. The different circumstances of these writings may explain this contrast in part. 'Infallibility' was written shortly after the Restoration and is an expression of Locke's conformism. 'Critical Notes' and 'Ecclesia' were written during troubled times, when it appeared that England might some day have a Catholic king.

More important, however, is whether this contrast goes deeper, that is, whether it is an expression of a profound change in Locke's practical religious epistemology, what that change involved, and how it occurred. This is too big a subject to consider here, and to consider it properly requires a review of almost everything that Locke wrote. But it is appropriate to raise it here, for a proper understanding of Locke's ecclesiology turns on a right understanding of his religious epistemology.

The next selection consists of extracts from 'Critical Notes Upon Edward Stillingfleet's *Mischief* and *Unreasonableness of Separation*', written in 1681 but never published. The manuscript, which consists of 168 pages, is mostly in the hand of James Tyrrell, with parts written by an amanuensis and by Locke himself. It has long been thought to have been authored jointly by Locke and Tyrrell, but John Marshall has made a convincing case for Locke's sole authorship.[70] It offers the most complete account of Locke's theory of the Church.

Edward Stillingfleet, the future bishop of Worcester and theological critic of Locke's *Essay*, published in 1680 a sermon entitled *The Mischief of Separation*, which was soon followed by a longer work, *The*

[69] On the young Locke's conservatism, see Philip Abrams, *John Locke, Two Tracts on Government* (Cambridge, 1967), Introduction.
[70] See Marshall, *John Locke*, 97–110.

xlii INTRODUCTION

Unreasonableness of Separation. Building upon principles stated in an earlier work,[71] Stillingfleet argued that separation from the Church of England was—on grounds of Scripture, reason and precedent— unreasonable and morally impermissible. He defined separation as 'withdrawal from constant Communion' with the Church of England (the practice of occasional communion was unacceptable to him) to form separate congregations for the sake of purity of worship or a more satisfactory means of edification. The only acceptable basis for separation would be corruption such as would overthrow the being and constitution of the Church, corruption of the sort, he supposed, that justified separation from the Church of Rome. He noted that this was not among the reasons currently given to justify separation from the Church of England.[72] Stillingfleet's aim was the peace and unity of 'whole Churches'. A whole Church is coextensive with some imperial domain or nation state.

by *whole Churches*, I mean, the *Churches* of such *Nations,* which upon the decay of the *Roman Empire,* resumed their just Right of government to themselves, and upon owning Christianity, incorporated into one Christian Society, under the same Common Ties and Rules of Order and Government.[73]

Regular communion with a whole Church was the duty of every Christian; where conscience resisted, he counselled passive obedience.

Locke's critical remarks add up to a defence of Congregationalism, but it is a qualified and partial defence of it. As the last extract makes vividly clear, independent churches can be as abusive of the rights of individual Christians as any established Church. Whereas established churches try to keep their members by force, independent sects entrap them in dogmatic confessions. Rather, the standpoint that he takes in these notes is not one of a Congregationalist but of an individual Christian, who, while recognizing the practical necessity of religious societies, maintains a liberty to enter or leave them, so far as his religious duty directs him and his judgement, informed by reason and Scripture, advises him.

'Ecclesia' is the title of a notebook entry dated 1682, hence roughly contemporary with 'Critical Notes'. It consists of an extract drawn from Book I, chapter 15 of Richard Hooker's *Laws of Ecclesiastical Polity*, followed by four inferences drawn from it by Locke.

[71] *Irenicum. A Weapon-Salve for the Churchs Wounds, or the Divine Right of Particular Forms of Church-Government* (London, 1662).
[72] *The Unreasonableness of Separation*, 2nd edn. (London, 1681), 33.
[73] *The Mischief of Separation* (London, 1680), 16.

INTRODUCTION   xliii

Locke reflects upon the distinction Hooker draws in this chapter between the Church as a supernatural society and as a merely natural or social one. Although Locke describes the distinction correctly, his interest in it does not coincide with Hooker's. Hooker's point in this passage is that there are some supernatural positive laws and that among them some are immutable and some not. He contradicts the common belief that all positive laws are human inventions and that they and only they are mutable. His distinction between a natural and a positive law is epistemic. Natural laws are deducible from natural reasons, positive laws are not. Supernatural positive laws, therefore, are made known to mankind by revelation, and are 'appointed of God to supplie the defect of those natural wayes of salvation, by which we are not now able to attaine thereunto'. In short, they compensate for the deficiencies of natural religion. From this distinction between human and divine positive law, Hooker infers that positive divine laws are immutable unless they are changed by God himself. The 'eternall Gospell' is one such positive divine law that must not be changed 'as long as the world doth continue'. Although these are not matters that concerned Locke when he was writing this manuscript, they must have entered his mind, for, as we shall see, they are fundamental to the argument of *The Reasonableness of Christianity*.[74]

Here, in this manuscript, Locke's interest is entirely in the limitation of ecclesiastical and civil power, so far as they impinge on religion. It is the idea of toleration that guides Locke's thoughts here, which he founds on the distinction Hooker drew between the Church as a supernatural society and as a mere human society whose origins are natural and historical: viz. human inclination and consent, viz. the sort of church whose origin and utility Locke described in *Critical Notes*. From Hooker's distinction he infers that the Church is a voluntary society, and it is from this characteristic of the Church, which Hooker does not mention, that he draws his four inferences: (1) that membership in a church is voluntary and cannot be enforced; (2) that ceremonial practices cannot be required of individuals against their conscience; (3) that the natural or political bond of Christians in the Church is by consent; (4) not sociability but the rational principle that God ought to be worshipped in public is the only proper motive for constituting a church.

'Error' was written in 1698 as an entry in one of Locke's commonplace books. The particular circumstances that occasioned it are unknown to me. The general context is sectarian differences among Christian

[74] For a fuller version of the text from which Locke has drawn his extract, see below, p. 264, note on 80.1.

xliv INTRODUCTION

churches. The title may be meant to invoke the sceptical conclusion, that where there is a diversity of irreconcilable opinions not all can be right and all may be wrong. Locke, however, does not offer sceptical counsel, viz. that to avoid error, one must suspend judgement. Instead, he maintains that when honest enquiry produces an erroneous result, there is no fault, for the duty of Christians is just to enquire after truth and not implicitly to accept certain creedal propositions. The peevish tone of this piece suggests that Locke was feeling the effects of the charges of heterodoxy brought against him by John Edwards, Edward Stillingfleet, and others whom he alludes to but does not name. The conclusions of the *Reasonableness* are repeated here: the duties of the Christian are to believe that Jesus Christ has been 'sent from God to be the Saviour of the world' and sincerely to endeavour to obey his law.

6. The Reasonableness of Christianity

Locke began work on what was to become *The Reasonableness of Christianity* during the winter of 1694–5. In June 1695, he signed a contract with Awnsham and John Churchill, his publishers, for its publication. The first copies appeared in August 1695. *A Vindication of the Reasonableness of Christianity* was published around October 1695.

As already remarked, sometime before December 1694, Locke had engaged in a course of theological enquiry. In designing a list of themes that he might explore, he represented theology to himself as a comprehensive domain that included under its head almost every field of learning. The *Reasonableness* seems to be the product of a different project. We cannot be certain why Locke put aside the one to pursue the other, or even whether that is a fair description of his intellectual movements. We can be sure, however, that he began the work that would produce the *Reasonableness* during the winter of 1694–5, and that he had completed a manuscript by early May. We learn this from Locke's letter to Limborch dated 10 May 1695. He writes of having started an enquiry into the content of the Christian faith, and he remarks that he has confined this enquiry to one source, the Bible, especially to the New Testament and even more especially to the Gospels, ignoring, for the time being, 'the opinions and orthodoxies of sects and systems whatever they may be'. He does not give a title to his work, but the description fits.[75]

From the letter to Limborch, the title of the work, and an examination of the work itself, two themes appear to preponderate. The first is the

[75] *Correspondence*, vol. v, no. 1901.

INTRODUCTION xlv

propositional content of Christian faith. The second is indicated in the title, which can be reformulated as a proposition: Christianity as delivered in Scripture is reasonable. What is 'delivered' here is fundamental doctrine. I shall first elaborate on each in turn.

Christian Faith, as Locke presents it in the *Reasonableness*, is not a sum of doctrine, rather it is restricted to 'the faith that justifies', the creedal part of the Gospel or Christian proclamation presented in the New Testament, which is a necessary condition of justification. It consists of a single albeit complex proposition, whose summary version is that Jesus is the Messiah. 'Justification by faith' with 'Scripture only' as its foundation are familiar Protestant themes, and there is no doubt that Locke considered his work as belonging to the Reformation, if by this one means not that it exemplifies the Reformed tradition (of Luther and more particularly Calvin), but that it continues the Reformation.[76] This seems right, for what is most noteworthy about the *Reasonableness* is its originality with respect to its method and result and to its overall conception of Christianity.

First, let us consider the originality of Locke's method and its result. He was outspoken about the latter. In his letter to Limborch he describes the outcome of his biblical study as a moment of intellectual discovery.

From an intent and careful reading of the New Testament the conditions of the New Covenant and the teaching of the Gospel became clearer to me, as it seemed to me, than the noontide light, and I am fully convinced that a sincere reader of the Gospel cannot be in doubt as to what the Christian faith is.[77]

In his open letter to Samuel Bold, published in the Preface to the second *Vindication*, he expresses a joyous surprise at the singularity of his discovery. He comments on the 'reasonableness of the doctrine' and wonders that he had never come across it 'in my little reading'. This 'awed me with the apprehension of singularity; until going on in the gospel-history, the whole tenour of it made it so clear and visible, that I more wondered that every body did not see and embrace it'.[78] From the content, it is clear that what Locke means by 'reasonableness' here is not the context of the doctrine of faith, for that Jesus is the Messiah is a matter of fact, but the clarity and simplicity of it and the wisdom displayed in its promulgation.

Locke could have said as much about the method that led to this

---

[76] In a letter to Limborch (*Correspondence*, vol. v, no. 1826), Locke describes Tillotson as a great pillar of the Reformed church.

[77] *Correspondence*, vol. v, no. 1901.　　[78] Second *Vindication* (1697), p. A7ʳ.

xlvi INTRODUCTION

discovery: the limitation of his enquiry to the four Gospels and Acts which contained, so he believed, eyewitness accounts of the preaching and propagation of the Gospel by Jesus and the apostles.

Among the singular features of Locke's method is his preference for the expression 'law of faith'. The expression is biblical or, more precisely, Pauline,[79] but it was not ordinarily used by the Reformers, and where they did use it they gave it a different sense from the one given it in the *Reasonableness*. Luther, for example, commenting on Romans 3: 27, where the distinction between the law of works and the law of faith is made, defines it not as a rule, but as a gift. It is the capacity, supernaturally bestowed, to do whatever God requires.[80] Calvin comments on this same verse that 'the word *law* is here improperly applied to faith'.[81] Locke's usage is closer to that of the Westminster Divines, who characterize the expression as a Hebraism and define it as the doctrine of faith, which is to be believed, or as a new covenant 'which doth strip man of all worth and righteousness of his own, and cloath him by grace with that of Christ'.[82] The use that Locke gives the term may have come to him after reading Hooker. In book I, chapter 15 of the *Laws*, the very passage that Locke commented on in 'Ecclesia', after drawing a distinction between mutable and immutable divine laws, Hooker cites the Gospel as an instance of an immutable law:

And this doth seeme to have bene the verie cause why saint *John* doth so peculiarlie tearme the doctrine that teacheth salvation by Jesus Christ, *Evangelium æternum, an eternal Gospell,* because there can be no reason wherefore the publishing thereof should be taken away, and any other in stead of it proclaymed, as long as the world doth continue. . .[83]

[79] It is noteworthy that two distinctions on which the argument of the *Reasonableness* depends (law of works/law of faith; First Adam/Second Adam), derive from St Paul.

[80] *Lectures on Romans*, trans. and ed. Wilhelm Pauck (London, 1961), 118.

[81] *The Epistles of Paul the Apostle to the Romans and to the Thessalonians*, trans. Ross Mackenzie (Grand Rapids, 1961), 79.

[82] *Annotations upon all the Books of the Old and New Testament*, ii (3rd edn.; London, 1657). The authors of these annotations were members of the Westminster Assembly of Divines, appointed by Parliament in 1643 to revise the doctrine, liturgy, and constitution of the English Church. Richard Baxter (1615–91) used the expression, and reproved Protestants who denied that Christ was a lawgiver and Roman Catholics who affirmed it but misrepresented Christ's law. Cf. *Catholic Theologie* (London, 1675). In the Second Part, sect. IV, p. 43, Baxter observes that Christ's law consists of two parts: '1. The Law of Nature (called by many moral) as commanding the love of God and its attendant Duties. 2. And the remedying Law which is more proper to the Redeemer called *the Law of Faith*' (italics are Baxter's).

[83] *Of the Laws of Ecclesiastical Polity, The Folger Edition of the Works of Richard Hooker*, general ed. W. Speed Hill, 4 vols. (Cambridge, Mass., 1977–82), i. 132 (ed. Georges Edelen).

INTRODUCTION

xlvii

Hooker does not use the expression 'law of faith' as Locke does. Moreover, he did not regard acceptance of Jesus as Messiah as a matter of faith, but as an act of submission to one's Lord. The rule of faith, which is one of the three marks of Christians everywhere (the other two are 'one baptism' and 'one Lord'), consists of the baptismal creed, and is the faith of the Church everywhere and always.[84] Locke's political reconception of faith as an act of submission, whether done with Hooker in mind or not, lends cogency to the separation of faith in Jesus as Messiah from all the other doctrines of the faith. It also makes his version of Christianity immune from controversies over orthodoxy, a fact that he recognized and celebrated.[85]

The logical difference between submission to a ruler and acceptance of propositions or doctrines is conceptually neat. This distinction makes it evident that Locke was most likely led by other motives than minimalist ones as he searched the Scriptures for the faith that justifies.[86]

Another original feature of Locke's method of enquiry is the assurance that it brings. The historical construction of the history of the propagation of the Gospel is also taken to be evidence of the wisdom of God, which in turn assures the reader of the truth of the Gospel message. This is a wonderful economy of effort. I have not found anything like it in the theological writings of the authors with whom Locke was most familiar or of their contemporaries, be they Calvinist, Arminian, or Socinian.[87]

The second theme of *The Reasonableness of Christianity* is the assertion that Christianity *as delivered in the Scriptures* is reasonable. This qualification is important for two reasons. First, Locke intended that his idea of Christianity be derived solely from Scripture. It is only this complex idea, free of the obscurities of dogma and tradition and the

---

[84] *Laws*, i. 196 f.   [85] *Reasonableness*, 209, below.

[86] Characteristic of the distinctiveness of acceptance of Jesus as Messiah is Locke's comment on Matt. 28: 18, 'All power is given unto to me in heaven and in earth': 'By this & several other texts of the New Testament it is plain that god has given his kingdom into the hands of his son & invested him in it at his resurrection. Hence arises the necessity of beleiving in Jesus i e ~~beleiving~~ receiving him for the Messiah & Lord by all to whom the gospel is preachd because we cannot now enter into the Kingdom of god without entering into the Kingdom of the Messiah who is in possession of the Kingdom of god & declared Lord of all things. Whereas before this to return into the Kingdom of god from the Kingdom of Sathan it was enough to return to him by an acknowledgment & dependence on him & an obedience to his law in whose hands the Kingdom then was. JL'. This comment is written in Locke's interleaved English Bible (LL 309; Bodleian shelf mark, BOD Locke 16.25), p. 694.

[87] Calvin, Turretin, Ames, Perkins, Episcopius, Limborch, Crellius, the Racovian Catechism.

xlviii   INTRODUCTION

rhetoric of sectarian conflict, that Locke declares reasonable. Secondly, in Locke's mind, it was just the plainness and simplicity of the law of faith as presented in the gospel preaching that he believed would recommend it to Deists who, offended by the moral repugnancy of Calvinism, especially its idea of God, rejected the whole of the Christian revelation.[88] But it is not the rule of faith only that Locke hoped would commend Christianity to reasonable persons, it was the whole Gospel (faith, repentance, and renewed moral endeavour under a less rigorous standard of judgement) that Locke declares reasonable.

What sort of reasonableness did Locke intend here? John Higgins-Biddle has observed that Locke uses the word only once in the text of the *Reasonableness*. When carefully considered, its occurrence, almost two-thirds through the work, seems just right.

These two, Faith and Repentance; *i. e.* believing Jesus to be the *Messiah,* and a good Life; are the indispensible Conditions of the New Covenant to be performed by all those, who would obtain Eternal Life. The Reasonableness, or rather Necessity of which, that we may better comprehend, we must a little look back to what was said in the beginning.[89]

The reference is to the beginning of the *Reasonableness,* where Locke outlines the history of redemption framed between the two figures of Adam and Christ, notes what was lost by the former and what was restored by the latter, and narrates the events in between. I think that in this context, the meaning that Locke attaches to 'reasonableness' becomes clear. Christianity is reasonable because it is advantageous, because unlike other religious or philosophical doctrines, it effectively restores immortality and allows more moderate conditions of justification. The qualifier that he offers, 'Necessity', then, must be taken in an instrumental or prudential sense. Christianity is the only reliable remedy for frail, mediocre mankind who remain under the rigour of the moral law, be it the law of works or the law of nature. The law of faith is, in Hooker's sense, a positive law 'designed to supplie the defect of those natrurall wayes of salvation, by which we are not now able to attaine thereunto'.[90]

To prove the reasonableness of Christianity, Locke not only refers his readers to the narrative at the beginning of his book, but he retells it, now making explicit the advantages of Christianity and defending the

---

[88] See my 'Introduction' to the Thoemmes edn. of the *Reasonableness*. Also Higgins-Biddle's introduction to the *Reasonableness*, pp. xv–xlii.

[89] Below, p. 169.

[90] Hooker, *Laws,* bk. I, ch. 15.

INTRODUCTION   xlix

wisdom and goodness of God. The argument of this second part of the
Reasonableness warrants careful review.[91] It will, I think, make possible a
clearer assessment of Locke's supposed failure to found and develop
morality merely on the basis of the light of nature.

The benefit that Jesus Christ has gained for mankind is immortality.
His fitness to be the restorer of mankind to this state is vouchsafed in
Scripture. The advantage of Christianity is that it makes available this
benefit to everyone who enters the Kingdom of the Messiah by accepting
him as their Lord. Yet Locke makes clear that this faith alone is not
sufficient to secure the benefit. Obedience to the moral law, which is
required of every person whether Christian or not, remains an absolute
condition. The advantage of entering the Kingdom of Christ is that this
need not be a perfect obedience, so long as it is sincere. Christianity is, like
the religion of nature, a moral religion, but a more convenient one, a
surer way to eternal bliss, which any reasonable person must recognize.[92]

The other advantage of Christianity is that it provides a more
comprehensive and rigorous moral doctrine than has ever been published
to mankind, and we have this from the Messiah's 'own Mouth'. These are
'the Laws of the Kingdom'. Locke observes that, according to Jesus'
accounts, at the Last Judgment the punishment of the wicked is based
entirely upon their misdeeds. Faith, when not accompanied by repentance
and a sincere endeavour to obey the law, is of no advantage.[93]

Thus far, it would appear that the advantage of Christianity can be
gained only by those who have received the Gospel. But this brings into
question the justice of God. What about those who lived before the
coming of the Messiah? The standard case of Abraham is cited as an
example of a particular promise evoking faith which, like faith in the
Messiah, counts for righteousness. But Locke goes further than this.
There are 'Believers of old' who 'either by the light of Nature, or
particular Promises' pleased God by trusting in his mercy. Christianity,
in this respect, appears not so much as an altogether supernatural

[91] The *Reasonableness* divides into two main parts and an appendix. According to
Higgins-Biddle's chapter notations, the first part, which is an account of the history and
propagation of the Gospel, runs from ch. I to ch. X. The second part, which treats the
advantages of Christianity and some related problems of theodicy, comprises chs. XI–
XIV. The appendix, which explains why the New Testament epistles were not used as
primary resources, comprises ch. XV. I have removed the chapter breaks made by
Higgins-Biddle and put the numeration of chapters in the margin. For a justification of
this modification of the critical text, see my review of Higgins-Biddle's edition of
Reasonableness, *The Locke Newsletter*, 31 (2000).

[92] This paragraph summarizes ch. XI below, pp. 166–75.

[93] This paragraph summarizes ch. XII below, pp. 175–86.

l INTRODUCTION

religion, but as the paradigm of a less rigorous religion of nature. These two modes of religion become in Locke's thinking not rivals but complementary moments in the providential government of the world.

The original question is asked a second time: what about those who will never hear about the Gospel even after the Messiah has come? The answer comes easily this time: the light of nature is sufficient. 'The same spark of the Divine Nature and Knowledge in Man [viz. the light of nature or the rational nature of mankind], which making him a Man; shewed him also the way of Attoning the merciful, kind, compassionate Author and Father of him and his Being, when he had trangressed that Law.' But this reasonable answer must leave Christians wondering what need there is of Christ. Locke's answer is a long historical argument, which might be summarized as the story of 'moral man and immoral society'.[94] The failure of natural religion is due not to a human incompetence to discover God and the divine law in nature, but, given the frailty and mediocrity of our nature that makes us vulnerable to such things, to priestcraft and power politics and the cowardice of those who should have known better. Locke makes clear that so far as it concerns morality Christianity teaches nothing that reason could not have discovered on its own.

Now we may return to the problem of Locke's failure to found morality. If Locke turned to revelation because he was unable to found morality by the mere light of nature, he was acting foolishly and against what he should have known, for Christianity, at least as Locke conceived it, requires a viable natural religion if it is itself to be reasonable, and not only reasonable but just and universal.

From the very beginning, with his Oxford writings, his translation of Nicole's *Discourses*, and the numerous religious writings that followed these, Locke was working as a Christian philosopher, whose loyalties were not divided between Christianity and natural religion, but who embraced both in correlation. His writings are evidence that he never departed from this position. Therefore, when Locke refused to complete the task of founding morality on rational principles, we must not suppose that he did so out of disillusionment, for Locke continued to rely on this possibility in his defence of Christianity. What other reason might he have had? Dissatisfaction with the results of his earlier efforts, and a reluctance to continue with a difficult but not impossible task: these perhaps are closer to the truth.

[94] The expression is the title of the celebrated book by Reinhold Niebuhr (New York, 1932).

INTRODUCTION   li

Locke wrote *A Vindication of the Reasonableness of Christianity, &c*, in response to charges made against him, as the anonymous author of the *Reasonableness*, by John Edwards (1637–1726), an Anglican divine of moderate Calvinist outlook but intemperate disposition. He was a biblical scholar of modest accomplishment, and, like his father, a zealous defender of orthodoxy.[95] Edwards charged that Locke's book was Socinian in outlook and intention. For Edwards, Socinianism was more of a programme than a doctrine, whose aim was to unburden the Christian conscience of creedal obligations.[96] He argued that the ultimate consequence of this programme was atheism. To support this charge, Edwards observed that the author of the *Reasonableness* advocated a minimalist creed, reducing the Christian faith to a single article and assuring his readers that Christians need believe no more than this; that he denied the doctrine of original sin; that he failed to assert Jesus Christ's divine nature; that he wilfully ignored biblical evidence of the Trinity; that he denied the satisfaction of Christ; that he wilfully ignored the New Testament epistles in going about to show what the Christian faith is; that he was a mob-pleaser, who fashioned a version of Christianity within the limits of vulgar understanding. This last accusation was not merely rhetorical: from a Calvinist standpoint, the understanding of the mob, corrupted by original sin, unreformed by grace, and untutored by evangelical doctrine, must tend towards atheism.[97] Locke's reaction was swift, but the consequence of this was only to embroil him in a continuing conflict which a second *Vindication*, longer by half than the work it was supposed to defend, failed to end.

The charge of Socinianism, I think, is false, as the interpretation of the *Reasonableness* given above should show. Locke's reasons for writing his

---

[95] See below, p. 269, note on 211.6.

[96] Socinianism takes its name from the latinized surname (Socinus) of the liberal Italian Reformers Lelio Sozini (1525–62) and his nephew Fausto Sozzini (1539–1604). Doctrinally, Socinianism was characterized by a strict adherence to biblical authority in the formulation of doctrine, by the reliance on reason over tradition in the interpretation of Scripture, by anti-trinitarianism (hence the name Unitarianism, which was preferred by English Socinians), and by a more relaxed attitude to dogmatic formulas. The theological outlook of Socinianism is most accessible in the *Racovian Catechism* (1st edn. 1605; see bibliography), which was named after the Polish city of Racow, where a Socinian community flourished during the first half of the 17th cent. See E. M. Wilbur, *A History of Unitarianism* (Cambridge, Mass., 1946); also Herbert John MacLachlan, *Socinianism in Seventeenth-Century England* (Oxford, 1951).

[97] In this paragraph I have borrowed some lines from my introduction to the Thoemmes Key Text edition of the *Reasonableness* and its *Vindications*.

lii INTRODUCTION

book were various and complex, but there is no evidence, beyond mere suspicion, that he ever intended to propagate Socinianism.[98] Nevertheless, while suspicion about the intentions of the author of the *Reasonableness* may be unwarranted, the first *Vindication* lends it credibility. Locke misquotes Edwards for the sake of rhetorical advantage; he lies when he asserts that he never read Socinian literature and hence can't be familiar with the biblical interpretation of Socinian authors; he mockingly dismisses the idea of satisfaction; his claim that certain prelates are in agreement with his views is only a partial truth, and he ignores, perhaps wilfully, the differences between him and his supposed prelatal allies; finally, he is overall evasive.[99]

The suspicion that reading the first *Vindication* raises, however, is misdirected if it looks to Locke's intentions as author of the *Reasonableness*. It thus fails to consider the fact that Locke had no other choice but to be evasive. For it is obvious that the *Reasonableness* has much in common with Socinianism, so far as they both reject the a priori constraints of orthodoxy and insist on establishing faith on historical principles. But these were not principles peculiar to Socinianism. If anything, Locke's conception of them was clearer and his application of them more decisive. If the exercise of these principles overthrew orthodoxy, then one would have to conclude that many who were not Socinian, and who subscribed to orthodox creeds and submitted to orthodox ecclesiastical authority, had a part in it. The tendency of liberal defenders of Christianity towards heterodoxy may tell us more about the adequacy of the basic sources of Christian belief than about the intentions of its defenders.

7. *Fall and Redemption*

The selections in this last section closely surround the *Reasonableness* in time of composition. They are also close to it thematically, all having to do with the history of redemption.

Original sin comes first in the history of redemption. The document that bears this title, 'Peccatum originale', is dated 1692. It consists of a sequence of questions concerning the imputation of Adam's first sin to his posterity. The manuscript is not in Locke's hand, but the title, two or three corrections, and the name 'Proast', which appears at the end of the

---

[98] On Locke's Socinianism, see my 'Locke's Theology, 1694–1794'.

[99] For documentation, see the notes on the text. I shall give a full account of Locke's strategy in this text in *Locke's Vindications and other Theological Writings*.

INTRODUCTION

liii

manuscript, were inscribed by him. Locke probably dictated the text to an amanuensis. 'Proast' most likely refers to Jonas Proast, who had recently published a second critique of Locke's views on toleration, a rejoinder to Locke's second *Letter*.[100] Although there is nothing in Proast's letter that precisely coincides with the issues addressed in 'Peccatum originale', and nothing also among his other writings, Proast does appeal to the corruption of human nature as a reason to justify the use of civil force in establishing religion.[101] At the time this manuscript was written, not only Locke but his friend and ally, Archbishop Tillotson, were engaged in a controversy that involved Proast, who was a zealous member of the High Church party at Oxford.[102] This manuscript may represent another aspect of the controversy.

'Peccatum originale' presents an account of the doctrine of imputation that anticipates Locke's treatment of it in the *Reasonableness*. Imputation is the transmission of the guilt of Adam's sin and of the punishment due to it to his posterity. In the *Reasonableness*, Locke rejects this doctrine, because it is inconsistent with divine goodness and justice. In justification of this, Locke remarks that only if Adam's posterity, including the 'Millions' who never heard of him, had made him their representative, would God be justified in imputing Adam's sin to them.[103]

The main question addressed in the text is whether it can be truly said that God imputes Adam's sin to his descendants. Locke's concern is with analytic truth, hence whether it can be said consistently that God imputes Adam's sin to his posterity and that God is truthful and just. It all depends on what one means by 'imputation'. Locke distinguishes in scholastic fashion between a proper or formal sense of imputation and an effective sense and explains the distinction 'in plainer sense' as one between the attribution or non-attribution of guilt among Adam's descendants. The latter would be unjust, because it would involve

---

[100] *A Third Letter concerning Toleration* (Oxford, 1691). Proast's *Letter* was published anonymously.

[101] Ibid. 6. See also Harris, *The Mind of John Locke*, 294. On Proast's writings, cf. Richard Vernon, 'Locke's Antagonist, Jonas Proast', *The Locke Newsletter*, 24 (1993), 95; Mark Goldie, 'John Locke, Jonas Proast and Religious Toleration 1688–1692', 146.

[102] See Goldie, *Locke: Political Essays, passim*.

[103] See below, p. 92. The reference to Adam here is an interesting supplement to Locke's dispute with Filmer, who was a favourite among Proast and his High Church Oxford friends. For a thoughtful account of the connection between Locke's political and religious thought in respect to the role of Adam, cf. also Harris, *The Mind of John Locke*, ch. 10 *passim*.

liv INTRODUCTION

punishment without requisite judgement. The bulk of the analysis is of the formal or proper sense of imputation and the conclusion seems to be that there is no coherent way justly to attribute guilt to agents and punish them for an action they did not perform. The only consequence of Adam's sin that Locke allows may be justly passed on to posterity is death.[104]

A refinement of this conclusion is presented in the next document, 'Homo ante et post lapsum', dated a year later. Although death is a punishment to Adam, it is not so to his posterity; rather, for them, it is just the consequence of being a living corporeal being, which in itself is no bad thing. This doctrine is easier to defend against charges of inconsistency with the moral attributes of God, if mortality is Adam's natural state. Adam was not created immortal, but was provided in paradise with the means of attaining it. This account is consistent with Locke's discussion of Adam early in the *Reasonableness*. It does not fit with what Locke says later: that as Son of God and bearer of the divine image, Adam was immortal.[105] If Locke recognized this inconsistency, he did not bother to resolve it.[106] Another noteworthy feature of this document is the account given in it of the state of nature before the Fall of Adam. In this state, the first humans were burdened with no immoral passions; 'instinct and reason' were sufficient guides of life and, it would seem, had no need of any sort of law. Sin entered the world only after 'a probationary law' was given, and with the violation of this law came a knowledge of good and evil.

The next selection, 'Resurrectio et quae sequitur', is an interpretation of parts of 1 Cor. 15 that concern the resurrection. Wainwright gives good reasons for dating it to *c.* 1699.[107] 1 Cor. 15. 20–1 represents the central theme or leitmotiv of the *Reasonableness*. Here Locke looks beyond the conclusion of that work and considers the end of the history of redemption and the end of history. The end begins with resurrection, which, according to Locke who follows St Paul, is not just one event but a sequence of them: Christ's resurrection followed by the resurrection of the righteous and, finally, the resurrection of the damned. Locke contends, rightly, that St Paul treats only the resurrection of the righteous (those who are justified by faith, or, were there any, by works). This resurrection is a miraculous

[104] Cf. *Reasonableness*, 94.3–13.
[105] Compare *Reasonableness*, 91 f. with 169 f.
[106] Cf. 'Christianae religionis brevis delineatio', 242.1–7.
[107] Wainwright, *Paraphrase and Notes*, ii. 679.

INTRODUCTION   lv

transformation of beings from a state of corruption to one of incorruption, which is everlasting life. The resurrection of the wicked, however, is otherwise. Here Locke reaffirms his position that the punishment for wickedness is death, which, however, is preceded by a terrible punishment. The manuscript breaks off just as Locke was about to consider the state of the blessed after the resurrection. Mixed in with this discussion, Locke makes mention of apocalyptic events.

The analysis of the Epistle of the Hebrews has no date. It was written on a quire made up of two quarto sheets folded, sewn, and inserted in a polyglot New Testament that Locke had interleaved. Similar analyses of several Pauline epistles are also inserted in this New Testament. These were obviously done in preparation for *A Paraphrase and Notes*. Locke believed that Hebrews was probably written by St Paul, and so it seems very likely that this document was preparatory to a paraphrase of and notes on Hebrews. A date of *c.*1700, therefore, fits such an account.[108]

Locke's interpretation of Hebrews follows his theory of the epistolary part of the New Testament developed in the *Reasonableness*, viz. that the epistles are works of counsel and edification addressed to Christian communities, and although they contain fundamental doctrines, it is not their primary purpose to teach them, but to apply them with other pertinent truths to the problems and circumstances of these communities.[109] Perhaps most noteworthy is the discussion here of the priestly office of Christ, which is a central theme of the letter to the Hebrews. In the *Reasonableness*, Locke emphasized the Messianic or kingly office of Christ, and although he admits that Scripture attributes to him the additional offices of priest and prophet, he observes that Jesus never claimed the title of priest and only incidentally spoke of himself as a prophet.[110] Here the priestly office is given prominence, because it fits the circumstances of Jewish Christians who were schooled in the Mosaic religion. Jesus Christ is styled as a priest whose priestly function has been brought to perfection by the sacrifice of himself once and for all. The author of Hebrews, Locke observes, argues for the superiority of the new covenant over the old, and of the Christian over the Mosaic revelation. It is curious that Locke seems to accept without question the claim in

---

[108] On Locke's assignment of Hebrews to St Paul, see the note in his interleaved New Testament (LL 2864), p. 249: 'St Paul is with reason judgd the author. St Peter tells us 2 Pet: III. 15 that St Paul writ an Epistle to the Hebrews & in that place seems to refer to Heb X. 35 – 39.' But see also *Reasonableness*, ed. Higgins-Biddle, p. 165, l. 35 and n. 1, p. 166. It should be noted that, in this piece, Locke does not identify St Paul as the author.

[109] See below, pp. 205 ff.   [110] See below, p. 175.

lvi INTRODUCTION

Hebrews that the Mosaic religion was delivered through the mediation of angels and not directly by God himself. It is also noteworthy that in the account of this, Locke merely asserts the superiority of the Messiah over angels but does not attribute essential divinity to him.[111]

These notes on Hebrews provide a further view of Locke's Christology. Whatever his final judgement about the doctrine of Satisfaction, he never doubted that the death of Christ, along with the resurrection, is a supreme moment in the history of redemption, that it was a supererogatory act by means of which Jesus Christ won the right to rule his supernatural kingdom and, as second Adam, regained the possibility of immortality that Adam had lost. However, Locke does not speak here of Christ's death as sacrificial, as an action necessary to cleanse the stain of sin or as a means of placating divine disfavour, a necessity that would warrant priestcraft. The context in which Locke interprets this letter allows him to keep the aspect of an expiatory death of Christ on the margins of his idea of Christianity.[112]

Also of interest are Locke's notes on the meaning of 'perfect' in Hebrews. He assigns it both a moral and an ontological sense: it is a state of perfect righteousness and pure conscience as well as an unchangeable state of happiness.

'Christianae Religionis Synopsis', or, to use its secondary title, 'Christianae Religionis brevis delineatio', is dated 1702. It comes fittingly at the end of this collection. The occasion and purpose of its composition is nowhere stated. Wainwright conjectures that it was composed after Locke completed the manuscript on the Corinthian letters and before he began on Romans. Perhaps he composed this summary of Christianity in order to take his bearings. The account of Christianity conforms essentially to the *Reasonableness*. The main difference, if it is such, is the attempt to rationalize the inconsistency of Adam's original state. Here we have it that Adam was made immortal and only became mortal as a consequence of his first sin. Otherwise, this summary highlights the same elements of Locke's Christianity: Adam and Christ, the two covenants, the historical incompetence of natural religion, and the necessity of revelation and the duty of Christians.

---

[111] See below, 238.17–28.
[112] For additional comments on Locke's opinions concerning the doctrine of Satisfaction, see p. 271.

INTRODUCTION

II

The writings collected below should make clear that Locke's interest in religion and theology was neither peripheral nor pursued merely for the sake of appearances. The industrious manner of his pursuit of various theological questions and his ongoing engagement in biblical study should dispel all suspicion about the latter. Rather, we discover here that religious concern was one of the main determinants of his intellectual pursuits, so that his various philosophical enquiries inevitably impinge upon or lead back to theology. This concern, viz. about attaining immortal bliss, helps to engender a commitment to practise moral religion, natural or revealed. But on account of Adam's sin, which made us mortal, and of human frailty, which makes perfect obedience to the divine law a virtual impossibility, mere natural religion is insufficient, and thus revealed religion, and in particular Christianity, remains the only sure means of satisfying this religious concern. It is fitting, therefore, that the history of redemption should be the concluding theme of these writings, for in Locke's view, Christianity is more than a doctrine or a discipline, it is both of these made certain and efficacious by historical events in which humanity receives a new ancestor, one who is not merely mankind's biological progenitor, but its true representative and head. It was on account of this history that the prospect of eternal happiness for himself and his kind was for Locke not an idle hope but an assurance beyond doubt.

In the light of these conclusions, it is perhaps appropriate to consider Locke not merely as a progenitor of the Enlightenment, but as one of the last of the Reformers. His rejection of the dogmatic exclusiveness of the Protestant sects does not put him outside the Reformation, but, together with his fidelity to the Protestant principle of *sola scriptura*, arguably places him within it as one of its advocates. This is not the place, however, to present this argument, for it would require a retelling of the history of the Reformation. Suffice it to say that Locke, not having our perspective on the Enlightenment or on the later developments of evangelical Christianity, would not have found the designation of Protestant Reformer unfitting even while he protested his unworthiness of it.

I

THEOLOGY, ITS SOURCES, AND THE PRAGMATICS OF ASSENT

The first two selections, *Theologie* and *Indifferency*, are drawn from the critical text of *Of the Conduct of the Understanding* established by Paul Schuurman (Dissertation (University of Keele, 2000), 193–4, 221–3). I am grateful to Dr Schuurman for permission to use his meticulous edition. I have made only slight modifications of format. Schuurman's text is divided into paragraphs rather than sections, although the latter, which appear in all previous editions of the *Conduct*, have been retained by him. Hence the double numeration. There is a further complication in the numbering of sections that users of the 1706 edition and its facsimile reprint (Bristol, 1993) should be aware of. Because of a misnumbering of sections in the 1706 edition, § 22 in that edition should have been numbered 23; and § 34 should have been numbered 35. These errors have been corrected in subsequent editions. The selection from *An Essay concerning Human Understanding* is from the Nidditch edition, pp. 489–90.

THEOLOGIE

(§ 23) (49.) There is indeed one Science (as they are now destinguishd) incomparably above all the rest where it is not by corruption narrowed into a trade or faction for meane or ill ends and secular interests, I meane Theologie, which conteining the knowledg of god and his creatures, our 5
duty to him and our fellow creatures and a view of our present and future state is the comprehension of all other knowledg directed to its true end i.e. the honour and veneration of the Creator and the happynesse of man kinde. This is that noble study which is every mans duty and every one that can be called a rational creature is capable of. The workes of nature 10
and the words of the Revelation displai it to mankinde in Characters soe large and visible that those who are not quite blind may in them read and see the first principles and most necessary parts of it and from thence as they have time helps and industry may be inabled to goe on to the more abstruse parts of it and penetrate into those infinite depths filld with the 15
treasures of wisdom and knowledg. This is that Science which would truly enlarge mens minds were it studyed or permitted to be studyed every where with that freedom, love of truth and charity which it teaches, and were not made contrary to its nature the occasion of strife faction, malignity and narrow impositions. But I shall say noe more here of this 20
but that it is undoubtedly a wrong use of my understanding to make it the rule and measure of an other mans, a use which it is neither fit for nor capable of.

4 THEOLOGY, SOURCES, AND PRAGMATICS OF ASSENT

INDIFFERENCY

(68) Men deficient in knowledg are usualy in one of these three states either wholy ignorant: or as doubting of some proposition they have either imbraced formerly, or at present are inclined to: or lastly they doe
5 with assurance hold and professe without ever haveing examined and being convinced by well grounded arguments. The first of these are in the best state of the three by haveing their mindes yet in their perfect freedom and indifferency the likelier to pursue truth the better, haveing noe bias yet clapd on to mislead them.
10 (§ 35) For ignorance with an indifferency for truth is nearer to it, than opinion with ungrounded inclination which is the great source of Error. And they are more in danger to goe out of the way who are marching under the conduct of a guide that tis an hundred to one will mislead them, than he that has not yet taken a step and is likelyer to be prevaild on
15 to enquire after the right way. The last of the three sorts are in the worst condition of all . For if a man can be perswaded and fully assured of any thing for a truth without haveing examined, what is there that he may not imbrace for truth? and if he has given himself up to beleive a lie what means is there left to recover one who can be assured without examining?
20 To the other two This I crave leave to say. That as he that is ignorant is in the best state of the two, soe he should pursue truth in a method suitable to that state. i.e. by enquiring directly into the nature of the thing it self without mindeing the opinions of others or troubleing himself with their questions or disputes about it but to see what he himself can sincerely
25 searching after truth finde out. He that proceeds upon others principles in his enquiry into any sciences though he be resolved to examin them and judg of them freely, does yet at least put himself on that side and post himself in a party which he will not quit till he be beaten out. by which the minde is insensibly engaged to make what defence it can and soe is
30 unawares biassed. I doe not say but a man should embrace some opinion when he has examined, else he examines to noe purpose, But the surest and safest way is to have noe opinion at all till he has examined and that without any the least regard to the opinions or Systems of other men about it. For example were it my Businesse to understand physick would
35 not the safer and readier way be to consult nature her self and informe my self in the history of diseases and their cures than espouseing the principles of The Dogmatists, Methodists or Chymists engage in all the disputes concerning either of those systemes and suppose it true till I

THEOLOGY, SOURCES, AND PRAGMATICS OF ASSENT 5

have tried what they can say to beat me out of it. Or supposeing that Hippocrates or any other booke infallibly conteines the whole art of physick would not the direct way be to study read and consider that booke weigh and compare the parts of it to finde the truth rather than espouse the doctrines of any party who though they acknowledg his authority have already interpreted and wiredrawn all his text to their owne sense the tincture whereof when I have imbibed I am more in danger to misunderstand his true meaning than if I had come to him with a minde unprepossessed by doctors and commentators of my sect, whose reasonings interpretation and language which I have been used to will of course make all chime that way and make another and perhaps the genuine meaning of the author seeme harsh straind and uncouth to me. For words haveing naturaly none of their owne cary that signification to the hearer that he is used to put upon them what ever be the sense of him that uses them. This I thinke is visibly soe and if it be, he that begins to have any doubt of any of his tenets which he received without examination ought as much as he can to put himself wholy into this state of ignorance in reference to that question and throwing wholy by all his former notions and the opinions of others examin with a perfect indifferency the question in its source without an inclination to either side, or any regard to his or others unexamined opinions. This I owne is noe easy thing to doe, But I am not enquiring the easy way to opinion but the right way to truth which they must follow who will deale fairly with their own understandings and their own soules.

Essay III, ix, 23: The Volumes of Interpreters, and Commentators on the Old and New Testament, are but too manifest proofs of this. Though every thing said in the Text be infallibly true, yet the Reader may be, nay cannot chuse but be very fallible in the understanding of it. Nor is it to be wondred, that the Will of GOD, when cloathed in Words, should be liable to that doubt and uncertainty, which unavoidably attends that sort of Conveyance, when even his Son, whilst cloathed in Flesh, was subject to all the Frailties and Inconveniencies of human Nature, Sin excepted. And we ought to magnify his Goodness, that he spread before all the World, such legible Characters of his Works and Providence, and given all Mankind so sufficient a light of Reason, that they to whom this Written Word never came, could not (whenever they set themselves to search) either doubt of the Being of a GOD, or of the Obedience due to Him. Since then the Precepts of Natural Religion are plain, and very intelligible to all Mankind, and seldom come to be controverted; and

6 THEOLOGY, SOURCES, AND PRAGMATICS OF ASSENT

other revealed Truths, which are conveyed to us by Books and Languages, are liable to the common and natural obscurities and difficulties incident to Words, methinks it would become us to be more careful and diligent in observing the former, and less magisterial, positive, and imperious, in imposing our own sense and interpretations of the latter.

2

MORALITY AND RELIGION

Of Ethick in General

1. Happyness & misery are the two great springs of humane actions & through the different ways we finde men so busy in the world they all aime at happynesse & desire to avoid misery as it appears to them in different places & shapes.

2. I doe not remember that I have heard of any nation of men who have not acknowledgd that there has been right & wrong in mens actions as well as truth & falshood in their sayings. some measures there have been every where owned though very different some rules & boundarys to mens actions by which they were judgd to be good or bad, nor is there I thinke any people amongst whome there is noe distinction between virtue & vice. Some kinde of morality is to be found every where received I will not say perfect & exact but yet enough to let us know that the notion of it is more or lesse every where & that even where politique societys & magistrates are silent men yet are under some laws to which they owe obedience.

3. But however morality be the great businesse & concernment of mankinde & soe deserves our most attentive application & study, yet in the very entrance this occurs very strange & worthy our consideration that Morality hath been generally in the world treated as a science destinct from Theologie. Religion. & Law & that it has been the proper province of philosophers a sort of men different both from Divines Priests & Lawyers whose profession it has been to explaine & teach this knowledg to the world. A plain argumt to me of ~~an impression in the minds of~~ some discovery still amongst men of the law of nature, & a secret apprehension of another rule of action which rational creatures had a concernment to conforme to besides what either the priest pretended was the immediate command of their god (for all their heathen ceremonies of worship pretended to revelation reason faileing in the support of them) or the Lawyer told them was the command of the government.

4. But yet these philosophers seldom deriving these rules up to their originall nor urgeing them as the commands of the great god of Heaven & Earth & such as according to which he would retribute to men after this life; the utmost inforcemts they could adde to them, were reputation & disgrace by these names of virtue & vice which they endeavoured by

MORALITY AND RELIGION

their authority to make names of weight to their schollers & the rest of
the people Were there no humane law noe punishment noe obligation of
civill or divine sanctions there would yet still be such species of actions in
the world of Justice Temperence & Fortitude Drunkenesse & Theft
which would also be thought some of them good some bad, there would
be destinct notions of vertues & vices. For to each of these names there
would belong a complex Ideas or otherwise all these & the like words
which expresse morall things in all languages would be empty
insignificant sounds & all moral discourses would be perfect Jargon.
But all the knowledg of virtue & vice which a man atteind to this way
would amount to noe more then takeing the definitions or the
significations of the words of any language either from the more skilled
in that language or the common usage of the Country to know how to
apply them & call particular actions in that country by their right names
& soe in effect would be noe more but the skill how to speake properly or
at most know which actions in the Country he lives in are thought
laudible or disgracefull i.e. are calld virtues & vices the generall rule
whereof & the most constant that I can finde is that those actions are
esteemed virtuous which are thought absolutely necessary to the
preservation of society & those that disturbe or dissolve the bonds of
community are every where esteemed ill & vitious.

5. This would necessarily fall out for were there noe obligation or
Superior law at all besides that of Society since it cannot be Supposed
that any men should associate togeather & unite in the same community
& at the same time allow that for commendable i e count it a virtue nay
not discountenance & treate such actions as blameable i e count them
vices which tend to the dissolution of that society in which they were
united but all other actions that are not thought to have such an
immoderate influence on society I finde not (as far as I have been
conversant in historys) but that in some Countrys or Societys they are
virtues in others vices & in others indifferent according as the authority
of some offend wise men in some places or in inclinaton or fashion of the
people in other places hath happend to establishe them virtues or vices so
that the Ideas of virtue taken up this way teach us noe more then to
speake properly according to the fashon of the Country we are in
without any great improvemt of our knowledge more then what men
meant by such words & this is the knowledg conteind in the common
Ethicks of the Schools & this is noe more but to know the right names of
certain complex modes & the skill of Speaking properly.

6 The Ethicks of the schoolls built upon the Authority of Aristotle but

OF ETHICK IN GENERAL

perplexd a great deale more with hard words & uselesse destinctions telling us what he or they are pleased to call vertues & vices teach us noe thing of morality but only to understand their names, or call actions as they or Aristotle does which is in effect but to speake their language properly The end and use of Morality being to direct our lives, & by shewing us what actions are Good & what bad prepare us to doe the one & avoid the other, those that pretend to teach Morals mistake their businesse & become only language masters when they doe not doe this, when they teach us only to talke & dispute, call actions by names they prescribe, when they doe not shew the inforcemt that may draw us to virtue & deture us from vice.

7. Moral actions are only those that depend upon the choise of an understanding & free agent. And an understanding free agent naturally follows that which causes pleasure to it & flies that which causes pain. i.e naturally seekes happynesse & shuns misery. That then which causes him paine is bad to him. And that which causes the greater pleasure is the greater good & that which causes the greater pain the greater evill. For happynesse & misery consisting only in pleasure & pain either of minde or body or both according to the interpretation I have given above of those words L 2 c. 21 noe thing can be good or bad to any one but as it tends to their happynesse or misery. as it serves to produce in them pleasure or pain. For good & bad being relative termes doe not denote any thing in the natue of the thing but only the relation it bares to an other in its aptnesse & tendency to produce in it, pleasure or pain. And thus we see & say that which is good for one man is bad for an other.

8. Now though it be not soe apprehended generally yet tis from this tendency to produce to us pleasure or pain that Morall good or Evil has its name as well as naturall. that perhaps twill not be found soe erroneous as perhaps at first sight it will seeme strange if one should affirme That there is noe thing Morally Good which does not produce pleasure to a man, nor noe thing morally Evill that does not bring pain to him. ~~Why does a man pay an other a debt he owes him when he wants the mony to supply his own conveniencys or necessitys. Or why does another forbeare his neighbours wife. It will perhaps be answerd because there is Morall rectitude & goodnesse in the one. & moral turpitude or Ilnesse in the other. Good words. This moral rectitude which when considerd is but conformity to the natural law of god, would signify noething & moral goodnesse be noe reason to direct my action were there not really pleasure that would follow from the doeing of it & pain avoided greater than is to be found in the action it self. Were there noe lesse of pleasure,~~

MORALITY AND RELIGION

~~noe paine to follow from a mans satisfying his appetite as he could would~~
~~he not be a foole to endure the paine of hunger, when his neighbours~~
~~barne or stall could furnish him if noe evill would follow from his takeing~~
~~what was not his but the danger of a surfet~~ The difference between
5 morall & natural good & evill is only this that we call that natural good &
evill which by the natural efficiency of this thing produces pleasure or
peine in us & that is morally Good or Evill which by the appointmt of an
Intelligent Being that has power draws pleasure or peine after it not by
any natural consequence but by the intervention of that power. Thus
10 drinkeing to Excesse when it produces the headache or sicknesse is a
natural evil; but as it is a transgression of a law by which punishmt is
annexd to it, it is a Morall Evill. For rewards & punishmts are the good
and evill whereby Superiors enforce the observance of their laws it being
impossible to set any other motive or restraint to the actions of a free
15 understanding agent but the consideration of good or evill, that is
pleasure or pain, that will follow from it.

9. Who ever treats of Morality soe as to give us only the definitions of
Justice & temperence Theft & Incontinency &c. & tells which are vertues
which are vices does only setle certeine complex Ideas of Modes with
20 their names to them whereby we may learne to understand others well
when they talke by their rules & speake intelligibly & properly to others
who have been informed in their doctrine. But whilst they discourse
never soe acutely of temperence or Justice but shew noe law of a superior
that prescribes temperence to the observation or breach of which laws
25 there are rewards and punishmts annexd the force of morality is lost &
evaporates only into words & desputes & nicetys. And however Aristotle
or Anacarsis, Confucius or any amongst us shall name this or that action
a virtue or vice their Authoritys are all of them a like & they exercise but
what power every one has which is to shew what complex Ideas their
30 words shall stand for. For without shewing a law that commands or
forbids them Morall goodnesse will be but an empty sound, & those
Actions which ~~Aristotle~~ the schools have calld virtues or vices, may by
the same authority be cald by contrary names in an other country, & if
there be noe thing more then their decisions & determinations in the case
35 they will be still neverthelesse indifferent as to any mans practise, which
will by such kinde of determinations be under noe obligation to observe
them.

10. But there is an other sort of Morality or Rules of our actions which
though they may in many parts be coincident & agreeable with the
40 former yet have a different foundation & we come to the knowledge of

OF ETHICK IN GENERAL

them a different way these notions or standards of our actions not being Ideas of our own makeing to which we gives names but depend upon some thing without us & soe not made by us but for us & these are the rules set to our actions by the declard will or laws of another who hath power to punish our aberrations. These are properly & truely the rules of 5 good and evill because the conformity or disagreement of our actions with these bring upon us good or evill these influence our lives as the other doe our words & there is as much difference between those two as between living well & attaining happiness on the one hand compard with speaking properly & understanding of words on the other. The notion of 10 one, men have, by makeing to themselves a Collection of simple Ideas called by those names which they take to be names of virtues & vices; The notion of the other we come by from the rules set us by a Superior power

11. but because we cannot come to the knowledge of these rules without 1° makeing known a lawgiver to all mankinde with power & will 15 to reward & punish & 2° without shewing how he hath declard his will & law I must only at present suppose this rule till a fit place to speake of these viz god & the law of nature & only at present mention what is imediately to the purpose in hand 1°. That this rule of our actions set us by our lawmaker is conversant about & ultimately terminates in these 20 simple Ideas before mentioned v. g. thou shalt love thy neighbour as thy selfe 2° that the law being known or supposed knowne by us the relation of our actions to it. i e the agreementt or disagreementt of any thing we doe to that rule is as Easy & clearly knowne as any other relation 3° that we have morall Ideas as well as others that we come by them the same 25 way & that they are nothing but collections of simple Ideas. Only we are carefully to retain that destinction of moral actions that they have a double consideration 1° as they have their proper denominations as liberality modesty frugality Jesting &c. & thus they are but modes i e actions made up of such a precise collection of simple Ideas but tis not 30 thereby determined that they are either good or bad virtue or vice v.g. 2° As they refer to a law with which they agree or disagree soe are they good or bad virtues or vices Εὐτραπελία was a name amongst the Greeks of such a peculiar sort of action i.e. of such a collection of Simple Ideas concurring to make them up but whether this collection of simple Ideas 35 called εὐτραπελία be a virtue or vice is known only compareing it to that rule which determines virtue or vice & this is that consideration that properly belongs to actions i e their agreemt with a rule. In one any action is only a Collection of simple Ideas & soe is a possitive Complex Idea in the other it stands in relation to a law or rule & according as it 40

MORALITY AND RELIGION

agrees or disagrees is virtue or vice Soe Education & piety feasting & gluttony are modes alike being but certain complex Ideas calld by one name but when they are Considered as virtues & vices & rules of life carying an obligation with them they relate to a law & soe come under the consideration of relation.

~~That which to the mind as the greater Good at that time determines its choise~~

12. To establish morality therefor upon its proper basis & such foundations as may carry an obligation with them we must first prove a law which always supposes a law maker one that has a superiority & right to ordeyne & also a power to reward & punish according to the tenor of the law establishd by him. This Soverain Law maker who has set rules & bounds to the actions of men is god their maker whose existence we have already proved

The next thing then to shew is that there are certain rules certain dictates which it is his will all men should conforme their actions to, & that this will of his is sufficiently promulgated & made know to all man kinde.

92

Ethica

Noe thing can attract a rational agent nor be a cause of it of action but good. That good is only pleasure or greater pleasure or the means to it. Pleasures are all of the minde none of the body. but some consist in motions of the body some in contemplations & satisfactions of the minde separate or abstract & independent from any motions or 5 affections of the body. And these later are both the greatest & more lasting. The former of these we will for shortnesse sake ⟨call⟩ pleasures of the senses the other pleasures of the soule. or rather material & immaterial pleasures. Material pleasures last not beyond the present application of the object to the senses and make but a small part of the life 10 of the most voluptious man. Those of taste cease as soon as the stomach is full & a satiated appetite loathes the most exquisite dishes. Parfumes make men weary in a little time or which is the same are not smelt. Few are so delighted with musick that when it is grown familiar to them either minde it not or at least do not prefer this discourse of a friend to it as any 15 one may observe in himself & others. And for seeing though it be the most capacious & most emploid of all our senses, yet the pleasure of it lies not soe much in the delight the eyes have in the object before it, but in other things annexd to them as the knowledg & choise of things serviceable to the other parts of our lives & in the power of seeing so 20 usefull to us in all the parts of our lives. So that all the pleasures of the senses taken together even that too which modestie speaks not openly of I thinke one may say that the most voluptious man has not his senses affected by them & so has not pleasure from them $\frac{1}{4}$ part of his time perhaps when examined it will be found much lesse the rest the body lies 25 fallow or unaffected with pleasure. Perhaps it will be that though the bodily sensation be so short yet the enjoyment & pleasure is longer as of a splendid entertainment. The satisfaction lasts longer than the meale it began before it and ends not with it. Let it be so, which shews that even in those material sensual pleasures, contemplation makes up the greatest 30 part & when the senses have done the minde by thought continues a pleasure wherein the senses have noe share. The use I make of this is that even in voluptious men the minde without the body makes the greatest

16 MORALITY AND RELIGION

part of their happynesse or else the greatest part of their lives they only
are destitute of happynesse.

If then happynesse be our interest & businesse tis evident the way to it
is to love our neighbour as our self for by that means we enlarge & secure
5 our pleasures since then all the good we doe redoubts upon our selves &
gives us an undecaying & uninterrupted pleasure. who ever spared a
meale to save the life of a starveing man much more a friend which all
men are to us whom we love but had more and much more lasting
pleasure in it than he that eat it! The other pleasure died as he eat &
10 ended with his meal. but to him that gave it tis a feast as often as he
reflects on it.

Next pleasures of the minde are the greatest as well as the most lasting.
who ever was so bruitish as would not quit the greatest sensual pleasure
to save a childs life whom he loved what is this but pleasure of thought
15 remote from any sensual delight. Love all the world as you would do
your child or self & make this universal & how much short will it make
the earth of heaven.

Happynesse therefore is annexed to our loving others & to our doeing
our duty, to acts of love & charity or he that will deny it to be soe here
20 because every one observes not this rule of universal love & charity. He
brings in a necessity of another life (wherein god may put a distinction
between those that did good & sufferd & those who did evil & enjoyd by
their different treatment there) & soe enforces morality the stronger
laying a necessity on gods justice by his rewards & punishment he made
25 the good the gainers the wicked loosers.

98
Sacerdos

There were two sorts of Teachers amongst the ancients. Those who professed to teach them the arts of propitiation & atonement & those were primarily their Priests who for the most part made them selves the mediators betwixt the gods & men wherein they performed all or the principal part, at least noething was done without them. The Laity had but a small part in the performance unlesse it were in the charge of it & that was wholy theirs. The cheif at least the essential & sanctifying part of the ceremony was always the priest & the people and doe noething without them. The ancients had another sort of teachers who were calld philosophers. These had their schools professd to instruct those who would applie to them, the knowledg of things & the rules of virtue. These mixed not in with the publique religious worship or ceremonies but left them entirely to the priest, as the priests left the instruction of men in natural & moral knowledg wholy to the philosophers. These two parts or provinces of knowledg thus under the governmt of two different sorts of men, seem to be founded upon the supposition of two clearly distinct originals. viz Revelation & Reason. For the priests never for any of their ceremonies or forms of worship pleaded Reason: But always urged their sacred observances from the pleasure of the gods, antiquity & tradition, which at last resolves all their establishd rites into noe thing but Revelation[1] The philosophers on the other side pretended to noe thing but reason in all that they said & from thence owned to fetch all their doctrines. Though how little their lives answerd their owne rules whilst they studied ostentation & vanity rather than solid virtue Cicero tells us Tusc. Quest. l. 2 c. 4.

Jesus Christ bringing by revelation from heaven the true Religion to mankinde reunited these two again Religion and Morality as the inseparable parts of the worship of god, which ought never to have been separated, wherein for the obteining the favour & forgivenesse of the deity the chief part of what man could doe consisted in a holy life, & little or noe thing at all was left to outward ceremonie. which was therefore almost wholy cashiered out of true religion: and only two very plain & simple institutions introduced. all pompous rites being wholy abolishd,

18 MORALITY AND RELIGION

& no more of outward performances commanded but just soe much as decency & order requird in actions of publique assemblys. This being the state of this true Religion comeing immediately from god him self, The Ministers of it who also call them selves priests have assumed to them selves the parts both of the heathen priests & philosophers: And claim a right not only to performe all the outward acts of the Christian religion in publique & to regulate the ceremonies to be used there: But also to teach men their dutys of Morality towards one another & towards them selves & to prescribe to them in the conduct of their lives.

[1] cum de religione agitur T: Coruncan⟨i⟩um. P. Scipionem. P. Scaevolam pontifices maximos, non Zenonem aut Cleanthem, aut Chrysippum sequor . . . A te philosopho rationem accipere debeo religionis: majoribus autem nostris, etiam nulla ratione reddita credere Cic: de Nat deor: l. 3 ap Bayle pensées diverses § 127.

3

ADVERSARIA
THEOLOGICA 94

94
Adversaria Theologica

All of the entries in the 'Adversaria', with the exception of Locke's index, are printed below. Page numbers are given in brackets above the entries. For the reader's convenience, I have included translations of the names of topics in brackets. For translations of other passages, see the notes.

[1]
Deus [God]
  Unus [One]
  Trinus [Three]
  Omnipotens [Omnipotent]   5
  Omnisciens [Omniscient]
  Benignus [Good]
[2]
Spiritus [Spirit]
  Quando creati [When created?]   10
  Natura [Nature]
  Species [Kinds]
  Facultates [Faculties or Powers]
  Lapsus [Fall]
  Crimen [Offence]   15
  Supplicium [Punishment]
  Potestas [Power]
Anima humana [The human soul]
  Præexistentia [Preexistence]
  Revolutio [Revolution]   20
  Creatio [Creation]
  Traductio [Traduction]
Anima brutorum [The soul of animals]
[3]
Materia [Matter]   25
  creata [Created]
  Qualis [What kind?]
  Quanta [How much?]

22 ADVERSARIA THEOLOGICA

Mundus aspectabilis [Visible World]
  Antiquitas [Antiquity]
Systema nostrum [Our planetary system]
  Sol [Sun]
5 Planetae [Planets]
  Terra [Earth]
[4]
Homo [Man]
  Innocens [Innocent]
10 Lapsus [Fall]
  Intellectus [Understanding]
  Voluntas [Will]
  Libertas [Liberty]
  Sensus [Sense]
15 Peccatum Adami [Adam's sin]
    quid [What?]
    quomodo affecit Adamum [How it affected Adam]
        posteros eius reatu [How it affected his posterity:
        by accusation]
20   imputatione [by imputation]
    infectione [by infection]
  post mortem [After death]
  pseuchopannuchia [psychopannychia, viz. Soul sleep]
  Resurrectio [Resurrectio]
25 Paradisus [Paradise]
  Gehenna [Gehenna, Hell]
  Annihilatio [Annihilation]
[5]
Christus [Christ]
30 Deus [God]
  Primus creaturarum [First born of Creatures]
  Homo [Man]
  Redimit [He redeems]
    a quo [from what?]
35   quomodo [how?]
    pretio [by payment]
    gratia [by grace]
    spiritu [by the spirit]
    quos [who?]
40   credentes [believers]

ADVERSARIA THEOLOGICA

quae credenda ad salutem [what one must believe to be saved]
sanctos [saints]
quae agenda ad salutem [what one must do to be saved]
Spiritus Sanctus [The holy spirit]
   quis [who?]
   quomodo operatur [how it works]
     in quos [in whom?]
[6]
Revelatio [Revelation]
   Necessaria [Its necessity]
   Theopneusta [Divine inspiration]
   Modi [Modes]
   Certitudo [Certainty]
   Miracula [Miracles]
Biblia [Scripture]
   Lex Mosaica [Mosaic Law]
   Evangelium [The Gospel]
[7]
Ethica sive Hominis officium [Ethics or the duty of man]
   Erga Deum [Towards God]
     Spiritus bonos [Good Spirits]
       malos [Evil Spirits]
     Rempublicam [The State]
     Magistratus [Magistrates]
     Parentes [Parents]
     Conjuges [Spouses]
     Liberos [Freemen]
     Affines [Family members]
     Dominos [Masters]
     Servos [Servants]
     Herum [Heads of households]
     Famulos [Family Members]
     Vicinos [Neighbours]
     Homines [Mankind in general]
     Seipsum [Oneself]
[12]

Trinitas

1 Gen. I. 26. Let us ⟨make man⟩
2 Man is become as one of us. Gen III 22 & Gen XI. 6. 7. Isa. VI. 8
3

24 ADVERSARIA THEOLOGICA

[13]

Non Trinitas

Because it subverteth the unity of god. introducing 3 gods

Because it is inconsistent with the rule of prayer directed in the Sacred
5 Scripture: For if god be 3 persons how can we pray to him through his
son for his spirit?

The father alone is the most high god Luk I. 32. 35.

There is but one first independent cause of all things which is the most
high god Romans XI. 36

10 The Lord shall be one & his name one Zec XIV. 9

The Lord our god the Lord is one Mar XII. 29

'Tis life eternal to know thee [father] the only true god & Jesus Christ
whom thou has sent Joh XVII 3. If the holy spirit were god the
knowledg of him would be necessary too to eternal life. It is eternal life to
15 know Christ as sent, not as eternaly begotten, nor as co essential to the
father. Bidle $\frac{1}{24}$

1 Cor VIII. 5. 6

There is one spirit manifestly distinguished from god i.e. one created
spirit by way of excellency. 1° the holy spirit. 2° There is one Lord
20 distinguished from god & therefor made else there would be 2 unmade
Lords i e one made Lord by way of Excellency which is Jesus. Eph IV. 4–
6, Act II. 22. 23. 33. 36 Mat XXIV. 36. Mar XIII. 32

Rom XV. 6

Joh VI. 27

25 Jam III. 9

Joh VIII. 54. The Jews know noe god but the father & that was St
Pauls god 2 Tim I. 3. Act III. 13. V. 30. 31 XXII. 14 Nehemiah. IX. 6
Thou art Lord alone. Thou denoteth a single person

1 Let us make man noe more proves the speaker to be more persons
30 than one, than the like forme Mark VI. 30 Joh. III. 11. 2 Cor X. 1. 2.
This, if any thing, proves only that there was some other person with
god, whom he imploid as in the creation of other things soe of man viz.
the Spirit vs. 2. Psal CIV. 30. Job. XXVI. 13. XXXIII. 4

2 Gen III. 22 This was spoken also to the Holy Spirit as also that Gen
35 XI. 6. 7. Isa VI. 8

3

[14]

Cultus

All the congregation blessed the Lord god of their fathers, & bowed
40 down their heads & worshiped the Lord & the King. 1 Chr XXIX. 20

ADVERSARIA THEOLOGICA

[15]
Propitiatio Placamen

Ipsi deo nihil minus gratum quam non omnibus patere ad se placandum et colendum viam. Cicero de leg.

[26]
Christus Deus Supremus

1 If Christ were not god he could not satisfie our sins

2 He is called the mighty god Isa IX. 6

3 ὢν ἐπὶ πάντων θεὸς εὐλογητός εἰς τοὺς αἰῶνας. Rom IX. 5

[27]
Christus non Deus supremus

Because we are to honour him for that the father hath committed all judgment to him. Joh V. 22. 23 But the highest is to be honourd with the highest honour for him self & for noe other but his own sake

Because the love to the father is made the ground & reason of love to the son 1 Joh. V. 1

He is the Son of the most high Luke I. 32 & thereby distinguishd from the Most high

The father is greater than he Joh. XIV. 38

Phil. II. 5–8 vid. Bidle $\frac{5}{24}$ noe body can be equal with him self equality is always between two itd.

I Cor VIII. 6. By whom are all things. i e pertaining to our Salvation itd. 7. God has made him Lord Act II. 39. Phil. II. 9. 10

The glory & thanks which we give to Christ & the faith & hope that we place in him doe not rest in him but through him tend to god the father. Phil. II. 9. 10. 1. Pet. I. 21 Joh. XII. 44. Rom. I. 8. XVI. 27. & therefor he is not equal to god

He shall deliver up the Kingdom & be subject to the father 1 Cor XV. 24. 25. 28. Ans: He shall be subject according to his human nature. Resp (1) This distinction is not to be found in gods word. (2) It begs the question for it supposes two natures in Christ which is the thing in question (3) It makes two persons in Christ, for he is to be subiect who ruled & subdued, i e a person, for noe other can be a King, & therefor they must grant that the person of Christ which they hold to be a person of supream Deity delivereth up his Kingdom & becomes subiect. Or that his humane nature is a person. The later of these subverts the Trinitarian doctrine, the former it self itd. 7 (4) Tis said the Son him self shall be subiect: But how can the son him self become subject if only a humane nature added to the son is subiected & not the very person of the son? Bidle $\frac{8}{24}$

26 ADVERSARIA THEOLOGICA

God has exalted him & made him Lord. Phil. II 9–11 & raised him from the dead Rom X. 9. IV 24

If the eternall son of god coequall & coessential with the father were conceived & borne of the Virgin Mary. How said the Angel to Joseph
5 that which is conceived in her is of the holy Spirit? Mat I. 20. Bidle $\frac{11}{24}$
Luk I 35 Act X. 38 Luk. XXII. 48 Mat XVII. 46

1 How can God satisfie god? If one person satisfies an other, then he that satisfies is still unsatisfied or forgives itd. 12
Joh XX. 17. Eph. I. 7. Heb. I. 8. 9.
10 2 A mighty god for in the Hebrew El Gibbor not Hael Haggibbor as the Lord of Hosts is called Jer XXXII. 18. Besides the words in the close of vs. 7 distingish Christ from the Lord of hosts makeing his god head depend on the bounty of the Lord of hosts. Bidel $\frac{5}{24}$

3 A god over all for θεὸς there ⟨in Rom. IX. 5⟩ is without an article &
15 soe signifies not the supreme deity.
[28]

Christus merus homo

Christ was foreknown before the foundation of the world 1 Pet I. 20 How coud he be foreknown had he then had a being? Bidle $\frac{4}{24}$
20 Adam is the Type of him that was to come Rom V. 14. was Adam the type of him that created him or had then a being? itd. for the Greek is τοῦ μέλλοντος he that was to be.

There is one god. & one mediator of god & man, the man Christ Jesus 2 Tim: II. 5
25 The most excellent things that in Sacred Scripture are attributed to him are attributed to him under the notion & name of a Man as Mediator. Ascension into heaven before his death John III. 13. To have heard the truth from god Joh VIII. 40. To be beleived on to eternal life Joh III. 14. 15. To forgive sins Mat IX. 6–8. To have all judgment Joh. V. 22. 23.
30 27. Lord of the Sabbath. Mar II. 28 To be author of the Resurrection 1 Cor XV. 21 22. A quickening spirit vs. 45 The Lord from heaven vs. 47 To gather his elect. sending his angels Math XXIV. 30. 31 To reward every man according to his doeing XVI. 27. come in his Kingdom vs. 28. To have an everlasting dominion given him that all nations may serve
35 him Dan VII. 13. 14 Bidle $\frac{9}{24}$

He was to be raised up a prophet from the midst of the Israelites. Deut XVIII. 15 therefor did not exist in or before Moses's time
Act II. 22. 23. 36.
Joh. X 33–36. Did the godhead of Christ consist in a divine nature,
40 besides his humane it would have been necessary for answering the Jews

ADVERSARIA THEOLOGICA

here to have declared it. itd. 11 But he sayth he is god because the father had sanctified & sent him

If the eternal son of god equall with the father were conceived & borne of the virgin Mary how said the Angel to Joseph that which is conceived in her is of the holy Spirit Mat I 20. Luk I. 35. Act X: 38. Luk XXII. 48. Mat XXII. 46

[29]

Christus non merus homo

Because his spirit was in the ancient prophets 1 Pet. I. 11 JL

[30]

Spiritus Sanctus Deus

1 Father son & holy ghost equal because ranked togeather Mat XXVIII. 19

2 The Holy Spirit unlesse omnipresent could not dwell in soe many at once, & if omnipresent he is god

[31]

Spiritus Sanctus Non Deus

The cheif of ministring spirits. Heb. I. 14. cum 1 Pet. I. 12. Heb. I. 7. cum Act II. 2–4. As there is one Principal spirit among the Evil Angels caled Satan or the Adversary 1 Pet. V. 8. Unclean spirit Zach. XIII. 2. Evil spirit of god 1 Sam XVI. 15. 16 Spirit of god itd. 23: So there is one principal spirit among the good Angels, called Advocate Joh. XVI. 7. Holy spirit Eph. IV. 30 the good Spirit of god Neh. IX. 20. The Spirit Act X. 19. Spirit of god 1 Cor VII. 40.

Inferior to god by the whole tenour of the Scripture Neh: IX. 6. 20. Joh. XVI. 7. 8. Rom VIII 26. 27. Act XIX. 2. Eph IV. 4–6. 1 Cor XII. 3. 4 &c Luk III. 21. 22. 1 Cor II. 11–13 Rev. XXII. 12. 17. Act V. 32. Gal III. 5. 1 Cor. VIII. 4. Bidle $\frac{12}{16}$

Because distinguishd in Scripture from god. Person & Essence of god not distinct. 1° Because noe foundation in Sacred Scripture for such a distinction. 2° Noe distinct conception but of the sounds. 3° If the person be distinct from the Essence of god, it must be something finite & then god is finite; or infinite & then there are two infinites in god & consequently two gods. 4° To talk of God impersonaly is ridiculous Persona est suppositum intelligens

Because he speaketh not of himself but heareth from an other what he shall speak Joh. XVI. 13. 14

Because he is the gift of god Act. XII. 17 Neh. IX. 20 Rom V. 5

Because he changes place Luk III. 22. 23 Joh. I. 32

Because he prayeth to god. Rev. XXII. 12. 17

28 ADVERSARIA THEOLOGICA

Because men have been disciples & beleivers in god without beleiving in the Holy ghost Act XIX. 2. Rom. X. 14. Bidle $\frac{1}{16}$

1 Not equal because ranked togeather Mat XXV III. 19 vid. 1 Tim V. 21 Luk. IX. 26. <u>Into the name</u> of the holy Spirit i e into the holy Spirit into the guidance of the holy spirit itd. 8

2 If the Spirit be omnipresent & consequently god because he dwels in soe many, will not Satan by the same argument be omnipresent. vid. Mar. IV. 15. 1 King XXII. 22. 23. 2 Tim. II. last. 2 Cor IV. 4. Rev. I. 13. Joh. VIII. 38 Rev. XII. 9. XX. 2.3. The Spirit is not omni present Joh. XV. 26 Gal. IV. 6. 1 Pet. I. 12. Joh. I. 32. Luk III. 21. 22. The spirit dwelleth in the Saints by his gifts & effects, but not by his substance. If it were by his person & substance he would then fill all the world, & then he would dwell in all men alike. Bidle $\frac{16}{16}$

We are noe where in Scripture commanded expresly to love & honour the holy Spirit He is inferior to Christ Joh. XVI. 13–15. Evident by the benefits we receive from the one & the other. From the Spirit wisdome, knowledg, Faith, Gift of healeing, working of miracles, Prophesie Discerning of Spirits, Tongues, Interpretation of Tongues 1 Cor XII. 8–10 From Christ Remission of sins. Col III. 13. He is the pledg of our heavenly inheritance Eph. I. 14. The heavenly inheritance Mat XXV. 34. Luc XXII. 29 Joh. XVII. 2. From the Spirit assurance that we are the children of god Rom. VIII. 16. From Christ a power to become the sons of god Joh. I. 12. The Spirit is given upon Repentence. Christ gives repentence it self Act. V. 31

[32]

Anima humana Immaterialis

2 Cor XII. 2. An in corpore an extra corpus nescio

Mat X. 28. LXII. 4. 5. Fear not them that can kill the body but are not able to kill the Soule

Then shall the dust return to the earth as it was & the spirit shall return unto god who gave it. Eccles. XII. 7.

Father into thy hands I commend my spirit Luc XIII. 46

Lord Jesus receive my spirit. Act VII. 59

Si anima sit crasis corporea, quae dissoluto corpore tota perit, fieri utique non potest ut idem numero homo post mortem resurgat. Hactenus Episcopius $\frac{354}{440}$

1 We cannot conceive one material atom to think nor any Systeme of Atoms or particles to think JL

2 ψυχή In many places of the new Testament signifies only the animal life & thought in this present world without reference to any material or

ADVERSARIA THEOLOGICA

immaterial being or substance wherein it resides. So Math II. 20. VI. 25. XX. 28 Mar. X. 45. Luc XIV. 26. Joh: X. 11. XII. 25. Acts XX. 24. Act XXVII. 10. 22. Rom XI. 3. XVI. 4. 1 Cor. XV. 44. 45. Here the Apostle tels us of a spiritual body & an animal body. by which it appears that matter is capable of animality & spirituality ~~wherein then lies the difference between body soul & spirit?~~ And maybe considerd in three states 1st simply Body is insensible matter. σῶμα ψυχικόν that state of a thinkeing being in this life which depending on nourishment & the assistance & supply of new matter is corruptible. ~~Spirit~~ σῶμα πνευματικόν such a state of a sensible thinkeing being or body as has life & vigor durable in it self without need of any supplie from without & soe not liable to corruption. This the context in this XV Cor seems plainly to make out for speakeing of the different state of a man before & after the resurrection he says the one is a body animal corruptible & mortal the other is a body spiritual incorruptible & immortal as appears to any one who diligently considers what is said from vs. 40. to vs. 55. For the Apostle makes noe destinction here of soule & body material & immaterial as if one died & the other continued liveing the one was raised & the other not but he speaks of the whole man as dyeing & the whole man as raisd & this man what is he before the resurrection? vs. 44 he tels that he is σῶμα ψυχικὸν, an animal body sown in corruption. vs. 42 liable to be corrupted & dissolvd, sown in dishonour vs. 43 opposd to glory, which vss. 40 & 41 is the state of celestial bodys that shine & last & are not thought liable to corruption. The one made of grosse earth vss. 47 flesh & bloud, 50. The man after resurrection what is he? A spiritual body, vss. 44. 45. incorruptible, vss. 42, 52. in glory, vss. 43. & 40, 41. coelestial, vss. 39. 47. 48. 49. & tis plain that tis the same that is corruptible which puts on incorruption. vs. 53. Soe that immortality is not at all oweing nor built on immateriality as in its own nature incorruptible. The Apostle knew not that argument which is soe much insisted on but quite the contrary and says this corruptible must be changed & put on incorruption & this mortal put on immortality. Which corruptible & mortal is not meant of the body in contra distinction to the soule but of the whole man as is plain by the preceding part of this Chapter particularly vss. 18. 19. 22. 35. 36. 37. That which is sewn is the whole seed that which dies is the whole seed. If any one think that from St Pauls way of speakeing 2 Cor. V. 1. 2. 3. 4. he may conclude that there is in us an immaterial immutable substance distinct from the body I desire him to compare 1 Cor XV. 35. 36. 37. 38 & then see whether by that argument he must not as well conclude that in a grain of wheat there

30 ADVERSARIA THEOLOGICA

is an immaterial substance which is cald the grain of wheat as well as in the other place tis an immaterial substance which is cald we vid. Jo. V. 28. 29. And it is further remarkeable that in the whole new testament there is noe such thing as any mention of the resurrection of the body how ever it crept into the creed, but every where the resurrection is spoke of as the whole man. The resurrection is opposd to the state of insensibility & death in a man as is plain by the discourse between Martha & our Saviour Joh XI. 21–26 & Act. II. 31 οὐ κατελείφθη ἡ ψυχὴ αὐτοῦ εἰς ἅδου i e he should not be left in a state of the dead or of insensibility. JL

[33]

Anima humana Materialis

The life of the flesh is in the bloud, & I have given it to you upon the altar to make an attonement for your souls: for it is the bloud that makes an attonement for the soule Lev. XVII. 11

But flesh with the life thereof, which is the bloud thereof, shall you not eat. And surely your bloud of your lives will I require: at the hands of every beast will I require it; and at the hand of man, at the hand of every mans brother will I require the life of man. Gen IX. 4. 5.

1 We can conceive noe movable substance without extension, for what is not exended is no where. i e is not JL From this & the opposite we must conclude there is something in the nature of Spirits or thinking beings which we cannot conceive JL

2 Vid. the other page

[34]

Credenda necessario ad Salutem

Animae Immaterialitas. Aliter credi non potest resurrectio eiusdem numero hominis. Epis. $\frac{354}{440}$

[36]

Homo lapsus Liber

Liber est qui potest agere vel non agere JL

Ubicunque necessitas mera dominatur ibi religioni non est locus Epis $\frac{357}{440}$

In libero agente potentia ad agendum simul est cum potentia ad non agendum sed agens ipse se determinare potest ad agendum aut non agendum prout vult vel cum ad agendum se determinavit ab agendo cessare et actionem suam cohibere aut suspendere JL

[37]

Homo lapsus non liber

[38]

Adami ⟨Hominis⟩ Status ante Lapsum

ADVERSARIA THEOLOGICA 31

Anima non rasa tabula uti infantium omnium post nascendorum sed scientia actuali praedita earum rerum omnium quas in statu isto scire homini intererat et capacitate ad scientiam ulteriorem adipiscendam. sive per ratiocinationem, sive per experientiam sive per revelationem. Cum hac scientia consistebat 1° ignorantiam quarundam rerum. Ignorabat 5 enim se nudum esse. Nesciebat adhuc bonum et malum &c: 2° potentia errandi et patiendi seductionem. The serpent beguiled Eve Gen III. 13. 2 Cor XI. 3. 1 Tim II. 14. 3° potentia uxorem impensius et inordinatius amandi Gen III. 12. 1 Tim. II. 13
[40] 10

Lex operum. Rom. III. 27

The law of works is that law which requires perfect obedience: & by which a man cannot be justified without a perfect obedience This law admitting of noe remission or abatement of a compleat & exact performance of every title of it. Such an entire obedience is termed 15 Δικαιοσύνη Justice which we translate Righteousnesse Rom II. 26 IV. 6. V. 18. X. 6. Gal. II. 21. Tit. III. 5. 2 Pet. III. 13. Rom. IV. 5. 9. 22. Gal III. 6 Jam II. 23

The language of that Law is you shall keep my statutes & my judgment which if a man doe he shall live in them Lev: XVIII. 5. Ezek. XX. 11. 20 Rom X. 5. Gal. III. 12 but if ye transgresse ye shall die

This law of workes conteins both the positive Law given to Adam & that given by Moses & the Law of Nature, as is evident from Rom II. 14. 15. III. 9. 20. 23
[41] 25

Lex fidei Rom. III. 27.

The Law of Faith is that law, whereby god Justifies a man for beleiveing though by his workes he be not Just. though he come short of perfect obedience to the law of workes. And in this case Faith is by god counted to him for <u>Righteousnesse</u>. i e compleat performance of the law. 30 Rom IV. 3. 5. 6. 7. 8. 23. 24.

This faith for which God Justified Abraham or counted him perfectly Just what was it? It was the beleiveing god when god engagd his promise to him in the covenant he made with him. This is plain to any one who considers these places togeather. Gen XV. 6 <u>He beleived in</u> 35 <u>the Lord</u>. i e ffirmely relyd on the Lord with an assurance of the accomplishment of what he promised. Rom. IV. 3. 18–23. Gal. III. 6. Jam. II. 23.

But will the beleiving that Abraham when he was old should have a child & that his seed should possesse the Land of Canaan, which was 40

32   ADVERSARIA THEOLOGICA

what Abraham beleived be such a faith as for which god will Justifie us, Since god ~~imputed~~ accounted it to him for righteousnesse? Noe. But the Apostle tells us Rom IV. 12 It must be such a faith in us as his was. i e a sure beleif of what god requires us now to beleive under the Gospel. for
5   he tells us vs. 24 This was writ for our instruction
    [42]

Satisfactio Christi. Aff:

    [43]

Satisfactio Christi Neg:

10   Jesus Christ suffered for his owne sake & for ours. He sufferd for his owne sake. (1) ffor the joy that was set before him. i e to obtain the glorious & eternal rewards of a chearful suffering in the cause & for the glory of god Heb XII. 2. (2) Because it became him, for whom are all Things & by whom are all Things i e God in bringing many sons to glory
15   to make the Captain of our Salvation i e Christ perfect through sufferings. Heb. II. 10 He sufferd for our Sakes on many accounts (1) Effectualy to recommend mankind to the mercy, forgivenese & favour of god on the conditions of faith & newness of life on our parts The Unitarians acknowledg that the Lord Christ made him self a voluntary
20   expiatory sacrifice for our sins as may be seen in the Racovian Catechisme, in the Epistles of Schiltingius & Raurus as also in all our late prints in English. What we deny is this: That this Sacrifice was by way of true & proper satisfaction, or full & equate payment to the justice of God. We say, this sacrifice (as all other Sacrifices) was only an oblation
25   or application to the mercy of god: A sacrifice it was which it pleased god to accept for us though he might have refused it. And for this reason tis said all along in the Holy Scripture that god forgives to us our sins; & not that he received a Satisfaction, or an equivalent for them. Considerations $\frac{11}{61}$
30   [44]

Electio

    I cannot see of what use the Doctrine of Election & Perseverence is unlesse it be to lead men into praesumption & a neglect of their dutys being once perswaded that they are in a state of grace, which is a state
35   they are told they can not fall from. For since noe body can know that he is Elected but by haveing true ffaith & noe body can know when he has such a faith that he can not fall from Common & Saving faith (as they are distinguished) being soe a like that he that has faith cannot distinguish whether it be such as he can fall from or noe. Vid. Calv: Inst. l. 3. c. 2
40   § 12 Who is elected or had faith from which he cannot fall can only be

ADVERSARIA THEOLOGICA

known by the event at the last day & therefor is in vain talked of now till the marks of such a faith be certainly given JL

[46]

Redemptio & Ransom

By Christs sufferings & death we are redeemd not from punishment but from Sin primarily & from punishment because free from sin Tit. II. 14. Gal. I. 4. Eph. V. 25. 1 Pet I. 18 Heb. IX. 14. Col. I. 21. 22. Rom. VI. 6. 10. 1 Pet II. 24. 25. Col. II. 14. 1 Pet. IV. 2. 2 Cor V. 14. 15. Christ by his death redeems us from sin in that his death is a demonstration of the truth of his doctrine & the great argument to bring them into an obedience to the Gospel whereby they leave sin & soe scape punishment To restore the law of nature or natural religion almost blotted out by corruption god yields his son to death which is therefor cald a Ransome 1 Cor. VI. 20. 1 Tim II. 6. Hosea. XIII. 14. The first & principal end of Christs death is by being a proof of the Gospel to be a motive to holynesse, & for all such as it thus works on god accepts it as a Sacrifice & forgives their sins. Heb. V. 5. 8. 9. 10. 1 Jo: II. 1. 2. Tis gods acceptance not its merit makes it expiatory Psal LI. 17. Num. XXV. 13

4

INSPIRATION, REVELATION, SCRIPTURE, AND FAITH

Dec. 87
Immediate Inspiration

An inward inspiration or revelation
Q. Whether it be destinguished from a strong persuasion & in what.
Whether reason or revelation has given us rules of destinction. If reason
what are they, if revelation produce them. If there be no destinction.
Such inspirations can be of noe use either for direction or counsel since 5
they cannot be distinguished from illusions.

You suppose them necessary to divine faith which distinction of faith
into divine & humane being noe where that I know made use of in
scripture, is either an uselesse destinction or needs explication, for if
divine faith has any thing different from humane it must be either in the 10
act of assent or the object, or the grounds. the act is every where the
same, the object makes it not divine, for the divils when their faith is
exercised about the diety it still is not divine though they beleive &
tremble. as to the reasons of assent, if it be upon a divine traditional
revelation received upon rational motives, that is noe more then may be 15
had from the scripture in the ordinary way without the inspiration by
you spoken of. If that be only divine which is had by immediate
inspiration that cannot be had from hearing noe more than sight in a
blinde man from discourse. & Pauls powerfull reasoning on the schools
of Tyranny &c. was to noe purpose. 20

Besides this supposition takes away all faith, for though sense &
perception & knowledg conteine a certainty greater then faith, yet they
are not faith. faith is of things not seen & faith shall be swallowed up in
vision & therefor vision puts an end to faith. faith hope & charity but the
greatest of these is charity because that shall last when the other two shall 25
be abolished for a man can be noe more said to beleive what he certainly
knows then to hope for what he actually possesses.

But I imagine the originall of this mistake arises from not rightly
considering the language of the scripture. Tis evident that the Jewish
nation who as they derive all the originall of all things from the great god 30
they worshipd that made the heavens & the earth soe they attributed all
things to him in an more immediate manner & soe it became the ordinary
idiom of their language to ascribe to the Spirit of god som things that were

38 INSPIRATION, REVELATION, SCRIPTURE, AND FAITH

brought about in the ordinary course of providence. Such a way of speakeing is not only not unusuall but very consistent with the notions of a deity in whom we live move & have our being & has noe impropriety in it but when straind to some extraordinary & immediate influences where the effect requires noe such supernatural cause & the end might be obteind without it. That things brought about by the ordinary course of providence & humane meanes are yet thus ascribed to the Spirit of god is very evident in the old Testament or else we must suppose the spirit of god descend to the meane offices of teaching the arts of weaving & embroidery. as in the case of Aholiab &c. besides many other places in ye old testament where the Spirit of god is named & yet it would be folly to ascribe the thing donne to any extraordinary or supernaturall power. The Spirit of the Lord makes the hindes to calve. This way of speakeing continued downe in that nation to our saviours time & was the language still of the Jews & therefor we are not soe much to wonder that it is soe frequently made use of by the apostles in the new testament wherein many things are ascribed to the spirit which need not the supposition of an immediate & supernaturall influence, which yet in some cases I doe not deny

But to what purpose is it made use of (in the sense you talk of it of an internall supernaturall perception) is this the only foundation of true & saveing faith & the only meanes of salvation, if soe 1° the scripture is uselesse, & Abraham did amisse to send Dives's brethren to Moses & the Prophets which he tooke to be the proper meanes of beleiving soe as to keep men from that place of torment & by addeing that if they will not beleive them, they will not beleive one sent from the dead, where we may take notice that that faith is taken in the ordinary plain sense of assenting upon rational grounds of examination & enquiry & that such an one whether <u>divine</u> or noe was sufficient to keepe men from the place of torment

Q They will not beleive whether it be $\theta\acute{\epsilon}\chi o\upsilon\sigma\iota$

2° If such inspirations be absolutely necessary to salvation your assemblies & preachings are vain & to as litle purpose as to preach to a blinde man & endeavour to perswade him to open his eyes

But to this you have insinuated an answer & that is, that preaching excites those Ideas which are antecedentally in the minde but this has the double weaknesse 1° that it supposes there are latent Ideas in the minde which were never introduced which will always remain upon you to be proved. 2° If there be such Ideas naturall in every mans minde & preaching which is noe thing but discourse & reasoning be the ordinary

IMMEDIATE INSPIRATION 39

way to excite them, this has noe thing of extraordinary or supernaturall influence but is produced by an ordinary course of cause & effect as other ways of reasoning & discourse

But granting that it is an immediate influence of the Spirit joyning with or makeing use of preaching to produce divine faith what will this advantage your cause or what ground of pretence can your church have to it before any other, for this internal perception being a thing impossible to be made knowne to any but he that has & feels it, if you have had & felt such an influence upon your owne minde tis impossible you should know whether any other Quaker (Iust not that name with any disrespect but as I do al objects as that by which things are distinguished in discourse) ever had any such, & if you presume the spirit of god by preaching produces amongst you impressions which noe body can know but he that receives, why may not other societys of Christians presume the same as well as yours, & how can yu with any modesty or reason deny it them soe that this pretence to the spirit gives you noe advantage above other churches, nor can be any proofe of your being more in the right than others or that you have more of the spirit, noe more then it is a proof the church of roome is more infallible then others because she more boldly pretends to it. This sort of revelation can be of use only to particular persons & not to any church.

The utmost that this argument can prove is only that there may be such an inspiration (which noe body can deny that considers an omnipotent agent & author of us & all our facultys which he can alter & enlarge as seems good to him) but can never prove that any man or sect of men have it one more than another & soe all this great discourse of the Spirit leaves man kind just in the same that they were before.

If faith be to have this ground of inward immediate inspiration, the command of being able to render a reason of ones faith is impracticable

This takes away also all reasoning about religion, since it would be ridiculous to goe about to reason a man into a new sense which yet he has not.

Three questions 1° Whether god can do it? affirmativ. 2° Whether he often does it? Ignorativ 3° Whether we are to expect it as the necessary ground of saveing faith? Negativ. As to the 3d of these that there was any such revelation in the old testament either practised or promised remains to be proved. all the revelations I read of there were either prescriptions of actions to be performed or predictions of events to happen but not of opinions internally to be beleived & the members of that church had their directions not from an internall impulse but an externall rule

40 INSPIRATION, REVELATION, SCRIPTURE, AND FAITH

This inspiration is either of some new Ideas or of some proposition to be assented to or of some duty to be performed 1° Of the first the author speaks doubtfully since he supposes the Ideas innate, but by the revelation excited. 2° if some doctrine to be beleived which was before revealed in Scripture & consequently its Ideas known before v.g. that Jesus was the messias promised, then all that is due to inspiration is only an impulse to assent, which is that only which the man feels but whether that impulse be from god & his spirit or noe that cannot be known by the assent it self since such firme assent may be from impulse from ye evill one or naturall temper but must be known from some other rule either of reason or revelation. which must distinguish those emotions of the minde as proceeding from severall causes else the most extravagant boundlesse enthusiasme must passe for revelation. the same also must be said of any proposition of speculation not conteind in the scripture, or any action to be donne wherein if the termes be before known all that can depend on inspiration is noe thing but such a ~~strong~~ degree of assent to the truth of the proposition if it be speculative, or rectitude of the action if it be practical, which has noe ground in reason. for if the assent be founded in reason there is noe pretence for revelation soe that all that a man can comprehend that one so inspired sees or perceives or feels by a new sort of sensation is only the vehemence of the impulse where with he feels his minde caryd to the assent of such a proposition or performance of such an action beyond what reason moves him to. if it be any thing else those that have experience of such immediate communications ought to tell us. For as there were need of signes to convince those they were sent to, that the prophets were messengers sent from god, soe there was need also of some signe some way of distinction where by the messenger him self might be convinced that his message was from god. Thus god spoke to Moses not by a bare influence on his minde, but out of a bush all on fire that consumed not & if after Moses we have not an account of the like ~~proofs~~ instances of some particular marke of their calling from god yet this is noe argument against the necessity of such a distinguishing character for al things are not to be concluded as not donne that are not mentioned in Scripture[1] some way or other or else it may happen that the voice of man may be taken for the voice of god or the voice of god was taken for the voice of man 1 Sam III. 4. 5. But secondly from the time of Moses there appears to have been a regular order & succession of prophets set a part there unto Deutr XVIII. 15. 18 There were schools & sons of the prophets. And the ~~calling~~ being a prophet seems to have been a kinde of profession to which men were set

IMMEDIATE INSPIRATION

apart, & were prepared there unto by certain application & endeavour of their owne is plaine from their schools &c: which is also plainly intimated Numb: XII. 6. which study & preparation where in it consisted & what use it was of towards this guift of prophesy is not impossible to be guessed Though there were some extraordinarily cald to it as appears Amos. VII. 14.

Q. Spirit of illusion to beleive a lye

[1] besides that which we have of the succeeding prophets conteins not the history of the prophets when nor how they were calld or prepard to that worke but only an imperfect collection of their prophesies made by some after compilers

92

Scriptura Sacra

Scriptura Sacra) A vindication of the Divine Authoritie & inspiration of the writeings of the old & new Testam^t by. Wm Lowth 8° [Lon] Ox. 92 p. 288

All the books have not an equall inspiration— 1 Q what is equal
5 inspiration? If the New be inspired the old is, because of the testimony given to the old by the new. 2 Inspired because designed by god for the perpetuall use & instruction of the church & to be a rule of the christian faith in all ages 3. Q Whether by the same reason they must not be very plain & their sense infallibly intelligble to those to whom they are to be a
10 rule?

An inspired writeing is what is writ by the incitation, direction & assistance of god & designed by him for the perpetual use of the church. 3. Q What is meant by Incitation. Direction & Assistance in the case. Q. Whether that may not be inspired which is not designed for the
15 perepetuall use of the church?

God designed to provide a means for preserveing the doctrine of Christ to the end of the world. 5. Q. Will it thence follow that all that St Luc writ was inspired?

Writing the best ordinary means of conveying doctrine to after
20 ages. For god never works more miracles than needs must 6 Q. Whether therefor all in the new testament was appointed by god to be written?

Oral tradition ~~or particular revelation~~ not soe good. particular revelation not pretended to but by Enthusiasts. 9 Q. Whether the
25 name Enthusiasts answers their arguments for particular revelation?

By writeings preserved in the ordinary methods of providence men may as well know the revealed will of god, as they can know the history of former ages & the opinions of philosophers &c. 9. Q. Will as well serve the turne? for that is with great uncertainty.

30 God made use of writeing for the instruction of the Jewish church: B. Moses by gods direction wrote his law in a booke 10. Q. Whether then your argument be not the Old testament was inspired therefor the New is? vid. p. 3

SCRIPTURA SACRA 43

'Tis natural to suppose that the Apostles should take care to provide some certain of instruction for the Christian church in conformity to the Jewish. 11. Q. Whether the author writ this whether he thought not of it as an humane contrivance.

St Matthew writ particularly for the use of the Jews he had preached to. 12 Q. Whether then he had any thoughts that it should be an universal rule?

A Discourse of Miracles

To discourse of Miracles without defining what one means by the word Miracle, is to make a shew, but in effect to talk of nothing.

A Miracle then I take to be a sensible Operation, which being above the comprehension of the Spectator, and in his Opinion contrary to the establish'd Course of Nature, is taken by him to be Divine.

He that is present at the fact, is a Spectator: He that believes the History of the fact, puts himself in the place of a Spectator.

This Definition, 'tis probable, will not escape these two Exceptions.

1. That hereby what is a Miracle is made very uncertain; for it depending on the Opinion of the Spectator, that will be a Miracle to one which will not be so to another.

In answer to which, it is enough to say, that this Objection is of no force, but in the Mouth of one who can produce a definition of a Miracle not liable to the same exception, which I think not easie to do; for it being agreed, that a Miracle must be that which surpasses the force of Nature in the establish'd, steady Laws of Causes and Effects, nothing can be taken to be a Miracle but what is judg'd to exceed those Laws. Now every one being able to judge of those Laws only by his own acquaintance with Nature, and notions of its Force (which are different in different Men) it is unavoidable that That should be a Miracle to one, which is not so to another.

2. Another Objection to this Definition, will be, that the notion of a Miracle thus enlarged, may come sometimes to take in Operations that have nothing extraordinary or supernatural in them, and thereby invalidate the use of Miracles for the attesting of Divine Revelation.

To which I answer, not at all, if the Testimony which Divine Revelation receives from Miracles be rightly consider'd.

To know that any Revelation is from God, it is necessary to know that the Messenger that delivers it is sent from God, and that cannot be known but by some credentials given him by God himself. Let us see then whether Miracles, in my sense, be not such credentials, and will not infallibly direct us right in the search of Divine Revelation.

It is to be consider'd, that Divine Revelation receives Testimony from no other Miracles, but such as are wrought to witness his Mission from God who delivers the Revelation. All other Miracles that are done in the

A DISCOURSE OF MIRACLES 45

World, how many or great soever, Revelation is not concern'd in. Cases wherein there has been, or can be need of Miracles for the confirmation of Revelation are fewer than perhaps is imagin'd. The heathen World amidst an infinite and uncertain jumble of Deities, Fables and Worships had no room for a divine Attestation of any one against the rest. Those owners of many Gods were at liberty in their Worship; and no one of their Divinities pretending to be the one only true God, no one of them could be suppos'd in the Pagan Scheme to make use of Miracles to establish his Worship alone, or to abolish that of the others; much less was there any use of Miracles to confirm any Articles of Faith, since no one of them had any such to propose as necessary to be believ'd by their Votaries. And therefore I do not remember any Miracles recorded in the *Greek* or *Roman* Writers, as done to confirm any one's Mission and Doctrine. Conformable hereunto we find St. *Paul*, I *Cor.* i. 22. takes notice that the *Jews* ('tis true) requir'd Miracles but, as for the *Greeks* they look'd after something else; they knew no need or use there was of Miracles to recommend any Religion to them. And indeed it is an astonishing Mark how far the God of this World had blinded Mens Minds, if we consider that the Gentile World receiv'd and stuck to a Religion, which, not being deriv'd from Reason, had no sure Foundation in Revelation. They knew not its Original nor the Authors of it, nor seem'd concern'd to know from whence it came, or by whose Authority deliver'd; and so had no mention or use of Miracles for its Confirmation. For though there were here and there some pretences to Revelation, yet there were not so much as pretences to Miracles that attested it.

If we will direct our Thoughts by what has been, we must conclude that Miracles as the credentials of a Messenger delivering a Divine Religion, have no place but upon a supposition of one only true God; and that it is so in the nature of the thing, and cannot be otherwise, I think will be made to appear in the sequel of this Discourse. Of such who have come in the name of the one only true God, professing to bring a Law from him we have in History a clear account but of three, *viz. Moses, Jesus* and *Mohamet.* For what the *Persees* say of their *Zoroaster,* or the *Indians* of their *Brama* (not to mention all the wild Stories of the Religions farther East) is so obscure or so manifestly fabulous, that no account can be made of it. Now of the three before mention'd, *Mahomet* having none to produce, pretends to no Miracles for the vouching his Mission; so that the only Revelations that come attested by Miracles, being only those of *Moses* and *Christ*, and they confirming each other, the business of Miracles, as it stands really in matter of Fact, has no manner

46 INSPIRATION, REVELATION, SCRIPTURE, AND FAITH

of difficulty in it; and I think the most scrupulous or sceptical cannot from Miracles raise the least doubt against the Divine Revelation of the Gospel.

But since the Speculative and Learned will be putting of Cases which never were, and it may be presum'd never will be; since Scholars and Disputants will be raising of Questions where there are none, and enter upon Debates whereof there is no need; I crave leave to say, that he who comes with a Message from God to be deliver'd to the World, cannot be refus'd belief if he vouches his Mission by a Miracle, because his credentials have a right to it. For every rational thinking Man must conclude as *Nicodemus* did, *We know that thou art a teacher come from God, for no Man can do these signs which thou dost, except God be with him.*

For example, *Jesus* of *Nazareth* professes himself sent from God: He with a word calms a Tempest at Sea: This one looks on as a Miracle, and consequently cannot but receive his Doctrine: Another thinks this might be the effect of Chance, or Skill in the Weather and no Miracle, and so stands out; but afterwards seeing him walk on the Sea, owns that for a Miracle and believes: Which yet upon another has not that force, who suspects it may possibly be done by the assistance of a Spirit: But yet the same Person seeing afterwards our Saviour cure an inveterate Palsie by a word, admits that for a Miracle, and becomes a Convert: Another over looking it in this instance, afterwards finds a Miracle in his giving sight to one born Blind, or in raising the Dead, or his raising himself from the Dead, and so receives his Doctrine as a Revelation coming from God. By all which it is plain, that where the Miracle is admitted, the Doctrine cannot be rejected; it comes with the assurance of a Divine Attestation to him that allows the Miracle, and he cannot question its Truth.

The next thing then is, what shall be a sufficient inducement to take any extraordinary Operation to be a Miracle, *i.e.* wrought by God himself for the attestation of a Revelation from him.

And to this I answer, the carrying with it the Marks of a greater power than appears in opposition to it. For

1. First, This removes the main Difficulty where it presses hardest, and cleares the matter from doubt, when extraordinary and supernatural Operations are brought to support opposite Missions, about which methinks more Dust has been rais'd by Men of leisure than so plain a matter needed. For since God's Power is paramount to all, and no opposition can be made against him with an equal force to his; and since his Honour and Goodness can never be suppos'd to suffer his Messenger and his Truth to be born down by the appearance of a greater Power on

A DISCOURSE OF MIRACLES 47

the side of an Impostor, and in favour of a Lie; wherever there is an opposition, and two pretending to be sent from Heaven clash, the signs which carry with them the evident marks of a greater Power, will always be a certain and unquestionable evidence that the Truth and Divine Mission is on the side on which they appear. For though the discovery how the lying wonders are or can be produc'd, be beyond the Capacity of the Ignorant, and often beyond the Conception of the most knowing Spectator, who is therefore forc'd to allow them in his apprehension to be above the force of natural Causes and Effects; yet he cannot but know they are not Seals set by God to his Truth for the attesting of it, since they are oppos'd by Miracles that carry the evident marks of a greater and superior Power, and therefore they cannot at all shake the Authority of one so supported. God can never be thought to suffer that a Lie, set up in opposition to a Truth coming from him, should be back'd with a greater Power than he will shew for the Confirmation and Propagation of a Doctrine which he has reveal'd, to the end it might be believ'd. The producing of Serpents, Blood and Frogs by the *Egyptian* Sorcerers and by *Moses*, could not to the Spectators but appear equally miraculous; which of the Pretenders then had their Mission from God? And the truth on either side could not have been determin'd if the matter had rested there. But when *Moses*'s Serpent eat up theirs, when he produc'd Lice which they could not, the decision was easie. 'Twas plain *Jannes* and *Jambres* acted by an inferior Power, and their operations, how marvellous and extraordinary soever, could not in the least bring in question *Moses*'s Mission; that stood the firmer for this opposition, and remain'd the more unquestionable after this, than if no such signs had been brought against it.

So likewise the number, variety and greatness of the Miracles wrought for the confirmation of the Doctrine deliver'd by *Jesus Christ*, carry with them such strong marks of an extraordinary Divine Power, that the Truth of his Mission will stand firm and unquestionable, 'till any one rising up in opposition shall do greater Miracles than he and his Apostles did. For any thing less will not be of weight to turn the Scales in the Opinion of any one, whether of an inferior or more exalted understanding. This is one of those palpable Truths and Trials of which all Mankind are judges; and there needs no assistance of Learning, no deep thought to come to a certainty in it. Such care has God taken that no pretended Revelation should stand in competition with what is truly Divine, that we need but open our Eyes to see and be sure which came from him. The marks of his over-ruling Power accompany it; and

48 INSPIRATION, REVELATION, SCRIPTURE, AND FAITH

therefore to this day we find, that wherever the Gospel comes, it prevails to be beating down the strong Holds of *Satan*, and the dislodging the Prince of the Power of Darkness, driving him away with all his living wonders; which is a standing Miracle, carrying with it the Testimony of Superiority.

What is the uttermost Power of natural Agents or created Beings, Men of the greatest reach cannot discover; but that it is not equal to God's Omnipotency is obvious to every one's Understanding; so that the superior Power is an easie, as well as sure guide to Divine Revelation, attested by Miracles, where they are brought as Credentials to an Embassy from God.

And thus upon the same grounds of superiority of Power, uncontested Revelation will stand to.

For the explaining of which, it may be necessary to premise,

1. That no Mission can be look'd on to be Divine, that delivers any thing derogating from the Honour of the one, only, true, invisible God, or inconsistent with natural Religion and the rules of Morality: Because God having discover'd to Men the Unity and Majesty of his Eternal Godhead, and the truths of natural Religion and Morality by the light of Reason, he cannot be suppos'd to back the contrary by Revelation; for that would be to destroy the evidence and use of Reason, without which Men cannot be able to distinguish Divine Revelation from Diabolical Imposture.

2. That it cannot be expected that God should send any one into the World on purpose to inform Men of things indifferent, and of small moment, or that are knowable by the use of their natural Faculties. This would be to lessen the Dignity of his Majesty in favour of our Sloth, and in prejudice to our Reason.

3. The only case then wherein a Mission of any one from Heaven can be reconciled to the high and awful Thoughts Men ought to have of the Deity, must be the Revelation of some supernatural Truths relating to the Glory of God, and some great concern of Men. Supernatural Operations attesting such a Revelation may with reason be taken to be Miracles, as carrying the marks of a superior and over-ruling Power, as long as no Revelation accompanied with marks of a greater Power appears against it. Such supernatural signs may justly stand good, and be receiv'd for Divine, *i.e.* wrought by a Power superior to all, 'till a Mission attested by Operations of a greater force shall disprove them: Because it cannot be suppos'd God should suffer his Prerogative to be so far usurp'd by any inferior Being as to permit any Creature, depending on

A DISCOURSE OF MIRACLES 49

him, to set his Seals, the marks of his Divine Authority, to a Mission coming from him. For these supernatural signs being the only means God is conceived to have to satisfie Men as rational Creatures of the Certainty of any thing he would reveal, as coming from himself, can never consent that it should be wrested out of his hands, to serve the Ends and establish the Authority of an inferior Agent that rivals him. His Power being known to have no equal, always will, and always may be safely depended on, to shew its superiority in vindicating his Authority, and maintaining every Truth that he has reveal'd. So that the marks of a superior Power accompanying it, always have been, and always will be a visible and sure guide to Divine Revelation; by which Men may conduct themselves in their examining of revealed Religions, and be satisfied which they ought to receive as coming from God; though they have by no means ability precisely to determine what is, or is not above the force of any created Being; or what Operations can be perform'd by none but a Divine Power, and require the immediate Hand of the Almighty. And therefore we see 'tis by that our Saviour measures the great Unbelief of the *Jews*. John xv. 24. saying, *If I had not done among them the works which no other Man did, they had not sin, but now have they both seen and hated both me and my father*; declaring, that they could not but see the Power and Presence of God in those many Miracles he did, which were greater than every any other Man had done. When God sent *Moses*, to the Children of *Israel* with a Message, that now according to his promise he would redeem them by his hand out of *Egypt*, and furnish'd him with signs and Credentials of his Mission; it is very remarkable what God himself says of those Signs, *Exod.* iv. 8. *And it shall come to pass, if they will not believe thee, nor hearken to the voice of the first sign* (which was turning his Rod into a Serpent) that *they will believe, and the voice of the latter sign* (which was the making his Hand leprous by putting it in his Bosom;) God farther adds, *v.* 9. *and it shall come to pass, if they will not believe also these two signs, neither hearken unto thy voice, that thou shalt take of the water of the river and pour it upon the dry land: And the water which thou takest out of the river shall become blood upon the dry land.* Which of those Operations was or was not above the force of all created Beings, will, I suppose, be hard for any man, too hard for a poor Brick-maker to determine; and therefore the Credit and certain Reception of the Mission, was annex'd to neither of them, but the prevailing of their Attestation was heighten'd by the increase of their number; two supernatural Operations shewing more power than one, and three more than two. God allow'd that it was natural, that the marks of greater Power should have a greater Impression on the Minds and

50 INSPIRATION, REVELATION, SCRIPTURE, AND FAITH

Beliefs of the Spectators. Accordingly the *Jews*, by this estimate judg'd of the Miracles of our Saviour, *John* vii. 31. where we have this account, *And many of the people believed on him, and said, when Christ cometh will he do more miracles than these which this Man hath done?* This perhaps, as it is the plainest, so it is also the surest way to preserve the Testimony of Miracles in its due force to all sorts and degrees of People. For Miracles being the Basis on which divine Mission is always establish'd, and consequently that Foundation on which the Believers of any divine Revelation must ultimately bottom their Faith, this use of them would be lost, if not to all Mankind, yet at least to the simple and illiterate (which is the far greatest part) if Miracles be defin'd to be none but such divine Operations as are in themselves beyond the power of all created Beings, or at least Operations contrary to the fix'd and establish'd Laws of Nature. For as to the latter of those, what are the fix'd and establish'd Laws of Nature, Philosophers alone, if at least they can pretend to determine. And if they are to be Operations performable only by divine Power, I doubt whether any Man learn'd or unlearn'd, can in most cases be able to say of any particular Operation that can fall under his Senses, that it is certainly a Miracle. Before he can come to that certainty, he must know that no created being has a power to perform it. We know good and bad Angels have Abilities and Excellencies exceedingly beyond all our poor Performances or narrow Comprehensions. But to define what is the utmost extent of Power that any of them has, is a bold undertaking of a Man in the dark, that pronounces without seeing, and sets bounds in his narrow Cell to things at an infinite distance from his Model and Comprehension.

Such definitions therefore of Miracles, however specious in Discourse and Theory, fail us when we come to use, and an application of them in particular cases. 1701/2.

These Thoughts concerning Miracles, were occasion'd by my reading Mr. Fleetwood's Essay on Miracles, and the Letter writ to him on that Subject. The one of them defining a Miracle to be an extraordinary operation performable by God alone: And the other writing of Miracles without any definition of a Miracle at all.

J. LOCKE

An Essay for the understanding of St Paul's epistles by consulting St Paul himself

To go about to explain any of St. *Paul's* Epistles, after so great a Train of Expositors and Commentators, might seem an Attempt of Vanity, censurable for its Needlessness, did not the daily and approv'd Examples of pious and learned Men justify it. This may be some Excuse for me to the Publick, if ever these following Papers should chance to come abroad: But to my self, for whose Use this Work was undertaken, I need make no Apology. Though I had been conversant in these Epistles, as well as in other Parts of Sacred Scripture, yet I found that I understood them not; I mean the doctrinal and discursive parts of them: Though the practical Directions, which are usually drop'd in the latter Part of each Epistle, appear'd to me very plain, intelligible, and instructive.

I did not, when I reflected on it, very much wonder that this part of Sacred Scripture had Difficulties in it, many Causes of Obscurity did readily occur to me. The Nature of Epistolary Writings in general, disposes the Writer to pass by the mentioning of many Things, as well known to him to whom his Letter is address'd, which are necessary to be laid open to a Stranger, to make him comprehend what is said: And it not seldom falls out, that a well Penn'd Letter which is very easy and intelligible to the Receiver, is very obscure to a Stranger, who hardly knows what to make of it. The Matters that St. *Paul* writ about, were certainly things well known to those he writ to, and which they had some peculiar Concern in, which made them easily apprehend his Meaning, and see the Tendency and Force of his Discourse. But we having now at this distance no Information of the Occasion of his writing, little or no Knowledge of the Temper and Circumstances those he writ to were in, but what is to be gather'd out of the Epistles themselves, it is not strange that many things in them lie conceal'd to us, which no doubt they who were concern'd in the Letter understood at first sight. Add to this, that in many places 'tis manifest he answers Letters sent, and Questions propos'd to him, which if we had, would much better clear those Passages that relate to them, than all the learned Notes of Criticks and Commentators, who in aftertimes fill us with their Conjectures; for very often, as to the Matter in hand, they are nothing else.

52 INSPIRATION, REVELATION, SCRIPTURE, AND FAITH

The Language wherein these Epistles are writ, are another; and that no small occasion of their Obscurity to us now: The Words are *Greek*; a Language dead many Ages since: A Language of a very witty volatile People, Seekers after Novelty, and abounding with Variety of Notions and Sects, to which they applied the Terms of their common Tongue with great Liberty and Variety: And yet this makes but one small part of the Difficulty in the Language of these Epistles; there is a Peculiarity in it, that much more obscures and perplexes the Meaning of these Writings, than what can be occasion'd by the Looseness and Variety of the Greek Tongue. The Terms are *Greek*, but the Idiom or Turn of the Phrases may be truly said to be *Hebrew* or *Syriack*. The Custom and Familiarity of which Tongues do sometimes so far influence the Expressions in these Epistles, that one may observe the Force of the Hebrew Conjugations, particularly that of *Hiphil* given to Greek Verbs, in a way unknown to the *Grecians* themselves. Nor is this all; the Subject treated of in these Epistles is so wholly new, and the Doctrines contained in them so perfectly remote from the Notions that Mankind were acquainted with, that most of the important Terms in it have quite another Signification from what they have in other Discourses: So that putting all together, we may truly say, that the New Testament is a Book written in a Language peculiar to it self.

To these Causes of Obscurity common to St. *Paul*, with most of the other Penmen of the several Books of the New Testament, we may add those that are peculiarly his, and owing to his Stile and Temper. He was, as 'tis visible, a Man of quick Thought, warm Temper, mighty well vers'd in the Writings of the Old Testament, and full of the Doctrine of the New: All this put together, suggested Matter to him in abundance on those Subjects which came in his way: So that one may consider him when he was writing, as beset with a Crowd of Thoughts, all striving for Utterance. In this Posture of Mind it was almost impossible for him to keep that slow Pace, and observe minutely that Order and Method of ranging all he said, from which results an easie and obvious Perspicuity. To this Plenty and Vehemence of his may be imputed those many large Parentheses which a careful Reader may observe in his Epistles. Upon this account also it is, that he often breaks off in the Middle of an Argument, to let in some new Thought suggested by his own Words; which having pursued and explained as far as conduced to his present Purpose, he reassumes again the Thread of his Discourse, and goes on with it, without taking any notice that he returns again to what he had been before saying, though sometimes it be so far off, that it may well

THE UNDERSTANDING OF ST PAUL'S EPISTLES   53

have slipt out of his Mind, and requires a very attentive Reader to observe, and so bring the disjointed Members together, as to make up the Connection, and see how the scatter'd Parts of the Discourse hang together in a coherent well-agreeing Sense, that makes it all of a Piece.

Besides the disturbance in perusing St. *Paul's* Epistles, from the Plenty and Vivacity of his Thoughts, which may obscure his Method, and often hide his Sense from an unwary, or over-hasty Reader; the frequent changing of the Personage he speaks in, renders the Sense very uncertain, and is apt to mislead one that has not some Clue to guide him; sometimes by the Pronoun *I*, he means himself; sometimes any Christian; sometimes a Jew, and sometimes any Man, *etc*. If speaking of himself in the first Person Singular has so various meanings; his use of the first Person Plural is with a far greater Latitude, sometimes designing himself alone, sometimes those with himself whom he makes Partners to the Epistle; sometimes with himself comprehending the other Apostles, or Preachers of the Gospel, or Christians: Nay, sometimes he in that way speaks of the Converted *Jews*, other times of the Converted *Gentiles*, and sometimes of others, in a more or less extended Sense, every one of which varies the meaning of the Place, and makes it to be differently understood. I have forborn to trouble the Reader with Examples of them here. If his own Observation hath not already furnished him with them, the following Paraphrase and Notes I suppose will satisfie him in the point.

In the current also of his Discourse, he sometimes drops in the Objections of others, and his Answers to them, without any Change in the Scheme of his Language, that might give Notice of any other speaking besides himself. This requires great Attention to observe, and yet if it be neglected or overlook'd, will make the Reader very much mistake, and misunderstand his Meaning, and render the Sense very perplex'd.

These are intrinsick difficulties arising from the Text it self, whereof there might be a great many other named, as the uncertainty, sometimes, who are the Persons he speaks to, or the Opinions or Practices which he has in his Eye, sometimes in alluding to them, sometimes in his Exhortations and Reproofs. But those above mentioned being the chief, it may suffice to have opened our Eyes a little upon them, which, well examin'd, may contribute towards our Discovery of the rest.

To these we may subjoyn two external Causes that have made no small increase of the Native and Original Difficulties that keep us from an easie and assur'd Discovery of St. *Paul's* Sense, in many parts of his Epistles, and those are,

First, The dividing of them into Chapters and Verses, as we have done,

54 INSPIRATION, REVELATION, SCRIPTURE, AND FAITH

whereby they are so chop'd and minc'd, and as they are now Printed, stand so broken and divided, that not only the Common People take the Verses usually for distinct Aphorisms, but even Men of more advanc'd Knowledge in reading them, lose very much of the strength and force of the Coherence, and the Light that depends on it. Our Minds are so weak and narrow, that they have need of all the helps and assistances can be procur'd, to lay before them undisturbedly, the Thread and Coherence of any Discourse; by which alone they are truly improv'd and lead into the Genuine Sense of the Author. When the Eye is constantly disturb'd with loose Sentences, that by their standing and separation, appear as so many distinct Fragments; the Mind will have much ado to take in, and carry on in its Memory and uniform Discourse of dependent Reasonings, especially having from the Cradle been used to wrong Impressions concerning them, and constantly accustom'd to hear them quoted as distinct Sentences, without any limitation or explication of their precise Meaning from the Place they stand in, and the Relation they bear to what goes before, or follows. These Divisions also have given occasion to the reading these Epistles by parcels and in scraps, which has farther confirm'd the Evil arising from such partitions. And I doubt not but every one will confess it to be a very unlikely way to come to the Understanding of any other Letters, to read them Peicemeal, a Bit to day, and another Scrap to morrow, and so on by broken Intervals; Especially if the Pause and Cessation should be made as the Chapters the Apostles Epistles are divided into do end sometimes in the middle of a Discourse, and sometimes in the middle of a Sentence. It cannot therefore but be wondred, that that should be permitted to be done to Holy Writ, which would visibly disturb the Sense and hinder the Understanding of any other Book whatsoever. If *Tully*'s Epistles were so printed, and so used, I ask whither they would not be much harder to be understood, less easy and less pleasant to be read by much than now they are?

How plain soever this Abuse is, and what Prejudice soever it does to the Understanding of the Sacred Scripture, yet if a Bible was printed as it should be, and as the several Parts of it were writ, in continued Discourses where the Argument is continued, I doubt not but the several Parties would complain of it, as an Innovation, and a dangerous Change in the publishing those holy Books. And indeed those who are for maintaining their Opinions, and the Systems of Parties by Sound of Words, with a Neglect of the true Sense of Scripture, would have reason to make and foment the Outcry. They would most of them be immediately disarm'd of their great Magazine of Artillery wherewith

THE UNDERSTANDING OF ST PAUL'S EPISTLES 55

they defend themselves, and fall upon others, if the Holy Scripture were but laid before the Eyes of Christians in its due Connection and Consistency, it would not then be so easy to snatch out a few Words, as if they were separate from the rest, to serve a Purpose, to which they do not at all belong, and with which they have nothing to do. But as the matter now stands, he that has a mind to it, may at a cheap rate be a notable Champion for the Truth, that is, for the Doctrines of the Sect that Chance or Interest has cast him into. He need but be furnished with Verses of Sacred Scripture, containing Words and Expressions that are but flexible (as all general obscure and doubtful ones are) and his System that has appropriated them to the Orthodoxie of his Church, makes them immediately strong and irrefragable Arguments for his Opinion. This is the Benefit of loose Sentences, and Scripture crumbled into Verses, which quickly turn into independent Aphorisms. But if the Quotation in the Verse produc'd, were consider'd as a part of a continued coherent Discourse, and so its Sense were limited by the Tenour of the Context, most of these forward and warm Disputants would be quite strip'd of those, which they doubt not now to call Spiritual Weapons, and they would have often nothing to say that would not shew their Weakness, and manifestly fly in their Faces. I crave leave to set down a Saying of the Learned and Judicious Mr. *Selden*, 'In interpreting the Scripture, says he, many do as if a Man should see one have Ten Pounds, which he rekon'd by *1, 2, 3, 4, 5, 6, 7, 8, 9, 10*. meaning Four was but four Unites, and five five Unites, *etc.* and that he had in all but Ten Pounds: The other that sees him, takes not the Figures together, as he doth, but picks here and there; and thereupon reports that he had five Pounds in one Bag, and six Pounds in another Bag, and nine Pounds in another Bag, *etc.* when as in truth he has but ten Pounds in all. So we pick out a Text here and there, to make it serve our turn; whereas if we take it altogether, and consider what went before, and what followed after, we should find it meant no such thing.' I have heard sober Christians very much admire why ordinary illiterate People, who were Professors, that shew'd a Concern for Religion, seem'd much more conversant in St *Paul's* Epistles, than in the plainer, and as it seem'd to them much more intelligible Parts of the New Testament; They confessed that tho' they read St. *Paul's* Epistles with their best Attention, yet they generally found them too hard to be master'd, and they labour'd in vain so far to reach the Apostle's Meaning all along in the Train of what he said, as to read them with that Satisfaction that arises from a feeling that we understand and fully comprehend the Force and Reasoning of an Author; and therefore they could not imagin

56 INSPIRATION, REVELATION, SCRIPTURE, AND FAITH

what those saw in them, whose Eyes they thought not much better than their own. But the Case was plain, These sober inquisitive Readers had a mind to see nothing in St. *Paul's* Epistles but just what he meant; whereas those others of a quicker and gayer Sight could see in them what they pleased. Nothing is more acceptable to Phansie than plyant Terms and Expressions that are not obstinate, in such it can find its account with Delight, and with them be illuminated, Orthodox, infallible at pleasure, and in its own way. But where the Sense of the Author goes visibly in its own Train, and the Words, receiving a determin'd Sense from their Companions and Adjacents, will not consent to give Countenance and Colour to what is agreed to be right, and must be supported at any rate, there Men of establish'd Orthodoxie do not so well find their Satisfaction. And perhaps if it were well examin'd, it would be no very extravagant Paradox to say, that there are fewer that bring their Opinions to the Sacred Scripture to be tried by that infallible Rule, than bring the Sacred Scripture to their Opinions, to bend it to them, to make it as they can a cover and Guard of them. And to this Purpose its being divided into Verses, and brought as much as may be into loose and general Aphorisms, makes it most useful and serviceable. And in this lies the other great Cause of Obscurity and Perplexedness, which has been cast upon St. *Paul's* Epistles from without.

St. *Paul's* Epistles, as they stand translated in our English Bibles, are now by long and constant Use become a part of the English Language, and common Phraseology, especially in Matters of Religion; This every one uses familiarly, and thinks he understands, but it must be observed, that if he has a distinct meaning when he uses those Words and Phrases, and knows himself what he intends by them, it is always according to the Sense of his own System, and the Articles or Interpretations of the Society he is engaged in. So that all this Knowledge and Understanding which he has in the Use of these Passages of Sacred Scripture, reaches no farther than this, that he knows (and that is very well) what he himself says, but thereby knows nothing at all what St. *Paul* said in them. The Apostle writ not by that Man's System, and so his Meaning cannot be known by it. This being the ordinary way of understanding the Epistles, and every Sect being perfectly Orthodox in its own Judgment: What a great and invincible Darkness must this cast upon St. *Paul's* Meaning to all those of that way, in all those Places where his Thoughts and Sense run counter to what any Party has espoused for Orthodox; as it must unavoidably to all but one of the different Systems, in all those Passages that any way relate to the Points in Controversie between them.

THE UNDERSTANDING OF ST PAUL'S EPISTLES   57

This is a Mischief which, however frequent and almost natural, reaches so far, that it would justly make all those who depend upon them, wholly diffident of Commentators, and let them see, how little Help was to be expected from them in relying on them for the true Sense of the Sacred Scripture, did they not take care to help to cozen themselves, by choosing to use and pin their Faith on such Expositors as explain the Sacred Scripture in favour of those Opinions that they before hand have voted Orthodox, and bring to the Sacred Scripture not for Trial, but Confirmation. No Body can think that any Text of St. *Paul's* Epistles has two contrary Meanings, and yet so it must have to two different Men, who taking two Commentators of different Sects for their respective Guides into the Sense of any one of the Epistles, shall build upon their respective Expositions. We need go no further for a Proof of it, than the Notes of the two Celebrated Commentators on the New Testament, Dr. *Hammond* and *Beza*, both Men of Parts and Learning, and both thought by their Followers Men mighty in the Sacred Scriptures. So that here we see the hopes of great Benefit and Light from Expositors and Commentators, is in a great part abated, and those who have most need of their Help, can receive but little from them, and can have very little Assurance of reaching the Apostle's Sense by what they find in them, whilst Matters remain in the same State they are in at present. For those, who find they need Help, and would borrow Light from Expositors, either consult only those who have the good luck to be thought sound and Orthodox, avoiding those of different Sentiments from themselves in the great and approved Points of their Systems, as dangerous and not fit to be medled with; or else with Indifferency look into the Notes of all Commentators promiscuously. The first of these take Pains only to confirm themselves in the Opinions and Tenents they have already, which whether it be the way to get the true Meaning of what St. *Paul* deliver'd, is easy to determin. The others with much more Fairness to themselves, tho with reaping little more Advantage (unless they have something else to guide them into the Apostle's Meaning than the Comments themselves) seek Help on all hands, and refuse not to be taught by any one, who offers to enlighten them in any of the dark Passages. But here tho they avoid the Mischief which the others fall into, of being confin'd in their Sense, and seeing nothing but that in St. *Paul's* Writings, be it right or wrong; yet they run into as great on the other side, and instead of being confirm'd in the meaning, that they thought they saw in the Text, or distracted with an hundred, suggested by those they advised with; and so instead of that one Sense of the Scripture

58 INSPIRATION, REVELATION, SCRIPTURE, AND FAITH

which they carried with them to their Commentators, return from them with none at all.

This indeed seems to make the Case desperate: For if the Comments and Expositions of pious and learned Men cannot be depended on, whither shall we go for Help? To which I answer, I would not be mistaken, as if I thought the Labours of the Learned in this Case wholly lost, and fruitless. There is great Use and Benefit to be made of them, when we have once got a Rule to know which of their Expositions, in the great Variety there is of them, explains the Words and Phrases according to the Apostle's Meaning. Till then 'tis evident, from what is above said, they serve for the most part to no other Use, but either to make us find our own Sense, and not his in St. *Paul's* Words; or else to find in them no settled Sense at all.

Here it will be ask'd, how shall we come by this Rule you mention? Where is that Touchstone to be had, that will shew us whether the Meaning we our selves put, or take as put by others upon St. *Paul's* Words in his Epistles, be truly his Meaning or no? I will not say the way which I propose, and have in the following Paraphrase follow'd, will make us infallible in our Interpretations of the Apostle's Text: But this I will own, that till I took this way, St. *Paul's* Epistles to me, in the ordinary way of reading and studying them, were very obscure Parts of Scripture, that left me almost every where at a loss; and I was at a great Uncertainty in which of the contrary Senses, that were to be found in his Commentators, he was to be taken. Whether what I have done has made it any clearer and more visible now, I must leave others to judge. This I beg leave to say for my self, that if some very sober judicious Christians, no Strangers to the Sacred Scriptures, nay learned Divines of the Church of *England,* had not professed that by the Perusal of these following Papers, they understood the Epistles better much than they did before, and had not with repeated Instances pressed me to publish them, I should not have consented they should have gone beyond my own private Use, for which they were at first designed, and where they made me not repent my Pains.

If any one be so far pleased with my Endeavours, as to think it worth while to be informed, what was the Clue I guided my self by through all the dark Passages of these Epistles, I shall minutely tell him the Steps by which I was brought into this way, that he may judge whether I proceeded rationally, upon right Grounds or no, if so be any thing in so mean an Example as mine may be worth his notice.

After I had found by long Experience, that the reading of the Text and

THE UNDERSTANDING OF ST PAUL'S EPISTLES   59

Comments in the ordinary way proved not so successful as I wish'd to the end propos'd, I began to suspect that in reading a Chapter as was usual, and thereupon sometimes consulting Expositors upon some hard Places of it, which at that time most affected me, as relating to Points then under Consideration in my own Mind, or in Debate amongst others, was not a right Method to get into the true Sense of these Epistles. I saw plainly, after I began once to reflect upon it, that if any one now should write me a Letter, as long as St. *Paul*'s to the *Romans*, concerning such as Matter as that is, in a Stile as Foreign, and Expressions as dubious as his seem to be, if I should divide it into fifteen or sixteen Chapters, and read of them one to day, and another to morrow, *etc.* it was ten to one I should never come to a full and clear Comprehension of it. The way to understand the Mind of him that writ it, every one would agree, was to read the whole Letter through from one end to the other, all at once, to see what was the main Subject and Tendency of it: or if it had several Views and Purposes in it, not dependent one of another, nor in a Subordination to one chief Aim and End, to discover what those different Matters were, and where the Author concluded one, and began another; and if there were any Necessity of dividing the Epistle into Parts, to make the Boundaries of them.

In Prosecution of this Thought, I concluded it necessary, for the understanding of any one of St. *Paul*'s Epistles, to read it all through at one Sitting, and to observe as well as I could the Drift and Design of his writing it. If the first reading gave me some Light, the second gave me more; and so I persisted on reading constantly the whole Epistle over at once, till I came to have a good general View of the Apostle's main Purpose in writing the Epistle, the chief Branches of his Discourse wherein he prosecuted it, the Arguments he used, and the Disposition of the whole.

This, I confess, is not to be obtained by one or two hasty Readings; it must be repeated again and again, with a close Attention to the Tenour of the Discourse, and a perfect Neglect of the Divisions into Chapters and Verses. On the contrary, the safest way is to suppose, that the Epistle has but one Business, and one Aim, till by a frequent Perusal of it, you are forced to see there are distinct independent Matters in it, which will forwardly enough shew themselves.

It requires so much more Pains, Judgment and Application, to find the Coherence of obscure and abstruse Writings, and makes them so much the more unfit to serve Prejudice and Pre-occupation when found, that it

60 INSPIRATION, REVELATION, SCRIPTURE, AND FAITH

is not to be wondered that St. *Paul's* Epistles have with many passed rather for disjointed, loose pious Discourses, full of Warmth and Zeal, and Overflows of Light, rather than for calm strong coherent Reasonings, that carried a Thread of Argument and Consistency all
5 through them.

But this muttering of lazy or ill disposed Readers, hindered me not from persisting in the Course I had began; I continued to read the same Epistle over and over, and over again, till I cam to discover, as appeared to me, what was the Drift and Aim of it; and by what Steps and Arguments
10 St. *Paul* prosecuted his Purpose. I remembred that St. *Paul* was miraculously called to the Ministry of the Gospel, and declared to be a chosen Vessel; that he had the whole Doctrine of the Gospel from God by immediate Revelation, and was appointed to be the Apostle of the *Gentiles*, for the propagating of it in the Heathen World. This was enough
15 to perswade me, that he was not a Man of loose and shattered Parts, uncapable to argue, and unfit to convince those he had to deal with. God knows how to choose fit Instruments for the Business he employs them in. A large Stock of Jewish Learning he had taken in at the Feet of *Gamaliel*, and for his Information in Christian Knowledge, and the Mysteries and
20 Depths of the Dispensation of Grace by Jesus Christ, God himself had condescended to be his Instructer and Teacher. The Light of the Gospel he had received from the Fountain and Father of Light himself, who, I concluded, had not furnished him in this extraordinary manner, if all this plentiful Stock of Learning and Illumination had been in danger to have
25 been lost, or proved useless, in a jumbled and confused Head; nor have laid up such a Store of admirable and useful Knowledge in a Man, who for want of Method and Order, Clearness of Conception, or Pertinency in Discourse, could not draw it out into Use with the greatest Advantages of Force and Coherence. That he knew how to prosecute his Purpose with
30 Strength of Argument and close Reasoning, without incoherent Sallies, or the intermixing of things foreign to his Business, was evident to me from several Speeches of his recorded in the *Acts*: And it was hard to think that a Man that could talk with so much Consistency and Clearness of Conviction, should not be able to write without Confusion, inextricable
35 Obscurity, and perpetual Rambling. The Force, Order and Perspicuity of those Discourses could not be denied to be very visible. How then came it that the like was thought much wanting in his Epistles? and of this there appear'd to me this plain Reason: The Particularities of the History in which these Speeches are inserted, shew St. *Paul's* end in Speaking, which
40 being seen, casts a Light on the whole, and shews the Pertinency of all that

THE UNDERSTANDING OF ST PAUL'S EPISTLES   61

he says. But his Epistles not being so circumstantiated; there being no concurring History that plainly declares the Disposition St. *Paul* was in, what the Actions, Expectations, or Demands of those to whom he writ, required him to speak to, we are no where told. All this and a great deal more necessary to guide us into the true meaning of the Epistles, is to be 5 had only from the Epistles themselves, and to be gather'd from thence with stubborn Attention, and more than common Application.

This being the only safe Guide (under the Spirit of God, that dictated these Sacred Writings) that can be rely'd on, I hope I may be excused, if I venture to say, that the utmost ought to be done to observe and trace out 10 St. *Paul's* Reasonings; to follow the Thread of his Discourse in each of his Epistles; to shew how it goes on still directed with the same View, and pertinently drawing the several Incidents towards the same Point. To understand him right, his Inferences should be strictly observed; and it should be carefully examined from what they are drawn, and what they 15 tend to. He is certainly a coherent, argumentative, pertinent Writer, and Care I think should be taken in expounding of him, to shew that he is so. But tho I say he has weighty Aims in his Epistles, which he steadily keeps in his Eye, and drives at in all that he says, yet I do not say that he puts his Discourses into an artificial Method, or leads his Reader into a 20 Distinction of his Arguments, or gives them notice of new Matter by Rhetorical or study'd Transitions. He has no Ornaments borrow'd from the Greek Eloquence; no Notions of their Philosophy mix'd with his Doctrine to set it off. The *inticing Words of Man's Wisdom*, whereby he means all the studied Rules of the Grecian Schools, which made them 25 such Masters in the Art of Speaking, he, as he says himself, *I Cor. 2. 4.* wholly neglected. The Reason whereof he gives in the next Verse, and in other places. But tho Politeness of Language, Delicacy of Stile, Fineness of Expression, laboured Periods, artificial Transitions, and a very methodical ranging of the Parts with such other Imbellishments as 30 make a Discourse enter the Mind smoothly, and strike the Phansie at first hearing, have little or no place in his Stile, yet Coherence of Discourse, and a direct Tendency of all the Parts of it, to the Argument in hand, are most eminently to be found in him. This I take to be his Character, and doubt not but he will be found to be so upon diligent Examination. And 35 in this if it be so, we have a Clue, if we will take the Pains to find it, that will conduct us with Surety through those seemingly dark Places, and imagined Intricacies in which Christians have wander'd so far one from another, as to find quite contrary Senses.

Whether a superficial Reading, accompanied with the common 40

62 INSPIRATION, REVELATION, SCRIPTURE, AND FAITH

Opinion of his invincible Obscurity, has kept off some from seeking in him the Coherence of a Discourse tending with close strong reasoning to a Point; Or a seemingly more honourable Opinion of one that had been wrap'd up into the Third Heaven, as if from a Man so warm'd and illuminated as he had been, nothing could be expected but Flashes of Light, and Raptures of Zeal, hinder'd others to look for a Train of Reasoning, proceeding on regular and cogent Argumentation from a Man rais'd above the ordinary pitch of Humanity to an higher and brighter way of Illumination; Or else whether others were loth to beat their Heads about the Tenor and Coherence in St. *Paul's* Discourses, which if found out, possibly might set him at a manifest and irreconcileable Difference with their Systems, 'tis certain that whatever hath been the Cause, this way of getting the true Sense of St. *Paul's* Epistles, seems not to have been much made use of, or at least so throughly pursued as I am apt to think it deserves.

For, granting that he was full stor'd with the Knowledge of the things he treated of: For he had Light from Heaven, it was God himself furnished him, and he could not want; Allowing also that he had Ability to make use of the Knowledge had been given him for the end for which it was given him, *viz.* the Information, Conviction, and Conversion of others; and accordingly that he knew how to direct his Discourse to the Point in hand, we cannot widely mistake the Parts of his Discourse imploy'd about it, when we have any where found out the Point he drives at: Where-ever we have got a View of his Design, and the Aim he proposed to himself in Writing, we may be sure that such or such an Interpretation does not give us his genuine Sense, it being nothing at all to his present purpose. Nay among various Meanings given a Text, it fails not to direct us to the best, and very often to assure us of the true. For it is no Presumption, when one sees a Man arguing for this or that Proposition, if he be a sober Man, Master of Reason or common Sense, and takes any care of what he says, to pronounce with Confidence in several Cases, that he could not talk thus or thus.

I do not yet so magnifie this Method of studying St. *Paul's* Epistles, as well as other Parts of Sacred Scripture, as to think it will perfectly clear every hard Place, and leave no Doubt unresolved. I know Expressions now out of use, Opinions of those times, not heard of in our days, Allusions to Customs lost to us, and various Circumstances and Particularities of the Parties, which we cannot come at, *etc.* must needs continue several Passages in the dark now to us at this distance, which shon with full Light to those they were directed to. But for all that the

THE UNDERSTANDING OF ST PAUL'S EPISTLES 63

studying of St. *Paul*'s Epistles in the way I have proposed, will, I humbly conceive, carry us a great length in the right understanding of them, and make us rejoyce in the Light we receive from those most useful Parts of Divine Revelation, by furnishing us with visible Grounds that we are not mistaken, whilst the Consistency of the Discourse, and the Pertinency of it to the Design he is upon, vouches it worthy of our great Apostle. At least I hope it may be my Excuse for having indeavoured to make St. *Paul* an Interpreter to me of his own Epistles.

To this may be added another Help which St. *Paul* himself affords us towards the attaining the true meaning contained in his Epistles. He that reads him with the Attention I propose, will easily observe, that as he was full of the Doctrine of the Gospel, so it lay all clear and in order open to his view. When he gave his Thoughts Utterance upon any Point, the Matter flow'd like a Torrent, but 'tis plain 'twas a Matter he was perfectly Master of: he fully possess'd the entire Revelation he had receiv'd from God, had throughly digested it; all the Parts were formed together in his Mind into one well contracted harmonious Body. So that he was no way at Uncertainty, nor ever in the least at a loss concerning any Branch of it. One may see his Thoughts were all of a piece in all his Epistles, his Notions were at all times uniform, and constantly the same, tho his Expressions very various. In them he seems to take great Liberty. This at least is certain, that no one seems less tied up to a Form of Words. If then having by the Method before proposed got into the Sense of the several Epistles, we will but compare what he says, in the Places where he treats of the same Subject, we can hardly be mistaken in his Sense, nor doubt what it was, that he believed and taught concerning those Points of the Christian Religion. I know it is not unusual to find a Multitude of Texts heaped up for the maintaining of an espoused Proposition, but in a Sense often so remote from their true Meaning, that one can hardly avoid thinking that those who so used them, either sought not or valued not the Sense; and were satisfied with the Sound where they could but get that to favour them. But a verbal Concordance leads not always to Texts of the same meaning; trusting too much thereto, will furnish us but with slight Proofs in many Cases, and any one may observe how apt that is to jumble together Passages of Scripture not relating to the same Matter, and thereby to disturb and unsettle the true meaning of Holy Scripture. I have therefore said that we should compare together Places of Scripture treating of the same Point. Thus indeed one part of the Sacred Text could not fail to give light unto another. And since the Providence of God hath so order'd it, that St. *Paul* has writ a great Number of Epistles, which

64 INSPIRATION, REVELATION, SCRIPTURE, AND FAITH

tho upon different Occasions, and to several Purposes, yet are all confined within the Business of his Apostleship, and so contain nothing but Points of Christian Instruction, amongst which he seldom fails to drop in, and often to inlarge on the great and distinguishing Doctrines of
5 our holy Religion; which, if quitting our own Infallibility in that Analogy of Faith which we have made to our selves, or have implicitly adopted from some other, we would carefully lay together, and diligently compare and study, I am apt to think would give us St. *Paul*'s System in a clear and indisputable Sense, which every one must acknowledge to be a
10 better Standard to interpret his Meaning by, in any obscure and doubtful Parts of his Epistles, if any such should still remain, than the System, Confession, or Articles of any Church or Society of Christians yet known, which however pretended to be founded on Scripture, are visibly the Contrivances of Men (fallible both in their Opinions and
15 Interpretations) and as is visible in most of them, made with partial Views, and adapted to what the Occasions of that time, and the present Circumstances they were then in, were thought to require for the Support or Justification of themselves. Their Philosophy also has its part in mis-leading Men from the true Sense of the Sacred Scripture. He that
20 shall attentively read the Christian Writers after the Age of the Apostles, will easily find how much the Philosophy they were tinctured with, influenced them in their Understanding of the Books of the Old and New Testament. In the Ages wherein Platonism prevailed, the Converts to Christianity of that School, on all occasions, interpreted Holy Writ
25 according to the Notions they had imbib'd from that Philosophy. *Aristotle*'s Doctrine had the same effect in its turn, and when it degenerated into the Peripateticism of the Schools, that too brought its Notions and Distinctions into Divinity, and affixed them to the Terms of the Sacred Scripture. And we may see still how at this day every ones
30 Philosophy regulates every ones Interpretation of the Word of God. Those who are possessed with the Doctrine of Aerial and Ætherial Vehicles, have thence borrowed an Interpretation of the Four first Verses of *2 Cor. 5.* without having any Ground to think that St. *Paul* had the least Notion of any such Vehicles. 'Tis plain that the teaching of Men
35 Philosophy, was no part of the Design of Divine Revelation; but that the Expressions of Scripture are commonly suited in those Matters to the Vulgar Apprehensions and Conceptions of the Place and People where they were delivered. And as to the Doctrine therein directly taught by the Apostles, that tends wholly to the seting up the Kingdom of Jesus Christ
40 in this World, and the Salvation of Mens Souls, and in this 'tis plain their

THE UNDERSTANDING OF ST PAUL'S EPISTLES   65

Expressions were conformed to the Ideas and Notions which they had received from Revelation, or were consequent from it. We shall therefore in vain go about to interpret their Words by the Notions of our Philosophy, and the Doctrines of Men deliver'd in our Schools. This is to explain the Apostles meaning by what they never thought of whilst they were writing, which is not the way to find their Sense in what they deliver'd, but our own, and to take up from their Writings not what they left there for us, but what we bring along with us in our selves. He that would understand St. *Paul* right, must understand his Terms in the Sense he uses them, and not as they are appropriated by each Man's particular Philosophy, to Conceptions that never enter'd the Mind of the Apostle. For Example, he that shall bring the Philosophy now taught and receiv'd to the explaining of *Spirit*, *Soul*, and *Body*, mentioned *1 Thess. 5. 23.* will I fear hardly reach St. *Paul's* Sense, or represent to himself the Notions St. *Paul* then had in his Mind. That is what we should aim at in reading him, or any other Author, and 'till we from his Words paint his very Ideas and Thoughts in our Minds, we do not understand him.

In the Divisions I have made, I have indeavour'd the best I could to govern my self by the Diversity of Matter. But in a Writer like St. *Paul*, it is not so easie always to find precisely where one Subject ends, and another begins. He is full of the Matter he treats and writes with Warmth, which usually neglects Method, and those Partitions and Pauses which Men educated in the Schools of Rhetoricians usually observe. Those Arts of Writing St. *Paul*, as well out of Design as Temper, wholly laid by: The Subject he had in hand, and the Grounds upon which it stood firm, and by which he inforced it, was what alone he minded, and without solemnly winding up one Argument, and intimating any way that he began another, let his Thoughts, which were fully possess'd of the Matter, run in one continued Train, wherein the Parts of his Discourse were wove one into another. So that it is seldom that the Scheme of his Discourse makes any Gap; and therefore without breaking in upon the Connection of his Language, 'tis hardly possible to separate his Discourse, and give a distinct View of his several Arguments in distinct Sections.

I am far from pretending Infallibility in the Sense I have any where given in my Paraphrase or Notes; That would be to erect my self into an Apostle, a Presumption of the highest Nature in any one that cannot confirm what he says by Miracles. I have for my own Information sought the true Meaning as far as my poor Abilities would reach. And I have unbiassedly imbraced what upon a fair Enquiry appear'd so to me. This I

66 INSPIRATION, REVELATION, SCRIPTURE, AND FAITH

thought my Duty and Interest in a Matter of so great Concernment to me. If I must believe for my self, it is unavoidable that I must understand for my self. For if I blindly and with an Implicit Faith take the Pope's Interpretation of the Sacred Scripture, without examining whether it be
5 Christ's Meaning, 'tis the Pope I believe in, and not in Christ; 'tis his Authority I rest upon; 'tis what he says I imbrace: For what 'tis Christ says, I neither know nor concern my self. 'Tis the same thing when I set up any other Man in Christ's place, and make him the Authentique Interpreter of Sacred Scripture to my self. He may possibly understand
10 the Sacred Scripture as right as any Man, but I shall do well to examin my self, whether that which I do not know, nay (which in the way I take) I can never know, can justifie me in making my self his Disciple, instead of Jesus Christ's, who of Right is alone and ought to be my only Lord and Master: and it will be no less Sacrilege in me to substitute to my self any
15 other in his room, to be a Prophet, to me, than to be my King or Priest.

The same Reasons that put me upon doing what I have in these Papers done, will exempt me from all Suspition of imposing my Interpretation on others. The Reasons that lead me into the Meaning which prevail'd on my Mind, are set down with it; as far as they carry Light and
20 Conviction to any other Man's Understanding, so far I hope my Labour may be of some Use to him; beyond the Evidence it carries with it, I advise him not to follow mine, nor any Man's Interpretation. We are all Men liable to Errors, and infected with them; but have this sure way to preserve our selves every one from danger by them, if laying aside Sloth,
25 Carelessness, Prejudice, Party, and a Reverence of Men, we betake our selves in earnest to the Study of the way to Salvation, in those holy Writings wherein God has reveal'd it from Heaven, and propos'd it to the World, seeking our Religion where we are sure it is in Truth to be found, comparing spiritual things with spiritual things.

5

THE NATURE AND AUTHORITY OF THE CHURCH

Infallibility

The original of this document is in Latin. The English translation that follows is mine. It is based on the critical text prepared by John C. Biddle from the original manuscript in the British Public Records Office (PRO 30/24/47/33) and published in the *Journal of Church and State*, 19 (1977), 316–26. I have checked Biddle's transcription with a print made from a microfilm of the text. The manuscript is untitled. Locke's endorsement merely states its conclusion and marks the date: 'Infallible interpreters of Scripture not necessary, 1661'. Biddle called it 'Essay on Infallibility'. But an even shorter title, 'Infallibility', is mostly used and is adopted here.

Question: Whether it is necessary to grant that there be an Infallible Interpreter of Holy Scripture in the Church? Answer: Denied.

Although in any state and human society the right of making laws is the highest and greatest power, certainly next to this and almost equal to it is the authority of interpreting them. For what is the point of writing 5 dumb and silent rules of law, if anyone is permitted to attach new meaning to their expressions to suit his taste, and to twist words into a remotely contrived interpretation to fit his case and his opinion? Perspicacious priests, observing these two powers, have usurped both of them, so that they might establish a complete dominion over the conduct 10 and consciences of men, a dominion to which they zealously lay claim. They force upon the church traditions of their own that spring forth spontaneously as the occasion requires, and they argue that these traditions have the force of law and are binding on human consciences. They set up the Roman pontiff as the sole infallible interpreter of Holy 15 scripture. Nor does it matter much what god himself has dictated to his people on Mount Sinai, or Christ our lawgiver has commanded on the Mount of Olives, so long as the seven hills of Rome are higher than both and rule over them. When heaven itself does not have enough light to guide our steps, it is necessary to be blind. Does god himself, who has 20 made language and the organs of speech, who has given to men the use of discourse, so speak to mortals that he cannot be understood without an interpreter? Who will interpret the mind of god better than god himself? Are god's words obscure and uncertain, and men's clear and

70   THE NATURE AND AUTHORITY OF THE CHURCH

certain? Is he who first made the souls of mortals not able to instruct them? Does Christ so address waves and tempests that they understand, and so speak to men that only they do not? Do the eyes of the blind hear his words, which open ears cannot grasp? And does he so instruct
5 ignorant and pitiful mortals that diseases understand his command more than the diseased? God sent Prophets, Apostles, even his own son clothed in human form and not unacquainted with our ignorance and imbecility, that he might teach men what he willed to be done, so that mortals might know what sort of worship and reverence is owed to the
10 deity, and what sort of unity and common laws ought to prevail among them. Nor after so many messengers is it necessary to add an interpreter. Therefore, it is agreed that it is not necessary to grant that there be an Infallible Interpreter of holy Scripture in the Church.

1° Because there has been no such infallible interpreter since the time
15 of the Apostles, for the inference from fact to necessity is valid here, for there is little doubt that god, who has promised that he will preserve his church until the end of the age, will also provide that it will not lack whatever it needs. Besides, disagreements among Christians concerning divine things sufficiently show that there has been no infallible
20 interpreter, and the difference of opinions, which present not only a variety of propositions but also mutually contradictory ones, have vexed diverse members of the church separated in different regions of the world and divided them into parties. Perhaps priests will say that this is only a quarrel or dispute of the true church, that is their own, with ignorant and
25 heretical people. Yet it is indeed sufficiently obvious to anyone even moderately informed in ecclesiastical history that there are enormous discrepancies in the opinions of the Roman church and its infallible interpreter concerning faith and morals, and interpretations of Holy Scripture.

30   2° That which is utterly useless both to the faith and peace of the church is not necessary. For let it be granted that there be an infallible interpreter of Holy Scripture, however ⟨......⟩ he may have been, he will be able to offer nothing to unravel the faith, nothing to establish peace among Christians, unless he infallibly show that he is infallible, but
35 since he cannot prove this about himself, for anyone's testimony about himself is not admissible, and since scripture is silent, it is not easy to see whence he can be identified, hence one may expect no remedy from here for so much disagreement and so many errors. For that everyone can err and that there is an infallible interpreter who is unknown and uncertain
40 amount to the same thing; what help is it to be certain of something

INFALLIBILITY   71

when you have doubts about the person? How anxiously you must hope from there for a cure for vice and ignorance, when you do not know whether he to whom you entrust yourself is a physician or a mountebank.

Besides, since scripture, whose interpreter we seek, was written down at different times and not in the same style, and includes a variety of arguments, a record of past events, rules of conduct, and articles of faith, it can be considered in many ways.

1° Hence, many things are contrived as a show and arrogance of learning, frivolous and worthless little questions that do not arise naturally from holy scripture, but are violently pressed out of the minds of wickedly deranged men, such as, What fruit was forbidden in paradise? Where was that pleasure garden located? and suchlike that neither want an interpreter nor merit a reader. Perhaps queries of this sort can occupy vacant minds, but they can scarcely detain sober and pious men, and although they may be hard to answer, they can be safely ignored. Besides they seem to have barely any relation to Scripture, which is the standard of faith and morals.

2° Hence, Holy Scripture contains within it profound mysteries of divine things that absolutely surpass human understanding, which, even if they are obscure, cannot have an interpreter, for, since to interpret is just to elicit the meaning of obscure utterances and to explicate less ordinary discourse in plain everyday speech, it is certain that interpretations of these mysteries are impossible, because God has proclaimed in the clearest words and with the greatest perspicuity what he wants men to know and what to believe. For, whoever tries to explain the trinity of persons in the divine nature in words other than those with which god has revealed it casts not so much light than darkness on scripture, and one can add to this the union of divine and human natures in the person of the mediator, the infinity of god, his eternity and not a few more, whose truth is certain and to be believed, but how they are such can neither be represented in discourse nor conceived in the mind. Whatever hinders us in such pursuits, it is certainly not the obscurity of words but the magnitude of the things themselves and the imbecility of our mind. Whoever desires to interpret these things ought to bring not copious words and a facility of speech but a new power of the human soul and a new understanding.

3° There are other things in holy writ, things most necessary for salvation, that are so clear and perspicuous that almost no one can doubt them, for it is the same to hear and to understand them. Such are the

72   THE NATURE AND AUTHORITY OF THE CHURCH

primary duties of the Christian man, justice, chastity, charity, benevolence, which certainly have little need of an interpreter, because they have been so clearly handed down that if any interpretation were added it would have been necessary to add another interpretation to that
5 interpretation.

4° There are some more general precepts and admonitions in holy writ like the one to the Corinthians οὐδὲ αὐτὴ ἡ φύσις (i e custom) διδάσκει ὑμᾶς ὅτι ἀνήρ μὲν ἐὰν κομᾷ ἀτιμία αὐτῷ ἐστι for scripture doesn't state precisely what hair is too long, hence this must be decided by the church.
10 And, chapter 14, πάντα εὐσχημόνως καὶ κατὰ τάξιν γινέσθω. Since these precepts concern things that are in themselves and by their nature indifferent, they can neither be applied to the practice of life and regulate human actions without an interpreter. In these cases and others like them, I affirm that it is both possible and necessary that an infallible
15 interpreter be granted in the Church, namely its fathers and leaders, who in these matters can be said to be infallible, but I would add, with an infallibility that is directive not definitive, for while it is clear that pastors of the church can go astray when they lead, the sheep surely are not able to go astray when they follow. For those who follow, the way is safe and
20 secure. For, since the duty of obedience for the multitude of Christians is certain and of little doubt, even if perchance the interpretation of the text of scripture should be in doubt, he errs least who follows what is certain, who applies himself to obedience, and is zealous for the peace of the church. Interpreters of this sort of divine law can be called infallible,
25 who, even if they perchance can be deceived, cannot mislead others.

However, in interpreting scripture, it is not very easy or straightforward to decide how much is to be allowed to each individual and how much to the authority of the church, what finally reason warrants and what the illumination of the holy spirit. Besides, the greatest caution
30 should be taken lest, having trusted too much in our reason, we neglect faith, and, by not having given due regard to the mysteries of the gospel, we embrace philosophy instead of religion. On the other hand, enthusiasm must be carefully avoided, lest while waiting for the inspiration of the holy spirit, we admire and worship our dreams. It is
35 beyond doubt that the interpretation of the Holy Bible derives much from learning, much from reason, and, lastly, much from the Holy Spirit illuminating the minds of men, but the most certain interpreter of Scripture is Scripture itself, and it alone is infallible.

'Critical Notes upon Edward Stillingfleet's Mischief *and* Unreasonableness of Separation'—*Extracts*

The title is not Locke's but has been adapted from Long's description of the manuscript, which has no title, in *A Summary Catalogue of the Lovelace Collection*, 33. All the extracts are from BOD MS Locke c. 34. Page numbers of the manuscript of Locke's 'Critical Notes' are inserted in brackets before each selection.

[19] The great businesse of Religion is to glorifye god, & find favour with him. this though it be the most intimate & peculiar concerne of every man within himself wherewith his neighbour hath nothing to doe (for what interest hath any one but that of charity, what way I take for the salvation of my soul?) yet since the actions of a private solitary life cannot 5 reach to all the instances & purposes of religion in its full entent. therefore men find themselves obliged, when they embrace any religion, to associate, to joyn in communion with some society, wherein that religion is professed.

[22] D^r: Ser: p. 17. makes the only end of a Church to be Government & 10 order which is as much as to say that the businesse of an Army is merely that it be commanded, his words are <u>for the true notion of a Church is no more than of a society of men united together for their Order and Government according to the Rules of the Christian Religion</u>. but there seems to me to be other ends why men enter into religious societyes, & I 15 think it is scarce to be imagined that every any man voluntarily enterd into any society merely to be governed, ~~but~~ the great end of every man is happynesse which Religion is alwayes thought more directly to serve to and though a great & principal part of it be a good life, in a mans common businesse, & transactions in the world, yet the great part of 20 Religion is to be managed in Society, that that alone hath got the name of religion, the several societyes concerning it being termed so many religions, & since this is not for nothing or barely for government, there must be some other great ends of religion to be attaind onely in societyes, which seem to me to be these, (1) edification, which consists in forming 25

74   THE NATURE AND AUTHORITY OF THE CHURCH

the understanding & subdueing of the will (2°) the publick worship of god. (3°) the propagation of truth, & the continuation of the Gospell downe to posterity one of these containing my duty to god the other to my neighbour, & the other to my self and these three at least ~~if I mistake not~~ are plainly set downe in scripture 1. for worship of god no man will require a proof for a thing so evident thorough out the whole Bible. for the 2^d see the 1° Tim 3. 15 & 3dly no body will deny let all things be done for edifying. 1 Cor. 14. 26 is as great a command, & of strict obligation as let all things be done decently & in order in the same chapter.

[75] The light of nature discovering to man that he is under the Government & disposal of an invisible & supreme being, teaches him also that he was concernd so to behave himself as not to offend, or as if he did so find means to reconcile & recover again the favour of that being which overrules all humane affairs & sovereignly despenses [76] good & evil in this world & on whom depends Eternall happiness & missery in an other: this knowledge of a God & his absolute Power over them puts all men upon thoughts of religion every where who had every where but reflected on there owne originall or the Constitution of the visible things of nature to any degree beyond brutes, & though morality be acknowledgd by them all to be a great part of that wherein god may be offended or pleased with us. Yet Morality being that law, which god hath planted in the nature of Man to preserve the being & welfare of himself & other men in this world, a great part of it has fallen under the Magistrates care, to whom the government of civill Societyes is committed, as the greatest means of the preservation of mankind in this world, & though Men are persuaded ⟨or⟩ convinced that the observance of that Law is a meanes also of pleaseing or displeaseing god & so a meanes too of procureing happynesse or misery in another world, yet it has not past under the name of Religion which has bin appropriated to those actions onely which are referred wholy to the pleaseing or displeaseing god without any concerneing at all my neighbour, Civil Society, or my owne preservation in this life for my praying to god in this or that fashion or useing any other ceremony in religion or speculative opinions concerneing things of another life impends not at all upon the health or possession good name or any other right of my neighbour which serves to his well being, or preservation in this world. Religion being then those opinions, & actions alone, which I entertaine, or performe, onely to please god, & such as have no concernement at all with my neighbour or the interest, or affaires of this

CRITICAL NOTES ON STILLINGFLEET 75

world, though many of these are outward & visible to others: are not within the civill Magistrates inspection and care, whose province is onely civil society, in order to mens well being in this world. This being the notion that Men have had of Religion as a transaction immediately between god, & them for the procureing his favour without concerneing 5 civill society at all, it has yet put men upon the necessity of uniteing into Societyes about it, there being many parts of it that could not be performed in the solitary recesses of a retired man. for Men finding it their duty to honour, and worship the god they served, were to doe it by publick acts of devotion. owneing to the world thereby that Deity by 10 solemne acts of worship to whom they payd the internal acts of veneration in [77] their hearts And twas from this that men were obliged to enter into societyes for Religion, with those who were of the same belief & way of worship with them selves. The Christian Religion when it came into the world proceeded upon the same grounds . . . 15

[78] These Religious societyes (at least among Christians) are calld Churches. which are onely voluntary societyes which men by their owne consent enter into for the ends of Religion above mentiond can have no other Government then that which the society it self shall agree of over its owne members. it being necessary to every society that has any thing 20 to doe to have some order & some distinction of offices amongst Men. & some Laws to governe the Members of the society. but these can reach none but those that are actuall members of that society which if they will not submit to the utmost power they have is turne them out of the society & to deny them the previledges of communicating with it. & on 25 the other side: as he entred freely into the society for the professing of the truth, the worshipping god, & his Edification may quit againe. when he thinks the constitution of that society serves ⟨or⟩ guides not to those ends, & is not so well as that of some other. For if I had the liberty to what religious society I would at first enter into for the salvation of my 30 owne soul I am for the same reason always at liberty to leave it agen when I judg it serves not to those ends or not so well as another Religion.

[86] All the arguments used from the Church, or established Church &c. amount to noe more but this, that there are a certain set of men in the world upon whose credit I must without farther examination to venture 35 my salvation. Soe that all the directions & precepts to examine doctrines, trie the spirits, take heed what you beleive, hold the truth, &c. are all to noe purpose, when all the measure & stamp of truth whereby I am to

76   THE NATURE AND AUTHORITY OF THE CHURCH

receive it will then be only the hand that delivers it, & not the appearances of rectitude it carries with it, this is to deale worse with men in their great eternall concernment of their souls, then in the short & triviall concernments of their estates. For though it be the allowed
5 prerogative of Princes to stamp silver & gold thereby make them currant mony, yet every man has the liberty to examine even those very pieces that have the magistrates stamp & imagine, & if they have the suspition and appearance of a false alloy they may avoid being cozend & not receive them. The stamp makes it neither good nor currant. the stamp is
10 but for security as much as may be that the metall is good but when that appears to be naught. but noe authority that I know on earth unlesse it be the infallible Church of Rome boldly claime a right to coine opinions into truths, & make them currant by their authority & yet in all places all men are unreasonably required to receive and professe doctrines for
15 truths because this governor, or that preist, says they are soe. But yet this how senseless soever helps not the case nor profits the opinions of any one sort of them. For if the Pope demands an obedient faith to him & his emissarys, the Bishops of England tell us that they & such as have Episcopal ordination under them are the true Church & are to be
20 beleived: the presbyterians tell us those of presbyterian ordination have noe lesse authority, & that in all matters of doctrine & discipline they are to be beleived. The Independents & anabaptists think they have as much reason to be heard as the former. And the Quakers think them selves the only true guides whilst they bid us be guided by the light within. All
25 these we have within our selves, every one of them calling on us to hearken to them ~~upon paine of damnation~~ as the sole deliverers of unmixed truth in doctrine & discipline. This they all doe severally with the same confidence and zeale, & for aught I know with the same divine authority for as for human authority I'm sure that weighs noething in the
30 case. If we will looke farther, & adde to these the Lutheran, Greeke, Armenian, Jacobite, and Abyssine Churches, & yet farther out of the borders of Christianity into the Jewish Synagogues and Mahumetan mosques the Mufti and the Rabbis are men of authority and think them selves as little deceivers or deceived as any of the rest. What will it availe
35 then to the Church of England Among soe many equall pretenders to say they are the true Church & must be beleived or have the magistrate on their side & must be obeyed? If they are to be beleived the true Church because Bishop G. or Dr. S. says so Mr. B or Dr. O will say as much for the presbyterian or independent. Cardinall H. and Mr. P for the papist
40 and Quakers & upon the same authority. for they are all men that say it,

CRITICAL NOTES ON STILLINGFLEET 77

endowd with the like facultys to know them selves & subject to the same frailtys of mistaking or imposing. If they will prove them selves to be in the right or to be the true Church. They take indeed the right course, but then they lay by their authority in proposeing, as I must lay it by in considering their arguments. they appeale to my reason, & that I must make use of to examine and judge. but then we are but just where we were at first seting out, & where we shall be, whether the church of England be or not be in the right whether its constitution be or be not jure divino, i e every one judging for himself of what church he thinks it best and safest to be.

[106] The D^r. presses the necessity of a national Church, as tending to the support of Religion, preserveing of Peace, & unity among Christians, & the preventing of dangerous errors, & endless confusions.
1. as to the support of Religion it is certain that a national Church tends to the support of the national Religion but with this serry addition: whether true or false, but if it is not the true religion it supports, it were better let alone, & it will hardly be our duty to be of it. or any bodyes duty to set it up: & where that national Church is besides ones that tend to support the true Religion I desire our Author to shew us
2. That it tends to the preserveing of Peace, & unity amongst Christians is just such a rule as the former for the peace & unity it preserves is amongst no other Christians but those of the same Church: for what unity has the Church of England more with the Church of Rome [107] then a gatherd congregation of Presbyterians. or what peace the attempts of more then one party in England if to make their Churches national by compelling others into them: hath produced amongst us, all true Christians & sober men may with sadnesse of thought consider. so that the tendency to peace here amounts to no more but this, that if all men of the nation were of the nationall Church they would be at peace about that matter. & so the same argument will hold for the universal Church. that if all Christians were agreed in one rule of faith, worship & Government of the Catholick Church it would mightily tend to Peace for there would be no more difference about that matter. but the question is whether the endeavouring to erect such an universal or national Church with a dominion upon mens consciences, & a pretended obligation that they ought to submit to it, will require better proofs then I have met with. but to speake truly of the matter the peace & unity of the Church is to be preservd only by Charity, & good will: & not by imposing of a rigid & stiff uniformity; it being no more to be hoped. to have men all of the

78   THE NATURE AND AUTHORITY OF THE CHURCH

same mind in these things then to have them all of the same looks, or complexions, nor does it tend any more to Peace without the inward persuasion of the mind goe along with it. then it does for men that are really at oddes to have the same Taylor, or danceing master; since it is the
5 unity & well wishes of the mind, & not any outward conformity of resemblance, that preserves peace, or unity in the world, which men may have if they follow Christian rules. with those that differ from them both in opinion & worship.

3. As to the tendency of a national Religion to prevent dangerous errors I
10 cannot see how it does so as long as I consider Spain France & Muscovy, not to reckon all other Christian Countreys besides England. though every one of those would use the same arguement for their national religion. & as for endlesse confusions I think it amounts but to a variety of opinions which whether it be worse, then unity in errour or
15 superstition at any thing els inconsistent with the gospell; from whence a man has no liberty of retreiving himself I leave everyone to consider. since experience shews us that national Churches or great numbers of Christians united into one Church are no more priviledged from Errour then great congregations. & where they assume to themselves an [108]
20 absolute power of imposeing are generaly lesse apt to be in the right. The question in short is whether it be best, that men should be compelld blindly to submit to, or publickly owne the doctrines & worship that others impose, right or wrong whether he beleives them or no: or that those who are in earnest concernd for their soules should seek out the
25 best way they could find to ~~their Salvation~~: the one is to put a mans greatest concernement his eternal happynesse or misery into his care whose greatest interest it is to look after it. The other to put it barely into the hands of Chance, or which is worse, often into the hands of those who make use of this power onely to serve the secular ends of their
30 ambition, & greatnesse, & I know not why it is not as reasonable to set over men Guardians who shall have the power to order all things as they thought fit for the preservation of their particular estates or healthes; for fear they should mistake or be negligent in them as Guardians over their soules, which must be saved onely in that way they prescribe them.

35 [161] The bonds given to their pastors in Independent Churches shew how in this contest churches are made like bird cages with trapp dores which give free admittance to all birds whether they have always been the wild inhabitants of the air, or are got loose from any other cages but when they are once in, they are to be kept there & are to have the liberty

CRITICAL NOTES ON STILLINGFLEET

of goeing out noe more And the reason is, because if this be permitted our volerys will be spoild, but the happynesse of the birds is not the business of these bird keepers.

82
Ecclesia

Hookers description of the church lib. 1 § 1 5 amounts to this That it is a supernatural but voluntary societie wherein a man associates himself to god angels & holy men. The original of it he says is the same as of other societies viz an inclination unto sociable life & a consent to the bond of
5 association which is the law & order they are associated in. That which makes it supernatural is the part of the bond of their association which is a law reveald concerning what worship god would have donne to him, which natural reason could not have discovered, soe that the worship of god soe far forth as it hath any thing in it more then the law of reason
10 doth teach may not be invented of men. From when I thinke it will follow 1° That the Church being a supernatural societie, & a societie by consent The secular power which is purely natural nor any other power can compel one to be of any particular church societie there being many such to be found. 2° That the end of entering into such societie being
15 only to obtain the favour of god by offering him an acceptable worship, noe body can impose any ceremonys unlesse positively & clearly by revelation injoyned any farther then every one who joyns in the use of them is perswaded in his conscience they are acceptable to god. for if his conscience condemns any part of unrevealed worship he cannot by any
20 sanction of men be obliged to it. 3° That since a part only of the bond of this association is a revealed law this part alone is unalterable & the other which is humane depends wholy upon consent & soe is alterable & a man is held by such laws or to such a particular societie noe longer then he him self doth consent. 4° Imagine that the original of this societie is not,
25 from our inclination as he says to a sociable life for that may be fully satisfied in other societies, but from the obligation man by the light of reason findes him self under to own & worship god publiquely in the world JL

98

Error

The great division amongst Christians is about Opinions. Every sect has its set of them & that is called Orthodoxie. And he who professes his assent to them though with an implicit faith & without examining he is Orthodox & in the way to salvation. But if he examines & thereupon questions any one of them, he is presently suspected of Heresie & if he 5 oppose them or hold the contrary he is presently condemnd as in a damnable Error & the sure way to perdition. Of this one may say there is nor can be nothing more wrong. For he that examines & upon a fair examination imbraces an error for a truth. has done his duty more than he who imbraces the profession (for the truths them selves he does not 10 imbrace) of the Truth without haveing examined whether it be true or noe. And he that has done his duty according to the best of his ability is certainly more in the way to heaven then he that has done noe thing of it For if it be our duty to search after truth he certainly that has searchd after it though he has not found it in some points has paid a more acceptable 15 obedience to the will of his maker then he that has not searchd at all, but professes to have found truth when he has neither searchd nor found it. For he that takes up the opinions of any church in the Lump without examining them has truly neither searchd after nor found truth but has only found those that he thinks have found truth, & soe receives what 20 they say with an implicit faith & soe pays them the homage that is due only to god, him who cannot be deceivd nor deceive. In this way the several churches (in which as ~~orthodoxie is preferd to Morals~~ one may observe opinions are preferd to life & orthodoxie is that which they are concernd for & not morals) put the terms of salvation on that which the 25 author of our Salvation does not put them in. The beleiving of a collection of certain propositions which are called & esteemd Fundamental articles because it has pleasd the compilers to put them into the Confession of faith, is made the condition of Salvation. But this beleiving is not in truth beleiving but a profession to beleive for it is enough to 30 joyn with those who make the same profession; & ignorance or disbeleif of some of those articles is well enough borne & a man is Orthodox enough & without any suspition till he begins to examin. As soon as it is

82 THE NATURE AND AUTHORITY OF THE CHURCH

perceived that he quits the implicit faith expected though disowned by the church, his Orthodoxie is presently questioned & he is marked out for a Heretick. In this way of an implicit faith I doe not deny but a man who beleives in God the father almighty & that Jesus Christ is his only Son
5 our Lord may be saved: because many of the articles of every sect are such as a man may be saved without the explicit beleif of. But how the several churches who place salvation in noe lesse then a knowledg & beleife of their several confessions can content them selves with such an implicit faith in any of their members I must owne I doe not see. The
10 truth is we cannot be saved without our performing some thing which is the explicit beleiving of what god in the gospel has made absolutely necessary to salvation to be explicitly beleived, & sincerely to obey what he has there commanded. To a man who beleives in Jesus Christ that he is sent from God to be the Saviour of the world The first step to
15 Orthodoxie is a sincere obedience to his law. Objection: But tis an ignorant day labourer, that cannot soe much as read & how can he study the Gospel & become Orthodox that way? Answer: A plough man that can not read is not soe ignorant but he has a confidence & knows in those few cases which concerne his own actions what is right & what is wrong
20 let him sincerely obey this light of nature it is the transcript of the moral law in the Gospel, and this, even though there be errors in it will lead him into all the truths in the Gospel that are necessary for him to know. For he that in earnest beleives Jesus Christ to be sent from God to be his Lord & ruler & does sincerly & unfeignedly sets upon a good life as far as he
25 know his dutys: & where he is in doubt in any matter that concerns him cannot faile to enquire of those better skild in Christs law to tell him what his Lord & master has commanded in the case & desire to have his law read to him concerning that duty which he finds him self concerned in for the regulation of his own actions. For as for other mens actions what is
30 right & wrong as to them that he is not concerned to know, his businesse is to live well him self & doe what is his particular duty. This is knowledg & Orthodoxie enough for him which will be sure to bring him to salvation, & an Orthodoxie which noe body can misse who in earnest resolves to lead a good life. And therefor I lay it down as a principle of
35 Christianity that the right & only way to Saveing Orthodoxie is the sincere & steady purpose of a good life. Ignorant of many things conteined in the Holy Scriptures we are all. Errors also concerning doctrines deliverd in scripture we have all of us not a few. these there for cannot be damnable if any shall be saved. And if they are dangerous tis
40 certain the ignorant & illiterate are safest for they have the fewest Errors

ERROR

that trouble not them selves with Speculations above their capacitys or beside their concerne. A good life in obedience to the law of Christ their Lord is their indispensable businesse, & if they informe them selves concerning that as far as their particular dutys lead them to enquire & oblige them to know, they have Orthodoxie enough, & will not be condemnd for ignorance in those speculations which they had neither parts, opportunity, nor leisure to know. Here we may see the difference between the Orthodoxie required by ~~the Gospel~~ Christianity & the Orthodoxie required by the several sects or as they are called Churches of Christians. The one is explicitly to beleive what is indispensably required to be beleived as absolutely necessary to Salvation, & to know & beleive the other doctrines of faith delivered in the word of god as a man has opportunity helps & parts: but to informe him self in the rules & measures of his owne duty as far as his actions are concernd & to pay a sincere obedience to them. But the other viz the Orthodoxie as requird by the several sects is a profession of beleiving the whole bundle of their respective articles set down in each churches Systeme, without knowing the rules of every ones particular dutys or requireing a sincere or strict obedience to them. For they are speculative opinions, confessions of faith that are insisted on in the several communions. they must be owned & subscribed to but the precepts & rules of morality & the observance of them I doe not remember there is much notice taken of, or any great stir made about a collection or observance of them in any of the termes of church communion. But it is also to be observed that this is much better fitted to get & retain church members then the other way, & is much more suited to that end, as much as it is easier to make Profession of beleiving a certain collection of opinions that one never perhaps soe much as read & several whereof one could not perhaps understand if one did read & study (For noe more is requird then a profession to beleive them expressed in an acquiescence that suffers one not to question or contradict any of them), Than it is to practise the dutys of a good life in a sincere obedience to those precepts of the gospel wherein his actions are concerned. Precepts not hard to be known by those willing & ready to obey them JL

6

THE REASONABLENESS
OF CHRISTIANITY

THE
REASONABLENESS
OF
Christianity,

As delivered in the

SCRIPTURES.

LONDON:

Printed for *Awnsham* and *John Churchil,*
at the *Black Swan* in *Pater-Noster-*
Row. 1695.

THE PREFACE [A2ʳ]

THE little Satisfaction and Consistency is to be found in most of the Systems of Divinity I have met with, made me betake my self to the sole Reading of the Scripture (to which they all appeal) for the understanding the Christian Religion. What from thence by an attentive and unbiassed search I have received, Reader, I here deliver to thee. If by this my Labour thou receivest any Light or Confirmation in the Truth, joyn with me in Thanks | to the Father of Lights for his Condescention to our Understandings. If upon a fair and unprejudiced Examination, thou findest I have mistaken the Sense and Tenor of the Gospel, I beseech thee, as a true Christian, in the Spirit of the Gospel (which is that of Charity) and in the words of Sobriety, set me right in the Doctrine of Salvation.

THE REASONABLENESS OF CHRISTIANITY, AS DELIVERED IN THE SCRIPTURES

I 'TIS obvious to any one who reads the New Testament, that the Doctrine of Redemption, and consequently of the Gospel, is founded upon the Supposition of *Adam*'s Fall. To understand therefore what we are restored to by Jesus Christ, we must consider what the Scripture shews we lost by *Adam*. This I thought worthy of a diligent and unbiassed search: Since I found the two Extreams, that Men run into on this Point, either on the one hand shook the Foundations of all Religion, or on the other made Christianity almost nothing. For whilst some Men would have all *Adam*'s Posterity doomed to Eternal Infinite Punishment for the Transgression of *Adam*, whom Millions had never heard of, and no one had authorized to tran|sact for him, or be his Representative; this seemed to others so little consistent with the Justice or Goodness of the Great and Infinite God, that they thought there was no Redemption necessary, and consequently that there was none, rather than admit of it upon a Supposition so derogatory to the Honour and Attributes of that Infinite Being; and so made Jesus Christ nothing but the Restorer and Preacher of pure Natural Religion; thereby doing violence to the whole tenor of the New Testament. And indeed both sides will be suspected to have trespassed this way, against the written Word of God, by any one, who does but take it to be a Collection of Writings designed by God for the Instruction of the illiterate bulk of Mankind in the way to Salvation; and therefore generally and in necessary points to be understood in the plain direct meaning of the words and phrases, such as they may be supposed to have had in the mouths of the Speakers, who used them according to the Language of that Time and Country wherein they lived, without such learned, artificial, | and forced senses of them, as are sought out, and put upon them in most of the Systems of Divinity, according to the Notions, that each one has been bred up in.

To one that thus unbiassed reads the Scriptures, what *Adam* fell from, is visible, was the state of perfect Obedience, which is called *Justice* in the New Testament, though the word which in the Original signifies *Justice*, be translated *Righteousness*: And by this Fall he lost Paradise, wherein was

92   THE REASONABLENESS OF CHRISTIANITY

Tranquility and the Tree of Life, *i. e.* he lost Bliss and Immortality. The Penalty annexed to the breach of the Law, with the Sentence pronounced by God upon it, shew this. The Penalty stands thus, *Gen.* II. 17. *In the day that thou eatest thereof thou shalt surely die.* How was this executed? He did eat, but in the day he did eat, he did not actually die, but was turned out of Paradise from the Tree of Life, and shut out for ever from it, *lest he should take thereof and live for ever.* This shews that the state of Paradise was a state of Immortality, of Life without end, which he lost that very day that he | eat: His Life began from thence to shorten, and wast, and to have an end; and from thence to his actual Death, was but like the time of a Prisoner between the Sentence past and the Execution, which was in view and certain. Death then enter'd and shewed his Face, which before was shut out, and not known. So St. *Paul, Rom.* V. 12. *By one man sin entred into the world, and death by sin*; *i. e.* a state of Death and Mortality: And 1 *Cor.* XV. 22. *In Adam all die*; *i. e.* by reason of his Transgression all Men are Mortal, and come to die.*

This is so clear in these cited places, and so much the current of the New Testament, that no body can deny, but that the Doctrine of the Gospel is, that Death came on all Men by *Adam*'s sin; only they differ about the signification of the word *Death*. For some will have it to be a state of Guilt, wherein not only he, but all his Posterity was so involved, that every one descended of him deserved endless torment in Hell-fire. I shall say nothing more here how far, in the apprehensions of Men, this consists with the Justice | and Goodness of God, having mentioned it above: But it seems a strange way of understanding a Law, which requires the plainest and directest words, that by *Death* should be meant Eternal Life in Misery. Could any one be supposed by a Law, that says, *For Felony you shall die*, not that he should lose his Life, but be kept alive in perpetual exquisite Torments? And would any one think himself fairly dealt with, that was so used?†

---

* De immortalitate per Adamum amissa et per Christum restituta, v: Jul: Firmicum Maternum, p. $\frac{51}{64}$.

† The Scripture speaks not to us so much in the tongue of the learned Sophies of the world as in the plainest and most vulgar dialect that may be, which the Jews constantly observed and took notice of, says Mr. Smith of Prophesie, Chap. 1. And again, It speaks with the most Idiotical sort of men in the most Idiotical way, ibidem. The reason of this plain and Idiotical stile Maimonides gives, *More Nevochim*, part I, chap. 33: For this reason the law speaks according to the language of the sons of men, because it is the most commodious and easie way of initiating and teaching Children, women and the common people, who have not ability to apprehend things according to the very nature and essence of them, etc. ibidem.

AS DELIVERED IN THE SCRIPTURES 93

To this they would have it be also a state of necessary sinning, and provoking God in every Action that men do: A yet harder sense of the word *Death* than the other. God says, *That in the day that thou eatest of* the forbidden Fruit, *thou shalt die*; *i. e.* thou and thy Posterity shall be ever after uncapable of doing any thing, but what shall be sinful and provoking to me, and shall justly deserve my wrath and indignation. Could a worthy man be supposed to put such terms upon the Obedience of his Subjects, much less can the Righteous God be supposed, as a Punishment of one sin wherewith he is displeased, to put Man under a ne|cessity of sinning continually, and so multiplying the Provocation? [6] The reason of this strange Interpretation we shall perhaps find in some mistaken places of the New Testament. I must confess by *Death* here I can understand nothing but a ceasing to be, the losing of all actions of Life and Sense.* Such a Death came on *Adam*, and all his Posterity by his first Disobedience in Paradise, under which *Death* they should have lain for ever, had it not been for the Redemption by Jesus Christ. If by *Death* threatned to *Adam* were meant the Corruption of Humane Nature in his Posterity, 'tis strange that the New Testament should not any where take notice of it, and tell us, that Corruption seized on all because of *Adam*'s Transgression, as well as it tells us so of *Death*. But as I remember every ones sin is charged upon himself only.

Another part of the Sentence was, *Cursed is the ground for thy sake; in sorrow shalt thou eat of it all the days of thy life, in the sweat of thy face shalt thou eat bread, till thou return unto the ground: For out of it wast thou taken; Dust thou art, and to dust shalt* | *thou return*, Gen. III. 17– [7] 19. This shews that Paradise was a place of Bliss as well as Immortality, without toyl, and without sorrow. But when Man was turned out, he was exposed to the drudgery, anxiety, and frailties of this Mortal Life, which should end in the *Dust*, out of which he was made, and to which he should return; and then have no more life or sense than the *Dust* had, out of which he was made.

As *Adam* was turned out of *Paradise*, so all his Posterity were born out of it, out of the reach of the Tree of Life, All like their Father *Adam* in a state of Mortality, void of the Tranquility and Bliss of *Paradise*. Rom. V. 12. *By one man sin entered into the world, and death by sin.* But here will occur the common Objection, that so many stumble at: How doth it consist with the Justice and Goodness of God, that the Posterity of

---

* *Psa.* VI. 5. LVI. 13. LXXXIX. 48. 2 *Sam.* XIV. 14. *Job* XIV. 14. Animas esse Mortales, Justin Martyr, Dialogus cum Tryphone, circa initium $\frac{173}{490}$.

94 THE REASONABLENESS OF CHRISTIANITY

Adam should suffer for his sin; the Innocent be punished for the Guilty? Very well, if keeping one from what he has no right to, be called a *Punishment*. The state of Immortality in Paradise is not due to the [8] Posterity of *Adam* more than to any | other Creature. Nay, if God afford 5 them a Temporary Mortal Life, 'tis his Gift, they owe it to his Bounty, they could not claim it as their Right, nor does he injure them when he takes it from them. Had he taken from Mankind any thing, that was their Right; or did he put Men in a state of Misery worse than not being, without any fault or demerit of their own; this indeed would be hard to 10 reconcile with the Notion we have of Justice, and much more with the Goodness and other Attributes of the Supream Being, which he has declared of himself, and Reason as well as Revelation must acknowledge to be in him; unless we will confound Good and Evil, God and Satan. That such a state of extream irremediable Torment is worse than no 15 Being at all, if every ones own sense did not determine against the vain Philosophy, and foolish Metaphysicks of some Men; yet our Saviour's peremptory decision, *Matt*. XXVI. 24. has put it past doubt, that one may be in such an estate, that it had been *better for him not to have been* [9] *born*. But that such a temporary Life as we now | have, with all its Frailties 20 and ordinary Miseries, is better than no Being, is evident by the high value we put upon it our selves. And therefore though *all die in Adam*, yet none are truly *punished* but for their own deeds. *Rom*. II. 6. *God will render to every one*, how? *according to his deeds. To those that obey unrighteousness, indignation and wrath, tribulation and anguish upon every* 25 *soul of man that doth evil*, v. 9. 2 *Cor*. V. 10. *We must appear before the Judgment-seat of Christ, that every one may receive the things done in his body, according to that he has done, whether it be good or bad*. And Christ himself, who knew for what he should condemn Men at the last day, assures us in the two places where he describes his proceeding at the great Judgment, 30 that the Sentence of Condemnation passes only on the *workers of Iniquity*, such as neglected to fulfil the Law in acts of Charity, *Mat*. VII. 23. *Luke* XIII. 27. *Mat*. XXV. 42. And again, *John* V. 29. our Saviour tells the Jews that *all shall come forth of their graves, they that have done good to the resurrection of life, and they that have done evil unto the resurrection of* 35 *damnation*. But here is no Condemnation of any one, for what his forefather *Adam* had done, which 'tis not likely should have been omitted, if [10] that should have been a cause, why | any one was adjudged to the *fire* with the *Devil and his Angels*. And he tells his Disciples, that when he comes again with his Angels in the Glory of his Father, *that then he will render to* 40 *every one according to his works*, Mat. XVI. 27.

AS DELIVERED IN THE SCRIPTURES 95

II *Adam* being thus turned out of Paradise, and all his Posterity born out of it, the consequence of it was, that all men should die, and remain under Death for ever, and so be utterly lost.

From this estate of Death Jesus Christ restores all mankind to Life; 1 *Cor.* XV. 22. *As in* Adam *all die, so in Christ shall all be made alive.* How this shall be, the same Apostle tells us in the foregoing *v.* 21. *By man death came, by man also came the Resurrection from the dead.* And so our Saviour him self tells us *John* V. 21. *For as the Father raiseth up the dead and makes them alive even so the Son maketh alive whom he will.* Whereby it appears, that the Life, which Jesus Christ restores to all men, is that Life, which they receive again at the Resurrection. Then they recovered from Death, which otherwise all mankind should have continued under lost for ever, as appears by St. *Paul's* Arguing, 1 *Cor.* XV. concerning the Resurrection.

And thus men are by the Second | *Adam* restored to Life again: That so by *Adam's* sin they may none of them lose any thing, which by their own Righteousness they might have a Title to. For Righteousness, or an exact obedience to the Law, seems by the Scripture to have a claim of Right to Eternal Life, *Rom.* IV. 4. *To him that worketh*; *i. e.* does the works of the Law, *is the reward not reckoned of Grace, but OF DEBT.* And *Rev.* XXII. 14. *Blessed are they who do his Commandments, that they may HAVE RIGHT to the Tree of Life, which is in the Paradise of God.* If any of the Posterity of *Adam* were just, they shall not lose the Reward of it, Eternal Life and Bliss, by being his Mortal Issue: Christ will bring them all to Life again; And then they shall be put every one upon his own Tryal, and receive Judgment, as he is found to be Righteous or no. And *the righteous*, as our Saviour says, *Mat.* XXV. 46. *shall go into eternal life.* Nor shall any one miss it, who has done what our Saviour directed the Lawyer, who asked, *Luke* X. 25. *What he should do to inherit eternal life? Do this, i. e.* what is required by the Law, *and thou shalt live.* |

On the other side, it seems the unalterable purpose of the Divine Justice, that no unrighteous Person, no one that is guilty of any breach of the Law, should be in Paradise; But that the wages of sin should be to every man, as it was to *Adam*, an Exclusion of him out of that Happy state of Immortality, and bring Death upon him. And this is so conformable to the Eternal and established Law of Right and Wrong, that it is spoke of too as if it could not be otherwise. St. *James* says, *Chap.* I. 15. *Sin when it is finished bringeth forth death*, as it were by a Natural and necessary production. *Sin entred into the World, and death by sin*, says St. *Paul, Rom.* V. 12. and VI. 23. *The wages of sin is Death.* Death

96   THE REASONABLENESS OF CHRISTIANITY

is the Purchase of any, of every sin. *Gal.* III. 10. *Cursed is every one who continueth not in all things which are written in the Book of the Law to do them.* And of this St. *James* gives a Reason, *Chap.* II. 10, 11. *Whosoever shall keep the whole Law, and yet offend in one point, he is guilty of all: For he*
5 *that said, Do not commit Adultery, said also, do not Kill: i. e.* He that offends
[13] in any one Point, sins | against the Authority which established the Law.

Here then we have the standing and fixed measures of Life and Death. Immortality and Bliss belong to the Righteous; Those who have lived in an exact Conformity to the Law of God, are out of the reach of Death:
10 But an Exclusion from Paradise, and loss of Immortality, is the Portion of Sinners, of all those who have any way broke that Law, and failed of a Compleat Obedience to it by the guilt of any one Transgression. And thus Mankind by the Law are put upon the issues of Life or Death; As they are *Righteous*, or *Unrighteous*; *Just* or *Unjust*; *i. e.* Exact Performers,
15 or Transgressors of the Law.

But yet *all having sinned*, Rom. III. 23. *and come short of the glory of God, i. e.* the Kingdom of God in Heaven, which is often called his Glory, *both Jews and Gentiles*, v. 9. So that *by the deeds of the Law no one could be justified*, v. 20. it follows, that no one could then have Eternal Life and
20 Bliss. |

[14]   Perhaps it will be demanded, Why did God give so hard a Law to Mankind, that to the Apostles time no one of *Adam*'s Issue had kept it? As appears by *Rom.* III. and *Gal.* III. 21, 22.

Answer. It was such a Law as the Purity of God's Nature required, and
25 must be the Law of such a Creature as Man, unless God would have made him a Rational Creature, and not required him to have lived by the Law of Reason, but would have countenanced in him Irregularity and Disobedience to that Light which he had; and that Rule, which was suitable to his Nature: Which would have been, to have authorized
30 Disorder, Confusion, and Wickedness in his Creatures. For that this Law was the *Law of Reason*, or as it is called *of Nature*, we shall see by and by: And if Rational Creatures will not live up to the Rule of their Reason, who shall excuse them? If you will admit them to forsake Reason in one point, why not in another? Where will you stop? To disobey God in any
35 part of his Commands (and 'tis he that Commands what Reason does) is
[15] direct Rebellion; which if dispensed with in | any Point, Government and Order are at an end; And there can be no bounds set to the Lawless Exorbitancy of unconfined men. *The Law therefore was*, as St. *Paul* tells us, *Rom.* VII. 12. *holy, just, and good,* and such as it ought, and could not
40 otherwise be.

AS DELIVERED IN THE SCRIPTURES 97

This then being the case, that whoever is guilty of any sin, should certainly die,* and cease to be, the benefit of Life restored by Christ at the Resurrection would have been no great Advantage, (for as much as here again Death must have seized upon all mankind, because all had sinned; For the Wages of Sin is every where Death,† *Rom.* VI. 23. as well after as before the Resurrection) if God had not found out a way to Justifie

* *Prov.* XIV. 32. *Job* VII. 21, 8. *Psa.* XXXIX. 13. That Death (*i. e.* a cessation of sense and perception) shall at last (after what length of torment appears not) be the punishment of the unrighteous is plain from *Gal.* VI. 8. where *corruption* is set in opposition to *life everlasting*, the one the fruit of righteousness and the other of unrighteousness. And by it cannot be understood ἀφθαρσίαν, immortality, under eternal torment. What is meant by φθορά may be seen and our translators tell us, *Col.* II. 22. 2 *Pet.* II. 12. And that it is put for the destruction or ceasing to be of any thing may be seen by the signification of φθάρτος, ἄφθαρτος, and ἀφθαρσία, *Rom.* I. 23. 1 *Cor.* IX. 25. XV. 50–54. 1 *Tim.* I. 17. ἄφθαρτος is translated immortal and 2 *Tim.* I. 10. ἀφθαρσία immortality. Another place that shews Death so constantly used for the state the unrighteous are at last destined to is a final cessation of life, *i. e.* of all sense perception and activity is 2 *Thess.* I. 9. There it is said the punishment of those that know not God and obey not the gospel shall be *everlasting destruction.* Further our Saviour, *Luke* XX. 35, 36. declares the particular privilege of the righteous to be that they *cannot die any more*; that this is spoken distinguishingly of the righteous is apparent in the text. For it is spoken to those that are *thought worthy* and therefore it must mean the first resurrection or resurrection to life. For to the resurrection in general there is no dignation required; and it is spoken of the *Children of God*, which all that rise from the dead are not.

That *everlasting punishment* does not necessarily signifie a life in eternal torments the late Excellent Archibishop Tillotson has clearly evinced in his sermon on *Mat.* XXV. 46.

St. John declareth it also to be the privilege of the saints to be eternal in these words, 1 *Epis.* II. 17. *The world passeth away and the lust thereof but he that doeth the will of God abideth forever.* 'Tis plain here that the difference he puts between *those that do the will of God* and others is that they *abide* or remain *forever.* Μένειν εἰς τὸν αἰῶνα signifies to have an eternal duration without the least intimation of happiness or misery annext, an expression which St. *John* would not certainly have appropriated as a privilege to *those who do the will of God*, if it had equally belonged to others; there were other ways enough to have expressed it, if the difference had not lain in this. The same words are used by St. *Peter* to express the eternal durations of the gospel. 1 *Pet.* I. 25.

† Without pardon of sin we cannot take one step towards eternal life. For Death, the fruit and punishment of sin, will still remain unless sin be pardoned: and then what hope can we have of eternal life? which is therefore perhaps called by the name of Righteousness, *Gal.* V. 5. because it includes our perfect justification, and absolution from the guilt of sin without which we could not attain it. Patrick $\frac{147}{657}$.

98 THE REASONABLENESS OF CHRISTIANITY

some, *i. e.* so many, as obeyed another Law, which God gave, which in the New Testament is called *the Law of Faith*, Rom. III. 27. and is opposed to *the Law of Works*. And therefore the Punishment of those
4 who would not follow him was to lose their Souls,* *i. e.* their Lives, *Mark*
[16] VIII. 35–38. as is plain, considering the occasion it was spoke on. |
III The better to understand *the Law of Faith*, it will be convenient in the first place to consider *the Law of Works*. *The Law of Works* then, in short, is that Law, which requires perfect Obedience, without any remission or abatement; So that by that Law a man cannot be Just, or justified
10 without an exact performance of every tittle. Such a perfect Obedience in the New Testament is termed δικαιοσύνη, which we translate *Righteousness*.

The Language of this Law is, Do this and live, Transgress and die. *Lev.* XVIII. 5. *Ye shall keep my statutes and my judgments, which if a man do he*
15 *shall live in them.* Ezek. XX. 11. *I gave them my statutes, and shewed them my judgements, which if a man do he shall even live in them. Moses*, says St. *Paul*, Rom. X. 5. *describeth the righteousness which is of the Law, that the man which doth those things shall live in them.* Gal. III. 12. *The Law is not of Faith, but that man that doth them shall live in them.* On the other side,
20 Transgress and die; no dispensation, no atonement. *V.* 10. *Cursed is every*
[17] *one that continueth not in all | things which are written in the book of the law to do them.*

Where this Law of Works was to be found, the New Testament tells us, (*viz.*) in the Law delivered by *Moses. John* I. 17. *The Law was given by*
25 *Moses, but Faith and Truth came by Jesus Christ.* Cap. VII. 19. *Did not Moses give you the Law*, says our Saviour, *and yet none of you keep the Law.* And this is the Law which he speaks of, where he asks the Lawyer, *Luke* X. 26. *What is written in the Law? how readest thou?* v. 28. *This do and thou shalt live.* This is that which St. *Paul* so often stiles the *Law*, without any
30 other distinction, *Rom.* II. 13. *Not the hearers of the Law are just before God,*

---

* Ψυχὴ in the New Testament ordinarily signifies life, *Luke* XII. 20. *Mat.* X. 39. XVI. 25, 26: Hammond 1 *Thess.* V. 23.

Animas esse mortales, Justin Martyr, Dialogus cum Tryphone, $\frac{173}{490}$, $\frac{171}{490}$· Οὐδὲ μὴν ἀθάνατον χρὴ λέγειν αὐτήν [ψυχήν]. καταλείπει ἡ ψυχὴ τὸ σῶμα, καὶ ὁ ἄνθρωπος
35 οὐκ ἔστιν, οὕτως καὶ ὅταν δέῃ τὴν ψυχὴν μηκέτι εἶναι, ἀπέστη ἀπ᾽ αὐτῆς τὸ ζωτικὸν πνεῦμα καὶ οὐκ ἔστιν ἡ ψυχὴ ἔτι, ἀλλὰ καὶ αὐτὴ ὅθεν ἐλήφθη ἐκεῖσε χωρεῖ πάλιν.

Αἱ αὐταὶ ψυχαὶ ἐν πᾶσι ζώοις εἰσί, itidem p. 171.

Ψυχαὶ οὐκ ἀθάνατοι, τῶν εὐσεβῶν ἄξιαι τοῦ θεοῦ φανεῖσαι οὐκ ἀποθνήσκουσι ἔτι, αἱ δὲ ἄδικαι καὶ πονηραὶ κολάζονται, ἔστ᾽ ἂν αὐτὰς καὶ εἶναι καὶ κολάζεσθαι ὁ θεὸς θέλῃ,
40 itidem p. 172.

AS DELIVERED IN THE SCRIPTURES   99

but the doers of the Law are justified. 'Tis needless to quote any more places, his Epistles are all full of it, especially this to the *Romans*.

But the Law given by *Moses* being not given to all Mankind, How are all men sinners; since without a Law there is no Transgression? To this the Apostle, *v.* 14. Answers, *For when the Gentiles which have not the Law,* *do* (*i. e.* find it reasonable to do) *by nature the | things contained in the Law; these having not the Law, are a Law unto themselves: Which shew the work of the Law written in their hearts, their Consciences also bearing witness, and amongst one another their thoughts accusing or excusing.* By which, and other places in the following Chapter, 'tis plain, that under the Law of Works is comprehended also the Law of Nature, knowable by Reason, as well as the Law given by *Moses. For*, says St. *Paul*, Rom. III. 9, 23. *we have proved both Jews and Gentiles, that they are all under sin: For all have sinned, and come short of the glory of God*: Which they could not do without a Law.

Nay, whatever God requires any where to be done without making any allowance for Faith, that is a part of the Law of Works. So the forbidding *Adam* to eat of the Tree of Knowledge was part of the Law of Works. Only we must take notice here, That some of God's Positive Commands being for peculiar Ends, and suited to particular Cir- cumstances of Times, Places, and Persons, have a limited and only temporary Obligation by vertue of God's | positive Injunction; such as was that part of *Moses*'s Law which concerned the outward Worship, or Political Constitution of the Jews, and is called the Ceremonial and Judaical Law, in contradistinction to the Moral part of it; Which being conformable to the Eternal Law of Right, is of Eternal Obligation, and therefore remains in force still under the Gospel; nor is abrogated by the *Law of Faith*, as St. *Paul* found some ready to infer, *Rom.* III. 31. *Do we then make void the Law through Faith? God forbid; yea, we establish the Law.*

Nor can it be otherwise: For were there no *Law of Works*, there could be no *Law of Faith*. For there could be no need of Faith, which should be counted to men for Righteousness, if there were no Law to be the Rule and Measure of Righteousness, which men failed in their Obedience to. Where there is no Law, there is no Sin; all are Righteous equally with or without Faith.

The Rule therefore of Right is the same that ever it was, the Obligation to observe it is also the same: The difference between the *Law of Works* and | the *Law of Faith* is only this; that the *Law of Works* makes no allowance for failing on any occasion. Those that obey are Righteous, those that in any part disobey are unrighteous, and must not expect Life

100 THE REASONABLENESS OF CHRISTIANITY

the Reward of Righteousness. But by the *Law of Faith*, Faith is allowed to
supply the defect of full Obedience; and so the Believers are admitted to
Life and Immortality as if they were Righteous. Only here we must take
notice, that when St. *Paul* says, that the Gospel establishes the Law, he
5 means the Moral part of the Law of *Moses*: For that he could not mean
the Ceremonial or Political part of it, is evident by what I quoted out of
him just now, where he says, *The Gentiles that do by nature the things*
contained in the Law, their Consciences bearing witness. For the Gentiles
neither did nor thought of the Judaical or Ceremonial Institutions of
10 *Moses*, 'twas only the Moral part their Consciences were concerned in. As
for the rest, St. *Paul* tells the *Galatians*, Cap. IV. they are not under that
part of the Law, which *v.* 3. he calls *Elements of the World*; and *v.* 9. *weak*
[21] *and beggarly* | *elements*. And our Saviour himself in his Gospel-Sermon on
the Mount, tells them, *Mat.* V. 17. That whatever they might think, he
15 was not come *to dissolve the Law*, but to make it more full and strict: For
that that is meant by πληρῶσαι is evident from the following part of that
Chapter, where he gives the Precepts in a stricter sense than they were
received in before. But they are all Precepts of the Moral Law which he
reinforces. What should become of the Ritual Law he tells the Woman of
20 *Samaria* in these words, *John* IV. 21, 23. *The hour cometh when you shall*
neither in this Mountain, nor yet at Jerusalem *worship the Father. But the*
true Worshippers shall worship the Father in spirit and in truth, for the Father
seeketh such to worship him.

Thus then as to the Law in short. The Civil and Ritual part of the Law
25 delivered by *Moses* obliges not Christians, though to the Jews it were a
part of the Law of Works; it being a part of the Law of Nature, that man
ought to obey every Positive Law of God, whenever he shall please to
[22] make any such addition to the Law of his Nature. | But the Moral part of
Moses's Law, or the Moral Law, (which is every where the same, the
30 Eternal Rule of Right) obliges Christians and all men every where, and is
to all men the standing Law of Works. But Christian Believers have the
Privilege to be under the *Law of Faith* too; which is that Law whereby
God Justifies a man for Believing, though by his Works he be not Just or
Righteous, *i. e.* though he came short of Perfect Obedience to the Law
35 of Works. God alone does, or can, Justifie or make Just those who by
their Works are not so: Which he doth by counting their Faith for
Righteousness, *i. e.* for a compleat performance of the Law. *Rom.* IV. 3.
Abraham believed God, and it was counted to him for righteousness. v. 5. *To*
him that believeth on him that justifieth the ungodly, his faith is counted for
40 *righteousness. v.* 6. *Even as* David *also describeth the blessedness of the man*

AS DELIVERED IN THE SCRIPTURES 101

unto whom God imputeth righteousness without works; *i. e.* without a full measure of Works, which is exact Obedience. v. 7. Saying, *Blessed are they whose iniquities are forgiven, and whose sins are covered.* v. 8. *Bles|sed is the* [23] *man to whom the Lord will not impute sin.*

This Faith for which God justified *Abraham*, what was it? It was the believing God when he engaged his Promise in the Covenant he made with him. This will be plain to any one who considers these places together, *Gen.* XV. 6. *He believed in the Lord*, or *believed the Lord*. For that the *Hebrew* Phrase *believing in*, signifies no more but *believing*, is plain from St. *Paul's* citation of this place, *Rom.* IV. 3. where he repeats it thus: *Abraham believed God*, which he thus explains, *v.* 18-22. *who against hope, believed in hope, that he might become the Father of many Nations: According to that which was spoken, so shall thy seed be. And being not weak in faith, he considered not his own body now dead, when he was about an hundred years old, nor yet the deadness of* Sarah's *womb. He staggered not at the promise of God through unbelief; but was strong in faith, giving glory to God. And being fully perswaded, that what he had promised, he was also able to perform. And therefore it was imputed to him for righteousness.* | By which it is clear, that the Faith which God counted to [24] *Abraham* for Righteousness, was nothing but a firm belief of what God declared to him, and a steadfast relying on him for the accomplishment of what he had promised.

Now this, says St. *Paul*, v. 23, 24. *was not writ for his* [Abraham's] *sake alone, But for us also*; teaching us, that as *Abraham* was justified for his Faith, so also ours shall be accounted to us for Righteousness, if we believe God as *Abraham* believed him. Whereby 'tis plain is meant the firmness of our Faith without *staggering*, and not the believing the same Propositions that *Abraham* believed; *viz.* that though he and *Sarah* were old, and past the time and hopes of Children, yet he should have a Son by her, and by him become the Father of a great People, which should possess the Land of *Canaan*. This was what *Abraham* believed, and was counted to him for Righteousness. But no body I think will say, that any ones believing this now, shall be imputed to him for Righteousness. The Law of Faith then, in short, is for | every one to believe what God [25] requires him to believe, as a condition of the Covenant he makes with him; and not to doubt of the performance of his Promises. This the Apostle intimates in the close here, *v.* 24. *But for us also, to whom it shall be imputed, if we believe on him that raised up Jesus our Lord from the dead.* We must therefore examine and see what God requires us to believe now under the Revelation of the Gospel: For the belief of one invisible,

102   THE REASONABLENESS OF CHRISTIANITY

Eternal, Omnipotent God, maker of Heaven and Earth, *etc.* was required before, as well as now.

IV What we are now required to believe to obtain Eternal Life, is plainly set down in the Gospel. St. *John* tells us, *John* III. 36. *He that believeth on the*
5 *Son, hath eternal life; and he that believeth not the Son, shall not see life.* What this *believing on him* is, we are also told in the next Chapter. *The woman saith unto him, I know that the Messiah cometh: When he is come, he will tell us all things. Jesus said unto her, I that spake unto thee am he. The woman*
[26] *then went into the City, and saith to the men, come see a man that hath | told*
10 *me all things that ever I did. Is not this the Messiah? And many of the* Samaritans *believed on him: for the saying of the woman, who testified, he told me all that ever I did. So when the* Samaritans *were come unto him, many more believed because of his words, and said to the woman; We believe not any longer because of thy saying, for we have heard our selves, and we know that this*
15 *Man is truly the Saviour of the World, the Messiah,* John IV. 25, 26, 29, 39, 40, 41, 42.

By which place it is plain, that *believing on the Son* is the *believing that Jesus was the Messiah;* giving Credit to the Miracles he did, and the Profession he made of himself. For those who were said to BELIEVE
20 ON HIM for the saying of the Woman, *v.* 39. tell the Woman, that they now believed not any longer because of her saying; but that having heard him themselves, they knew, *i. e.* BELIEVED past doubt THAT HE WAS THE MESSIAH.

This was the great Proposition that was then controverted concerning
[27] Jesus of *Nazareth,* whether he was the | *Messiah* or no; And the assent to
26 that, was that which distinguished Believers from Unbelievers. When many of his Disciples had forsaken him, upon his declaring that he was the Bread of Life which came down from Heaven, *He said to the Apostles, will ye also go away? Then* Simon Peter *answered him; Lord, to whom shall we*
30 *go? Thou hast the words of eternal life. And we believe, and are sure thou art the Messiah, the Son of the living God,* John VI. 69. This was the Faith which distinguished them from Apostates and Unbelievers, and was sufficient to continue them in the rank of Apostles: And it was upon the same Proposition, *That Jesus was the Messiah, the Son of the living God,*
35 owned by St. *Peter,* that our Saviour said, he would build his Church. *Mat.* XVI. 16–18.

To convince men of this he did his Miracles: And their assent to, or not assenting to this, made them to be, or not to be of his Church; Believers, or not Believers. *The Jews came round about him, and said unto him, how*
40 *long dost thou make us doubt? If thou be the Messiah tell us plainly. Jesus*

AS DELIVERED IN THE SCRIPTURES   103

answered | *them; I told you, and ye believed not: The works that I do in my* [28]
*Father's name they bear witness of me. But ye believe not, because ye are not of
my sheep,* John X. 24–26. Conformable hereunto St. *John* tells us, *That
many deceivers are entred into the world, who confess not* that Jesus, the
Messiah, is come in the flesh, which passage might perhaps be better   5
rendered thus, *That Jesus is the Messiah who is come in the flesh.* v: *Mat.*
X. 32. And so I think 1 *John* IV. 2, 3. ought to be translated. *This is a
deceiver, and an Antichrist, whosoever abideth not in the Doctrine of the
Messiah has not God. He that abideth in the Doctrine of the Messiah, i. e.* that
Jesus is he, *hath both the Father and the Son,* 2 John 7, 9, 10. That this is   10
the meaning of the place, is plain from what he says in his foregoing
Epistle, *Whosoever believeth that Jesus is the Messiah, is born of God,* 1 John
V. 1. And therefore drawing to a close of his Gospel, and shewing the
end for which he writ it, he has these words: *Many other signs truly did
Jesus in the presence of his Disciples, which are not written in this book; but these*   15
*are written, that ye may believe that Jesus is the Messiah, the Son of God; and
that believing ye might have life through his name,* John XX. 30, 31.
Whereby it is plain, that the Gospel | was writ to induce men into a belief [29]
of this Proposition, *that Jesus of Nazareth was the Messiah;* Which if they
believed, they should *have life.*   20

Accordingly the great Question amongst the Jews was, whether he were
the *Messiah* or no: And the great Point insisted on and promulgated in the
Gospel was, that he was the *Messiah.* The first glad tidings of his Birth,
brought to the Shepherds by an Angel, was in these words: *Fear not, for
behold I bring you good tidings of great joy, which shall be to all people; For to you*   25
is born this day in the City of David *a Saviour, who is the Messiah the Lord,*
Luke II. 11. Our Saviour Discoursing with *Martha* about the means of
attaining Eternal Life, saith to her, *John* XI. 27. *Whosoever believeth in me
shall never die. Believest thou this? She said unto him, Yea, Lord, I believe that
thou art the Messiah, the Son of God, which should come into the world.* This   30
Answer of hers sheweth what it is to believe in Jesus Christ, so as to have
Eternal Life, *viz.* to believe that he is the *Messiah* the Son of God, whose
coming was foretold by the Prophets. | And thus *Andrew* and *Philip* express [30]
it: Andrew *says to his Brother* Simon, *we have found the Messiah, which is,
being interpreted, the Christ.* Philip *saith to* Nathanael, *we have found him of*   35
whom Moses *in the Law, and the Prophets did write, Jesus of* Nazareth, *the Son
of* Joseph, *John* I. 41, 45. According to what the Evangelist says in this
place, I have, for the clearer understanding of the Scripture, all along put
Messiah for *Christ. Christ* being but the Greek name for the Hebrew
Messiah, and both signifying *The Anointed.*   40

104   THE REASONABLENESS OF CHRISTIANITY

And that he was the *Messiah*, was the great Truth he took pains to convince his Disciples and Apostles of; appearing to them after his Resurrection: As may be seen, *Luke* XXIV. which we shall more particularly consider in another place. There we read what Gospel our
5 Saviour Preach'd to his Disciples and Apostles; And That, as soon as he was risen from the Dead, twice the very day of his Resurrection.

V And if we may gather what was to be believed by all Nations, from what
[31] was preached unto them; we may | observe, that the Preaching of the Apostles every where in the *Acts* tended to this one Point, to prove that
10 Jesus was the *Messiah*. Those infallible observers of all Christ's commands can not be supposed negligent performers of this solemn one which he left with them at parting or to have executed this last commission by halves. And therefore we may certainly know what they were to teach all nations by what we find in their history they actually did teach all nations
15 where they preached. Indeed, now after his Death, his Resurrection was also commonly required to be believed as a necessary Article, and sometimes solely insisted on: It being a mark and undoubted Evidence of his being the *Messiah*, and necessary now to be believed by those who would receive him as the *Messiah*. For since the *Messiah* was to be a
20 Saviour and a King, and to give Life and a Kingdom to those who received him, as we shall see by and by, there could have been no Pretence to have given him out for the *Messiah*, and to require men to believe him to be so, who thought him under the Power of Death, and Corruption of the Grave. And therefore those who believed him to be
25 the *Messiah*, must believe that he was risen from the Dead: And those who believed him to be risen from the Dead, could not doubt of his being the *Messiah*. But of this more in another place.

Let us see therefore how the Apostles preached Christ, and what they |
[32] proposed to their Hearers to believe. St. *Peter* at *Jerusalem, Acts* II. by his
30 first Sermon, converted Three Thousand Souls. What *was his word,* which, as we are told, *v.* 41. *they gladly received, and thereupon were baptized?* That may be seen from *v.* 22 to *v.* 36. In short this; Which is the Conclusion drawn from all that he had said, and which he presses on them as the thing they were to believe, *viz. Therefore let all the House of*
35 Israel *know assuredly, that God hath made that same Jesus, whom ye have crucified, Lord and Messiah,* v. 36.

To the same purpose was his Discourse to the Jews in the Temple, *Acts* III. the design whereof you have, *v.* 18. *But those things that God before had shewed by the mouth of all his Prophets, that the Messiah should suffer, he*
40 *hath so fulfilled.*

AS DELIVERED IN THE SCRIPTURES 105

In the next Chapter, *Acts* IV. *Peter* and *John* being examined about the Miracle on the lame Man, profess it to have been done in the Name of Jesus of *Nazareth*, who was the *Messiah*, in whom alone there was Salvation, *v.* 10–12. The same thing | they confirm to them again, *Acts* [33] V. 29–32. *And daily in the Temple, and in every House they ceased not to* 5 *teach and preach Jesus the Messiah*, v. 42.

What was *Stephen*'s Speech to the Council, *Acts* VII. but a Reprehension to them, that they were the Betrayers and Murderers of the *Just One*? Which is the Title by which he plainly designs the *Messiah*, whose coming was foreshewn by the Prophets, *v.* 51, 52. And that the 10 *Messiah* was to be without sin (which is the import of the word Just) was the Opinion of the Jews, appears from *John* IX. *v.* 22. compared with 24.

Acts VIII. *Philip* carries the Gospel to *Samaria. Then* Philip *went down to* Samaria, *and preached to them.* What was it he preached? You have an account of it in this one word, *The Messiah*, v. 5. This being that alone 15 which was required of them, to believe that *Jesus* was the *Messiah*; which, when they believed, they were baptized. *And when they believed* Philip's *Preaching the Gospel of the Kingdom of God, and the name of Jesus the Messiah, they were baptized both Men and Women*, v. 12. |

Philip being sent from thence, by a special call of the Spirit, to make an [34] Eminent Convert, out of *Isaiah* preaches to him Jesus, *v.* 35. And what it 21 was he preached concerning *Jesus*, we may know by the Profession of Faith the Eunuch made, upon which he was admitted to Baptism, *v.* 37. *I believe that Jesus Christ is the Son of God*: which is as much as to say, I believe that he, whom you call Jesus Christ, is really and truly the *Messiah* 25 that was promised. For that believing him to be the *Son of God*, and to be the *Messiah*, was the same thing, may appear by comparing *John* I. 45. with *v.* 49. where *Nathanael* owns Jesus to be the *Messiah* in these terms: *Thou art the Son of God; Thou art the King of Israel.* So the Jews, *Luke* XXII. 70. asking Christ, whether he were the *Son of God*; plainly demand 30 of him, whether he were the *Messiah*? Which is evident by comparing that with the three preceding Verses. They ask him, *v.* 67. whether he were the *Messiah*? He answers, *If I tell you, you will not believe*; but withal tells them, that from thenceforth he should be in Pos|session of the [35] Kingdom of the *Messiah*, expressed in these words, *v.* 69. *Hereafter shall* 35 *the Son of Man sit on the right hand of the power of God*: Which made them all cry out, *Art thou then the Son of God? i. e.* Dost thou then own thy self to be the *Messiah*? To which he replies; *Ye say that I am.* That the *Son of God* was the known Title of the *Messiah* at that time amongst the Jews, we may see also from what the Jews say to *Pilate*, John XIX. 7. *We have a* 40

106   THE REASONABLENESS OF CHRISTIANITY

Law, and by our Law he ought to die, because he made himself THE SON OF GOD; *i. e.* by making himself the *Messiah*, the Prophet which was to come, but falsely; and therefore he deserves to die by the Law, *Deut.* XVIII. 20. That this was the common signification of *the Son of God*, is
5 farther evident from what the Chief Priests, mocking him, said, when he was on the Cross, *Mat.* XXVII. 42. *He saved others, himself he cannot save: If he be the King of* Israel, *let him now come down from the Cross, and we will believe him. He trusted in God, let him deliver him now, if he will have him;*
[36] *for he said, I am the SON OF GOD;* | *i. e.* he said, he was the *Messiah*: But
10 'tis plainly false; for if he were, God would deliver him: For the *Messiah* is to be King of *Israel*, the Saviour of others; but this Man cannot save himself. The Chief Priests mention here the two Titles then in use whereby the Jews commonly designed the *Messiah, viz. Son of God*, and *King of Israel*. That of *Son of God*, was so familiar a compellation of the
15 *Messiah*, who was then so much expected and talked of, that the *Romans* it seems, who lived amongst them, had learned it; as appears from *v.* 54. *Now when the Centurion, and they that were with him, watching Jesus, saw the Earthquake, and those things that were done, they feared greatly, saying, Truly this was the SON OF GOD*; this was that extraordinary Person that was
20 looked for.

    Acts IX. St. *Paul* exercising the Commission to Preach the Gospel, which he had received in a Miraculous way, *v.* 20. *Straitway preached Christ in the Synagogues, that he is the Son of God; i. e.* that Jesus was the *Messiah*: For Christ in this place is evidently a Proper Name. And that
[37] this was it which | *Paul* preached, appears from *v.* 22. *Saul increased the*
26 *more in strength, and confounded the Jews who dwelt in* Damascus, *proving that this is the very Christ, i. e.* the *Messiah*.

    Peter, when he came to *Cornelius* at *Cesarea*; who by a Vision was ordered to send for him, as *Peter* on the other side was by a Vision
30 commanded to go to him; What does he teach him? His whole Discourse, *Acts* X. tends to shew what he says God commanded the Apostles *to Preach unto the People, and to testifie; That it is he* [Jesus] *which was ordained of God to be the Judge of the quick and the dead.* And that it was *to him that all the Prophets give witness, that through his name whosoever*
35 *believeth in him shall have remission of sins, v.* 42, 43. This is *the Word which God sent to the Children of* Israel; *that WORD which was published throughout all* Judea, *and began from* Galilee, *after the Baptism which* John *preached, v.* 36, 37. And these are the *words* which had been promised to
39 *Cornelius*, Acts XI. 14. *Whereby he and all his house should be saved*: Which
[38] *words* amount only to thus | much, That *Jesus was the Messiah*, the Saviour

AS DELIVERED IN THE SCRIPTURES 107

that was promised. Upon their receiving of this (for this was all was taught them) the Holy Ghost fell on them, and they were baptized. 'Tis observable here, that the Holy Ghost fell on them before they were baptized; which in other places Converts received not till after Baptism. The reason whereof seems to be this; That God by bestowing on them the Holy Ghost, did thus declare from Heaven, that the Gentiles, upon believing *Jesus* to be the *Messiah*, ought to be admitted into the Church by Baptism as well as the Jews. Whoever reads St. *Peter's* Defence, *Acts* XI. when he was accused by those of the Circumcision, that he had not kept that distance which he ought with the uncircumcised, will be of this Opinion; and see by what he says, *v.* 15, 16, 17. That this was the ground, and an irresistible Authority to him for doing so strange a thing, as it appeared to the Jews (who alone yet were Members of the Christian Church) to admit Gentiles into their Communion, upon their believing. And therefore | St. *Peter*, in the foregoing Chapter, *Acts* X. before he would Baptize them, proposes this Question *to those of the Circumcision, which came with him, and were astonished, because that on the Gentiles also was poured out the gift of the Holy Ghost: Can any one forbid water, that these should not be baptized, who have received the Holy Ghost as well as we?* v. 47. And when some of the Sect of the *Pharisees*, who believed, thought *it needful that the converted* Gentiles *should be circumcised, and keep the Law of Moses*, Acts XV. Peter *rose up and said unto them, Men and Brethren, you know that a good while ago God made choice amongst us, that the Gentiles*, viz. *Cornelius*, and those here converted with him, *by my mouth should hear the Gospel, and believe. And God, who knoweth the hearts, bear them witness, giving them the Holy Ghost, even as he did unto us, and put no difference between us and them, purifying their hearts by Faith*, v. 7–9. So that both Jews and Gentiles, who believed Jesus to be the *Messiah*, received thereupon the Seal of Baptism; whereby they were owned to be his, and distinguished | from Unbelievers. From what is above-said, we may observe, That this Preaching Jesus to be the *Messiah*, is called *the Word*, and *the Word of God*; and believing it, *receiving the Word of God. Vid.* Acts X. 36, 37. and XI. 1, 19, 20. And *the Word of the Gospel*, Acts XV. 7. And so likewise in the History of the Gospel, what *Mark*, Chap. IV. 14, 15. calls simply the *Word*, St. *Luke* calls *the Word of God*, *Luke* VIII. 11. And St. *Matthew, Chap.* XIII. 19. *the Word of the Kingdom*; which were, it seems, in the Gospel-writers Synonymous terms, and are so to be understood by us.

But to go on: *Acts* XIII. *Paul* Preaches in the Synagogue at *Antioch*, where he makes it his business to convince the Jews, that *God, according to*

108   THE REASONABLENESS OF CHRISTIANITY

his promise, had of the seed of David *raised to* Israel *a Saviour, Jesus,* v. 23.
That he was *He* of whom the Prophets writ, *v.* 25–29. *i. e.* the *Messiah*:
And that as a demonstration of his being so, God had raised him from the
Dead, *v.* 30. From whence he argues thus, *v.* 32, 33. *We Evangelize to*

[41]   *you,* or bring you this Gospel, *how that the Promise which was made | to our*

6 *Fathers, God hath fulfilled the same unto us, in that he hath raised up Jesus*
again; as it is also written in the second Psalm, Thou art my Son, this day have
I begotten thee. And having gone on to prove him to be the *Messiah*, by his
Resurrection from the Dead, he makes this Conclusion; *v.* 38, 39. *Be it*

10 *known unto you therefore, men and brethren, that through this man is*
preached unto you forgiveness of sins; and by him all who believe are justified
from all things, from which they could not be justified by the Law of Moses.
This is in this Chapter called *the Word of God* over and over again:
Compare *v.* 42. with 44, 46, 48, 49. And *Chap.* XII. *v.* 24.

15   *Acts* XVII. 2–4. At *Thessalonica, Paul, as his manner was, went into the*
Synagogue, and three Sabbath-days reasoned with the Jews out of the
Scriptures; opening and alledging, that the Messiah *must needs have suffered,*
and risen again from the dead: And that this Jesus, whom I preach unto you, is
the Messiah. *And some of them believed, and consorted with* Paul *and* Silas:

[42] *But the Jews which believed not, set | the City in an uproar.* Can there be any

21 thing plainer, than that the assenting to this Proposition, that Jesus was
the *Messiah*, was that which distinguished the Believers from the
Unbelievers? For this was that alone which, three Sabbaths, *Paul*
endeavoured to convince them of, as the Text tells us in direct words.

25   From thence he went to *Berea,* and preached the same thing: And the
Bereans are commended, *v.* 11. for searching the Scriptures, whether
those things, *i. e.* which he had said, *v.* 2, 3. concerning Jesus his being
the *Messiah*, were true or no.

    The same Doctrine we find him Preaching at *Corinth, Acts* XVIII. 4–6.

30 *And he reasoned in the Synogogue every Sabbath, and perswaded the Jews and*
the Greeks. And when Silas *and* Timotheus *were coming from* Macedonia,
Paul *was pressed in spirit, and testified to the Jews, that Jesus was the* Messiah.
And when they opposed themselves, and blasphemed, he shook his raiment, and
said unto them, your blood be upon your own heads, I am clean; from

35 *henceforth I will go unto the Greeks. |*

[43]   Upon the like occasion he tells the Jews at *Antioch, Acts* XIII. 46. *It*
was necessary that the Word of God should first have been spoken to you: But
seeing you put it off from you, we turn to the Gentiles. 'Tis plain here, St.
Paul's charging their Blood on their own heads, is for opposing this

40 single Truth, that *Jesus* was the *Messiah*; that Salvation or Perdition

AS DELIVERED IN THE SCRIPTURES 109

depends upon believing or rejecting this one Proposition. I mean, this is all is required to be believed by those who acknowledge but one Eternal and Invisible God, the maker of Heaven and Earth, as the Jews did. For that there is something more required to Salvation, besides believing, we shall see hereafter. In the mean time, it is fit here on this occasion to take notice, that though the Apostles in their Preaching to the Jews, and the *Devout*, (as we translate the word Σεβόμενοι, who were Proselytes of the Gate, and the worshippers of one Eternal and Invisible God,) said nothing of the believing in this one true God, the maker of Heaven and Earth; because it was needless to press this to those who believed and professed it | already (for to such, 'tis plain, [44] were most of their Discourses hitherto). Yet when they had to do with Idolatrous Heathens, who were not yet come to the knowledge of the one only true God; they began with that, as necessary to be believed; it being the Foundation on which the other was built, and without which it could signifie nothing.

Thus *Paul* speaking to the Idolatrous *Lystrians*, who would have sacrificed to him and *Barnabas*, says, *Acts* XIV. 15. *We Preach unto you, that you should turn from these vanities unto the living God, who made Heaven, and Earth, and the Sea, and all things that are therein. Who in times past suffered all Nations to walk in their own ways. Nevertheless he left not himself without witness in that he did good, and gave us rain from Heaven, and fruitful seasons, filling our hearts with food and gladness.*

Thus also he proceeded with the Idolatrous *Athenians, Acts* XVII. Telling them, upon occasion of the Altar dedicated to the unknown God, *Whom ye ignorantly worship, him declare I unto | you; God who made the* [45] *World, and all things therein: Seeing that he is Lord of Heaven and Earth, dwelleth not in Temples made with hands. — Forasmuch then as we are the Offspring of God, we ought not to think that the Godhead is like unto Gold, or Silver, or Stone, graven by art, and man's device. And the times of this ignorance God winked at; But now commandeth all men every where to repent: Because he hath appointed a day in which he will judge the World in Righteousness, by that man whom he hath ordained: Whereof he hath given assurance unto all men, in that he hath raised him from the dead.* So that we see, where any thing more was necessary to be proposed to be believed, as there was to the Heathen Idolaters, there the Apostles were careful not to omit it.

Acts XVIII. 4. *Paul at Corinth reasoned in the Synagogue every Sabbathday, and testified to the Jews, that Jesus was the* Messiah. *Ver.* 11. *And he continued there a year and six months, teaching the Word of God amongst*

110   THE REASONABLENESS OF CHRISTIANITY

[46] *them*; *i. e.* The good News, that Jesus was | the *Messiah*; as we have already shewn is meant by the *Word of God*.

Apollos, another Preacher of the Gospel, when he was instructed in the way of God more perfectly, what did he teach but this same Doctrine? As 5 we may see in this account of him, *Acts* XVIII. 27. That *when he was come into* Achaia, *he helped the Brethren much who had believed through grace. For he mightily convinced the Jews, and that publickly, shewing by the Scriptures that Jesus was the* Messiah.

St. *Paul*, in the Account he gives of himself before *Festus* and *Agrippa*, 10 professes this alone to be the Doctrine he taught after his Conversion: For, says he, *Acts* XXVI. 22. *Having obtained help of God, I continue unto this day, witnessing both to small and great, saying none other things than those which the Prophets and* Moses *did say should come: That the* Messias *should suffer, and that he should be the first that should rise from the dead, and* 15 *should shew light unto the People, and to the Gentiles.* Which was no more than to prove that Jesus was the *Messiah*. This is that, which, as we have [47] above observed, is called | the *Word of God*; *Acts* XI. 1. compared with the foregoing Chapter, from *v.* 34. to the end. And XIII. 42. compared with 44, 46, 48, 49. And XVII. 13. compared with *v.* 11, 3. It is also called *the* 20 *Word of the Gospel, Acts* XV. 7. And this is that *Word of God*, and that *Gospel*, which, whereever their Discourses are set down, we find the Apostles preached; and was that Faith, which made both Jews and Gentiles Believers and Members of the Church of Christ; purifying their hearts, *Acts* XV. 9. And carrying with it Remission of sins, *Acts* X. 43. So 25 that all that was to be believed for Justification, was no more but this single Proposition; That *Jesus of* Nazareth *was the Christ, or the Messiah*. All, I say, that was to be believed for Justification: For that it was not all that was required to be done for Justification, we shall see hereafter.

VI Though we have seen above from what our Saviour has pronounced 30 himself, *John* III. 36. *That he that believeth on the Son, hath everlasting life;* [48] *and he that believeth not the Son, shall not see life, but the wrath of God abi\deth on him*; And are taught from *John* IV. 39. compared with *v.* 42. *That believing on him, is believing that he is the* Messiah, *the Saviour of the World*; And the Confession made by St. *Peter, Mat.* XVI. 16. That he is *the* 35 Messiah, *the Son of the living God*, being the Rock, on which our Saviour has promised to build his Church; Though this, I say, and what else we have already taken notice of, be enough to convince us what it is we are in the Gospel required to believe to Eternal Life, without adding what we have observed from the Preaching of the Apostles; Yet it may not be amiss, for 40 the farther clearing this matter, to observe what the Evangelists deliver

AS DELIVERED IN THE SCRIPTURES

concerning the same thing, though in different words; Which therefore perhaps are not so generally taken notice of to this purpose.

We have above observed, from the words of *Andrew* and *Philip* compared, That the *Messiah*, and *him of whom* Moses *in the Law and the Prophets did write*, signifie the same thing. We shall now consider that place, *John* I. a little further. *Ver.* 41. *Andrew* says to | *Simon, We have found the Messiah. Philip*, on the same occasion, *v.* 45. *says to* Nathanael, *We have found him, of whom* Moses *in the Law and the Prophets did write, Jesus of* Nazareth, *the Son of* Joseph. *Nathanael*, who disbelieved this, when upon Christ's speaking to him, he was convinced of it, declares his assent to it in these words; *Rabbi, thou art the Son of God, thou art the King of Israel.* From which it is evident, that to believe him to be *Him of whom* Moses *and the Prophets did write*, or to be the *Son of God*, or to be the *King of Israel*, was in effect the same as to believe him to be the *Messiah*: And an assent to that, was what our Saviour received for believing. For upon *Nathanael*'s making a Confession in these words, *Thou art the Son of God, thou art the King of Israel*; *Jesus answered and said to him, Because I said to thee, I saw thee under the Fig-tree, dost thou BELIEVE? Thou shalt see greater things than these*, v. 50. I desire any one to read the latter part of the first of *John*, from *v.* 25. with attention, and tell me, whether it be not plain, that this Phrase, *The Son of | God*, is an Expression used for the *Messiah*. To which let him add *Martha*'s declaration of her Faith, *John* XI. 27. in these words; *I believe that thou art the Messiah, THE SON OF GOD, who should come into the World*; And that passage of St. *John, Chap.* XX. 31. *That ye might believe that Jesus is the Messiah, THE SON OF GOD; and that believing, ye might have life through his name*: And then tell me whether he can doubt that *Messiah* and *Son of God* were Synonymous terms, at that time, amongst the Jews.

The Prophecy of *Daniel, Chap.* IX. where he is called *Messiah the Prince*; And the mention of his Government and Kingdom, and the deliverance by him, in *Isaiah, Daniel*, and other Prophesies, understood of the *Messiah*; were so well known to the Jews, and had so raised their hopes of him about this time, which by their account was to be the time of his coming to restore the Kingdom to *Israel*, That *Herod* no sooner heard of the *Magi*'s enquiry after *him that was born King of the Jews, Mat.* II. But he forthwith *demanded of the chief Priests and Scribes, where the | Messiah should be born*, v. 4. Not doubting, but if there were any King born to the Jews, it was the *Messiah*: Whose Coming was now the general Expectation, as appears, *Luke* III. 15. *The people being in expectation, and all men musing in their hearts of* John, *whether he were the*

112   THE REASONABLENESS OF CHRISTIANITY

Messiah *or not*. And when the Priests and Levites sent to ask him who he was; He understanding their meaning, answers, *John* I. 20. That he was *not the Messiah*: But he bears witness that Jesus *is the Son of God, i. e.* the *Messiah, v.* 34.

5   This looking for the *Messiah* at this time, we see also in *Simeon*; who is said to be *waiting for the consolation of Israel, Luke* II. 25. And having the Child Jesus in his Arms, he says he had *seen the Salvation of the Lord*, v. 30. And *Anna coming at the same instant into the Temple, she gave thanks also unto the Lord, and spake of him to all them that looked for Redemption in*

10   *Israel,* v. 38. And of *Joseph* of *Arimathea*, it is said, *Mark* XV. 43. That *he also expected the Kingdom of God*: By all which was meant the Coming of

[52]   the *Messiah*. And *Luke* XIX. 11. | 'tis said, *They thought that the Kingdom of God should immediately appear.*

This being premised, let us see what it was that *John the Baptist*

15   preached, when he first entred upon his Ministry. That St. *Matthew* tells us, *Chap*. III. 1, 2. *In those days came* John the Baptist *preaching in the Wilderness of* Judea, *saying, Repent, for the Kingdom of Heaven is at hand.* This was a declaration of the Coming of the *Messiah*; the *Kingdom of Heaven* and the *Kingdom of God* being the same, as is clear out of several

20   places of the Evangelists; and both signifying the Kingdom of the *Messiah*. The Profession which *John the Baptist* made, when sent to the Jews, *John* I. 19. was, That *he was not the Messiah*; but that Jesus was. This will appear to any one, who will compare *v.* 26–34. with *John* III. 27, 30. The Jews being very inquisitive to know whether *John* were the *Messiah*;

25   he positively denies it, but tells them, he was only his Fore-runner; and that there stood one amongst them, who would follow him, whose Shoe-latchet he was not worthy to untie. The next day seeing Jesus, he

[53]   says, he was the | Man; and that his own Baptizing in Water, was only that *Jesus* might be manifested to the World; and that he knew him not,

30   till he saw the Holy Ghost descend upon him. He that sent him to Baptize having told him, that he on whom he should see the Spirit descend, and rest upon, he it was that should Baptize with the Holy Ghost; And that therefore he witnessed, that *this was the Son of God*, v. 34. *i. e.* the *Messiah*. And *Chap.* III. 26, *etc.* They came to *John the Baptist*, and

35   tell him, that *Jesus* baptized, and that all Men went to him. *John* answers, He has his Authority from Heaven; You know I never said, I was the *Messiah*, but that I was sent before him; He must increase, but I must decrease; For God hath sent him, and he speaks the words of God; And God hath given all things into the hands of his Son, *And he that believes on*

40   *the Son, hath eternal life*; The same Doctrine, and nothing else but what

AS DELIVERED IN THE SCRIPTURES 113

was preached by the Apostles afterwards: As we have seen all through the *Acts, v. g.* that Jesus was the *Messiah*. And thus it was | that *John* bears [54] witness of our Saviour, as Jesus himself says, *John* V. 3 3.

This also was the Declaration was given of him at his Baptism, by a voice from Heaven; *This is my beloved Son, in whom I am well pleased, Mat.* 5 III. 1 7. Which was a declaration of him to be the *Messiah; the Son of God* being (as we have shewed) understood to signifie the *Messiah*. To which we may add the first mention of him after his Conception, in the words of the Angel to *Joseph*; Mat. I. 2 1. *Thou shalt call his name Jesus,* or Saviour; *for he shall save his people from their sins.* It was a received Doctrine 10 in the Jewish Nation, that at the Coming of the *Messiah*, all their sins should be forgiven them. These words therefore of the Angel we may look on as a declaration, that Jesus was the *Messiah*; whereof these words, *his People,* are a further mark; which suppose him to have a People, and consequently to be a King. 1 5

VII After his Baptism, Jesus himself enters upon his Ministry. But before we examine what it was he proposed to be believed, we must observe, that | there is a three-fold declaration of the *Messiah*. [55]

1. By Miracles. The Spirit of Prophecy had now for many Ages forsaken the Jews: And though their Common-Wealth were not quite 20 dissolved, but that they lived under their own Laws, yet they were under a Foreign Dominion, subject to the *Romans.* In this state their account of the time being up, they were in expectation of the *Messiah*; and of deliverance by him in a Kingdom, he was to set up, according to their Ancient Prophesies of him: Which gave them hopes of an extraordinary 2 5 Man yet to come from God, who with an Extraordinary and Divine Power, and Miracles, should evidence his Mission, and work their Deliverance. And of any such extraordinary Person who should have the Power of doing Miracles, they had no other expectation but only of their *Messiah.* One great Prophet and worker of Miracles, and only One more, 30 they expected; who was to be the *Messiah.* And therefore we see the People justified their *believing in him, i. e.* their believing him to be the *Messiah,* because of the Mi|racles he did; *John* VII. 3 1. *And many of the* [56] *people believed in him, and said, when the* Messiah *cometh, will he do more Miracles than this man hath done?* And when the Jews, at the Feast of 3 5 Dedication, *John* X. 24, 2 5. coming about him, said unto him, *How long dost thou make us doubt? If thou be the* Messiah, *tell us plainly. Jesus answered them, I told you, and ye believed not; the works that I do in my Father's name, bear witness of me.* And *John* V. 3 6. He says, *I have a greater witness than that of* John; *for the works which the Father hath given me to do, the same* 40

114   THE REASONABLENESS OF CHRISTIANITY

works that I do, bear witness of me, that the Father hath sent me. Where, by the way, we may observe, that his being *sent by the Father*, is but another way of expressing the *Messiah*; Which is evident from this place here, *John* V. compared with that of *John* X. last quoted. For there he says, that
5 his Works bear witness of him: And what was that witness? *viz.* That he was the *Messiah.* Here again he says, that his Works bear witness of him: And what is that witness? *viz. That the Father sent him.* By which we are |
[57] taught, that to be sent by the Father, and to be the *Messiah*, was the same thing, in this way of declaring himself. And accordingly we find, *John*
10 IV. 53. and XI. 45. and elsewhere, many hearkened and assented to his Testimony, and believed on him, seeing the things that he did.

2. Another way of declaring the Coming of the *Messiah*, was by Phrases and Circumlocution, that did signifie or intimate his Coming; though not in direct words pointing out the Person. The most usual of
15 these were, *The Kingdom of God, and of Heaven*; because it was that which was oftnest spoken of the *Messiah*, in the Old Testament, in very plain words: And a Kingdom was that which the Jews most looked after, and wished for. In that known place, *Isa.* IX. *The GOVERNMENT shall be upon his shoulders; he shall be called the PRINCE of Peace: Of the increase of*
20 *his GOVERNMENT and Peace there shall be no end: Upon the THRONE of* David, *and upon his KINGDOM, to order it, and to establish it with*
[58] *Judgment, and with Justice, from henceforth even for ever.* | Micah V. 2. *But thou*, Bethlehem Ephratah, *though thou be little among the thousands of* Judah, *yet out of thee shall He come forth unto me, that is to be the RULER in*
25 *Israel.* And *Daniel*, besides that he calls him *Messiah the PRINCE, Chap.* IX. 25. In the account of his Vision *of the Son of Man, Chap.* VII. 13, 14. says, *There was given him Dominion, Glory, and a KINGDOM, that all People, Nations, and Languages, should serve him: His Dominion is an everlasting Dominion, which shall not pass away; and his KINGDOM that*
30 *which shall not be destroyed.* So that the Kingdom of God, and the Kingdom of Heaven, were common Phrases amongst the Jews, to signifie the times of the *Messiah.* Luke XIV. 15. *One of* the Jews *that sat at meat with him, said unto him, Blessed is he that shall eat bread in the Kingdom of God. Chap.* XVII. 20. The Pharisees demanded, *When the*
35 *Kingdom of God should come?* And St. *John Baptist* came, *saying, Repent, for the Kingdom of Heaven is at hand*: A Phrase he would not have used in Preaching, had it not been understood. |
[59] There are other Expressions that signified the *Messiah*, and his Coming; which we shall take notice of as they come in our way.
40 3. By plain and direct words, declaring the Doctrine of the *Messiah*;

AS DELIVERED IN THE SCRIPTURES 115

speaking out that Jesus was He: As we see the Apostles did, when they went about Preaching the Gospel, after our Saviour's Resurrection. This was the open clear way, and that which one would think the *Messiah* himself, when he came, should have taken; especially if it were of that moment that upon mens believing him to be the *Messiah*, depended the 5 forgiveness of their sins. And yet we see that our Saviour did not: But on the contrary, for the most part, made no other discovery of himself, at least in *Judea*, and at the beginning of his Ministry, but in the two former ways, which were more obscure; Not declaring himself to be the *Messiah*, any otherwise than as it might be gathered from the Miracles he did, and 10 the conformity of his Life and Actions with the Prophesies of the Old Testament concerning him; and from some general Dis|courses of the [60] Kingdom of the *Messiah* being come, under the name of the *Kingdom of God*, and *of Heaven*. Nay, so far was he from publickly owning himself to be the *Messiah*, that he forbid the doing of it: *Mark* VIII. 27–30. *He* 15 *asked his Disciples, whom do men say that I am? And they answered*, John the Baptist; *but some say*, Elias; *and others, one of the Prophets.* (So that it is evident, that even those who believed him an extraordinary Person, knew not yet who he was, or that he gave himself out for the *Messiah*; though this was in the third Year of his Ministry, and not a year before his Death.) 20 *And he saith unto them, but whom say ye that I am? And* Peter *answered, and said unto him, Thou art the* Messiah. *And he charged them that they should tell no man of him.* Luke IV. 41. *And Devils came out of many, crying, Thou art the* Messiah, *the Son of God: And he rebuking them, suffered them not to speak, that they knew him to be the* Messiah. *Mark* III. 11, 12. *Unclean spirits, when* 25 *they saw him, fell down before him, and cryed, saying, Thou art the Son of God: And he straitly char|ged them that they should not make him known.* Here [61] again we may observe from the comparing of the two Texts, that *Thou art the Son of God*; or, *Thou art the Messiah*; were indifferently used for the same thing. But to return to the matter in hand. The Devils are forbid by 30 him as well as the Apostles to make him known. For we may conceive this forwardness in them to declare him to be the Messiah not out of any kindness to that doctrine or desire it should be received, but did it either to bring scandal on it by their owning of it or else, which seems rather to be the reason, they willingly published it to raise him enemies and to 35 disturb the work of his ministry by hastening his death.

VIII This concealment of himself will seem strange, in one who was come to bring Light into the World, and was to suffer Death for the Testimony of the Truth. This reservedness will be thought to look as if he had a mind to conceal himself, and not to be known to the World for the *Messiah*; 40

116   THE REASONABLENESS OF CHRISTIANITY

nor to be believed on as such. But we shall be of another mind, and
conclude this proceeding of his according to Divine Wisdom, and suited
to a fuller Manifestation and Evidence of his being the *Messiah*; When we
consider, that he was to fill out the time foretold of his Ministry; And,
5 after a Life illustrious in Miracles and Good Works, attended with
Humility, Meekness, Patience, and Suffering, and every way conformable to the Prophesies of him, should be led as a sheep to the slaughter,
[62] and with all quiet and submission be | brought to the Cross, though there
were no guilt nor fault found in him. This could not have been, if as soon
10 as he appeared in Publick, and began to Preach, he had presently
professed himself to have been the *Messiah*; the King that owned that
Kingdom he published to be at hand. For the *Sanhedrim* would then have
laid hold on it, to have got him into their Power, and thereby have taken
away his Life; at least, they would have disturbed his Ministry, and
15 hindred the Work he was about. That this made him cautious, and avoid,
as much as he could, the occasions of provoking them, and falling into
their hands, is plain from *John* VII. 1. *After these things Jesus walked in
Galilee*; out of the way of the Chief Priests and Rulers; *for he would not walk
in Jewry, because the Jews sought to kill him*. Thus, making good what he
20 foretold them at *Jerusalem*, when at the first Passover after his beginning
to Preach the Gospel, upon his Curing the man at the Pool of *Bethesda*,
they sought to kill him, *John* V. 16. *Ye have not*, says he, v. 38. *his word*
[63] *abiding amongst you: For whom he hath sent, him ye | believe not*. This was
spoken more particularly to the Jews of *Jerusalem*, who were the forward
25 men, zealous to take away his Life: And it imports, that because of their
Unbelief and Opposition to him, the *Word of God, i. e.* the Preaching of
the Kingdom of the *Messiah*, which is often called the Word of God, did
not stay amongst them: He could not stay amongst them, Preach and
explain to them the Kingdom of the *Messiah*.
30   That the Word of God, here, signifies *the Word of God* that should
make Jesus known to them to be the *Messiah*, is evident from the
Context: And this meaning of this place is made good by the event. For
after this, we hear no more of Jesus at *Jerusalem*, till the Pentecost come
twelve month; though 'tis not to be doubted but that he was there the
35 next Passover, and other Feasts between, but privately. And now at
Jerusalem, at the Feast of *Pentecost*, near fifteen Months after, he says very
little of any thing, and not a word of the Kingdom of Heaven being
come, or at hand; nor did he any Miracle there. And returning to
[64] *Jerusalem* at the Feast | of Tabernacles, it is plain, that from this time till
40 then, which was a Year and a half, he had not Taught them at *Jerusalem*.

AS DELIVERED IN THE SCRIPTURES 117

For, 1. It is said, *John* VII. 2, 15. That he teaching in the Temple at the Feast of Tabernacles, *The Jews marvelled, saying, How knoweth this man letters, having never learned?* A sign they had not been used to his Preaching: For if they had, they would not now have marvelled.

2. *Ver.* 19. He says thus to them: *Did not* Moses *give you the Law, and* 5 *yet none of you keep the Law? Why go you about to kill me? One work,* or miracle, *I did* here amongst you, *and ye all marvel.* Moses *therefore gave unto you Circumcision, and ye on the Sabbath-day circumcise a man: If a man on the Sabbath-day receive Circumcision, that the Law of* Moses *should not be broken, are ye angry with me, because I have made a man every way whole on* 10 *the Sabbath-day?* Which is a direct defence of what he did at *Jerusalem* a Year and a half before. The work he here speaks of we find reported, *John* V. 1–16. He had not preached to them there from that time till this: but had made good what he then | told them, *v.* 38. *Ye have not the Word of* [65] *God remaining among you, because whom he hath sent ye believe not.* 15 Whereby, I think, he signifies his not staying and being frequent amongst them at *Jerusalem,* Preaching the Gospel of the Kingdom there; because their great Unbelief, Opposition, and Malice to him would not permit his stay and Preaching in that place.

This was manifestly so in fact. For the first Miracle he did at *Jerusalem,* 20 which was at the second Passover after his Baptism, brought him in danger of his Life: Hereupon we find he forbore Preaching again there till the Feast of Tabernacles, immediately preceding his last Passover: So that till half a Year before his Passion, he did but one Miracle, and preached but once publickly, at *Jerusalem.* These Tryals he made there: 25 But found their unbelief such, that if he had staid and persisted to Preach the good tidings of the Kingdom, and to shew himself by Miracles among them, he could not have had time and freedom to do those Works which his Father had given him to finish, as he says, *v.* 36. of this fifth of St. *John.* 30

The words *After these things Jesus walked in Galilee* which I above took notice of out of *John* VII. give us occasion also to observe and admire the peculiar providence of God suited here unto in ordering his habitation in *Galilee* though he were born in *Judæa,* where he might preach and do miracles more out of the sight and reach of the *Sanhedrim,* till the fulness 35 of time made it no prejudice to his ministry to provoke them by his doctrine and miracles at *Jerusalem.* |

When upon the curing of the withered Hand on the Sabbath-day, *The* [66] Pharisees *took Counsel with the* Herodians, *how they might destroy him; Jesus withdrew himself with his Disciples to the Sea: And a great multitude from* 40

118   THE REASONABLENESS OF CHRISTIANITY

Galilee *followed him, and from* Judea, *and from* Jerusalem, *and from* Idumea, *and from beyond* Jordan, *and they about* Tyre *and* Sidon, *A great multitude; when they had heard what great things he did, came unto him, and he healed them all, and* CHARGED THEM THAT THEY SHOULD
5   NOT MAKE HIM KNOWN: *That it might be fulfilled what was spoken by the Prophet* Isaiah, *saying: Behold my servant whom I have chosen; my beloved, in whom my soul is well pleased: I will put my spirit upon him, and he shall shew Judgment to the Gentiles. He shall not strive, nor cry, neither shall any man hear his voice in the streets,* Mat. XII. *and* Mark III.

10   And *John* XI. 47. Upon the News of our Saviour's raising *Lazarus* from the Dead, *The Chief Priests and* Pharisees *convened the* Sanhedrim, *and said,*
[67]   *what do we? For this man does many* | *Miracles.* v. 53. *Then from that day forth they took counsel together for to put him to death.* v. 54. *Jesus therefore walked no more openly amongst the Jews.* His Miracles had now so much declared him
15   to be the *Messiah,* that the Jews could no longer bear him, nor he trust himself amongst them; *But went thence unto a Country near to the Wilderness, into a City called* Ephraim, *and there continued with his Disciples.* This was but a little before this last Passover, as appears by the following words, *v.* 55. *And the Jews Passover was nigh at hand*: And he could not,
20   now his Miracles had made him so well known, have been secure the little time that remained till his hour was fully come; if he had not with his wonted and necessary caution withdrawn, *And walked no more openly amongst the Jews,* till his time (at the next Passover) was fully come; And then again he appeared amongst them openly.

25   Nor would the *Romans* have suffered him, if he had gone about Preaching that he was the King whom the Jews expected. Such an
[68]   Accusation would have been forwardly brought against | him by the Jews, if they could have heard it out of his own mouth; And That had been his Publick Doctrine to his followers, Which was openly preached
30   by the Apostles after his Death, when he appeared no more. And of this they were accused, *Acts* XVII. 5–9. *But the Jews which believed not, moved with envy, took unto them certain lewd fellows of the baser sort, and gathered a company, and set all the City in an uproar; And assaulted the House of* Jason, *and sought to bring them out to the people. And when they found them* [Paul
35   and Silas] *not, they drew* Jason *and certain brethren unto the Rulers of the City, crying, these that have turned the World upside down, are come hither also, whom* Jason *hath received: And these all do contrary to the decrees of* Cæsar, *saying, that there is another King, one Jesus. And they troubled the People and the Rulers of the City, when they heard these things: And when they*
40   *had taken Security of* Jason *and the other, they let them go.*

AS DELIVERED IN THE SCRIPTURES 119

Though the Magistrates of the World had no great regard to the talk of a King, who had suffered Death, | and appeared no longer any where; Yet [69] if our Saviour had openly declared this of himself in his Life-time, with a train of Disciples and Followers every where owning and crying him up for their King, the *Roman* Governour of *Judea* could not have forborn to 5 have taken notice of it, and have made use of their Force against him. This the Jews were not mistaken in; and therefore made use of it as the strongest Accusation, and likeliest to prevail with *Pilate* against him for the taking away his Life; It being Treason, and an unpardonable Offence, which could not scape Death from a *Roman* Deputy, without the 10 Forfeiture of his own Life. Thus then they Accuse him to *Pilate, Luke* XXIII. 2. *We found this fellow perverting the Nation, and forbidding to give Tribute to* Cæsar, *saying, that he himself is the Messiah, a King*, or rather *Messiah the King*.

Our Saviour indeed, now that his time was come, (and he in Custody, 15 and forsaken of all the World, and so out of all danger of raising any Sedition or Disturbance,) owns himself, to *Pilate*, to be a King; after having first | told *Pilate, John* XVIII. 36. *That his Kingdom was not of this* [70] *World*: And for a Kingdom in another World, *Pilate* knew that his Master at *Rome* concerned not himself. But had there been any the least 20 appearance of truth in the Allegations of the Jews, that he had perverted the Nation; forbidding to pay Tribute to *Cæsar*, or drawing the People after him, as their King; *Pilate* would not so readily have pronounced him Innocent. But we see what he said to his Accusers, *Luke* XXIII. 13, 14. *Pilate, when he had called together the Chief Priests and Rulers of the* 25 *People, said unto them, You have brought this man unto me, as one that perverteth the People; and behold, I having examined him before you, have found no fault in this man, touching those things whereof you accuse him: No, nor yet* Herod, *for I sent you to him; and lo, nothing worthy of death is done by him*. And therefore finding a man of that mean Condition, and innocent 30 Life, (no mover of Seditions, or disturber of the Publick Peace,) without a Friend or a Follower, he would have dismissed him, as a King of no conse|quence; as an innocent man, falsely and maliciously accused by the [71] Jews.

How necessary this Caution was in our Saviour, to say or do nothing 35 that might justly offend, or render him suspected to the *Roman* Governour; and how glad the Jews would have been to have any such thing against him; we may see, *Luke* XX. 20. The Chief Priests and the Scribes *watched him, and sent forth spies, who should feign themselves just men, that might take hold of his words, that so they might deliver him unto the* 40

120   THE REASONABLENESS OF CHRISTIANITY

Power and Authority of the Governour. And the very thing wherein they hoped to entrap him in this place, was paying Tribute to *Cæsar*, which they afterwards falsely accused him of. And what would they have done, if he had before them professed himself to have been the *Messiah*, their
5 King and Deliverer?

And here we may observe the wonderful Providence of God, who had so ordered the state of the Jews at the time when his Son was to come into the World; that though neither their Civil Constitution, nor
[72] Religious Worship were dissolved, yet the Power of | Life and Death was
10 taken from them; Whereby he had an Opportunity to publish the Kingdom of the *Messiah*; that is, his own Royalty, under the name of the *Kingdom of God*, and *of Heaven*: Which the Jews well enough understood, and would certainly have put him to Death for, had the Power been in their own hands. But this being no matter of Accusation to the *Romans*,
15 hindred him not from speaking of the *Kingdom of Heaven*, as he did: Sometimes in reference to his appearing in the World, and being believed on by particular Persons; Sometimes in reference to the Power should be given him by the Father at his Resurrection; And sometimes in reference to his coming to Judge the World at the last day in the full Glory and
20 completion of his Kingdom. These were ways of declaring himself, which the Jews could lay no hold on, to bring him in danger with *Pontius Pilate*, and get him seized and put to Death.

Another Reason there was, that hindred him as much as the former from professing himself in express words to be the *Messiah*; and that was,
[73] that the | whole Nation of the Jews expecting at this time their *Messiah*,
26 and deliverance by him from the Subjection they were in to a Foreign Yoke, the body of the People would certainly, upon his declaring himself to be the *Messiah* their King, have rose up in Rebellion, and set him at the Head of them. And indeed, the miracles that he did, so much disposed
30 them to think him to be the *Messiah*, that though shrouded under the obscurity of a mean Condition, and a very private simple Life; though he assumed not to himself any Power or Authority, or so much as the Name of the *Messiah*; Nay, though his birth at *Bethlehem* being then concealed, he passed for a *Galilean*, which what an unanswerable argument it was to
35 the Jews that he could not be the *Messiah* may be seen, *John* VII. 41 and 52, yet he could hardly avoid being set up by a Tumult, and proclaimed their King. So *John* tells us, *Chap.* VI. 14, 15. *Then those men, when they had seen the Miracles that Jesus did, said, This is of a truth that Prophet that should come into the World. When therefore Jesus perceived that they would*
40 *come to take him by force to make him King, he departed again into a*

AS DELIVERED IN THE SCRIPTURES 121

Mountain himself alone. This was upon his feeding of Five Thousand | with [74]
five Barley Loaves and two Fishes. So hard was it for him, doing those
miracles which were necessary to testifie his Mission, and which often
drew great multitudes after him, *Mat.* IV. 25. to keep the heady and hasty
multitude from such Disorder, as would have involved him in it; and have 5
disturbed the course, and cut short the time of his Ministry; and drawn on
him the Reputation and Death of a Turbulent Seditious Malefactor:
Contrary to the design of his coming, which was to be offered up a Lamb
blameless, and void of Offence; his Innocence appearing to all the World,
even to him that delivered him up to be crucified. This it would have been 10
impossible to have avoided, if in his Preaching every where, he had openly
assumed to himself the Title of their *Messiah*; Which was all was wanting
to set the People in a flame; who, drawn by his miracles, and the hopes of
finding a Deliverer in so extraordinary a man, followed him in great
numbers. We read every where of multitudes; And in *Luke* XII. 1. of 15
Myriads that were gathered about him. This conflux | of People, thus [75]
disposed, would not have failed, upon his declaring himself to be the
Messiah, to have made a Commotion, and with Force set him up for their
King. It is plain therefore from these two Reasons, why, (though he
came to Preach the Gospel, and Convert the World to a belief of his 20
being the *Messiah*, and though he says so much of his Kingdom, under
the Title of the Kingdom of God, and the Kingdom of Heaven,) he yet
makes it not his business to perswade them that he himself is the *Messiah*,
nor does in his Publick Preaching declare himself to be him. He
inculcates to the People, on all occasions, that the Kingdom of God is 25
come. He shews the way of Admittance into this Kingdom, *viz.*
Repentance and Baptism; and teaches the Laws of it, *viz.* Good Life,
according to the strictest Rules of Vertue and Morality. But who the
King was of this Kingdom, he leaves to his miracles to point out to those
who would consider what he did, and make the right use of it, now; Or 30
to witness to those who should hearken to the Apostles hereafter, when
they | preached it in plain words, and called upon them to believe it, after [76]
his Resurrection, when there should be no longer room for fear that it
should cause any disturbance in Civil Societies and the Governments of
the World. But he could not declare himself to be the *Messiah*, without 35
manifest danger of Tumult and Sedition. And the miracles he did,
declared it so much, that he was fain often to hide himself, and withdraw
from the concourse of the People. The Leper that he cured, *Mark* I.
though forbid to say any thing, yet *blazed it so abroad, that Jesus could no
more openly enter into the City, but was without in desart places*, living in 40

122   THE REASONABLENESS OF CHRISTIANITY

retirement, as appears from *Luke* V. 16. And there *they came to him from every quarter*. And thus he did more than once.

This being premised, let us take a view of the Promulgation of the Gospel by our Saviour himself, and see what it was he taught the World, 5 and required men to believe.

IX The first beginning of his Ministry, whereby he shewed himself, seems to be at *Cana* in *Galilee*, soon after his Baptism; where he turned Water into [77] Wine: Of which St. *John, Chap.* II. 11. | says thus, *This beginning of Miracles Jesus made, and manifested his glory, and his Disciples believed in* 10 *him*. His Disciples here believed in him, but we hear not of any other Preaching to them, but by this Miracle, whereby he *manifested his Glory*; *i. e.* of being the *Messiah* the Prince. So *Nathanael*, without any other Preaching, but only our Saviour's discovering to him that he knew him after an extraordinary manner, presently acknowledges him to be the 15 *Messiah*; crying, *Rabbi, Thou art the Son of God; Thou art the King of Israel*.

From hence, staying a few days at *Capernaum*, he goes to *Jerusalem* to the Passover; and there he drives the Traders out of the Temple, *John* II. 12–15. saying, *Make not my Father's House a House of merchandize*. Where we see, he uses a Phrase, which by Interpretation signifies that he 20 was the *Son of God*, though at that time unregarded, *v*. 16. Hereupon the Jews demand, *What sign dost thou shew us, since thou doest these things? Jesus answered, Destroy ye this Temple, and in three days I will raise it again*. This [78] is an in|stance of what way Jesus took to declare himself: For 'tis plain by their Reply, the Jews understood him not, nor his Disciples neither; For 25 'tis said, *v*. 22. *When therefore he was risen from the dead, his Disciples remembred that he said this to them: And they believed the Scripture, and the saying of Jesus to them*.

This therefore we may look on, in the beginning, as a Pattern of Christ's Preaching, and shewing himself to the Jews; Which he generally 30 followed afterwards, *viz*. such a manifestation of himself, as every one at present could not understand; but yet carried such an Evidence with it to those who were well disposed now, or would reflect on it when the whole course of his Ministry was over, as was sufficient clearly to convince them that he was the *Messiah*.

35 The reason of this method used by our Saviour, the Scripture gives us here, at this his first appearing in Publick; after his entrance upon his Ministry; to be a Rule and Light to us in the whole course of it. For the [79] next Verse taking notice that many | believed on him, *because of his Miracles*, (which was all the Preaching they had,) 'Tis said, *v*. 24. *But Jesus* 40 *did not commit himself unto them, because he knew all men*; *i. e.* He declared

AS DELIVERED IN THE SCRIPTURES   123

not himself so openly to be the *Messiah*, their King, as to put himself into the Power of the Jews, by laying himself open to their malice; whom he knew would be so ready to lay hold on it to accuse him. For, as the next Verse 25. shews, he knew well enough what was in them. We may here farther observe, That *Believing in his Name*, signifies believing him to be 5 the *Messiah*. *V.* 23 tells us, That *many at the Passover believed in his name, when they saw the Miracles that he did.* What other Faith could these Miracles produce in them, who saw them, but that this was He, of whom the Scripture spoke, who was to be their Deliverer?

Whilst he was now at *Jerusalem*, *Nicodemus*, a Ruler of the Jews, comes 10 to him, *John* III. 1–21. to whom he Preaches Eternal Life by Faith in the *Messiah*, *v.* 15. and 17. But in general terms, without naming himself to be that *Messiah*; though his whole | Discourse tends to it. This is all we [80] hear of our Saviour the first Year of his Ministry; But only his Baptism, Fasting, and Temptation in the beginning of it; and spending the rest of 15 it after the Passover in *Judea* with his Disciples, Baptizing there. But *when he knew that the* Pharisees *reported that he made and baptized more Disciples than* John, *he left* Judea, and got out of their way again into *Galilee*, John IV. 1, 3.

In his way back, by the Well of *Sichar*, he discourses with the 20 *Samaritan* Woman; And after having opened to her the True and Spiritual Worship which was at hand, which the Woman presently understands of the times of the *Messiah*, who was then looked for; Thus she answers, *v.* 25. *I know that the Messiah cometh: When he is come, he will tell us all things.* Whereupon our Saviour, though we hear no such thing 25 from him in *Jerusalem* or *Judea*, or to *Nicodemus*, yet here to this *Samaritan* Woman, he in plain and direct words owns and declares, that he himself, who talked with her, was the *Messiah*, *v.* 26. |

This would seem very strange, that he should be more free and open to [81] a *Samaritan*, than he was to the Jews; were not the reason plain from 30 what we have observed above. He was now out of *Judea*, amongst a People with whom the *Jews* had no Commerce; *v.* 9. Who were not disposed out of Envy, as the *Jews* were, to seek his Life, or to Accuse him to the *Roman* Governour, or to make an Insurrection to set a *Jew* up for their King. What the Consequence was of his Discourse with this 35 *Samaritan* Woman, we have an Account, *v.* 28, 39–42. *She left her Water-pot, and went her way into the City, and saith to the men, Come, see a man who told me all things that ever I did: Is not this the Messiah? And many of the* Samaritans *of that City BELIEVED ON HIM for the saying of the Woman, which testified, He told me all that ever I did. So when the* Samaritans *were* 40

124   THE REASONABLENESS OF CHRISTIANITY

come unto him, they besought him that he would tarry with them: And he abode there two days. And many more believed because of his own word: And [82] *said unto the Woman, Now we believe not because of thy saying; For we | have heard him our selves; and we know,* (*i. e.* are fully perswaded,) *that it is* 5 *indeed the Messiah, the Saviour of the World.* By comparing *v.* 39. with 41. and 42. it is plain, that *believing on him* signifies no more than believing him to be the *Messiah.*

From *Sichar* Jesus goes to *Nazareth*, the place he was bred up in; and there Reading in the Synagogue a Prophecy concerning the *Messiah* out 10 of the LXI of *Isaiah*, he tells them, *Luke* IV. 21. *This day is this Scripture fulfilled in your ears.*

But being in danger of his Life at *Nazareth*, he leaves it, for *Capernaum*: And then, as St. *Matthew* informs us, *Chap.* IV. 17. *He began to Preach, and say, Repent, for the Kingdom of Heaven is at hand.* Or, 15 as St. *Mark* has it, *Chap.* I. 14, 15. *Preaching the Gospel of the Kingdom of God; and saying, The time is fulfilled, and the Kingdom of God is at hand, repent ye, and believe in the Gospel; i. e.* believe this good News. This removing to *Capernaum*, and seating himself there in the Borders of *Zabulon* and *Naphtali*, was, as St. *Matthew* observes, *Chap.* IV. 13–15. [83] That a | Prophecy of *Isaiah* might be fulfilled. Thus the Actions and 21 Circumstances of his Life answered the Prophesies, and declared him to be the *Messiah*. And by what St. *Mark* says in this place, it is manifest, that the Gospel which he preached and required them to believe, was no other but the good tidings of the Coming of the *Messiah*, and of his 25 Kingdom; the time being now fulfilled.

In his way to *Capernaum*, being come to *Cana*, a Noble-man of *Capernaum* came to him, *v.* 47. *And besought him that he would come down and heal his Son, for he was at the point of death.* v. 43. *Then said Jesus unto him, except ye see signs and wonders, you will not believe.* Then he returning 30 homewards, and finding that his Son began to *mend at the same hour in which Jesus said unto him, thy Son liveth;* he himself believed, and his whole House, v. 53.

Here this Noble-man is by the Apostle pronounced to be a *Believer*. And what does he *believe*? Even that which Jesus complains, *v.* 48. *They* 35 *would not BELIEVE*, except they saw Signs and Wonders: Which could [84] be nothing | but what those of *Samaria*, in the same Chapter, believed; *viz.* that he was the *Messiah*. For we no where in the Gospel hear of any thing else had been proposed to be believed by them.

Having done Miracles, and cured all their sick at *Capernaum*, he says, 40 *Let us go to the adjoyning Towns, that I may preach there also; for therefore*

AS DELIVERED IN THE SCRIPTURES 125

came I forth, Mark I. 38. Or, as St. *Luke* has it, *Chap.* IV. 43. He tells
the multitude, who would have kept him that he might not go from
them, *I must Evangelize,* or tell the good Tidings of the *Kingdom of God,*
to other Cities also; for therefore am I sent. And St. *Matthew, Chap.*
IV. 23. tells us how he executed this Commission he was sent on. *And* 5
Jesus went about all Galilee, *teaching in their Synagogues, and preaching the*
Gospel of the Kingdom, and curing all Diseases. This then was what he was
sent to Preach every where, *viz.* The Gospel of the Kingdom of the
Messiah; and by the Miracles and Good he did, let them know who was
the *Messiah.* 10

Hence he goes up to *Jerusalem,* to the second Passover since the
beginning | of his Ministry. And here discoursing to the Jews, who [85]
sought to kill him, upon occasion of the man, whom he had cured,
carrying his Bed on the Sabbath-day; and for making God his Father; He
tells them, that he wrought these things by the Power of God; and that 15
he shall do greater things: For that the Dead shall, at his Summons, be
raised; And that he, by a Power committed to him from his Father, shall
Judge them; And that he is sent by his Father; And that whoever shall
hear his Word, and believe in him that sent him, has Eternal Life. This,
though a clear Description of the *Messiah,* yet we may observe, that here 20
to the angry *Jews,* who sought to kill him, he says not a word of his
Kingdom, nor so much as names the *Messiah;* But yet that he is the Son
of God, and sent from God, He refers them to the Testimony of *John* the
Baptist, to the Testimony of his own Miracles, and of God himself in the
Voice from Heaven; and of the Scriptures, and of *Moses.* He leaves them 25
to learn from these the Truth they were to believe, *viz.* that he was the |
Messiah sent from God. This you may read more at large, *John* V. 1–47. [86]

The next place where we find him Preaching, was on the Mount,
Mat. V. and *Luke* VI. This is by much the longest Sermon we have of his
any where; and, in all likelihood, to the greatest Auditory. For it appears 30
to have been to the People gathered to him from *Galilee,* and *Judea,* and
Jerusalem, and from beyond *Jordan;* and that came out of *Idumea,* and
from *Tyre* and *Sidon;* mentioned *Mark* III. 7, 8. and *Luke* VI. 17. But in
this whole Sermon of his we do not find one word of Believing, and
therefore no mention of the *Messiah,* or any intimation to the People 35
who himself was. The reason whereof we may gather from *Mat.* XII. 16.
where Christ *forbids them to make him known;* which supposes them to
know already who he was. For that this XII. Chapter of *Matthew* ought
to precede the Sermon in the Mount, is plain, by comparing it with
Mark II. beginning at *v.* 13. to *Mark* III. 8. And comparing those 40

126   THE REASONABLENESS OF CHRISTIANITY

Chapters of St. *Mark* with *Luke* VI. And I desire my Reader once for all |
[87] here to take notice, that I have all along observed the order of time in our
Saviour's Preaching; and have not, as I think, passed by any of his
Discourses. In this Sermon our Saviour only teaches them what were the
5 Laws of his Kingdom, and what they must do who were admitted into it,
of which I shall have occasion to speak more at large in another place;
being at present only enquiring what our Saviour proposed as matter of
Faith to be believed.

After this, *John* the *Baptist* sends to him this Message, *Luke* VII. 19.
10 Asking, *Art thou he that should come, or do we expect another?* That is, in
short, art thou the *Messiah?* And if thou art, why dost thou let me, thy
Fore-runner, languish in Prison? Must I expect deliverance from any
other? To which Jesus returns this Answer, *v.* 22, 23. *Tell* John *what you
have seen and heard: The Blind see, the Lame walk, the Lepers are cleansed,*
15 *the Deaf hear, the Dead are raised, to the Poor the Gospel is preached; and
blessed is he who is not offended in me.* What it is to be *offended* or
[88] *scandalized in him,* we may see by comparing *Mat.* XIII. 21. and | *Mark*
IV. 17. with *Luke* VIII. 13. For what the two first call *scandalized,* the
last calls *standing off from,* or *forsaking; i. e.* not receiving him as the
20 *Messiah; (Vid. Mark* VI. 1–6.) or revolting from him. Here Jesus refers
John, as he did the Jews before, to the Testimony of his Miracles, to
know who he was; And this was generally his Preaching, whereby he
declared himself to be the *Messiah*: Who was the only Prophet to come,
whom the *Jews* had any expectation of; Nor did they look for any other
25 Person to be sent to them with the Power of Miracles, but only the
Messiah. His Miracles, we see by his Answer to *John* the *Baptist,* he
thought a sufficient declaration amongst them, that he was the *Messiah.*
And therefore, upon his curing the possessed of the Devil, the Dumb,
and Blind, *Mat.* XII. the People, who saw the Miracle, said, *v.* 23. *Is not*
30 *this the Son of David?* As much as to say, Is not this the *Messiah?* Whereat
the *Pharisees* being offended, said, He cast out Devils by *Beelzebub.* Jesus
shewing the falsehood and vanity of their Blasphemy, justifies the
[89] Con|clusion the People made from this Miracle; saying, *v.* 28. That his
casting out Devils by the Spirit of God, was an Evidence that the
35 Kingdom of the *Messiah* was come.

One thing more there was in the Miracles done by his Disciples, which
shewed him to be the *Messiah*; That they were done in his Name. *In the
name of Jesus of* Nazareth, *rise up and walk,* says St. *Peter* to the lame man
whom he cured in the Temple, *Acts* III. 6. And how far the Power of that
40 Name reached, they themselves seem to wonder, *Luke* X. 17. *And the*

AS DELIVERED IN THE SCRIPTURES 127

seventy returned again with joy, saying, Lord, even the Devils are subject to us in thy Name.

From this Message from *John* the *Baptist*, he takes occasion to tell the People, that *John* was the Fore-runner of the *Messiah*; That from the time of *John* the *Baptist* the Kingdom of the *Messiah* began; To which time all the Prophets and the Law pointed, *Luke* VII. and *Mat.* XI.

Luke VIII. 1. *Afterwards he went through every City and Village, preaching and shewing the good tidings of the | Kingdom of God.* Here we see, [90] as every where, what his Preaching was; and consequently what was to be believed.

Soon after, he Preaches from a Boat to the People on the shoar. His Sermon at large we may read, *Mat.* XIII. *Mark* IV. and *Luke* VIII. But this is very observeable, That this second Sermon of his here, is quite different from his former in the Mount. For that was all so plain and intelligible, that nothing could be more so: Whereas this is all so involved in Parables, that even the Apostles themselves did not understand it. If we enquire into the reason of this, we shall possibly have some Light from the different Subjects of these two Sermons. There he preached to the People only Morality; Clearing the Precepts of the Law from the false glosses which were received in those days; And setting forth the Duties of a good Life in their full Obligation and Extent, beyond what the Judiciary Laws of the *Israelites* did, or the Civil Laws of any Country could prescribe or take notice of. But here in this Sermon by the Sea-side, he speaks of nothing but the Kingdom of | the *Messiah*, which he does all [91] in Parables. One Reason whereof St. *Matthew* gives us, *Chap.* XIII. 35. *That it might be fulfilled which was spoken by the Prophet, saying, I will open my mouth in Parables, I will utter things that have been kept secret from the Foundations of the World.* Another reason our Saviour himself gives of it, *v.* 11, 12. *Because to you is given to know the Mysteries of the Kingdom of Heaven, but to them it is not given. For whosoever hath, to him shall be given, and he shall have more abundantly: But whosoever hath not, i. e.* improves not the Talents that he hath, *from him shall be taken away, even that that he hath.*

One thing it may not be amiss to observe; That our Saviour here in the Explication of the first of these Parables to his Apostles, calls the Preaching of the Kingdom of the *Messiah*, simply *the Word*; And *Luke* VIII. 21. *The Word of God*: From whence St. *Luke*, in the *Acts*, often mentions it under the name of the *Word*, and the *Word of God*, as we have elsewhere observed. To which I shall here add that of *Acts* VIII. 4. *Therefore they that | were scattered abroad, went every where preaching the* [92]

128   THE REASONABLENESS OF CHRISTIANITY

Word: Which Word, as we have found by examining what they preached all through their History, was nothing but this, That *Jesus was the Messiah*: I mean, This was all the Doctrine they proposed to be believed. For what they taught, as well as our Saviour, contained a great deal
5 more; but that concerned Practice, and not Belief. And therefore our Saviour says, in the place before quoted, *Luke* VIII. 21. *They are my Mother, and my Brethren, who hear the Word of God, and do it*: Obeying the Law of the *Messiah* their King, being no less required than their believing that Jesus was the *Messiah*, the King and Deliverer that was promised
10 them.

Mat. IX. 35. We have an Account again of this Preaching; what it was, and how. *And Jesus went about all the Cities and Villages, teaching in their Synagogues, and preaching the Gospel of the Kingdom; and healing every Sickness, and every Disease amongst the people.* He acquainted them that the
[93] Kingdom of the *Messiah* was come, and left | it to his Miracles to instruct
16 and convince them that he was the *Messiah*.

Mat. X. When he sent his Apostles abroad, their Commission to Preach we have, *v.* 7, 8. in these words: *As ye go, preach, saying, the Kingdom of Heaven is at hand; Heal the sick, etc.* All that they had to
20 Preach, was, that the Kingdom of the *Messiah* was come. Whosoever should not receive them, the Messengers of this good Tidings, nor hearken to their Message, incurred a heavier doom than *Sodom* and *Gormorrha* at the day of Judgment, *v.* 14, 15. But *v.* 32. *Whosoever shall confess me before men, I will confess him before my Father who is in*
25 *Heaven.* What this confessing of Christ is, we may see, by comparing *John* XII. 42. with IX. 22. *Nevertheless among the chief Rulers also many believed in him; But because of the* Pharisees *they did not CONFESS HIM, lest they should be put out of the Synagogue.* And Chap. IX. 22. *These words spake his Parents, because they feared the Jews: For the Jews had agreed already,*
30 *that if any man did CONFESS THAT HE WAS THE MESSIAH, he*
[94] *should | be put out of the Synagogue.* By which places it is evident, that to *confess* him, was to *confess* that he was the *Messiah*. From which give me leave to observe also (what I have cleared from other places, but cannot be too often remark'd, because of the different sense has been put upon
35 that Phrase;) *viz.* That *believing on* or *in him* (for ἐις αὐτὸν is rendred either way by the *English* Translation) signifies believing that he was the *Messiah*. For many of *the Rulers* (the Text says) *believed on him*; But they durst not confess what they believed, *for fear they should be put out of the Synagogue*. Now the Offence for which it was agreed that any one should
40 be put out of the Synagogue, was, if he *did confess that Jesus was the*

AS DELIVERED IN THE SCRIPTURES   129

Messiah. Hence we may have a clear understanding of that passage of St. *Paul* to the *Romans*, where he tells them positively, what is the Faith he Preaches; *Rom.* X. 8, 9. *That is the Word of Faith which we preach; That if thou shalt confess with thy mouth the Lord Jesus, and believe in thine heart, that God hath raised him from the dead, thou shalt be saved*: And that also of 5 St. *John*, 1 *Ep.* IV. | 14, 15. *We have seen, and do testifie, that the Father sent* [95] *the Son to be the Saviour of the World: Whosoever shall confess that Jesus is the Son of God, God dwelleth in him, and he in God.* Where confessing Jesus to be the Son of God, is the same with confessing him to be the *Messiah*: Those two Expressions being understood amongst the Jews to signifie 10 the same thing, as we have shewn already.

How calling him the Son of God came to signifie that he was the *Messiah*, would not be hard to shew. But it is enough that it appears plainly that it was so used, and had that import amongst the Jews at that time; Which if any one desires to have further evidenced to him, he may 15 add *Mat.* XXVI. 63. *John* VI. 69. and XI. 27. and XX. 31. to those places before occasionally taken notice of.

As was the Apostles Commission, such was their Performance; As we read, *Luke* IX. 6. *They departed, and went through the Towns, preaching the Gospel, and healing every where.* Jesus bid them Preach, *saying, The* 20 *Kingdom of Heaven is at hand.* And St. | *Luke* tells us, they went through [96] the Towns, Preaching the *Gospel*; A word which in *Saxon* answers well the *Greek* εὐαγγέλιον, and signifies, as that does, *Good news*. So that what the inspired Writers call the *Gospel*, is nothing but the good Tidings that the *Messiah* and his Kingdom was come; And so it is to be 25 understood in the New Testament; And so the Angel calls it *Good tidings of great joy, Luke* II. 10. Bringing the first News of our Saviour's Birth. And this seems to be all that his Disciples were at that time sent to Preach.

So *Luke* IX. 59, 60. To him that would have excused his present 30 Attendance, because of burying his Father; *Jesus said unto him, let the dead bury their dead, but go thou and preach the Kingdom of God.* When, I say, this was all they were to Preach, I must be understood, that this was the Faith they preached; But with it they joyned Obedience to the *Messiah*, whom they received for their King. So likewise when he sent out the 35 Seventy, *Luke* X. their Commission was in these words, *v. 9. Heal the sick, and say unto them, the Kingdom of God is come nigh unto you.* |

After the return of his Apostles to him, he sits down with them in a [97] Mountain; And a great multitude being gathered about them, St. *Luke* tells us, *Chap.* IX. 11. *The people followed him, and he received them, and* 40

130   THE REASONABLENESS OF CHRISTIANITY

spake unto them of the Kingdom of God; and healed them that had need of healing. This was his Preaching to this Assembly, which consisted of Five Thousand Men, besides Women and Children: All which great multitude he fed with five Loaves and two Fishes, *Mat.* XIV. 21. And
5 what this Miracle wrought upon them, St. *John* tells us, *Chap.* VI. 14, 15. *Then these men, when they had seen the miracle that Jesus did, said, This is of a truth that Prophet that should come into the World*; *i. e.* the *Messiah*. For the *Messiah* was the only Person that they expected from God, and this the time they looked for him. And hence *John* the *Baptist, Mat.* XI. 3. stiles
10 him, *He that should come*; As in other places, *Come from God*, or *Sent from God*, are Phrases used for the *Messiah*.

Here we see our Saviour keeps to his usual method of Preaching: He
[98] speaks to them of the Kingdom of God, and | does Miracles; by which they might understand him to be the *Messiah*, whose Kingdom he spake
15 of. And here we have the reason also, why he so much concealed himself, and forbore to own his being the *Messiah*. For what the consequence was, of the multitudes but thinking him so, when they were got together, St. *John* tells us in the very next words: *When Jesus then perceived that they would come and take him by force to make him a King, he departed again into*
20 *a mountain himself alone.* If they were so ready to set him up for their King, only because they gathered from his Miracles that he was the *Messiah*, whilst he himself said nothing of it; What would not the People have done; And what would not the Scribes and Pharisees have had an Opportunity to Accuse him of; if he had openly professed himself to
25 have been the *Messiah*, that King they looked for? But this we have taken notice of already.

From hence going to *Capernaum*, whither he was followed by a great part of the People, whom he had the day before so miraculously fed; He, |
[99] upon the occasion of their following him for the Loaves, bids them seek
30 for the Meat that endureth to Eternal Life: And thereupon, *John* VI. 22–69. declares to them his being sent from the Father; And that those who believed in him, should be raised to Eternal Life: But all this, very much involved in a mixture of Allegorical terms of eating, and of Bread, Bread of Life, which came down from Heaven, *etc.* Which is all
35 comprehended and expounded in these short and plain words, *v.* 47. and 54. *Verily, verily I say unto you, he that believeth on me, hath everlasting life, and I will raise him up at the last day.* The sum of all which Discourse is, that he was the *Messiah* sent from God; And that those who believed him to be so, should be raised from the Dead at the last day to Eternal Life.
40 These who he spoke to, were of those who the day before would by force

AS DELIVERED IN THE SCRIPTURES   131

have made him King; And therefore 'tis no wonder he should speak to them of himself, and his Kingdom and Subjects, in obscure and Mystical terms; and such as should offend those who looked for nothing but the Grandeur of a Temporal | Kingdom in this World, and the Protection [100] and Prosperity they had promised themselves under it. The hopes of such 5 a Kingdom, now that they had found a man that did Miracles, and therefore concluded to be the Deliverer they expected, had the day before almost drawn them into an open Insurrection, and involved our Saviour in it. This he thought fit to put a stop to; they still following him 'tis like with the same design. And therefore though he here speaks to them of 10 his Kingdom, it was in a way that so plainly bauk'd their Expectation; and shock'd them; that when they found themselves disappointed of those vain hopes, and that he talked of their eating his Flesh, and drinking his Blood, that they might have Life; the Jews said, *v.* 52. *How can this man give us his flesh to eat? And many, even of his Disciples, said, It* 15 *was an hard saying, who can bear it?* And so were scandalized in him, and forsook him, *v.* 60, 66. But what the true meaning of this Discourse of our Saviour was, the Confession of St. *Peter*, who understood it better and answered for the rest of the | Apostles, shews: When Jesus asked him, [101] *v.* 67. *Will ye also go away? Then* Simon Peter *answered him, Lord, to whom* 20 *shall we go? Thou hast the words of eternal life*; *i. e.* Thou teachest us the way to attain Eternal Life; And accordingly *We believe, and are sure that thou art the Messiah, the Son of the living God*. This was the eating his Flesh, and drinking his Blood, whereby those who did so had Eternal Life.

Sometime after this, he enquires of his Disciples, *Mark* VIII. 27. Who 25 the People took him for? They telling him, for *John* the *Baptist*, or one of the old Prophets risen from the Dead; He asked, what they themselves thought? And here again *Peter* answers in these words, *Mark* VIII. 29. *Thou art the Messiah*. Luke IX. 20. *The Messiah of God*. And *Mat*. XVI. 16. *Thou art the Messiah, the Son of the living God*: Which Expressions, we may 30 hence gather, amount to the same thing. Whereupon our Saviour tells *Peter, Mat*. XVI. 17, 18. That this was such a truth *As flesh and blood could not reveal to him, but only his Father who was in Heaven*; And that this was the Foun|dation on which he was *to build his Church*. By all the parts of [102] which passage it is more than probable, that he had never yet told his 35 Apostles in direct words that he was the *Messiah*; but that they had gathered it from his Life and Miracles. For which we may imagine to our selves this probable Reason; Because that if he had familiarly, and in direct terms, talked to his Apostles in private that he was the *Messiah* the Prince, of whose Kingdom he preached so much in publick every where, 40

132   THE REASONABLENESS OF CHRISTIANITY

Judas, whom he knew false and treacherous, would have been readily made use of to testifie against him, in a matter that would have been really Criminal to the *Roman* Governour. This perhaps may help to clear to us that seemingly abrupt reply of our Saviour to his Apostles, *John*
5 VI. 70. when they confessed him to be the *Messiah*. I will, for the better explaining of it, set down the passage at large. *Peter* having said, *We believe, and are sure that thou art the Messiah, the Son of the living God. Jesus answered them, Have not I chosen you twelve, and one of you is* διάβολος? This
[103] is a reply seeming | at first sight nothing to the purpose; when yet it is
10 sure all our Saviour's Discourses were wise and pertinent. It seems therefore to me to carry this sense, to be understood afterwards by the eleven (as that of destroying the Temple, and raising it again in three days was) when they should reflect on it after his being betray'd by *Judas*: You have confessed, and believe the truth concerning me; I am the *Messiah*
15 your King: But do not wonder at it, that I have never openly declared it to you: For amongst you twelve, whom I have chosen to be with me, there is one who is an Informer, or false Accuser, (for so the *Greek* word signifies, and may possibly here be so translated, rather than *Devil*) who, if I had owned my self in plain words to have been the *Messiah, the King of*
20 *Israel*, would have betrayed me, and informed against me.

That he was yet cautious of owning himself to his Apostles positively to be the *Messiah*, appears farther from the manner wherein he tells *Peter*, Mat. XVI. *v.* 18. that he will build his Church upon that Confession of
[104] his, that he was the *Mes|siah*. I say unto thee, *Thou art Cephas, or a Rock,*
25 *and upon this Rock I will build my Church, and the gates of Hell shall not prevail against it.* Words too doubtful to be laid hold on against him; as a Testimony that he professed himself to be the *Messiah*; Especially if we joyn with them the following words, *v.* 19. *And I will give thee the Keys of the Kingdom of Heaven; And what thou shalt bind on Earth, shall be bound in*
30 *Heaven; and what thou shalt loose on Earth, shall be loosed in Heaven.* Which being said Personally to *Peter*, render the foregoing words of our Saviour (wherein he declares the Fundamental Article of his Church to be the believing him to be the *Messiah*) the more obscure and doubtful, and less liable to be made use of against him; But yet such as might afterwards be
35 understood. And for the same reason he yet here again forbids the Apostles to say that he was the *Messiah, v.* 20.

From this time (say the Evangelists) Jesus *began to shew to his Disciples,* (*i. e.* his Apostles, who are often called Disciples) *that he must go to*
[105] Jerusalem, *and suffer many things from the Elders,* | *Chief Priests, and*
40 *Scribes; and be killed, and be raised again the third day*, Mat. XVI. 21.

AS DELIVERED IN THE SCRIPTURES 133

These, though all marks of the *Messiah*, yet how little understood by the Apostles, or suited to their expectation of the *Messiah*, appears from *Peter*'s rebuking him for it in the following words, *Mat.* XVI. 22. *Peter* had twice before owned him to be the *Messiah*, and yet he cannot here bear that he should Suffer, and be put to Death, and be raised again. 5 Whereby we may perceive, how little yet Jesus had explained to the Apostles what Personally concerned himself. They had been a good while witnesses of his Life and Miracles; and thereby being grown into a belief that he was the *Messiah*, were in some degree prepared to receive the Particulars that were to fill up that Character, and answer the Prophesies 10 concerning him. This from *henceforth* he began to open to them, (though in a way which the Jews could not form an Accusation out of) the time of the accomplishment of all, in his Sufferings, Death, and Resurrection, now drawing on. For this was in the last Year of his Life; he being to meet the Jews at | *Jerusalem* but once more at the Passover, who then [106] should have their will upon him; And therefore he might now begin to 16 be a little more open concerning himself: Though yet so, as to keep himself out of the reach of any Accusation, that might appear Just or Weighty to the *Roman* Deputy.

After his Reprimand to *Peter*, telling him That he *savoured not the things* 20 *of God, but of man*; *Mark* VIII. 34. He calls the People to him, and prepares those, who would be his Disciples, for Suffering; Telling them, *v.* 38. *Whoever shall be ashamed of me and my words in this adulterous and sinful Generation, of him also shall the Son of Man be ashamed when he cometh in the Glory of his Father with the holy Angels*: And then subjoyns, *Mat.* 25 XVI. 27, 28. two great and solemn Acts, wherein he would shew himself to be the *Messiah* the King: *For the Son of Man shall come in the Glory of his Father, with his Angels; and then he shall render every man according to his works*. This is evidently meant of the Glorious Appearance of his Kingdom, when he shall come to Judge the World at the last day; 30 Described | more at large, *Mat.* XXV. *When the Son of Man shall come in* [107] *his Glory, and all the holy Angels with him, then shall he sit upon the THRONE of his Glory. Then shall the KING say to them on his right hand,* etc. And thus we see what is called his Kingdom, *Mat.* XX. 21. is called his glory, *Mark* X. 37. 35

But what follows in the place above quoted, *Mat.* XVI. 28. *Verily, verily, there be some standing here, who shall not tast of Death, till they see the Son of Man coming in his Kingdom*; Importing that Dominion, which some there should see him exercise over the Nation of the Jews, was so covered, by being annexed to the preceding *v.* 27. (where he spoke of the 40

134   THE REASONABLENESS OF CHRISTIANITY

Manifestation and Glory of his Kingdom at the day of Judgment), That though his plain meaning here in *v.* 28. be, that the appearance and visible exercise of his Kingly Power in his Kingdom was so near, that some there should live to see it; Yet if the foregoing words had not cast a

5 shadow over these later, but they had been left plainly to be understood, as they plainly signified, that he should be a King; And that it was so near, that some there should see him in his Kingdom, this might have been laid

[108] hold on, and | made the matter of a plausible and seemingly just Accusation against him, by the Jews, before *Pilate.* This seems to be the

10 reason of our Saviour's inverting here the order of the two Solemn Manifestations to the World of his Rule and Power; thereby perplexing at present his meaning, and securing himself, as was necessary, from the malice of the Jews, which always lay at catch to intrap him, and accuse him to the *Roman* Governour; And would, no doubt, have been ready to

15 have alledged these words, *Some here shall not tast of Death, till they see the Son of Man coming in his Kingdom,* against him, as Criminal; had not their meaning been, by the former Verse, perplexed, and the sense at that time rendred unintelligible, and not applicable by any of his Auditors to a sense that might have been prejudicial to him before *Pontius Pilate.* For

20 how well the Chief of the Jews were disposed towards him, St. *Luke* tells us, *Chap.* XI. 54. *Laying wait for him, and seeking to catch something out of his mouth, that they might accuse him*: Which may be a reason to satisfie us

[109] of the seemingly | doubtful and obscure way of speaking used by our Saviour in other places; His Circumstances being such, that without such

25 a Prudent carriage and reservedness, he could not have gone through the Work which he came to do; Nor have performed all the parts of it, in a way correspondent to the Descriptions given of the *Messiah,* and which should be afterwards fully understood to belong to him, when he had left the World.

30   After this, *Mat.* XVII. 10, *etc.* He, without saying it in direct words, begins, as it were, to own himself to his Apostles to be the *Messiah*; by assuring them, that as the Scribes, according to the Prophecy of *Malachy, Chap.* IV. 5. rightly said, that *Elias* was to Usher in the *Messiah*; So indeed *Elias* was already come, though the Jews knew him

35 not, and treated him ill: Whereby *They understood that he spoke to them of* John *the* Baptist, *v.* 13. And a little after he somewhat more plainly intimates that he is the *Messiah,* Mark IX. 41. in these words: *Whosoever shall give you a cup of water to drink in my Name, because ye*

[110] *belong to the Messiah.* | This, as I remember, is the first place where our

40 Saviour ever mentioned the name of *Messiah*; and the first time that he

AS DELIVERED IN THE SCRIPTURES   135

went so far towards the owning, to any of the Jewish Nation, himself to be him.

In his way to *Jerusalem*, bidding one follow him, *Luke* IX. 59. who would first bury his Father, *v.* 60. *Jesus said unto him, let the dead bury their dead; but go thou and preach the Kingdom of God.* And *Luke* X. 1. Sending out the Seventy Disciples, he says to them, *v.* 9. *Heal the sick, and say, the Kingdom of God is come nigh unto you.* He had nothing else for these, or for his Apostles, or any one, it seems, to Preach; but the good News of the coming of the Kingdom of the *Messiah.* And if any City would not receive them, he bids them, *v.* 10. *Go into the streets of the same, and say, Even the very dust of your City, which cleaveth on us, do we wipe off against you: Notwithstanding, be ye sure of this, that the Kingdom of God is come nigh unto you.* This they were to take notice of, as that which they should dearly answer for; *viz.* That they had not with Faith received the good | Tidings [111] of the Kingdom of the *Messiah.*

After this, his Brethren say unto him, *John* VII. 2, 3, 4. (The Feast of Tabernacles being near) *Depart hence, and go into* Judea, *that thy Disciples also may see the works that thou doest: For there is no man that does any thing in secret, and he himself seeketh to be known openly. If thou do these things, shew thy self to the World.* Here his Brethren, which the next Verse tells us *did not believe in him,* seem to upbraid him with the Inconsistency of his carriage; as if he designed to be received for the *Messiah,* and yet was afraid to shew himself: To whom he justified his Conduct, (mentioned *v.* 1.) in the following verses; by telling them, *That the World* (meaning the Jews especially) *hated him, because he testified of it, that the works thereof are evil; And that his time was not yet fully come,* wherein to quit his reserve, and abandon himself freely to their Malice and Fury. Therefore, though he *went up unto the Feast,* it was *not openly; but as it were in secret, v.* 10. And here coming into the Temple about the middle of the | Feast, he [112] justifies his being sent from God; And that he had not done any thing against the Law in curing the man at the Pool of *Bethesda, v. John* V. 1– 16. on the Sabbath-day; Which, though done above a year and an half before, they made use of as a pretence to destroy him. But what was the true reason of seeking his Life, appears from what we have in this VII. *Chapter, v.* 25–34. *Then said some of them at* Jerusalem, *Is not this he whom they seek to kill? But lo, he speaketh boldly, and they say nothing unto him. Do the Rulers know indeed that this is the very Messiah? Howbeit, we know this man whence he is; But when the Messiah cometh, no man knoweth whence he is. Then cryed Jesus in the Temple, as he taught, ye both know me, and ye know whence I am: And I am not come of my self, but he that sent me is true, whom*

136   THE REASONABLENESS OF CHRISTIANITY

ye know not. But I know him, for I am from him, and he hath sent me. Then they sought [an occasion] *to take him, but no man laid hands on him, because his hour was not yet come. And many of the people believed on him, and said,*
[113] *when the Messiah cometh, will he do more miracles than these which this | man*
5 *hath done? The Pharisees heard that the people murmured such things concerning him; and the Pharisees and Chief Priests sent Officers to take him. Then said Jesus unto them, Yet a little while am I with you, and then I go to him that sent me: Ye shall seek me, and not find me; and where I am there ye cannot come. Then said the Jews among themselves, Whither will he go, that we*
10 *shall not find him?*

Here we find that the great fault in our Saviour, and the great Provocation to the Jews, was his being taken for the *Messiah*; and doing such things as made the People *believe in him*; *i. e.* believe that he was the *Messiah*. Here also our Saviour declares, in words very easie to be
15 understood, at least after his Resurrection, that he was the *Messiah*: For if he were *sent from God*, and did his Miracles by the Spirit of God, there could be no doubt but he was the *Messiah*. But yet this Declaration was in a way that the Pharisees and Priests could not lay hold on to make an Accusation of, to the disturbance of his Ministry, or the seizure of his
[114] Person, how much soever they desired it: For his time was | not yet
21 come. The Officers they had sent to Apprehend him, charmed with his Discourse, returned without laying hands on him, *v.* 45, 46. And when the Chief Priests asked them, *Why they brought him not?* They answered, *Never man spake like this man.* Whereupon the Pharisees reply, *Are ye also*
25 *deceived? Have any of the Rulers, or of the Pharisees believed on him? But this people, who know not the Law, are cursed.* This shews what was meant by *Believing on him*; *viz.* believing that he was the *Messiah*. For, say they, have any of the Rulers, who are skilled in the Law, or of the Devout and learned Pharisees, acknowledged him to be the *Messiah*? For as for those
30 who in the Division among the People concerning him, say, *That he is the Messiah*, they are ignorant and vile wretches, know nothing of the Scripture, and being accursed, are given up by God to be deceived by this Impostor, and to take him for the *Messiah*. Therefore, notwithstanding their desire to lay hold on him, he goes on; And *v.* 37, 38. *In the last and*
[115] *great day of the Feast, Jesus stood and cryed,* | *saying; If any man thirst, let him*
36 *come unto me and drink: He that believeth on me, as the Scripture hath said, out of his belly shall flow Rivers of living water.* And thus he here again declares himself to be the *Messiah*; But in the Prophetick stile; As we may see by the next Verse of the Chapter, and those places in the Old
40 Testament that these words of our Saviour refer to.

AS DELIVERED IN THE SCRIPTURES 137

In the next Chapter, *John* VIII. all that he says concerning himself, and what they were to believe, tends to this; *viz.* That he was sent from God his Father; And that if they did not believe that he was the *Messiah*, they should die in their sins: But this in a way, as St. *John* observes, *v.* 27. that they did not well understand. But our Saviour himself tells them, *v.* 28. *When ye have lift up the Son of Man, then shall ye know that I am he.*

Going from them, he Cures the Man born blind, whom meeting with again, after the Jews had questioned him, and cast him out, *John* IX. 3 5–3 8. Jesus *said to him, Dost thou believe on the Son of God? He answered, who is he, Lord, that I might believe on him? | And Jesus said unto him, Thou hast both seen him, and it is he that talketh with thee. And he said, Lord, I believe.* Here we see this man is pronounced a Believer, when all that was proposed to him to believe, was, that Jesus was *the Son of God*; Which was, as we have already shewn, to believe that he was the *Messiah*.

In the next Chapter, *John* X. 1–2 1. he declares the laying down of his Life for both Jews and Gentiles; But in a Parable, which they understood not, *v.* 6, 20.

As he was going to the Feast of the Dedication, the Pharisees ask him, *Luke* XVII. 20. *When the Kingdom of God, i. e.* of the *Messiah, should come?* He answers, that it should not come with Pomp, and Observation, and great Concourse; But that it was already begun amongst them. If he had stopt here, the sense had been so plain, that they could hardly have mistaken him; or have doubted, but that he meant, that the *Messiah* was already come, and amongst them; And so might have been prone to infer, that Jesus took upon him to be him. But here, as in | the place before taken notice of, subjoyning to this the future Revelation of himself, both in his coming to execute Vengeance on the Jews, and in his coming to Judgment mixed together, he so involved his sense, that it was not easie to understand him. And therefore the Jews came to him again in the Temple, *John* X. 2 3. and said, *How long dost thou make us doubt? If thou be the Christ tell us plainly. Jesus answered, I told you, and ye BELIEVED not: The works that I do in my Father's Name, they bear witness of me. But ye BELIEVED not, because ye are not of my sheep, as I told you.* The BELIEVING here, which he accuses them of not doing, is plainly their not BELIEVING him to be the *Messiah*, as the foregoing words evince, and in the same sense it is evidently meant in the following Verses of this Chapter. *Vid.* v. 4 1.

From hence *Jesus* going to *Bethabara*, and thence returning to *Bethany*; upon *Lazarus*'s Death, *John* XI. 2 5–27. Jesus said to *Martha, I am the Resurrection and the Life, he that believeth in me, though he were dead, yet he*

138   THE REASONABLENESS OF CHRISTIANITY

[118] *shall | live; and whosoever liveth, and believeth in me, shall not die for ever.* So I understand ἀποθάνῃ εἰς τὸν αἰῶνα, answerable to ζήσεται εἰς τὸν αἰῶνα of the *Septuagint*, *Gen.* III. 22 or *John* VI. 51. which we read right in our *English* Translation, *Live for ever.* But whether this saying of our Saviour
5 here can with truth be translated, *He that liveth and believeth in me, shall never die*, will be apt to be questioned. But to go on. *Believest thou this? She said unto him, Yea, Lord, I believe that thou art the* Messiah, *the Son of God, which should come into the World.* This she gives as a full Answer to our Saviour's Demands; This being that Faith, which whoever had, wanted
10 no more to make them Believers.

We may observe farther, in this same story of the raising of *Lazarus*, what Faith it was our Saviour expected; by what he says, *v.* 41, 42. *Father, I thank thee that thou hast heard me. And I know that thou hearest me always. But because of the people who stand by, I said it, that they may believe
15 that thou hast sent me.* And what the Consequence of it was, we may see,
[119] *v.* 45. *Then | many of the Jews who came to* Mary, *and had seen the things which Jesus did, believed on him*: Which belief was, that he was *sent from the Father*; which in other words was, that he was the *Messiah.* That this is the meaning, in the Evangelists, of the Phrase of *believing on him*, we have
20 a demonstration in the following words, *v.* 47, 48. *Then gathered the Chief Priests and Pharisees a Council, and said, what do we? For this man does many miracles; And if we let him alone, all men will BELIEVE ON HIM.* Those who here say, all men would BELIEVE ON HIM, were the Chief Priests and Pharisees his Enemies; who sought his Life; and therefore
25 could have no other sense nor thought of this Faith in him, which they spake of, but only the believing him to be the *Messiah*: And that that was their meaning, the adjoyning words shew. *If we let him alone, all the World will believe on him*; *i. e.* believe him to be the *Messiah. And the* Romans *will come and take away both our Place and Nation.* Which Reasoning of theirs
[120] was thus grounded. If we stand still, and let the People | *Believe on him*,
31 *i. e.* receive him for the *Messiah*; They will thereby take him and set him up for their King, and expect Deliverance by him; Which will draw the *Roman* Arms upon us, to the Destruction of us and our Country. The *Romans* could not be thought to be at all concerned in any other Belief
35 whatsoever, that the People might have on him. It is therefore plain, That *Believing on him*, was, by the Writers of the Gospel, understood to mean, *the believing him to be the Messiah. The* Sanhedrim *therefore*, v. 53, 54. *from that day forth consulted for to put him to death. Jesus therefore walked not yet* (for so the word ἔτι signifies, and so I think it ought here to be
40 translated) *boldly*, or open-fac'd *among the Jews*; *i. e.* of Jerusalem. Ἔτι

AS DELIVERED IN THE SCRIPTURES 139

cannot well here be translated *no more*, because within a very short time after, he appeared openly at the Passover, and by his Miracles and Speech declared himself more freely than ever he had done; And all the Week before his Passion Taught daily in the Temple, *Mat.* XX. 17. *Mark* X. 32. *Luke* XVIII. 31, *etc.* The meaning of this place | seems therefore to be [121] this: That his time being not yet come, he durst not yet shew himself 6 openly, and confidently, before the Scribes and Pharisees, and those of the *Sanhedrim* at *Jerusalem*, who were full of Malice against him, and had resolved his Death; *But went thence unto a Country near the Wilderness, into a City called* Ephraim, *and there continued with his Disciples*, to keep 10 himself out of the way till the Passover, *which was nigh at hand, v.* 55.

In his return thither, he takes the Twelve aside, and tells them before hand what should happen to him at *Jerusalem*, whither they were now going; And that all things that are written by the Prophets concerning the Son of Man, should be accomplished; That he should be betrayed to 15 the Chief Priests and Scribes; And that they should Condemn him to Death, and deliver him to the Gentiles; That he should be mocked, and spit on, and scourged, and put to Death; and the third day he should rise again. But St. *Luke* tells us, *Chap.* XVIII. 34. That the Apostles *understood none of these things, and this saying was hid from* | *them; neither knew they the* [122] *things which were spoken.* They believed him to be the Son of God, the 21 *Messiah* sent from the Father; But their Notion of the *Messiah* was the same with that which was entertained by the rest of the Jews; (*viz.*) That he should be a Temporal Prince and Deliverer. Accordingly we see, *Mark* X. 35. That even in this their last Journey with him to *Jerusalem*, two of 25 them, *James* and *John*, coming to him, and falling at his Feet, said, *Grant unto us, that we may sit, one on thy right hand, and the other on thy left hand, in thy Glory*; Or, as St. *Matthew* has it, *Chap.* XX. 21. *in thy Kingdom.* That which distinguished the Apostles from the unbelieving Jews was not any different Notion they had of the *Messiah* when he should come; But this, 30 that they believed he was come and that their master Jesus of Nazareth was he, the very *Messiah*: and so received him as their King and Lord.

And now the hour being come that the Son of Man should be glorified, he, without his usual Reserve, makes his Publick Entry into *Jerusalem, Riding on a Young Ass; As it is written, Fear not, Daughter of* 35 Sion, *behold, thy King cometh sitting on an Asses Colt.* But *these things*, says St. *John*, *Chap.* XII. 16. *his Disciples understood not at the first;* | *But when* [123] *Jesus was glorified, then remembred they that these things were written of him, and that they had done these things unto him.* Though the Apostles believed him to be the *Messiah*, yet there were many Occurrences of his Life which 40

140   THE REASONABLENESS OF CHRISTIANITY

they understood not, at the time when they happened, to be fore-told of the *Messiah*; which after his Ascension they found exactly to quadrate. Thus according as was foretold of him he rode into Jerusalem, *And all the People crying* Hosanna, *Blessed is the King of* Israel, *that cometh in the Name*
5 *of the Lord.* This was so open a Declaration of his being the *Messiah*, that *Luke* XIX. 39. *Some of the Pharisees from among the multitude said unto him, Master, rebuke thy Disciples.* But he was so far from stopping them, or disowning this their Acknowledgment of his being the *Messiah*, That he *said unto them, I tell you, that if these should hold their peace, the stones would*
10 *immediately cry out.* And again, upon the like occasion of their crying *Hosanna, to the Son of David*, in the Temple, *Mat.* XXI. 15, 16. When *the Chief Priests and Scribes were sore displeased, and said unto him, Hearest thou*
[124] *what they say? Jesus said unto | them, yea; Have ye never read, Out of the mouths of Babes and Sucklings thou hast perfected Praise?* And now, *v.* 14,
15 15. *He cures the Blind and the Lame* openly *in the Temple. And when the Chief Priests and Scribes saw the wonderful things that he did, and the Children crying in the Temple* Hosanna, *they were enraged.* One would not think, that after the multitude of Miracles that our Saviour had now been doing for above three Years together, that the curing the Lame and Blind
20 should so much move them. But we must remember, that though his Ministry had abounded with Miracles, yet the most of them had been done about *Galilee*, and in Parts remote from *Jerusalem*: There is but one left upon Record hitherto done in that City; And that had so ill a Reception, that they sought his Life for it; as we may read, *John* V. 16.
25 And therefore we hear not of his being at the next Passover, because he was there only privately, as an ordinary Jew: The reason whereof we may read, *John* VII. 1. *After these things, Jesus walked in* Galilee, *for he would not walk in* Jewry, *because the Jews sought to kill him.* |
[125]   Hence we may guess the reason why St. *John* omitted the mention of
30 his being at *Jerusalem* at the third Passover after his Baptism; probably because he did nothing memorable there. Indeed, when he was at the Feast of Tabernacles, immediately preceding this his last Passover, he cured the Man born blind: But it appears not to have been done in *Jerusalem* it self, but in the way as he retired to the Mount of *Olives*; for
35 there seems to have been no body by, when he did it, but his Apostles. Compare *v.* 2. with *v.* 8, 10. of *John* IX. This, at least, is remarkable; That neither the Cure of this Blind Man, nor that of the other Infirm Man, at the Passover above a twelve Month before at *Jerusalem*, was done in the sight of the Scribes, Pharisees, Chief Priests, or Rulers. Nor was it
40 without reason, that in the former part of his Ministry he was cautious of

AS DELIVERED IN THE SCRIPTURES 141

shewing himself to them to be the *Messiah*; But now that he was come to
the last Scene of his Life, and that the Passover brought | the appointed [126]
time wherein he was to compleat the Work he came for, in his Death and
Resurrection, he does many things in *Jerusalem* it self, before the face of
the Scribes, Pharisees, and whole Body of the Jewish Nation, to manifest 5
himself to be the *Messiah*. And, as St. *Luke* says, *Chap*. XIX. 47, 48. *He
taught daily in the Temple: But the Chief Priests, and the Scribes, and the
Chief of the People sought to destroy him; And could not find what they might
do, for all the People were very attentive to hear him.* What he taught, we are
not left to guess, by what we have found him constantly Preaching 10
elsewhere; But St. *Luke* tells us, *Chap*. XX. 1. *He taught in the Temple, and
Evangelized*; Or, as we translate it, *preached the Gospel*: Which, as we have
shewed, was the making known to them the Good News of the
Kingdom of the *Messiah*. And this we shall find he did, in what now
remains of his History. 15

In the first Discourse of his, which we find upon Record after this,
John XII. 20. *etc.* he fore-tells his Cruci|fixion; and the belief of all sorts, [127]
both *Jews* and *Gentiles*, on him after that. Whereupon the People say to
him, *v.* 34. *We have heard out of the Law, that the Messiah abideth for ever;
And how sayest thou, that the Son of Man must be lifted up? Who is this Son* 20
of Man? In his Answer he plainly designs himself, under the Name of
Light; which was what he had declared himself to them to be, the last
time that they had seen him in *Jerusalem*. For then at the Feast of
Tabernacles, but six Months before, he tells them in the very place
where he now is, *viz*. in the Temple, *I am the Light of the World;* 25
*whosoever follows me, shall not walk in darkness, but shall have the light of
Life*; As we may read, *John* VIII. 12. and IX. 5. He says, *As long as I am
in the World, I am the LIGHT of the World*. But neither here, nor any
where else, does he, even in these four or five last days of his Life
(though he knew his hour was come, and was prepared for his Death, 30
v. 27. And scrupled not to manifest himself to the Rulers of the Jews to
be the *Messiah*, by doing Miracles before them in the Tem|ple) ever [128]
once in direct words own himself to the Jews to be the *Messiah*;
Though by Miracles, and other ways, he did every where make it
known to them, so that it might be understood. 35

This could not be without some Reason; And the Preservation of his
Life, which he came now to *Jerusalem* on purpose to lay down, could not
be it. What other could it then be, but the same which had made him use
Caution in the former part of his Ministry; so to conduct himself, that he
might do the Work which he came for, and in all parts answer the 40

142 THE REASONABLENESS OF CHRISTIANITY

Character given of the *Messiah* in the Law and the Prophets? He had fulfilled the time of his Ministry; and now Taught, and did Miracles openly in the Temple, before the Rulers and the People, not fearing to be seized. But he would not be seized for any thing that might make him a
5 Criminal to the Government; And therefore he avoided giving those, who in the Division that was about him enclined towards him, occasion of Tumult for his sake; Or to the Jews his Enemies, matter of Just
[129] Accusation against him out of his own mouth, by | professing himself to be the *Messiah*, the King of *Israel* in direct words. It was enough, that by
10 words and deeds he declared it so to them, that they could not but understand him; Which 'tis plain they did, *Luke* XX. 16, 19. *Mat.* XXI. 45. But yet neither his Actions, which were only doing of Good; nor Words, which were Mystical and Parabolical; (As we may see, *Mat.* XXI. and XXII. And the Parallel places of *Mark* and *Luke*;) Nor any
15 of his ways of making himself known to be the *Messiah*, could be brought in Testimony, or urged against him, as opposite or dangerous to the Government. This preserved him from being Condemned as a Malefactor; and procured him a Testimony from the *Roman* Governour his Judge, that he was an Innocent Man, sacrificed to the Envy of the
20 *Jewish* Nation. So that he avoided saying that he was the *Messiah*, that to those who would consider his Life and Death after his Resurrection, he might the more clearly appear to be so.

It is farther to be remarked, that though he often appeals to the
[130] Testimony of his Miracles who he is, yet he never | tells the *Jews* that he
25 was born at *Bethlehem*; to remove the Prejudice that lay against him, whilst he passed for a *Galilean*, and which was urged as a Proof that he was not the *Messiah*, *John* VII. 41, 42. The healing of the Sick, and doing of Good miraculously, could be no Crime in him, nor Accusation against him: But the naming of *Bethlehem* for his Birth-place, might have
30 wrought as much upon the mind of *Pilate*, as it did on *Herod*'s; and have raised a Suspicion in the *Roman* Governour as Prejudicial to our Saviour's Innocence, as *Herod*'s was to the Children born there. His pretending to be born at *Bethlehem*, as it was liable to be explained by the *Jews*, could not have failed to have met with a sinister Interpretation in
35 the mind of *Pilate*; and would certainly have rendred *Jesus* suspected of some Criminal Design against the Government. And hence we see, that when *Pilate* asked him, *John* XIX. 9. *Whence art thou? Jesus gave him no answer.*

Whether our Saviour had not an Eye to this straitness, this narrow
40 room that was left to his Conduct, between the new Converts and the

AS DELIVERED IN THE SCRIPTURES   143

captious | Jews, when he says, *Luke* XII. 50. *I have a Baptism to be baptized* [131]
with, and πῶς συνέχομαι *how am I straitned till it be accomplished,* I leave to
be considered. *I am come to send fire on the Earth,* says our Saviour, *and
what if it be already kindled? i. e.* There begin already to be Divisions about
me, *v. John* VII. 12, 43. and IX. 16. and X. 19. And I have not the   5
freedom, the Latitude, to declare my self openly to be the *Messiah,*
though I am he, that must not be spoken out till after my Death. My way
to my Throne is closely hedged in on every side, and much straitned,
within which I must keep, till it bring me to my Cross in its due time and
manner; so that it do not cut short the time, nor cross the end of my   10
Ministry.

And therefore to keep up this inoffensive Character, and not to let it
come within the reach of Accident or Calumny, he withdrew with his
Apostles out of the Town every Evening; and kept himself retired out of
the way, *Luke* XXI. 37. *And in the day-time he was teaching in the Temple,* 15
*and every night he went out and abode in the Mount that is called the Mount of
Olives;* | That he might avoid all Concourse to him in the Night, and give [132]
no occasion of Disturbance, or Suspicion of himself in that great conflux
of the whole Nation of the *Jews,* now assembled in *Jerusalem* at the
Passover.   20

But to return to his Preaching in the Temple. He bids them, *John*
XII. 36. *To believe in the light whilst they have it.* And he tells them, *v.* 46. *I
am the light come into the World, that every one who believes in me should not
remain in darkness.* Which believing in him, was the believing him to be
the *Messiah,* as I have elsewhere shewed.   25

The next day, *Mat.* XXI. he rebukes them for not having believed *John*
the *Baptist,* who had testified that he was the *Messiah.* And then, in a
Parable, declares himself to be the *Son of God,* whom they should destroy;
And that for it God would take away the Kingdom of the *Messiah* from
them, and give it to the Gentiles. That they understood him thus, is plain 30
from *Luke* XX. 16. *And when they heard it, they said, God forbid.* And *v.* 19.
For they knew that he had spoken this Parable against them. |

Much to the same purpose was his next Parable concerning *the* [133]
Kingdom of Heaven, Mat. XXII. 1–10. That the Jews not accepting of the
Kingdom of the *Messiah,* to whom it was first offered, others should be 35
brought in.

The Scribes and Pharisees, and Chief Priests, not able to bear the
declaration he made of himself to be the *Messiah*; (by his Discourses and
Miracles *before* them, ἔμπροσθεν αὐτῶν, *John* XII. 37. which he had
never done before) impatient of his Preaching and Miracles; and being 40

144 THE REASONABLENESS OF CHRISTIANITY

not able otherwise to stop the increase of his Followers; (For, *said the Pharisees among themselves, perceive ye how ye prevail nothing? Behold, the World is gone after him, John* XII. 19. So that *the Chief Priests, and the Scribes, and the Chief of the People) sought to destroy him,* the first day of his
5 entrance into *Jerusalem, Luke* XIX. 47. The next day again they were intent upon the same thing, *Mark* XI. 17, 18. *And he taught* in the Temple; *And the Scribes, and the Chief Priests heard it, and sought how they might destroy him; For they feared him, because all the people were astonished at his Doctrine.* |

[134]   The next day but one, upon his telling them the Kingdom of the
11 *Messiah* should be taken from them; *The Chief Priests and Scribes sought to lay hands on him the same hour; and they feared the People, Luke* XX. 19. If they had so great a desire to lay hold on him, why did they not? They were the Chief Priests and the Rulers, the men of Power. The reason St.
15 *Luke* plainly tells us, in the next Verse: *And they watched him, and sent forth Spies, which should feign themselves just men, that they might take hold of his words; that so they might deliver him unto the Power and Authority of the Governour.* They wanted matter of Accusation against him, to the Power they were under. That they watched for; and that they would have been
20 glad of, if they could have *entangled him in his talk*; As St. *Matthew* expresses it, *Chap.* XXII. 15. If they could have laid hold on any word that had dropt from him, that might have rendred him guilty or suspected to the *Roman* Governour; That would have served their turn, to have laid hold upon him, with hopes to destroy him. For their Power
[135] not an|swering their Malice, they could not put him to Death by their
26 own Authority, without the Permission and Assistance of the Governour; as they confess, *John* XVIII. 31. *It is not lawful for us to put any man to Death.* This made them so earnest for a declaration in direct words, from his own mouth, that he was the *Messiah.* 'Twas not that they
30 would more have believed in him, for such a declaration of himself, than they did for his Miracles, or other ways of making himself known, which it appears they understood well enough. But they wanted plain direct words, such as might support an Accusation, and be of weight before an Heathen Judge. This was the Reason why they pressed him to speak out,
35 *John* X. 24. *Then came the Jews round about him, and said unto him, How long dost thou hold us in suspense? If thou be the Messiah, tell us PLAINLY,* παρρησία; *i. e.* in direct words: For that St. *John* uses it in that sense, we may see, *Chap.* XI. 11–14. Jesus saith to them, *Lazarus sleepeth.* His
39 Disciples said, *If he sleeps, he shall do well. Howbeit, Jesus spake of his Death;*
[136] *but they* | *thought he had spoken of taking of rest in sleep. Then said Jesus to*

AS DELIVERED IN THE SCRIPTURES 145

them plainly, παῤῥησία, Lazarus *is dead.* Here we see what is meant by παῤῥησία, PLAIN direct words, such as express the thing without a Figure; And so they would have had Jesus pronounce himself to be the *Messiah.* And the same thing they press again, *Mat.* XXVI. 63. The High-Priest adjuring him by the Living God, to tell them whether he were the 5 *Messiah,* the Son of God; As we shall have occasion to take notice by and by.

This we may observe in the whole management of their Design against his Life. It turned upon this; That they wanted and wished for a Declaration from him, in direct words, that he was the *Messiah*: 10 Something from his own mouth, that might offend the *Roman* Power, and render him Criminal to *Pilate.* In the 21st. Verse of this XX of *Luke, They asked him, saying, Master, we know that thou sayest and teachest rightly; neither acceptest thou the Person of any, but teachest the way of God truly. Is it lawful for us to give Tribute to* Cæsar *or no?* By this captious Question they 15 hoped to catch him, | which way soever he answered. For if he had said, [137] they ought to pay Tribute to *Cæsar*, 'twould be plain he allowed their Subjection to the *Romans*; And so in effect disowned himself to be their King and Deliverer: Whereby he would have contradicted, what his Carriage and Doctrine seemed to aim at, the Opinion that was spread 20 amongst the People, that he was the *Messiah.* This would have quash'd the Hopes, and destroyed the Faith of those who believed on him; and have turned the Ears and Hearts of the People from him. If on the other side, he answered *No,* it is not Lawful to pay Tribute to *Cæsar*; they had had out of his own mouth wherewithal to Condemn him before *Pontius* 25 *Pilate.* But St. *Luke* tells us, *v.* 23. *He perceived their Craftiness, and said unto them, Why tempt ye me? i. e.* Why do ye lay Snares for me? *Ye Hypocrites, shew me the Tribute-money*; So it is, *Mat.* XXII. 19. *Whose Image and Inscription has it? They said,* Cæsar's. *He said unto them, Render therefore to* Cæsar *the things that are* Cæsar's; *and to God the things that are* 30 *God's.* By the Wisdom and Caution of which unex|pected Answer, he [138] defeated their whole Design. *And they could not take hold of his words before the People; And they marvelled at his answer, and held their peace.* Luke XX. 26. *And leaving him, they departed, Mat.* XXII. 22.

He having by this Reply, (and what he answered to the *Sadducees* 35 concerning the Resurrection, And to the *Lawyer,* about the First Commandment, *Mark* XII.) Answered so little to their Satisfaction or Advantage; they durst ask him no more Questions, any of them. And now their mouths being stop'd, he himself begins to Question them about the *Messiah*; Asking the *Pharisees,* Mat. XXII. 41. *What think ye of* 40

146   THE REASONABLENESS OF CHRISTIANITY

the Messiah, whose Son is he? They say unto him, The Son of David. Wherein, though they answered right, yet he shews them in the following words, that however they pretended to be Studiers and Teachers of the Law, yet they understood not clearly the Scriptures concerning the *Messiah*; And
5 thereupon he sharply rebukes their Hypocrisie, Vanity, Pride, Malice, Covetousness, and Ignorance; And particularly tells them, *v.* 13. *Yet shut*
[139] *up the Kingdom of Heaven against | men: For ye neither go in your selves, nor suffer ye them that are entring, to go in.* Whereby he plainly declares to them, that the *Messiah* was come, and his Kingdom began; But that they
10 refused to believe in him themselves, and did all they could to hinder others from believing in him; As is manifest throughout the New Testament: The History whereof sufficiently explains what is meant here by *The Kingdom of Heaven,* Which the *Scribes* and *Pharisees* would neither go into themselves, nor suffer others to enter into. And they could not
15 choose but understand him, though he named not himself in the case.

Provoked anew by his Rebukes, they get presently to Council, *Mat.* XXVI. *Then assembled together the Chief Priest, and the Scribes, and the Elders of the People, unto the Palace of the High-Priest, who was called* Caiphas, *and consulted that they might take Jesus by subtilty, and kill him.*
20 *But they said, Not on the Feast-day, lest there by an Uproar among the People. For they feared the People,* says St. *Luke, Chap.* XXII. 2.

Having in the Night got Jesus into their Hands, by the Treachery of
[140] *Ju|das,* they presently led him away bound to *Annas,* the Father-in-Law of *Caiphas,* the High-Priest, probably having examined him, and getting
25 nothing out of him for his Purpose, sends him away to *Caiphas, v.* 24. where the Chief Priests, the Scribes and the Elders were assembled, *Mat.* XXVI. 57. *John* XVIII. 13, 19. *The High-Priest then asked Jesus of his Disciples, and of his Doctrine. Jesus answered him, I spake openly to the World; I ever taught in the Synagogue, and in the Temple, whither the Jews*
30 *always resort; And in secret have I said nothing.* A Proof that he had not in private to his Disciples declared himself in express words to be the *Messiah,* the Prince. But he goes on. *Why askest thou me? Ask Judas,* who has been always with me. *Ask them who heard me, what I have said unto them; behold, they know what I said.* Our Saviour we see here warily
35 declines, for the Reasons above mentioned, all Discourse of his Doctrine. The *Sanhedrim, Mat.* XXVI. 59. *Sought false Witness against him to put him to death*: But when *they found none that were sufficient,* or came up to the Point they desired; which was to have something against
39 him to take away his Life, (For so I think the words ἴσαι and ἴση mean,
[141] *Mark* XIV. 56, 59.) They try again | what they can get out of him himself,

AS DELIVERED IN THE SCRIPTURES 147

concerning his being the *Messiah*; Which if he owned in express words, they thought they should have enough against him at the Tribunal of the *Roman* Governour, to make him *Læsæ Majestatis reum*, and so to take away his Life. They therefore say to him, *Luke* XXII. 67. *If thou be the Messiah, tell us*. Nay, as St. *Matthew* hath it, the High-Priest adjures him by the 5 Living God to tell them whether he were the *Messiah*. To which our Saviour replies: *If I tell you, ye will not believe; And if I ask you, ye will not answer me, nor let me go*. If I tell you, and prove to you, by the Testimony given of me from Heaven, and by the Works that I have done among you, you will not believe in me, that I am the *Messiah*. Or if I should ask 10 you where the *Messiah* is to be Born; and what State he should come in; how he should appear, and other things that you think in me are not reconcileable with the *Messiah*; You will not answer me, and let me go, as one that has no pretence to be the *Messiah*, and you are not afraid should be received for such. But yet | I tell you, *Hereafter shall the Son of Man sit* [142] *on the right hand of the Power of God*, v. 70. *Then said they all, Art thou then* 16 *the Son of God? And he said unto them, ye say that I am*. By which Discourse with them, related at large here by St. *Luke*, it is plain, that the Answer of our Saviour, set down by St. *Matthew, Chap*. XXVI. 64. in these words, *Thou hast said*; And by St. *Mark, Chap*. XIV. 62. in these, *I am*; Is an 20 Answer only to this Question, *Art thou then the Son of God?* And not to that other, *Art thou the Messiah?* Which preceded, and he had answered to before: Though *Matthew* and *Mark*, contracting the story, set them down together, as if making but one Question; omitting all the intervening Discourse; Whereas 'tis plain out of St. *Luke*, that they were 25 two distinct Questions, to which *Jesus* gave two distinct Answers. In the first whereof, he, according to his usual Caution, declined saying in plain express words, that he was the *Messiah*; though in the latter he owned himself to be *the Son of God*. Which, though they being *Jews*, understood to signifie the *Messiah*; Yet he | knew could be no Legal or Weighty [143] Accusation against him before a Heathen; and so it proved. For upon his 31 answering to their Question, *Art thou then the Son of God? Ye say that I am*; They cry out, *Luke* XXII. 71. *What need we any further witnesses? For we our selves have heard out of his own mouth*: And so thinking they had enough against him, they hurry him away to *Pilate. Pilate* asking them, 35 *John*, XVIII. 29–32. *What Accusation bring you against this man? They answered, and said, if he were not a Malefactor, we would not have delivered him up unto thee*. Then said *Pilate* unto them, *Take ye him, and Judge him according to your Law*. But this would not serve their turn, who aimed at his Life, and would be satisfied with nothing else. *The Jews therefore said* 40

148   THE REASONABLENESS OF CHRISTIANITY

unto him, It is not lawful for us to put any man to death. And this was also, *That the saying of Jesus might be fulfilled which he spake, signifying what Death he should dye.* Pursuing therefore their Design, of making him appear to *Pontius Pilate* guilty of Treason against *Cæsar*, Luke XXIII. 2.

[144] *They | began to accuse him, saying; We found this Fellow perverting the*
6   *Nation, and forbidding to give Tribute to* Cæsar; *saying, that he himself is the Messiah the King*: All which were Inferences of theirs, from his saying, he was *the Son of God*: Which *Pontius Pilate* finding (for 'tis consonant, that he examined them to the precise words he had said) their Accusation had
10 no weight with him. However, the Name of King being suggested against Jesus, he thought himself concerned to search it to the bottom. *John* XVIII. 3 3–3 7. *Then* Pilate *entred again into the Judgment-Hall, and called Jesus, and said unto him, Art thou the King of the Jews? Jesus answered him, Sayest thou this of thy self, or did others tell thee of me?* Pilate *answered,*
15 *am I a Jew? Thine own Nation and the Chief Priest have delivered thee unto me: What hast thou done? Jesus answered, My Kingdom is not of this World: If my Kingdom were of this World, then would my servants fight, that I should not be delivered to the Jews: But my Kingdom is not from hence.* Pilate *therefore*
[145] *said unto him, Art thou a King then? Jesus answered, | Thou sayest that I am a*
20 *King. For this end was I born, and for this cause came I into the World, that I should bear witness to the Truth: Every one that is of the Truth heareth my voice.* In this Dialogue between our Saviour and *Pilate*, we may observe,

1. That being asked, whether he were *the King of the Jews?* He answers so, that though he deny it not, yet he avoided giving the least Umbrage,
25 that he had any Design upon the Government. For though he allows himself to be a King, yet to obviate any suspicion, he tells *Pilate His Kingdom is not of this World*; And evidences it by this, that if he had pretended to any Title to that Country, his followers, which were not a few, and were forward enough to believe him their King, would have
30 fought for him; if he had had a mind to set himself up by force, or his Kingdom were so to be erected. *But my Kingdom*, says he, *is not from hence*; Is not of this fashion, or of this place.

2. *Pilate*, being by his words and circumstances satisfied that he laid no Claim to his Province, or meant any Disturbance of the Government,
[146] was | yet a little surprized to hear a Man, in that poor Garb, without
36 Retinue, or so much as a Servant or a Friend, own himself to be a King; And therefore asks him, with some kind of wonder, *Art thou a King then?*

3. That our Saviour declares, that his great business into the World was, to testifie and make good this great Truth, that he was a King; *i. e.* in
40 other words, that he was the *Messiah*.

AS DELIVERED IN THE SCRIPTURES 149

4. That whoever were followers of Truth, and got into the way of Truth and Happiness, received this Doctrine concerning him, *viz.* That he was the *Messiah* their King.

Pilate being thus satisfied, that he neither meant, nor could there arise any harm from his pretence, whatever it was, to be a King; Tells the Jews, *v.* 38. *I find no fault in this man.* But the Jews were the more fierce, *Luke* XXIII. 5. saying, *He stirreth up the people* to Sedition, by *his Preaching through all* Jewry, *beginning from* Galilee *to this place.* And then *Pilate,* learning that he was of *Galilee, Herod's* Jurisdiction, sent him to *Herod;* to whom also *the Chief Priests and Scribes,* v. 10. *vehemently | accused him.* [147] *Herod* finding all their Accusations either false or frivolous, thought our Saviour a bare Object of Contempt; And so turning him only into Ridicule, sent him back to *Pilate:* Who calling unto him the Chief Priests, and the Rulers, and the People, *v.* 14. *Said unto them, Ye have brought this man unto me, as one that perverteth the People; And behold, I having examined him before you, have found no fault in this man, touching these things whereof ye accuse him; No, nor yet* Herod; *for I sent you to him: And so nothing worthy of Death is done by him*: And therefore he would have released him. *For he knew the Chief Priests had delivered him through envy, Mark* XV. 10. And when they demanded *Barrabbas* to be released, but as for Jesus, cryed, Crucifie him; *Luke* XXIII. 22. Pilate *said unto them the third time, Why? What evil hath he done? I have found no cause of death in him; I will therefore chastise him, and let him go.*

We may observe in all this whole Prosecution of the Jews, that they would fain have got it out of *Jesus*'s own mouth, in express words, that he | was the *Messiah*: Which not being able to do with all their Art and [148] Endeavour; All the rest that they could alledge against him, not amounting to a Proof before *Pilate,* that he claimed to be King of the Jews; or that he had caused or done any thing towards a Mutiny or Insurrection among the People; (for upon these two, as we see, their whole Charge turned) *Pilate* again and again pronounced him innocent: For so he did a fourth, and a fifth time; bringing him out to them, after he had whip'd him, *John* XIX. 4, 6. And after all, *When* Pilate *saw that he could prevail nothing, but that rather a Tumult was made, he took Water, and washed his hands before the multitude, saying, I am innocent of the Blood of this just man; see you to it, Mat.* XXVII. 24. Which gives us a clear reason of the cautious and wary Conduct of our Saviour; in not declaring himself, in the whole course of his Ministry, so much as to his Disciples, much less to the Multitude or the Rulers of the Jews, in express words, to be the *Messiah* the King: And why he kept himself always in Prophetical

150 THE REASONABLENESS OF CHRISTIANITY

[149] or Parabolical terms: (He and his Dis|ciples Preaching only the Kingdom of God, *i. e.* of the *Messiah*, to be come) And left to his Miracles to declare who he was; Though this was the Truth, which he came into the World, as he says himself, *John* XVIII. 37. to testifie, and which his Disciples
5 were to believe.

When *Pilate*, satisfied of his Innocence, would have released him; And the Jews persisted to cry out, *Crucifie him, Crucifie him, John* XIX. 6. Pilate *says to them, Take ye him your selves, and Crucifie him: For I do not find any fault in him.* The Jews then, since they could not make him a State-
10 Criminal, by alledging his saying that he was *the Son of God*; say, by their Law it was a Capital Crime, *v.* 7. *The Jews answered to* Pilate, *We have a Law, and by our Law he ought to die; because he made himself the Son of God,* *i. e.* because, by saying he is the *Son of God*, he has made himself the *Messiah*, the Prophet which was to come. For we find no other Law but
15 that against False Prophets, *Deut.* XVIII. 20. whereby *making himself the Son of God* deserved Death. After this, *Pilate* was the more desirous to release him, *v.* 12, 13. *But the Jews cried out, saying, If thou let this man go, thou art not* Cæsar's *Friend: Whosoever maketh himself a King, speaketh against* Cæsar. Here we see the stress of their Charge against Jesus;
[150] whereby | they hoped to take away his Life; *viz.* That he *made himself*
21 *King.* We see also upon what they grounded this Accusation, *viz.* Because he had owned himself to be *the Son of God.* For he had, in their hearing, never made or professed himself to be a King. We see here likewise the reason why they were so desirous to draw, from his own
25 mouth, a Confession in express words that he was the *Messiah*; *viz.* That they might have what might be a clear Proof that he did so. And last of all, we see the reason why, though in Expressions, which they understood, he owned himself to them to be the *Messiah*; yet he avoided declaring it to them, in such words as might look Criminal at *Pilate's*
30 Tribunal. He owned himself to be the *Messiah* plainly to the Under-standing of the *Jews*; But in ways that could not, to the Understanding of *Pilate*, make it appear that he laid claim to the Kingdom of *Judea*, or went about to make himself King of that Country. But whether his saying, that he was *the Son of God*, was Criminal by their Law, that *Pilate* troubled not
35 himself about. |

[151] He that considers what *Tacitus, Suetonius, Seneca, de Beneficiis, lib.* 3. *cap.* 26. says of *Tiberius* and his Reign, will find how necessary it was for our Saviour, if he would not dye as a Criminal and a Traytor, to take great heed to his words and actions; that he did, or said not any thing,
40 that might be offensive, or give the least Umbrage to the *Roman*

AS DELIVERED IN THE SCRIPTURES 151

Government. It behoved an Innocent Man, who was taken notice of for something Extraordinary in him, to be very wary under a jealous and cruel Prince, who encouraged Informations, and filled his Reign with Executions for Treason; Under whom words spoken innocently, or in jest, if they could be misconstrued, were made Treason, and prosecuted 5 with a Rigor, that made it always the same thing to be accused and condemned. And therefore we see, that when the *Jews* told *Pilate*, *John* XIX. 12. That he should not be a Friend to *Cæsar*, if he let *Jesus* go; (For that whoever made himself King, was a Rebel against *Cæsar*;) He asks them no more, whether they would take *Barrabbas*, and spare *Jesus*; But 10 (though | against his Conscience) gives him up to Death, to secure his [152] own Head.

One thing more there is, that gives us light into this wise and necessarily cautious management of himself, which manifestly agrees with it, and makes a part of it: And that is, the choice of his Apostles; 15 exactly suited to the design and fore-sight of the Necessity of keeping the declaration of the Kingdom of the *Messiah*, which was now expected, within certain general terms during his Ministry. It was not fit to open himself too plainly or forwardly, to the heady Jews, that he himself was the *Messiah*; That was to be left to the Observation of those who would 20 attend to the Purity of his Life, and the Testimony of his Miracles, and the Conformity of all with the Predictions concerning him. By these marks those he lived amongst were to find it out without an express promulgation that he was the *Messiah*, till after his Death. His Kingdom was to be opened to them by degrees, as well to prepare them to receive 25 it, as to enable him to be long enough amongst them; to perform what was the work of the *Messiah* to be done; and fulfil all those several parts of what | was foretold of him in the Old Testament, and we see applyed to [153] him in the New.

The *Jews* had no other thoughts of their *Messiah*, but of a Mighty 30 Temporal Prince, that should raise their Nation into an higher degree of Power, Dominion, and Prosperity than ever it had enjoyed. They were filled with the expectation of a Glorious Earthly Kingdom. It was not therefore for a Poor Man, the Son of a Carpenter, and (as they thought) born in *Galilee*, to pretend to it. None of the *Jews*, no not his Disciples, 35 could have born this; if he had expresly avowed this at first, and began his Preaching, and the opening of his Kingdom this way; Especially if he had added to it, that in a Year or two he should dye an ignominious Death upon the Cross. They are therefore prepared for the Truth by degrees. First, *John the Baptist* tells them, *The Kingdom of God* (a name by which 40

152   THE REASONABLENESS OF CHRISTIANITY

the Jews called the Kingdom of the *Messiah*) *is at hand*. Then our Saviour comes, and he tells them *of the Kingdom of God*; Sometimes that it is at
[154] hand, and upon some occasions, | that it is come; but says in his Publick Preaching little or nothing of himself. Then come the Apostles and
5 Evangelists after his Death, and they in express words teach what his Birth, Life, and Doctrine had done before, and had prepared the well-disposed to receive; *viz.* That *Jesus is the Messiah*.

    To this Design and Method of Publishing the Gospel, was the choice of the Apostles exactly adjusted; A company of Poor, Ignorant, Illiterate
10 Men; who, as Christ himself tells us, *Mat.* XI. 2 5. and *Luke* X. 2 1. Were not of the *Wise and Prudent* Men of the World: They were, in that respect, but meer Children. These, convinced by the Miracles they saw him daily do, and the unblameable Life he led, might be disposed to believe him to be the *Messiah*: And though they with others expected a
15 Temporal Kingdom on Earth, might yet rest satisfied in the truth of their Master (who had honoured them with being near his Person) that it would come, without being too inquisitive after the time, manner, or seat of his Kingdom; As men of Letters, more studied in their Rabbins,
[155] or men | of Business, more versed in the World, would have been
20 forward to have been. Men great, or wise, in Knowledge or ways of the World, would hardly have been kept from prying more narrowly into his Design and Conduct; Or from questioning him about the ways and measures he would take, for ascending the Throne; and what means were to be used towards it, and when they should in earnest set about it. Abler
25 men, of higher Births or Thought, would hardly have been hindred from whispering, at least to their Friends and Relations, that their Master was the *Messiah*; And that though he concealed himself to a fit Opportunity, and till things were ripe for it, yet they should ere long see him break out of his Obscurity, cast off the Cloud, and declare himself, as he was, King
30 of *Israel*. But the ignorance and lowness of these good poor men made them of another temper. They went along in an implicite trust on him, punctually keeping to his Commands, and not exceeding his Commis-sion. When he sent them to Preach the Gospel, He bid them Preach *The*
[156] *Kingdom of God* to be at hand; And that | they did, without being more
35 particular than he had ordered; or mixing their own Prudence with his Commands, to promote the Kingdom of the *Messiah*. They preached it, without giving, or so much as intimating that their Master was he: Which men of another Condition, and an higher Education, would scarce have forborn to have done. When he asked them, who they
40 thought him to be; And *Peter* answered, *The Messiah, the Son of God, Mat.*

AS DELIVERED IN THE SCRIPTURES 153

XVI. 16. He plainly shews, by the following words, that he himself had not told them so; And at the same time, *v.* 20. forbids them to tell this their Opinion of him, to any body. How obedient they were to him in this, we may not only conclude from the silence of the Evangelists concerning any such thing, published by them any where before his Death; but from the exact Obedience three of them paid to a like Command of his. He takes *Peter, James,* and *John* into a Mountain; And there *Moses* and *Elias* coming to him, he is transfigured before them: *Mat.* XVII. 9. He charges them, saying; *See that ye tell no man what you have | seen, till the Son of Man shall be risen from the dead.* And St. *Luke* tell us, what punctual Observers they were of his Orders in this case: *Chap.* IX. 36.*They kept it close, and told no man, in those days, any of those things which they had seen.*

Whether twelve other men, of quicker Parts, and of a Station or Breeding which might have given them any Opinion of themselves, or their own Abilities, would have been so easily kept from medling beyond just what was prescribed them, in a matter they had so much Interest in; and have said nothing of what they might in Humane Prudence have thought would have contributed to their Master's Reputation, and made way for his advancement to his Kingdom; I leave it to be considered. And it may suggest matter of Meditation, whether St. *Paul* was not for this reason, by his Learning, Parts, and warmer Temper, better fitted for an Apostle after, than during our Saviour's Ministry: And therefore, though a chosen Vessel, was not by the Divine Wisdom called till after Christ's Resurrection. |

I offer this only as a Subject of magnifying the Admirable Contrivance of the Divine Wisdom, in the whole Work of our Redemption, as far as we are able to trace it by the foot-steps which God hath made visible to Humane Reason. For though it be as easie to Omnipotent Power to do all things by an immediate over-ruling Will; and so to make any Instruments work, even contrary to their Nature, in subserviency to his ends; Yet his Wisdom is not usually at the expence of Miracles (if I may so say) but only in cases that require them, for the evidencing of some Revelation or Mission to be from him. He does constantly (unless where the confirmation of some Truth requires it otherwise) bring about his Purposes by means operating according to their Natures. If it were not so, the course and evidence of things would be confounded; Miracles would lose their name and force, and there could be no distinction between Natural and Supernatural.

There had been no room left to see and admire the Wisdom, as well as

154   THE REASONABLENESS OF CHRISTIANITY

[159] Innocence, of our Saviour; if he had rashly | every where exposed himself
to the Fury of the Jews, and had always been preserved by a miraculous
suspension of their Malice, or a miraculous rescuing him out of their
Hands. It was enough for him once to escape from the men of *Nazareth*,
5   who were going to throw him down a Precipice, for him never to Preach
to them again. Our Saviour had multitudes that followed him for the
Loaves; Who barely seeing the Miracles that he did, would have made
him King. If to the Miracles he did, he had openly added in express
words, that he was the *Messiah*, and the King they expected to deliver
10   them; he would have had more Followers, and warmer in the Cause, and
readier to set him up at the Head of a Tumult. These indeed, God, by a
miraculous Influence, might have hindred from any such Attempt: But
then Posterity could not have believed that the Nation of the *Jews* did at
that time expect the *Messiah*, their King and Deliverer; Or that *Jesus*, who
15   declared himself to be that King and Deliverer, shewed any Miracles
[160] amongst them, to convince them of it; Or did any thing worthy to | make
him be credited or received. If he had gone about Preaching to the
multitude which he drew after him, that he was the *Messiah, the King of
Israel*; and this had been evidenced to *Pilate*; God could indeed, by a
20   Supernatural Influence upon his mind, have made *Pilate* pronounce him
Innocent; And not Condemn Him as a Malefactor, Who had openly, for
three Years together, preached Sedition to the People, and endeavoured
to perswade them that he was the *Messiah their King*, of the Blood-Royal
of *David*, come to deliver them. But then I ask, whether Posterity would
25   not either have suspected the Story, or that some Art had been used to
gain that Testimony from *Pilate*? Because he could not (for nothing)
have been so favourable to *Jesus*, as to be willing to release so Turbulent
and Seditious a Man; to declare him Innocent; and to cast the blame and
guilt of his Death, as unjust, upon the Envy of the Jews.
30   But now the Malice of the Chief Priests, Scribes, and Pharisees; the
Headiness of the Mob, animated with hopes, and raised with miracles;
[161] *Judas's* | Treachery, and *Pilate's* care of his Government, and of the Peace
of his Province, all working Naturally as they should; *Jesus*, by the
admirable wariness of his Carriage, and an extraordinary Wisdom visible
35   in his whole Conduct, weathers all these Difficulties, does the Work he
comes for, uninterruptedly goes about Preaching his full appointed time,
sufficiently manifests himself to be the *Messiah* in all the Particulars the
Scriptures had foretold of him; And when his hour is come, suffers
Death; But is acknowledged both by *Judas* that betrayed, and *Pilate* that
40   condemned him, to dye innocent. For, to use his own words, *Luke*

AS DELIVERED IN THE SCRIPTURES 155

XXIV. 46. *Thus it is written, and thus it behoved the Messiah to suffer.* And of his whole Conduct, we have a Reason and clear Resolution in those words to St. *Peter, Mat.* XXVI. 53. *Thinkest thou that I cannot now pray to my Father, and he shall presently give me more than twelve Legions of Angels? But how then shall the Scripture be fulfilled, that thus it must be?* 5

X Having this clew to guide us, let us now observe how our Saviour's Preach|ing and Conduct comported with it, in the last Scene of his Life. [162] How cautious he has been in the former part of his Ministry, we have already observed. We never find him to use the Name of the *Messiah* but once, till he now came to *Jerusalem* this last Passover. Before this, his 10 Preaching and Miracles were less at *Jerusalem* (where he used to make but very short stays) than any where else. But now he comes six days before the Feast, and is every day in the Temple Teaching; And there publickly heals the Blind and the Lame, in the presence of the *Scribes, Pharisees,* and *Chief Priests.* The time of his Ministry drawing to an end, and his hour 15 coming, he cared not how much the Chief Priests, Elders, Rulers, and the *Sanhedrim* were provoked against him by his Doctrine and Miracles; He was as open and bold in his Preaching and doing the Works of the *Messiah* now at *Jerusalem,* and in the sight of the Rulers, and of all the People, as he had been before cautious and reserved there, and careful to 20 be little taken notice of in that place, and not to come in their way more than needs. | All that he now took care of, was, not what they should [163] think of him, or design against him, (for he knew they would seize him) But to say or do nothing that might be a just matter of Accusation against him, or render him Criminal to the Governour. But as for the Grandees 25 of the *Jewish* Nation, he spares them not, but sharply now reprehends their miscarriages publickly in the Temple; where he calls them, more than once, Hypocrites; As is to be seen, *Mat.* XXIII. And concludes all with no softer a Compellation, than *Serpents* and *Generation of Vipers.*

After this severe Reproof of the *Scribes* and *Pharisees,* being retired with 30 his Disciples into the *Mount of Olives,* over against the Temple; and there fore-telling the Destruction of it; His Disciples ask him, *Mat.* XXIV. 3. *etc. When it should be, and what should be the signs of his coming?* He says to them, *Take heed that no man deceive you: For many shall come in my Name;* *i. e.* taking on them the Name and Dignity of the *Messiah,* which is only 35 mine; saying, *I am the Messiah, and shall deceive many.* But be not you by them | mislead, nor by Persecution driven away from this Fundamental [164] Truth, That I am the *Messiah; For many shall be scandalized,* and Apostatize, *but he that endures to the end, the same shall be saved: And this Gospel of the Kingdom shall be preached in all the World: i. e.* The good 40

156 THE REASONABLENESS OF CHRISTIANITY

News of me, the *Messiah*, and my Kingdom, shall be spread through the World. This was the great and only Point of Belief they were warned to stick to; And this is inculcated again, *v.* 23–26. and *Mark* XIII. 21–23. with this Emphatical Application to them in both these Evangelists,

5 *Behold, I have told you before-hand*; remember ye are fore-warned.

This was in his Answer to the Apostles Enquiry concerning his *Coming, and the end of the World, v.* 3. For so we translate τῆς συντελείας τοῦ αἰῶνος; We must understand the Disciples here to put their Question, according to the Notion and way of speaking of the *Jews.* For they had

10 two *Worlds*, as we translate it, ὁ νῦν αἰὼν καὶ ὁ μέλλων αἰών; The *present World*, and the *World to come.* The Kingdom of God, as they called it, or

[165] the time of the *Mes|siah*, they called ὁ μέλλων αἰών, *the World to come*, which they believed was to put an end to *this world*: And that then the Just should be raised from the Dead; to enjoy, in that *new World*, a

15 Happy Eternity, with those of the Jewish Nation who should be then living.

These two things, *viz.* The visible and powerful appearance of his Kingdom, and the end of the World, being confounded in the Apostles Question, Our Saviour does not separate them, nor distinctly reply to

20 them apart; But leaving the Enquirers in the common Opinion, answers at once concerning his coming to take Vengeance of the *Jewish* Nation, and put an end to their Church, Worship, and Commonwealth; Which was their ὁ νῦν αἰών, *present World*, which they counted should last till the *Messiah* came: And so it did, and then had an end put to it. And to this he

25 joyns his last coming to Judgment, in the Glory of his Father, to put a final end to this World, and all the Dispensation belonging to the Posterity of *Adam* upon Earth. This joyning them together, made his

[166] Answer obscure, and | hard to be understood by them then; Nor was it safe for him to speak plainer of his Kingdom, and the Destruction of

30 *Jerusalem*; unless he had a mind to be accused for having Designs against the Government. For *Judas* was amongst them: And whether no other but his Apostles were comprehended under the name of *his Disciples*, who were with him at this time, one cannot determine. Our Saviour therefore speaks of his Kingdom in no other stile but that which he had all along

35 hitherto used, *viz. The Kingdom of God*; Luke XXI. 31. *When you see these things come to pass, know ye that the Kingdom of God is nigh at hand.* And continuing on his Discourse with them, he has the same Expression, *Mat.* XXV. 1. *Then the Kingdom of Heaven shall be like unto ten Virgins.* At the end of the following Parable of the Talents, he adds, *v.* 31. *When the*

40 *Son of Man shall come in his Glory, and all the holy Angels with him, then shall*

AS DELIVERED IN THE SCRIPTURES 157

he sit upon the Throne of his Glory, and before him shall be gathered all the Nations. And he shall set the Sheep on his right hand, and the Goats on his left. Then shall the KING | say, etc. Here he describes to his Disciples the [167] appearance of his Kingdom, wherein he will shew himself *a King* in Glory upon his Throne; But this in such a way, and so remote, and so 5 unintelligible to a Heathen Magistrate; That if it had been alledged against him, it would have seemed rather the Dream of a crazy Brain, than the Contrivance of an Ambitious or Dangerous man designing against the Government: The way of expressing what he meant, being in the Prophetick stile; which is seldom so plain; as to be understood, till 10 accomplished. 'Tis plain, that his Disciples themselves comprehended not what Kingdom he here spoke of, from their Question to him after his Resurrection, *Wilt thou at this time restore again the Kingdom to Israel?* It may be worth while on occasion of what our Saviour says here, *Mat.* XXV. 31. to observe that where he speaks of the appearance of his 15 Kingdom at the day of Judgment he names the Son of Man: But in other places speaking of his Kingdom under the title of the Kingdom of God and Kingdom of Heaven, he never mentions him self as King of that Kingdom, unless to the Eleven once just before his passion.

Having finished these Discourses, he takes Order for the Passover, and 20 eats it with his Disciples; And at Supper tells them, that one of them should betray him: And adds, *John* XIII. 19. *I tell it you now, before it come, that when it is come to pass, you may know that I am.* He does not say out the *Messiah*; *Judas* should not have that to | say against him if he would; [168] Though that be the sense in which he uses this Expression, ἐγώ εἰμι, *I am,* 25 more than once. And that this is the meaning of it, is clear from *Mark* XIII. 6. *Luke* XXI. 8. In both which Evangelists the words are, *For many shall come in my Name, saying,* ἐγώ εἰμι, *I am*: The meaning whereof we shall find explained in the parallel place of St. *Matthew, Chap.* XXIV. 5. *For many shall come in my Name, saying,* ἐγώ εἰμι ὁ Χριστός, *I am the Messiah.* 30 Here in this place of *John* XIII. Jesus fore-tells what should happen to him, *viz.* That he should be betrayed by *Judas*; adding this Prediction to the many other Particulars of his Death and Suffering, which he had at other times foretold to them. And here he tells them the reason of these his Predictions, *viz.* That afterwards they might be a confirmation to their 35 Faith. And what was it that he would have them believe, and confirmed in the belief of? Nothing but this, ὅτι ἐγώ εἰμι, *that he was the Messiah.* The same reason he gives, *John* XIV. 28. *You have heard, how I said unto you, I go away, and come again unto you: And | now I have told you before it come to pass,* [169] *that when it is come to pass, ye might believe.* 40

158   THE REASONABLENESS OF CHRISTIANITY

When *Judas* had left them, and was gone out, he talks a little freer to them of his Glory, and his Kingdom, than ever he had done before. For now he speaks plainly of himself, and his Kingdom, *John* XIII. 31. *Therefore when he* [Judas] *was gone out, Jesus said, Now is THE SON OF* 5 *MAN glorified, and God is also glorified in him. And if God be glorified in him, God shall also glorifie him in himself, and shall straitway glorifie him.* And *Luke* XXII. 29. *And I will appoint unto you a Kingdom, as my Father hath appointed unto ME; that ye may eat and drink with me at my Table in MY KINGDOM.* Though he has every where all along through his 10 Ministry preached the *Gospel of the Kingdom*; and nothing else but that and Repentance, and the Duties of a good Life; Yet it has been always *the Kingdom of God*, and *the Kingdom of Heaven*: And I do not remember, that any where, till now, he uses any such expression, as *MY KINGDOM*. But here now he speaks in the first Person, *I WILL* [170] *APPOINT YOU A | KINGDOM*; and *IN MY KINGDOM*: And this we 16 see is only to the Eleven, now *Judas* was gone from them.

With these Eleven, whom he was now just leaving, he has a long Discourse to comfort them for their loss of him; And to prepare them for the Persecution of the World; And to exhort them to keep his 20 Commandments, and to love one another. And here one may expect all the Articles of Faith should be laid down plainly; if any thing else were required of them to believe, but what he had taught them, and they believed already; *viz. That he was the Messiah*, John XIV. 1. *Ye believe in God, believe also in me.* v. 29. *I have told you before it come to pass, that when it* 25 *is come to pass, ye may believe.* It is believing on him, without any thing else. *John* XVI. 31. *Jesus answered them, Do you now believe?* This was in Answer to their professing, *v.* 30. *Now are we sure that thou knowest all things, and needest not that any man should ask thee: By this we believe that thou comest forth from God.* 30   John XVII. 20. *Neither pray I for these alone, but for them also which shall |* [171] *believe on me through their word.* All that is spoke of *Believing*, in this his last Sermon to them, is only *Believing on him*, or believing that *He came from God*; Which was no other than believing him to be the *Messiah*.

Indeed, *John* XIV. 9. Our Saviour tells *Philip, He that hast seen me, hath* 35 *seen the Father.* And adds, *v.* 10. *Believest thou not that I am in the Father, and the Father in me? The words that I speak unto you, I speak of my self: But the Father that dwelleth in me, he doth the works.* Which being in Answer to *Philip*'s words, *v.* 9. *Shew us the Father*, seem to import thus much: *No man hath seen God at any time*, he is known only by his Works. And that 40 he is my Father, and I the Son of God, *i. e.* the *Messiah*, you may know by

AS DELIVERED IN THE SCRIPTURES 159

the Works I have done; Which it is impossible I could do of my self, but by the Union I have with God my Father. For that by being *in God*, and *God in him*, he signifies such an Union with God, that God operates in and by him, appears not only by the words above-cited out of *v.* 10. (which can scarce otherwise be made coherent sense) but | also from the same Phrase used again by our Saviour presently after, *v.* 20. *At that day, viz.* after his Resurrection, when they should see him again, *ye shall know that I am in my Father, and you in me, and I in you*; *i. e.* By the works I shall enable you to do, through a Power I have received from the Father: Which whoever sees me do, must acknowledge the Father to be in me; And whoever sees you do, must acknowledge me to be in you. And therefore he says, *v.* 12. *Verily, verily I say unto you, He that believeth on me, the works that I do shall he also do, because I go unto my Father.* Though I go away, yet I shall be in you, who believe in me; And ye shall be enabled to do Miracles also for the carrying on of my Kingdom, as I have done; That it may be manifested to others that you are sent by me, as I have evidenced to you that I am sent by the Father. And hence it is that he says, in the immediately preceding *v.* 11. *Believe me that I am in the Father, and the Father in me; If not, believe me for the sake of the works themselves.* Let the Works that I have done convince you that I | am sent by the Father; That he is with me, and that I do nothing but by his Will, and by vertue of the Union I have with him; And that consequently I am the *Messiah*, who am anointed, sanctified, and separate by the Father to the Work for which he hath sent me.

To confirm them in this Faith, and to enable them to do such Works as he had done, he promises them the Holy Ghost, *John* XIV. 25, 26. *These things I have said unto you, being yet present with you.* But when I am gone, *the Holy Ghost, the Paraclet* (which may signifie Monitor as well as Comforter, or Advocate) *which the Father shall send you in my Name, he shall shew you all things, and bring to your remembrance all things which I have said.* So that considering all that I have said, and laying it together, and comparing it with what you shall see come to pass, you may be more abundantly assured that I am the *Messiah*, and fully comprehend that I have done and suffered all things foretold of the *Messiah*; and that were to be accomplished and fulfilled by him, according to the Scriptures. But be | not filled with grief that I leave you; *John* XVI. 7. *It is expedient for you that I go away: For if I go not away, the Paraclet will not come unto you.* One Reason why, if he went not away, the Holy Ghost could not come, we may gather from what has been observed concerning the Prudent and wary carriage of our Saviour all through his Ministry, that he might not

160   THE REASONABLENESS OF CHRISTIANITY

incur Death with the least suspicion of a Malefactor: And therefore though his Disciples believed him to be the *Messiah*, yet they neither understood it so well, nor were so well confirmed in the belief of it, as after that he being crucified and risen again, they had received the Holy
5   Ghost; And with the Gifts of the Holy Spirit, a fuller and clearer Evidence and Knowledge that he was the *Messiah*: They then were enlightned to see how his Kingdom was such as the Scriptures foretold, though not such as they, till then, had expected. And now this Knowledge and Assurance received from the Holy Ghost, was of use
10   to them after his Resurrection; when they could now boldly go about,
[175]   and openly Preach, as they did, that *Jesus* | was the *Messiah*; confirming that Doctrine by the Miracles which the Holy Ghost impowered them to do. But till he was dead and gone, they could not do this. Their going about openly Preaching, as they did after his Resurrection, that *Jesus* was
15   the *Messiah*; and doing Miracles every where to make it good, would not have consisted with that Character of Humility, Peace, and Innocence, which the *Messiah* was to sustain; if they had done it before his Crucifixion. For this would have drawn upon him the Condemnation of a Malefactor, either as a stirrer of Sedition against the Publick Peace; or
20   as a Pretender to the Kingdom of *Israel*. And hence we see, that they who before his Death preached only the *Gospel of the Kingdom*; that *the Kingdom of God was at hand*; As soon as they had received the Holy Ghost after his Resurrection, changed their stile, and every where in express words declare that *Jesus* is the *Messiah*, that *King* which was to come.
25   This, the following words here in St. *John* XVI. 8–14. confirm; Where he goes on to tell them; *And when he is come, he will convince the World of Sin:* |
[176]   *Because they believed not on me.* Your Preaching then, accompanied with Miracles, by the assistance of the Holy Ghost, shall be a Conviction to the World that the *Jews* sinned in not believing me to be the *Messiah*. *Of*
30   *Righteousness*, or Justice: *Because I go to my Father, and ye see me no more.* By the same Preaching and Miracles you shall confirm the Doctrine of my Ascension; and thereby convince the World that I was that *Just One*, who am therefore ascended to the Father into Heaven, where no unjust Person shall enter. *Of Judgment*: *Because the Prince of this World is judged.*
35   And by the same assistance of the Holy Ghost ye shall convince the World that the Devil is judged or condemned, by your casting of him out, and destroying his Kingdom, and his Worship where ever you Preach. Our Saviour adds, *I have yet many things to say unto you, but you cannot bear them now.* They were yet so full of a Temporal Kingdom,
40   that they could not bear the discovery of what a kind of Kingdom his

AS DELIVERED IN THE SCRIPTURES   161

was, nor what a King he was to be; And therefore he leaves them to
the coming of | the Holy Ghost, for a farther and fuller discovery of [177]
himself, and the Kingdom of the *Messiah*; For fear they should be
scandalized in him, and give up the hopes they had now in him, and
forsake him. This he tells them, *v.* 1. of this XVI. Chapter: *These things* 5
I have said unto you, that you may not be scandalized. The last thing he
had told them before his saying this to them, we find in the last Verses
of the precedent Chapter: *When the Paraclet is come, the Spirit of Truth,*
he shall witness concerning me. He shall shew you who I am, and
witness it to the World; And then *Ye also shall bear witness, because ye* 10
have been with me from the beginning. He shall call to your mind what I
have said and done, that ye may understand it, and know, and bear
Witness concerning me. And again here, *John* XVI. after he had told
them, they could not bear what he had more to say, he adds; *v.* 13.
Howbeit, when the Spirit of Truth is come, he will guide you into all Truth; 15
and he will shew you things to come: He shall glorifie me. By the Spirit,
when he comes, ye shall be fully instructed concerning me; And
though | you cannot yet, from what I have said to you, clearly [178]
comprehend my Kingdom and Glory; yet he shall make it known to
you wherein it consists: And though I am now in a mean state, and 20
ready to be given up to Contempt, Torment, and Death; So that ye
know not what to think of it; Yet the Spirit, when he comes, *shall*
glorifie me, and fully satisifie you of my Power and Kingdom; And that
I sit on the right hand of God, to order all things for the good and
increase of it, till I come again at the last day in fulness of Glory.   25

Accordingly, the Apostles had a full and clear sight and perswasion of
this, after they had received the Holy Ghost; And they preached it every
where boldly and openly, without the least remainder of doubt or
uncertainty. But that even so late as this they understood not his Death
and Resurrection, is evident from *v.* 17, 18. *Then said some of the Disciples* 30
among themselves, What is this that he saith unto us; A little while, and ye
shall not see me; And again, a little while, and ye shall see me; and because I go
to the Father? They said therefore, what is this that he saith, a little while? | *We* [179]
know not what he saith. Upon which he goes on to Discourse to them of
his Death and Resurrection, and of the Power they should have of doing 35
Miracles; But all this he declares to them in a Mystical and involved way
of speaking, as he tells them himself, *v.* 25. *These things have I spoken to you*
in Proverbs; *i. e.* In General, Obscure, Ænigmatical, or Figurative terms.
(All which, as well as Allusive Apologues, the Jews called Proverbs or
Parables.) Hitherto my declaring of my self to you hath been obscure, 40

162   THE REASONABLENESS OF CHRISTIANITY

and with reserve; And I have not spoken of my self to you in plain and direct words, because ye *could not bear it.* A *Messiah*, and not a King, you could not understand; And a King living in Poverty and Persecution, and dying the Death of a Slave and Malefactor upon a Cross, you could not
5 put together. And had I told you in plain words that I was the *Messiah*, and given you a direct Commission to Preach to others that I professedly owned my self to be the *Messiah*, you and they would have been ready to
[180] have made a Commotion, to have set me upon the Throne of my | Father *David*, and to fight for me, that your *Messiah*, your King, in whom are
10 your hopes of a Kingdom, should not be delivered up into the hands of his Enemies, to be put to Death; And of this, *Peter* will instantly give you a Proof. But *the time cometh when I shall no more speak unto you in Parables; but I shall shew unto you plainly of the Father.* My Death and Resurrection, and the coming of the Holy Ghost, will speedily enlighten you, and then
15 I shall make you know the Will and Design of the Father; What a Kingdom I am to have, and by what means, and to what end, *v.* 27. And this the Father himself will shew unto you; *For he loveth you, because ye have loved me, and have believed that I came out from the Father*; Because ye have believed that I am the *Son of God, the Messiah*; That he hath anointed
20 and sent me; Though it hath not been yet fully discovered to you, what kind of Kingdom it shall be, nor by what means brought about. And then our Saviour, without being asked, explaining to them what he had said; And making them understand better, what before they stuck at, and
[181] com|plained secretly among themselves that they understood not; They
25 thereupon declare, *v.* 30. *Now are we sure that thou knowest all things, and needest not that any man should ask thee.* 'Tis plain thou knowest mens Thoughts and Doubts before they ask. *By this we believe that thou comest forth from God. Jesus answered, Do ye now believe?* Notwithstanding that you now believe that I came from God, and am the *Messiah*, sent by him;
30 *Behold, the hour cometh, yea, is now come, that ye shall be scattered*; And as it is, *Mat.* XXVI. 31. and *shall all be scandalized in me.* What it is to be scandalized in him, we may see by what followed hereupon, if that which he says to St. *Peter, Mark* XIV. did not sufficiently explain it.
    This I have been the more particular in; That it may be seen, that in
35 this last Discourse to his Disciples (where he opened himself more than he had hitherto done; and where, if any thing more was required to make them Believers, than what they already believed, we might have expected they should have heard of it;) there were no new Articles proposed to
[182] them, but what | they believed before, *viz.* That he was the *Messiah*, the
40 Son of God, sent from the Father; Though of his manner of proceeding,

AS DELIVERED IN THE SCRIPTURES 163

and his sudden leaving the World, and some few particulars, he made them understand something more than they did before. But as to the main design of the Gospel, *viz.* That he had a Kingdom, that he should be put to Death, and rise again, and ascend into Heaven to his Father, and come again in Glory to Judge the World; This he had told them: 5 And so had acquainted them with the Great Counsel of God, in sending him the *Messiah*, and omitted nothing that was necessary to be known or believed in it. And so he tells them himself, *John* XV. 1 5. *Henceforth I call ye not Servants; for the Servant knoweth not what his Lord does: But I have called ye Friends; for ALL THINGS I have heard of my Father, I have made* 10 *known unto you*; though perhaps ye do not so fully comprehend them, as you will shortly, when I am risen and ascended.

To conclude all, in his Prayer, which shuts up this Discourse, he tells the | Father what he had made known to his Apostles; The Result [183] whereof we have *John* XVII. 8. *I have given unto them the words which thou* 15 *gavest me, and they have received them, and THEY HAVE BELIEVED THAT THOU DIDST SEND ME.* Which is in effect, that he was the *Messiah* promised and sent by God. And then he Prays for them, and adds, *v.* 20, 21. *Neither pray I for these alone, but for them also who shall believe on me through their word.* What that Word was, through which 20 others should believe in him, we have seen in the Preaching of the Apostles all through the History of the *Acts, viz.* This one great Point, that Jesus was the *Messiah.* The Apostles, he says, *v.* 25. *know that thou hast sent me; i. e.* are assured that I am the *Messiah.* And in *v.* 21. and 23. he Prays, *That the World may believe* (which *v.* 23. is called knowing) *that* 25 *thou hast sent me.* So that what Christ would have believed by his Disciples, we may see by this his last Prayer for them, when he was leaving the World, as well as by what he Preached whilst he was in it. |

And as a Testimony of this, one of his last Actions, even when he was [184] upon the Cross, was to confirm this Doctrine; by giving Salvation to one 30 of the Thieves that was crucified with him, upon his Declaration that he believed him to be the *Messiah*: For so much the words of his Request imported, when he said, *Remember me, Lord, when thou comest into thy Kingdom, Luke* XXIII. 42. To which Jesus replied, *v.* 43. *Verily I say unto thee, to day shalt thou be with me in Paradise.* An Expression very 35 remarkable: For as *Adam*, by sin, lost *Paradise; i. e.* a state of Happy Immortality; Here the believing Thief, through his Faith in *Jesus* the *Messiah*, is promised to be put in Paradise, and so re-instated in an Happy Immortality.

Thus our Saviour ended his Life. And what he did after his 40

164   THE REASONABLENESS OF CHRISTIANITY

Resurrection, St. *Luke* tells us, *Acts* I. 3. That he shewed himself to the Apostles *forty days*, *speaking* things *concerning the Kingdom of God*. This was what our Saviour preached in the whole Course of his Ministry, [185] before his Passion: And no other Mysteries of Faith does he now | 5 discover to them after his Resurrection. All he says, is concerning the Kingdom of God; And what it was he said concerning that, we shall see presently out of the other Evangelists; having first only taken notice, that when now they asked him, *v.* 6. *Lord, wilt thou at this time restore again the Kingdom to* Israel? *He said, unto them*, v. 7. *It is not for you to know the* 10 *Times, and the Seasons, which the Father hath put in his own power: But ye shall receive Power after that the Holy Ghost is come upon you; And ye shall be witnesses unto me unto the utmost parts of the Earth.* Their great business was to be Witnesses to *Jesus*, of his Life, Death, Resurrection, and Ascension; which put together, were undeniable Proofs of his being the 15 *Messiah*. This was what they were to Preach, and what he said to them concerning the Kingdom of God; As will appear by what is recorded of it in the other Evangelists.

When on the day of his Resurrection, he appeared to the two going to *Emmaus, Luke* XXIV. they declare, *v.* 21. what his Disciples Faith in him [186] was: *But we trusted that it had been He which should | have redeemed* Israel; 21 *i. e.* We believed that he was the *Messiah*, come to deliver the Nation of the *Jews*. Upon this *Jesus* tells them, they ought to believe him to be the *Messiah*, notwithstanding what had happened; Nay, they ought by his Suffering and Death to be confirmed in that Faith, that he was the 25 *Messiah*. And *v.* 26, 27. *Beginning at* Moses *and all the Prophets, he expounded unto them in all the Scriptures, the things concerning himself; How that the Messiah ought to have suffered these things, and to have entred into his Glory.* Now he applies the Prophesies of the *Messiah* to himself, which we read not that he did ever do before his Passion. And afterwards appearing 30 to the Eleven, *Luke* XXIV. 36. He said unto them, *v.* 44–47. *These words which I spoke unto you while I was yet with you, that all things must be fulfilled which are written in the Law of* Moses, *and in the Prophets, and in the Psalms concerning me. Then opened he their Understandings, that they might understand the Scripture, and said unto them; Thus it is written, and thus it* [187] *behoved the Messiah to suffer, and to rise from the | dead the third day; and that* 36 *Repentance, and Remission of Sins should be preached in his Name among all Nations, beginning at Jerusalem.* Here we see what it was he had preached to them, though not in so plain open words, before his Crucifixion; And what it is he now makes them understand; And what it was that was to be 40 preached to all Nations, *viz.* That he was the *Messiah*, that had suffered,

AS DELIVERED IN THE SCRIPTURES   165

and rose from the Dead the third day, and fulfilled all things that were written in the Old Testament concerning the *Messiah*; And that those who believed this, and repented, should receive Remission of their Sins through this Faith in him. Or, as St. *Mark* has it, *Chap.* XVI. 15. *Go into all the World, and Preach the Gospel to every Creature; He that believeth, and* 5 *is baptized, shall be saved; But he that believeth not, shall be damned*, v. 20. What the *Gospel, or Good News* was, we have shewed already, *viz.* The happy Tidings of the *Messiah* being come. *v.* 20. And *They went forth and preached every where, the Lord working with them, and confirming the Word with signs following.* What | the *Word* was which they preached, and the [188] Lord confirmed with Miracles, we have seen already out of the History of 11 their Acts.

I have already given an Account of their Preaching every where, as it is recorded in the *Acts*, except some few places, where the Kingdom of the *Messiah* is mentioned under the name of *the Kingdom of God*; Which I 15 forbore to set down, till I had made it plain out of the Evangelists, that That was no other but the Kingdom of the *Messiah*.

It may be seasonable therefore now, to add to those Sermons we have formerly seen of St. *Paul* (wherein he preached no other Article of Faith, but that *Jesus was the Messiah*, the King, who being risen from the Dead, 20 now Reigneth, and shall more publickly manifest his Kingdom, in judging the World at the last day) what farther is left upon Record of his Preaching. *Acts* XIX. 8. At *Ephesus*, Paul *went into the Synagogues, and spake boldly for the space of three months; disputing and perswading concerning the Kingdom of God.* And *Acts* XX. 25. At *Miletus* he thus takes leave of the 25 Elders of *Ephesus*: *And* | *now behold, I know that ye all among whom I have* [189] *gone Preaching the Kingdom of God, shall see my face no more.* What this Preaching the Kingdom of God was, he tells you, *v.* 20, 21. *I have kept nothing back from you, which was profitable unto you, but have shewed you, and have taught you publickly, and from House to House; Testifying both to the* 30 *Jews, and to the Greeks, Repentance towards God, and Faith towards our Lord Jesus Christ.* And so again, *Acts* XXVIII. 23, 24. *When they* [the Jews at Rome] *had appointed him* [Paul] *a day, there came many to him into his Lodging; To whom he expounded and testified the Kingdom of God; perswading them concerning Jesus, both out of the Law of Moses, and out of* 35 *the Prophets, from Morning to Evening. And some believed the things which were spoken, and some believed not.* And the History of the *Acts* is concluded with this Account of St. *Paul*'s Preaching: *And Paul dwelt two whole years in his own hired House, and received all that came in unto him, Preaching the Kingdom of God, and teaching those things which concern the Lord Jesus the* 40

166   THE REASONABLENESS OF CHRISTIANITY

[190] *Messiah.* We may | therefore here apply the same Conclusion, to the History of our Saviour, writ by the Evangelists; And to the History of the Apostles, writ in the *Acts*; which St. *John* does to his own Gospel, *Chap.* XX. 30, 31. *Many other signs did Jesus before his Disciples*; And in
5   many other places the Apostles preached the same Doctrine, *which are not written* in these Books; *But these are written, that you may believe that Jesus is the Messiah, the Son of God; and that believing, you may have life in his Name.*

What St. *John* thought necessary and sufficient to be *believed*, for the
10   attaining Eternal Life, he here tells us. And this, not in the first dawning of the Gospel; when, perhaps, some will be apt to think less was required to be believed, than after the Doctrine of Faith, and Mystery of Salvation, was more fully explained, in the Epistles writ by the Apostles. For it is to be remembred, that St. *John* says this not as soon as Christ was ascended;
15   For these words, with the rest of St. *John*'s Gospel, were not written till many Years after not only the other Gospels, and St. *Luke*'s History of
[191] the *Acts*; but in all appear|ance, after all the Epistles writ by the other Apostles. So that above Threescore Years after our Saviour's Passion; (for so long after, both *Epiphanius* and St. *Jerome* assure us this Gospel
20   was written) St. *John* knew nothing else required to be believed for the attaining of Life, but that *Jesus is the Messiah, the Son of God.*

XI   To this, 'tis likely, it will be objected by some, that to believe only that *Jesus* of *Nazareth* is the *Messiah*, is but an *Historical*, and not a Justifying or Saving Faith.
25   To which I Answer; That I allow to the makers of Systems and their followers, to invent and use what distinctions they please; and to call things by what names they think fit. But I cannot allow to them, or to any man, an Authority to make a Religion for me, or to alter that which God hath revealed. And if they please to call the believing that which our
30   Saviour and his Apostles preached and proposed alone to be believed, an *Historical* Faith; they have their liberty. But they must have a care how
[192] they deny it to be a Justifying or Saving Faith, when our | Saviour and his Apostles have declared it so to be, and taught no other which men should receive, and whereby they should be made Believers unto Eternal Life;
35   Unless they can so far make bold with our Saviour, for the sake of their beloved Systems, as to say, that he forgot what he came into the World for; And that he and his Apostles did not Instruct People right in the way and Mysteries of Salvation. For that this is the sole Doctrine pressed and required to be believed in the whole tenour of our Saviour's and his
40   Apostles Preaching, we have shewed through the whole History of the

AS DELIVERED IN THE SCRIPTURES 167

Evangelists and the *Acts*. And I challenge them to shew that there was any other Doctrine, upon their assent to which, or disbelief of it, men were pronounced *Believers*, or Unbelievers; And accordingly received into the Church of Christ, as Members of his Body, as far as meer believing could make them so, or else kept out of it. This was the only Gospel-Article of 5 Faith which was preached to them. And if nothing else was preached every where, the Apostles Argument will hold against any | other Articles [193] of Faith to be believed under the Gospel; *Rom.* X. 14. *How shall they believe that whereof they have not heard?* For to Preach any other Doctrines necessary to be believed, we do not find that any body was sent. 10

Perhaps it will farther be urged, That this is not a *Saving Faith*; Because such a *Faith* as this the Devils may have, and 'twas plain they had; For they believed and declared *Jesus* to be the *Messiah*. And St. *James, Chap.* II. 19. tells us, *The Devils believe, and tremble*; And yet they shall not be saved. To which I answer, 1. That they could not be saved by any *Faith*, 15 to whom it was not proposed as a means of Salvation, nor ever promised to be counted for Righteousness. This was an Act of Grace, shewn only to Mankind. God dealt so favourably with the Posterity of *Adam*, that if they would believe *Jesus* to be the *Messiah*, the promised King and Saviour; And perform what other Conditions were required of them by 20 the Covenant of Grace; God would Justifie them, because of this Belief. He would account this Faith to them for Righteousness, | and look on it [194] as making up the defects of their Obedience; Which being thus supplied by what was taken instead of it, they were looked on as Just or Righteous, and so inherited Eternal Life. But this Favour shewn to 25 Mankind, was never offered to the fallen Angels. They had no such Proposals made to them: And therefore whatever of this kind was proposed to men, it availed not Devils, whatever they performed of it. This Covenant of Grace was never offered to them.

2. I Answer; That though the Devils believed, yet they could not be 30 saved by the Covenant of Grace; Because they performed not the other Condition required in it, altogether as necessary to be performed as this of Believing, and that is *Repentance*. Repentance is as absolute a Condition of the Covenant of Grace, as Faith; and as necessary to be performed as that. *John the Baptist*, who was to prepare the way for the 35 *Messiah, Preached the Baptism of Repentance for the remission of sins*, Mark I. 4.

As *John* began his Preaching with *Repent, for the Kingdom of Heaven is* | *at hand, Mat.* III. 2. So did our Saviour begin his, *Mat.* IV. 17. *From that* [195] *time began Jesus to Preach, and to say, Repent, for the Kingdom of Heaven is at* 40

168   THE REASONABLENESS OF CHRISTIANITY

hand. Or, as St. *Mark* has it in that parallel place, *Mark* I. 14, 15. *Now after that* John *was put in Prison, Jesus came into* Galilee, *Preaching the Gospel of the Kingdom of God, and saying; The time is fulfilled, and the Kingdom of God is at hand: Repent ye, and believe the Gospel.* This was not
5 only the beginning of his Preaching, but the sum of all that he did Preach; *viz.* That men should *Repent,* and believe the good Tidings which he brought them; That *the time was fulfilled* for the coming of the *Messiah.* And this was what his Apostles preached, when he sent them out, *Mark* VI. 12. *And they going out, preached that men should Repent.* Believing
10 Jesus to be the *Messiah,* and Repenting, were so Necessary and Fundamental parts of the Covenant of Grace, that one of them alone is often put for both. For here St. *Mark* mentions nothing but their Preaching *Repentance*; as St. *Luke,* in the parallel place, *Chap.* IX. 6.
[196] mentions nothing but their | *Evangelizing,* or Preaching the Good News
15 of the Kingdom of the *Messiah*: And St. *Paul* often in his Epistles puts *Faith* for the whole Duty of a Christian. But yet the tenour of the Gospel is what Christ declares, *Luke* XIII. 3, 5. *Unless ye repent, ye shall all likewise perish.* And in the Parable of the Rich Man in Hell, delivered by our Saviour, *Luke* XVI. *Repentance* alone is the means proposed of avoiding
20 that place of Torment, *v.* 30, 31. And what the tenor of the Doctrine, which should be preached to the World, should be, He tells his Apostles after his Resurrection, *Luke* XXIV. 47. *viz. That Repentance and Remission of Sins should be preached in his Name,* who was the *Messiah.* And accordingly, believing *Jesus* to be the *Messiah,* and Repenting, was what
25 the Apostles preached. So *Peter* began, *Acts* II. 38. *Repent, and be baptized.* These two things were required for the Remission of Sins, *viz.* Entring themselves in the Kingdom of God; And owning and professing themselves the Subjects of *Jesus,* whom they believed to be the *Messiah,*
[197] and received for their Lord and King; For that was to *be bap|tized in his*
30 *Name*: Baptism being an initiating Ceremony known to the *Jews,* whereby those, who leaving Heathenism, and professing a submission to the Law of *Moses,* were received into the Common-wealth of *Israel.* And so it was made use of by our Saviour, to be that Solemn visible Act, whereby those who believed him to be the *Messiah,* received him as their
35 King, and professed Obedience to him, were admitted as Subjects into his Kingdom: Which in the Gospels is called the *Kingdom of God*; And in the *Acts* and Epistles often by another name, *viz.* The *Church.*

The same St. *Peter* Preaches again to the *Jews,* Acts III. 19. *Repent, and be converted, that your sins may be blotted out.*
40   What this Repentance was; which the New Covenant required as one

AS DELIVERED IN THE SCRIPTURES 169

of the Conditions to be performed by all those who should receive the Benefits of that Covenant; is plain in the Scripture, to be not only a sorrow for sins past, but (what is a Natural consequence of such sorrow, if it be real) a turning from them, into a new and contrary Life. And so they are joyned together, | *Acts* III.19. *Repent and turn about*; Or, as we render it, be converted. And *Acts* XXVI. *Repent and turn to God.* [198]

6

And sometimes *turning about* is put alone, to signifie Repentance, *Mat.* XIII. 15. *Luke* XXII. 32. Which in other words is well expressed by *Newness of Life*. For it being certain that he who is really sorry for his sins, and abhors them, will turn from them, and forsake them; Either of these 10 Acts, which have so Natural a connexion one with the other, may be, and is often put for both together. Repentance is an hearty sorrow for our past misdeeds, and a sincere Resolution and Endeavour, to the utmost of our power, to conform all our Actions to the Law of God. So that Repentance does not consist in one single Act of sorrow (though that 15 being the first and leading Act, gives denomination to the whole) But in *doing works meet for Repentance*, in a sincere Obedience to the Law of Christ, the remainder of our Lives. This was called for by *John the Baptist*, the Preacher of Repentance, *Mat.* III. 8. *Bring forth fruits meet for Repentance*. And by St. *Paul* here, *Acts* XXVI. 20. *Re|pent and turn to God,* [199] *and do works meet for Repentance*. There are works to follow belonging to 21 Repentance, as well as sorrow for what is past.

These two, Faith and Repentance; *i. e.* believing Jesus to be the *Messiah*, and a good Life; are the indispensible Conditions of the New Covenant to be performed by all those, who would obtain Eternal Life. 25 The Reasonableness, or rather Necessity of which, that we may the better comprehend, we must a little look back to what was said in the beginning.

Adam being the Son of God; and so St. *Luke* calls him, *Chap.* III. 38. had this part also of the *Likeness* and *Image* of the Father, *viz.* That he was 30 Immortal. But *Adam* transgressing the Command given him by his Heavenly Father, incurred the Penalty, forfeited that state of Immortality, and became Mortal. After this, *Adam* begot Children: But they were *in his own likeness, after his own image*; Mortal, like their Father. | 35

God nevertheless, out of his Infinite Mercy, willing to bestow Eternal [200] Life on Mortal Men, sends Jesus Christ into the World; Who being conceived in the Womb of a Virgin (that had not known Man) by the immediate Power of God, was properly the Son of God; According to what the Angel declared to his Mother, *Luke* I. 30–35. *The Holy Ghost* 40

170   THE REASONABLENESS OF CHRISTIANITY

shall come upon thee, and the Power of the Highest shall overshadow thee: Therefore also that Holy Thing which shall be born of thee, shall be called THE SON OF GOD. So that being the Son of God, he was, like his Father, *Immortal.* As he tells us, *John* V. 26. *As the Father hath life in himself, so* 5 *hath he given to the Son to have life in himself.* On which words the Bishop of Ely thus comments. *Here he teaches us to argue, that, if he be the SON of God, as the voice from heaven said he was, then he is by the same voice declared to have LIFE in him self: because the Father hath so, whom his SON, his only SON, doth perfectly resemble.*

10   And that Immortality is a part of the *Image*, wherein these (who were the immediate Sons of God, so as to have no other Father) were made like their Father, appears probable, not only from the places in *Genesis* concerning *Adam*, above taken notice of, but seems to me also to be intimated in some Expressions concerning *Jesus*, the Son of God. In the
[201] New Testament, *Col.* I. | 15. He is called *the Image of the invisible God.*
16   *Invisible* seems put in, to obviate any gross Imagination, that he (as Images use to do) represented God in any corporeal or visible Resemblance. And there is farther subjoyned, to lead us into the meaning of it, *The First-born of every Creature*; Which is farther explained,
20   *v.* 18. Where he is termed, *The First-born from the dead*: Thereby making out, and shewing himself to be the *Image* of the Invisible God; That Death hath no power over him: But being the Son of God, and not having forfeited that Son-ship by any Transgression, was the Heir of Eternal Life; As *Adam* should have been, had he continued in his filial
25   Duty. In the same sense the Apostle seems to use the word *Image* in other places, *viz. Rom.* VIII. 29. *Whom he did foreknow, he also did predestinate to be conformed to the Image of his Son, that he might be the first-born among many Brethren.* The *Image*, to which they were conformed, seems to be *Immortality* and Eternal Life. For 'tis remarkable that in both
30   these places St. *Paul* speaks of the Resurrection; And that Christ was *The* |
[202] *First-born among many Brethren*; He being by Birth the Son of God, and the others only by Adoption, as we see in this same Chapter, *v.* 15–17. *Ye have received the Spirit of Adoption, whereby we cry, Abba, Father: The Spirit it self bearing witness with our Spirits, that we are the Children of God. And if*
35   *Children, then Heirs; And Joynt-Heirs with Christ: If so be that we suffer with him, that we may also be glorified together.* And hence we see that our Saviour vouchsafes to call those, who at the Day of Judgment are through him entering into Eternal Life, his *Brethren; Mat.* XXV. 40. *In as much as ye have done it unto one of the least of these my Brethren.* And may we
40   not in this find a reason why God so frequently in the New Testament,

AS DELIVERED IN THE SCRIPTURES 171

and so seldom, if at all, in the Old, is mentioned under the single Title of THE FATHER? And therefore our Saviour says, *Mat.* XI. *No man knoweth the Father save the Son, and he to whomsoever the Son will reveal him.* God has now a Son again in the World, the First-born of many Brethren, who all now, by the Spirit of Adoption, can say, *Abba,* | Father. And we by Adoption, being for his sake made his Brethren, and the Sons of God, come to share in that Inheritance, which was his Natural Right; he being by Birth the Son of God: Which Inheritance is Eternal Life. And again, *v.* 23. *We groan within our selves, waiting for the Adoption, to wit, the Redemption of our Body;* Whereby is plainly meant the change of these frail Mortal Bodies, into the Spiritual Immortal Bodies at the Resurrection; *When this Mortal shall have put on Immortality,* 1 *Cor.* XV. 54. Which in that Chapter, *v.* 42–44. he farther expresses thus: *So also is the Resurrection of the dead. It is sown in Corruption, it is raised in Incorruption: It is sown in dishonour, it is raised in Glory: It is sown in Weakness, it is raised in Power: It is sown a Natural Body, it is raised a Spiritual Body, etc.* To which he subjoyns, *v.* 49. *As we have born the Image of the Earthy,* (*i. e.* As we have been Mortal, like Earthy *Adam* our Father, from whom we are descended, when he was turned out of Paradise) *We shall also bear the Image of the Heavenly;* Into whose Sonship and Inheritance be|ing adopted, we shall, at the Resurrection, receive that *Adoption* we expect, *Even the Redemption of our Bodies;* And after his *Image,* which is the *Image* of the Father, become Immortal. Hear what he says himself, *Luke* XX. 35, 36. *They who shall be accounted worthy to obtain that World, and the Resurrection from the Dead, neither marry, nor are given in marriage. Neither can they die any more; for they are equal unto the Angels, and are the SONS OF GOD, being the Sons of the Resurrection.* And he that shall read St. *Paul's* Arguing, *Acts* XIII. 32, 33. will find that the great Evidence that Jesus was the *Son of God,* was his Resurrection. Then the Image of his Father appeared in him, when he visibly entred into the state of Immortality. For thus the Apostle reasons; *We Preach to you, how that the Promise which was made to our Fathers, God hath fulfilled the same unto us, in that he hath raised up Jesus again; As it is also written in the second Psalm, Thou art my Son, this day have I begotten thee.*

This may serve a little to explain the *Immortality* of the Sons of God, who | are in this like their Father, made after his *Image* and Likeness. But that our Saviour was so, he himself farther declares, *John* X. 18. Where speaking of his Life, he says, *No one taketh it from me, but I lay it down of my self: I have power to lay it down, and I have power to take it up again.* Which he could not have had, if he had been a Mortal Man, the Son of a

172   THE REASONABLENESS OF CHRISTIANITY

Man, of the Seed of *Adam*; Or else had by any Transgression forfeited his Life. For *the wages of Sin is Death*: And he that hath incurred Death for his own Transgression, cannot lay down his Life for another, as our Saviour professes he did. For he was the Just One, *Acts* VII. 52. and III. 14. *Who*
5 *knew no sin.* 2 *Cor.* V. 21. *Who did no sin, neither was guile found in his mouth.* And thus, *As by Man came Death, so by Man came the Resurrection of the Dead. For as in* Adam *all die, so in Christ shall all be made alive.*

For this laying down his Life for others, our Saviour tells us, *John* X. 17. *Therefore does my Father love me, because I lay down my life, that I*
[206] *might take it again.* And this his Obedience | and Suffering was rewarded
11 with a Kingdom; which, he tells us, *Luke* XXII. *His Father had appointed unto him*; And which, 'tis evident out of the Epistle to the *Hebrews, Chap.* XII. 2. he had a regard to in his Sufferings: *Who for the joy that was set before him, endured the Cross, despising the shame, and is set down at the right*
15 *hand of the Throne of God.* Which Kingdom given him upon this account of his Obedience, Suffering, and Death, He himself takes notice of, in these words, *John* XVII. 1–4. *Jesus lift up his eyes to Heaven, and said, Father, the hour is come, glorifie thy Son, that thy Son also may glorifie thee. As thou hast given him power over all flesh, that he should give Eternal Life to as*
20 *many as thou hast given him. And this is Life Eternal, that they may know thee the only true God, and Jesus the Messiah, whom thou hast sent. I have glorified thee on Earth: I have finished the work which thou gavest me to do.* And St. *Paul,* in his Epistle to the *Philippians, Chap.* II. 8–11. *He humbled himself, and became obedient unto Death, even the death of the Cross. Wherefore God*
[207] *also hath highly | exalted him, and given him a name that is above every name:*
26 *That at the name of Jesus every knee should bow, of things in Heaven, and things in Earth, and things under the Earth; And that every Tongue should confess that Jesus Christ is Lord.*

Thus God, we see, designed his Son *Christ Jesus* a Kingdom, an
30 Everlasting Kingdom in Heaven. But *Though as in* Adam *all die, so in Christ all shall be made alive*; And all men shall return to Life again at the last day; Yet all men having sinned, and thereby *come short of the Glory of God,* as St. *Paul* assures us, *Rom.* III. 23. (*i. e.* Not attaining to the Heavenly Kingdom of the *Messiah,* which is often called the Glory of
35 God; as may be seen, *Rom.* V. 2. and XV. 7. and II. 7. *Mat.* XVI. 27. *Mark* VIII. 38. For no one who is unrighteous, *i. e.* comes short of perfect Righteousness, shall be admitted into the Eternal Life of that Kingdom; As is declared, 1 *Cor.* VI. 9. *The unrighteous shall not inherit the*
39 *Kingdom of God*;) And Death, the Wages of Sin, being the Portion of all
[208] those who had transgressed the Righteous Law of God; The | Son of

AS DELIVERED IN THE SCRIPTURES 173

God would in vain have come into the World, to lay the Foundations of a Kingdom, and gather together a select People out of the World, if, (they being found guilty at their appearance before the Judgment-seat of the Righteous Judge of all men at the last day) instead of entrance into Eternal Life in the Kingdom he had prepared for them, they should 5 receive Death, the just Reward of Sin, which every one of them was guilty of. This second Death would have left him no Subjects; And instead of those Ten Thousand times Ten Thousand, and Thousands of Thousands, there would not have been one left him to sing Praises unto his Name, saying, *Blessing, and Honour, and Glory, and Power, be unto him* 10 *that sitteth on the Throne, and unto the Lamb for ever and ever.* God therefore, out of his Mercy to Mankind, and for the erecting of the Kingdom of his Son, and furnishing it with Subjects out of every Kindred, and Tongue, and People, and Nation, proposed to the Children of Men, that as many of them as would believe *Jesus* his Son 15 (whom he sent into the World) to be the *Messiah*, the promised | Deliverer; And would receive him for their King and Ruler; should have [209] all their past Sins, Disobedience, and Rebellion forgiven them: And if for the future they lived in a sincere Obedience to his Law, to the utmost of their power; the sins of Humane Frailty for the time to come, as well as 20 all those of their past Lives, should, for his Son's sake, because they gave themselves up to him to be his Subjects, be forgiven them: And so their Faith, which made them be baptized into his Name; (*i. e.* Enroll themselves in the Kingdom of *Jesus* the *Messiah*, and profess themselves his Subjects, and consequently live by the Laws of his Kingdom) should 25 be accounted to them for Righteousness; *i. e.* Should supply the defects of a scanty Obedience in the sight of God; Who counting this Faith to them for Righteousness, or Compleat Obedience, did thus Justifie, or make them Just, and thereby capable of Eternal Life.

Now, that this is the Faith for which God of his free Grace Justifies 30 sinful Man; (For *'tis God alone that justifieth, Rom.* VIII. 33. *Rom.* III. 26.) We have | already shewed; by observing through all the History of our [210] Saviour and the Apostles, recorded in the Evangelists, and in the *Acts*, what he and his Apostles preached and proposed to be believed. We shall shew now, that besides believing him to be the *Messiah* their King, it was 35 farther required, that those who would have the Priviledge, Advantages, and Deliverance of his Kingdom, should enter themselves into it; And by Baptism being made Denizons, and solemnly incorporated into that Kingdom, live as became Subjects obedient to the Laws of it. For if they believed him to be the *Messiah* their King, but would not obey his Laws, 40

174   THE REASONABLENESS OF CHRISTIANITY

and would not have him to Reign over them, they were but greater Rebels; and God would not Justifie them for a Faith that did but increase their Guilt, and oppose Diametrically the Kingdom and Design of the *Messiah*; *Who gave himself for us, that he might redeem us from all Iniquity,*
5 *and purifie unto himself a peculiar People, zealous of good works, Titus* II. 14. And therefore St. *Paul* tells the *Galatians*, That that which availeth is
[211] *Faith*; But *Faith* | *working by Love*. And that *Faith* without *Works*, *i. e.* the Works of sincere Obedience to the Law and Will of Christ, is not sufficient for our Justification, St. *James* shews at large, *Chap.* II.
10   Neither indeed could it be otherwise; For Life, Eternal Life being the Reward of Justice or Righteousness only, appointed by the Righteous God (who is of purer Eyes than to behold Iniquity) to those only who had no taint or infection of Sin upon them, it is impossible that he should Justifie those who had no regard to Justice at all, whatever they believed.
15 This would have been to encourage Iniquity, contrary to the Purity of his Nature; and to have condemned that Eternal Law of Right, which is Holy, Just, and Good; Of which no one Precept or Rule is abrogated or repealed; nor indeed can be; whilst God is an Holy, Just, and Righteous God, and Man a Rational Creature. The Duties of that Law arising from
20 the Constitution of his very Nature, are of Eternal Obligation; Nor can it be taken away or dispensed with, without changing the Nature of
[212] Things, overturning the measures of | Right and Wrong, and thereby introducing and authorizing Irregularity, Confusion, and Disorder in the World. Christ's coming into the World was not for such an End as that;
25 But on the contrary, to reform the corrupt state of degenerate Man; And out of those who would mend their Lives, and bring forth Fruit meet for Repentance, erect a new Kingdom.

This is the Law of that Kingdom, as well as of all Mankind; And that Law by which all Men shall be judged at the last day. Only those who
30 have believed *Jesus* to be the *Messiah*, and have taken him to be their King, with a sincere Endeavour after Righteousness, in obeying his Law, shall have their past sins not imputed to them; And shall have that Faith taken instead of Obedience; Where Frailty and Weakness made them transgress, and sin prevailed after Conversion in those who hunger and
35 thirst after Righteousness (or perfect Obedience) and do not allow themselves in Acts of Disobedience and Rebellion, against the Laws of that Kingdom they are entred into. |

[213]   He did not expect, 'tis true, a Perfect Obedience void of all slips and falls: He knew our Make, and the weakness of our Constitutions too
40 well, and was sent with a Supply for that Defect. Besides, perfect

AS DELIVERED IN THE SCRIPTURES 175

Obedience was the Righteousness of the Law of Works; and then the Reward would be of Debt, and not of Grace; And to such there was no need of Faith to be imputed to them for Righteousness. They stood upon their own legs, were Just already, and needed no allowance to be made them for believing Jesus to be the *Messiah*, taking him for their King, and becoming his Subjects. But that Christ does require Obedience, sincere Obedience, is evident from the Laws he himself delivers (unless he can be supposed to give and inculcate Laws only to have them disobeyed) and from the Sentence he will pass when he comes to Judge.

The Faith required was, to believe *Jesus* to be the *Messiah*, the Anointed; who had been promised by God to the World. Amongst the *Jews* (to whom the Promises and Prophesies of the *Messiah* were more immediately delivered) | Anointing was used to three sorts of Persons, at [214] their Inauguration; Whereby they were set apart to three great Offices; *viz.* Of Priests, Prophets, and Kings. Though these three Offices be in Holy Writ attributed to our Saviour, yet I do not remember that he any where assumes to himself the Title of a Priest, or mentions any thing relating to his Priesthood; Nor does he speak of his being a Prophet but very sparingly, and once or twice, as it were, by the way: But the Gospel, or the Good News of the Kingdom of the *Messiah*, is what he Preaches every where, and makes it his great business to publish to the world. This he did, not only as most agreeable to the Expectation of the *Jews*, who looked for their *Messiah*, chiefly as coming in Power to be their King and Deliverer; But as it best answered the chief end of his Coming, which was to be a King, and as such to be received by those who would be his Subjects in the Kingdom which he came to erect. And though he took not directly on himself the Title of King till he was in Custody, and in the hands of *Pilate*; yet 'tis plain, | *King*, and *King of Israel*, were the Familiar [215] and received Titles of the *Messiah*. See *John* I. 49. *Luke* XIX. 38. Compared with *Mat.* XXI. 9. And *Mark* XI. 9. *John* XII. 13. *Mat.* XXI. 5. *Luke* XXIII. 2. Compared with *Mat.* XXVII. 11. And *John* XVIII. 33–37. *Mark* XV. 12. Compared with *Mat.* XXVII. 22. *Mat.* XXVII. 42.

XII What those were to do, who believed him to be the *Messiah*, and received him for their King, that they might be admitted to be partakers with him of this Kingdom in Glory, we shall best know by the Laws he gives them, and requires them to obey; And by the Sentence which he himself will give, when, sitting on his Throne, they shall all appear at his Tribunal, to receive every one his Doom from the mouth of this Righteous Judge of all Men.

176   THE REASONABLENESS OF CHRISTIANITY

What he proposed to his Followers to be believed, we have already seen; by examining his, and his Apostles Preaching, step by step, all through the History of the four Evangelists, and the *Acts of the Apostles*. The same Method will best and plainest shew us, whether he required of [216] those who be|lieved him to be the *Messiah*, any thing besides that Faith, 6 and what it was. For he being a King, we shall see by his Commands what he expects from his Subjects: For if he did not expect Obedience to them, his Commands would be but meer Mockery; And if there were no Punishment for the Transgressors of them, his Laws would not be the 10 Laws of a King, that had Authority to Command, and Power to Chastise the disobedient; But empty Talk, without Force, and without Influence.

We shall therefore from his Injunctions (if any such there be) see what he has made Necessary to be performed, by all those who shall be received into Eternal Life in his Kingdom prepared in the Heavens. And 15 in this we cannot be deceived. What we have from his own Mouth, especially if repeated over and over again, in different places and expressions, will be past Doubt and Controversie. I shall pass by all that is said by St. *John Baptist*, or any other, before our Saviour's entry upon his Ministry and Publick Promulgation of the Laws of his Kingdom. |

[217]   He began his Preaching with a Command to Repent; As St. *Mat.* tells 21 us, IV. 17. *From that time Jesus began to preach; saying, Repent, for the kingdom of heaven is at hand.* And *Luke* V. 32. he tells the Scribes and Pharisees, *I came not to call the righteous*; Those who were truly so, needed no help, they had a right to the Tree of Life, *but sinners to Repentance.*

25   In his Sermon in the Mount, *Luke* VI. and *Mat.* V, *etc.* He commands they should be exemplary in Good Works. *Let your light so shine amongst men, that they may see your good works, and glorify your Father which is in Heaven, Mat.* V. 16. And that they might know what he came for, and what he expected of them, he tells them, *v.* 17–20. *Think not that I am* 30 *come to dissolve* or loosen, *the Law, or the Prophets: I am not come to dissolve*, or loosen, but to *make it full*, or compleat; By giving it you in its true and strict sense. Here we see he confirms, and at once reinforces all the Moral Precepts in the Old Testament. *For verily I say to you, Till Heaven and Earth* [218] *pass, one jot or one tittle, shall in no wise* | *pass from the Law, till all be done.* 35 *Whosoever therefore shall break one of these least Commandments, and shall teach men so, he shall be called the least,* (*i. e.* as it is interpreted) Shall not be at all, *in the Kingdom of Heaven.* V. 20. *I say unto you, That except your Righteousness, i. e.* your Performance of the Eternal Law of right, *shall exceed the Righteousness of the Scribes and Pharisees, ye shall in no case enter* 40 *into the Kingdom of Heaven*: And then he goes on to make good what he

AS DELIVERED IN THE SCRIPTURES

said, *v.* 17. *viz. That he was come to compleat the Law, viz.* By giving its full and clear sense, free from the corrupt and loosning glosses of the Scribes and Pharisees, *v.* 22–26. He tells them, That not only Murder, but causeless Anger, and so much as words of Contempt, were forbidden. He Commands them to be reconciled and kind towards their Adversaries; And that upon Pain of Condemnation. In the following part of his Sermon, which is to be read *Luke* VI. and more at large, *Mat.* V, VI, VII. He not only forbids actual Uncleanness, but all irregular desires, upon pain of Hell-fire; Causless Divorces; Swearing | in Conversation, as well as Forswearing in Judgment; Revenge; Retaliation; Ostentation of Charity, of Devotion, and of Fasting; Repetitions in Prayer; Covetousness; Worldly Care, Censoriousness: And on the other side, Commands Loving our Enemies; Doing good to those that Hate us; Blessing those that Curse us; Praying for those that despightfully use us; Patience, and Meekness under Injuries; Forgiveness; Liberality; Compassion: And closes all his particular injunctions, with this general Golden Rule, *Mat.* VII. 12. *All things whatsoever ye would have that Men should do to you, do ye even so to them: For this is the Law and the Prophets.* And to shew how much he is in earnest, and expects Obedience to these Laws; He tells them *Luke* VI. 35. That if they obey, *Great shall be their REWARD*; they *shall be called, The Sons of the Highest.* And to all this, in the Conclusion, he adds this Solemn Sanction; *Why call ye me Lord, Lord, and do not the things that I say?* 'Tis in vain for you to take me for the *Messiah* your King, unless you obey me. *Not every one who calls me Lord, Lord, | shall enter into the Kingdom of Heaven,* or be Sons of God; *But he that does the Will of my Father which is in Heaven.* To such Disobedient Subjects, though they have Prophesied and done Miracles in my Name, I shall say at the day of Judgment; *Depart from me ye workers of Iniquity, I know you not.*

When *Mat.* XII. he was told, That his Mother and Brethren sought to speak with him, *v.* 49. *Stretching out his hands to his Disciples, he said, Behold my Mother and my Brethren; For whosoever shall do the Will of my Father, who is in Heaven, he is my Brother, and Sister, and Mother.* They could not be Children of the Adoption, and fellow Heirs with him of Eternal Life, who did not do the Will of his Heavenly Father. *Mark* IV. 13–20.

Mat. XV. and *Mark* VII. The Pharisees finding fault, that his Disciples eat with unclean hands, he makes this Declaration to his Apostles: *Do ye not perceive, that whatsoever from without entreth into a man, cannot defile him; because it enters not into his Heart, but his Belly. That which cometh out of the Man, that defileth the Man: For from within, out of the Heart of Men,*

178   THE REASONABLENESS OF CHRISTIANITY

[221] pro\ceed evil Thoughts, Adulteries, Fornications, Murders, Thefts, false Witnesses, Covetousness, Wickedness, Deceit, Lasciviousness, an evil Eye, Blasphemy, Pride, Foolishness. All these ill things come from within, and defile a Man.

5   He commands Self-denial, and the exposing our selves to Suffering and Danger, rather than to deny or disown him: And this upon pain of losing our Souls; which are of more worth than all the World. This we may read, *Mat.* XVI. 24–27. and the parallel places, *Mark* VIII. and *Luke* IX.

10   The Apostles disputing amongst them, who should be greatest in the Kingdom of the *Messiah, Mat.* XVIII. 1. He thus determines the Controversy: *Mark* IX. 35. *If any one will be first, let him be last of all, and Servant of all*; And setting a Child before them adds, *Mat.* XVIII. 3. *Verily I say unto you, Unless ye turn, and become as Children, ye shall not enter into*
15   *the Kingdom of Heaven.*

Mat. XVIII. 15. *If thy Brother shall trespass against thee, go and tell him his fault between thee and him alone: If he shall hear thee, thou hast gained thy*
[222] *Bro\ther. But if he will not hear thee, then take with thee one or two more, that in the mouth of two or three Witnesses every word may be established. And if he*
20   *shall neglect to hear them, tell it to the Church: But if he neglect to hear the Church, let him be unto thee as an Heathen and Publican.* Verse 21. *Peter said, Lord, how often shall my Brother sin against me, and I forgive him? Till seven times? Jesus said unto him, I say not unto thee, till seven times; but until seventy times seven.* And then ends the Parable of the Servant, who being
25   himself forgiven, was rigorous to his Fellow-Servant, with these words; *v.* 34. *And his Lord was wroth, and delivered him to the Tormentors, till he should pay all that was due unto him. So likewise shall my Heavenly Father do also unto you, if you from your hearts forgive not every one his Brother their Trespasses.*

30   *Luke* X. 25. To the Lawyer, asking him, *What shall I do to inherit Eternal Life? He said, What is written in the Law? How readest thou?* He answered, *Thou shalt love the Lord thy God with all thy heart, and with all thy*
[223] *soul, and with all thy strength, and with all thy | mind; And thy Neighbour as thy self.* Jesus said, *This do, and thou shalt live.* And when the Lawyer, upon
35   our Saviour's Parable of the good *Samaritan*, was forced to confess, that he that shewed Mercy, was his Neighbour; Jesus dismissed him with this Charge, *v.* 37. *Go, and do thou likewise.*

Luke XI. 41. *Give Alms of such things as ye have: Behold, all things are clean unto you.*

40   Luke XII. 15. *Take heed, and beware of Covetousness.* Verse 22. *Be not*

AS DELIVERED IN THE SCRIPTURES 179

sollicitous what ye shall eat, or what ye shall drink, nor what ye shall put on;
But not fearful, or apprehensive of want, *For it is your Father's pleasure to
give you a Kingdom. Sell that you have, and give Alms: And provide your
selves bags that wax not old, and Treasure in the Heavens that faileth not:
For where your Treasure is, there will your heart be also. Let your loyns be* 5
*girded, and your lights burning; And ye your selves like unto men that wait
for the Lord, when he will return. Blessed are those Servants, whom the Lord
when he cometh, shall find watching. Blessed is that Servant, whom the Lord
having made | Ruler of his Houshold, to give them their Portion of Meat in* [224]
due season, the Lord, when he cometh, shall find so doing. Of a truth I say 10
*unto you, that he will make him a Ruler over all that he hath. But if that
Servant say in his heart, my Lord delayeth his coming; And shall begin to
beat the Men-servants, and Maidens, and to eat and drink, and to be
drunken: The Lord of that Servant will come in a day when he looketh not for
him, and at an hour when he is not aware, and will cut him in sunder, and* 15
*will appoint him his Portion with Unbelievers. And that Servant who knew
his Lord's will, and prepared not himself, neither did according to his will,
shall be beaten with many stripes. For he that knew not, and did commit
things worthy of stripes, shall be beaten with few stripes. For unto whomsoever
much is given, of him shall be much required: And to whom men have* 20
committed much, of him they will ask the more.

Luke XIV. 11. *Whosoever exalteth himself, shall be abased: And he that
humbleth himself, shall be exalted.*

Verse 12. *When thou makest a Dinner or Supper, call not thy Friends, or
thy Bre|thren, neither thy Kinsmen, nor thy Neighbours; lest they also bid thee* [225]
again, and a recompence be made thee. But when thou makest a Feast, call the 26
*Poor and Maimed, the Lame, and the Blind; And thou shalt be blessed: For
they cannot recompence thee: For thou shalt be recompenced at the Resurrection
of the Just.*

Verse 33. *So likewise, whosoever he be of you, that is not ready to forego all* 30
that he hath, he cannot be my Disciple.

Luke XVI. 9. *I say unto you, make to your selves Friends of the Mammon of
Unrighteousness; That when ye fail, they may receive you into Everlasting
Habitations. If ye have not been faithful in the unrighteous Mammon, who
will commit to your trust the true Riches? And if ye have not been faithful in* 35
that which is another mans, who shall give you that which is your own?

Luke XVII. 3. *If thy Brother trespass against thee, rebuke him; And if he
repent, forgive him. And if he trespass against thee seven times in a day, and
seven times in a day turn again to thee, saying, I repent; Thou shalt forgive
him. |*
40

180   THE REASONABLENESS OF CHRISTIANITY

[226]   Luke XVIII. 1. *He spoke a Parable to them, to this end, that men ought always to pray, and not to faint.*

Verse 18. *One comes to him, and asks him, saying, Master, what shall I do to inherit Eternal Life? Jesus said to him, If thou wilt enter into Life, keep the* 5 *Commandments. He says, Which? Jesus said, Thou knowest the Commandments: Thou shalt not Kill; Thou shalt not commit Adultery; Thou shalt not Steal; Thou shalt not bear false Witness; Defraud not; Honour thy Father, and thy Mother; And thou shalt love thy Neighbour as thy self. He said, All these have I observed from my Youth. Jesus hearing this, loved him; and said* 10 *unto him, Yet lackest thou one thing: Sell all that thou hast, and give it to the Poor, and thou shalt have Treasure in Heaven; And come, follow me.* To understand this right, we must take notice, that this Young Man asks our Saviour, what he must do, to be admitted effectually into the Kingdom of the *Messiah?* The Jews believed, that when the *Messiah* came, those of 15 their Nation that received him, should not die; But that they, with those

[227] who being dead should then be | raised again by him, should enjoy Eternal Life with him. Our Saviour, in Answer to this Demand, tells the Young Man, that to obtain the Eternal Life of the Kingdom of the *Messiah*, he must keep the Commandments. And then enumerating 20 several of the Precepts of the Law, the Young Man says, he had observed these from his Childhood. For which, the Text tells us, Jesus loved him. But our Saviour, to try whether in earnest he believed him to be the *Messiah*, and resolved to take him to be his King, and to obey him as such, bids him give all he has to the Poor, and come, and follow him; and 25 he should have Treasure in Heaven. This I look on to be the meaning of the place. This, of selling all he had, and giving it to the Poor, not being a standing Law of his Kingdom; but a Probationary Command to this Young Man; to try whether he truly believed him to be the *Messiah*, and was ready to obey his Commands, and relinquish all to follow him, when 30 he his Prince required it.

And therefore we see, *Luke* XIX. 14. Where our Saviour takes notice of

[228] the | Jews not receiving him as the *Messiah*, he expresses it thus; *We will not have this man to Reign over us.* 'Tis not enough to believe him to be the *Messiah*, unless we also obey his Laws, and take him to be our King, to 35 Reign over us.

Mat. XXII. 11–13. He that had not on the Wedding-Garment, though he accepted of the Invitation, and came to the Wedding, was cast into utter Darkness. By the *Wedding-Garment*, 'tis evident Good Works are meant here. That Wedding-Garment of fine Linnen, clean and white, 40 which we are told, *Rev.* XIX. 8. is the δικαιώματα, *Righteous acts of the*

AS DELIVERED IN THE SCRIPTURES 181

Saints: Or, as St. *Paul* calls it, *Ephes*. IV. 1. *The walking worthy of the Vocation wherewith we are called*. This appears from the Parable it self: *The Kingdom of Heaven*, says our Saviour, *v*. 2. *Is like unto a King, who made a Marriage for his Son*. And here he distinguishes those who were invited, into three sorts. 1. Those who were invited, and came not; *i. e*. Those who had the Gospel, the Good News of the Kingdom of God proposed to them, but believed not. | 2. Those who came, but had not on a Wedding-Garment; *i. e*. Believed *Jesus* to be the *Messiah*, but were not new clad (as I may so say) with a true Repentance, and Amendment of Life; Nor adorned with those Vertues, which the Apostle, *Col*. III. requires to be put on. 3. Those who were invited, did come, and had on the Wedding Garment; *i. e*. Heard the Gospel, believed *Jesus* to be the *Messiah*, and sincerely obeyed his Laws. These three sorts are plainly designed here; whereof the last only were the Blessed, who were to enjoy the Kingdom prepared for them.

Mat. XXIII. *Be not ye called Rabbi: For one is your Master, even the Messiah, and ye all are Brethren. And call no man your Father upon the Earth: For one is your Father which is in Heaven. Neither be ye called Masters: For one is your Master, even the Messiah. But he that is greatest amongst you, shall be your Servant. And whosoever shall exalt himself, shall be abased; And he that shall humble himself, shall be exalted.*

Luke XXI. 34. *Take heed to your selves, lest your hearts be at any time | overcharged with surfeiting and drunkenness, and cares of this life.*

Luke XXII. 25. *He said unto them, The Kings of the Gentiles exercise Lordship over them; And they that exercise Authority upon them, are called Benefactors. But ye shall not be so. But he that is greatest amongst you, let him be as the younger; And he that is chief, as he that doth serve.*

John XIII. 34. *A new Commandment I give unto you, That ye love one another; As I have loved you, that ye also love one another. By this shall all men know that ye are my Disciples, if ye love one another.* This Command, of loving one another, is repeated again, *Chap*. XV. 12. and 17.

John XIV. 15. *If ye love me, keep my Commandments.* Verse 21. *He that hath my Commandments, and keepeth them, he it is that loveth me: And he that loveth me, shall be loved of my Father, and I will love him, and manifest my self to him.* Verse 23. *If a man loveth me, he will keep my words.* Verse 24. *He that loveth me not, keepeth not my sayings.* |

John XV. 8. *In this is my Father glorified, that ye bear much fruit; so shall ye be my Disciples.* Verse 14. *Ye are my Friends, if ye do whatsoever I command you.*

Thus we see our Saviour not only confirmed the Moral Law; and

182   THE REASONABLENESS OF CHRISTIANITY

clearing it from the corrupt glosses of the Scribes and Pharisees, shewed the strictness as well as obligation of its Injunctions; But moreover, upon occasion, requires the Obedience of his Disciples to several of the Commands he afresh lays upon them; With the enforcement of
5 unspeakable Rewards and Punishments in another World, according to their Obedience, or Disobedience. There is not, I think, any of the Duties of Morality, which he has not some where or other, by himself and his Apostles, inculcated over and over again to his Followers in express terms. And is it for nothing, that he is so instant with them to
10 bring forth Fruit? Does He their King Command, and is it an indifferent thing? Or will their Happiness or Misery not at all depend upon it,
[232] whether they obey or no? They were required to believe | him to be the *Messiah*; Which Faith is of Grace promised to be reckoned to them for the compleating of their Righteousness, wherein it was defective: But
15 Righteousness, or Obedience to the Law of God, was their great business; Which if they could have attained by their own Performances, there would have been no need of this Gracious Allowance, in Reward of their Faith: But Eternal Life, after the Resurrection, had been their due by a former Covenant, even that of Works; the Rule whereof was never
20 abolished, though the Rigour were abated. The Duties enjoyned in it were Duties still. Their Obligations had never ceased; nor a wilful neglect of them was ever dispensed with. But their past Transgressions were pardoned, to those who received *Jesus*, the promised *Messiah*, for their King; And their future slips covered, if renouncing their former
25 Iniquities, they entred into his Kingdom, and continued his Subjects, with a steady Resolution and Endeavour to obey his Laws. This Righteousness therefore, a compleat Obedience and freedom from Sin,
[233] are still sincerely to | be endeavoured after. And 'tis no where promised, That those who persist in a wilful Disobedience to his Laws, shall be
30 received into the eternal bliss of his Kingdom, how much soever they believe in him.

A sincere Obedience, how can any one doubt to be, or scruple to call, a Condition of the New Covenant, as well as faith; Whoever read our Saviour's Sermon in the Mount, to omit all the rest? Can any thing be
35 more express than these words of our Lord? *Mat.* VI. 14. *If you forgive Men their Trespasses, your Heavenly Father will also forgive you: But if ye forgive not Men their Trespasses, neither will your Father forgive your Trespasses.* And *John* XIII. 17. *If ye know these things, happy are ye if ye do them.* This is so indispensible a Condition of the New Covenant, that
40 believing without it will not do, nor be accepted; If our Saviour knew the

AS DELIVERED IN THE SCRIPTURES 183

Terms on which he would admit Men into Life. *Why call ye me Lord, Lord*, says he, *Luke* VI. 46. *and do not the things which I say?* It is not enough to believe him to be the *Messiah*, the *Lord*, without obeying him. For that these he speaks to here, | were Believers, is evident, from the [234] parallel place, *Mat.* VII. 21–23. where it is thus Recorded: *Not every one who says Lord, Lord, shall enter into the Kingdom of Heaven; but he that doth the Will of my Father, which is in Heaven.* No Rebels, or Refractory Disobedient, shall be admitted there; though they have so far believed in Jesus, as to be able to do Miracles in his Name; As is plain out of the following words. *Many will say to me in that day, Have we not Prophesied in thy Name, and in thy Name have cast out Devils; and in thy Name have done many wonderful Works? And then will I profess unto them, I never knew you, depart from me ye workers of iniquity.*

This part of the New Covenant, the Apostles also, in their Preaching the Gospel of the *Messiah*, ordinarily joined with the Doctrine of Faith.

St. *Peter* in his first Sermon, *Acts* II. when they were pricked in heart, and asked, *What shall we do?* says, *v.* 38. *REPENT, and be Baptized, every one of you, in the Name of Jesus Christ, for the Remission of Sins.* The same he says to them again in his next Speech, | *Acts* III. 26. *Unto you first, God* [235] *having raised up his Son Jesus, sent him to bless you.* How was this done? *IN TURNING AWAY EVERY ONE FROM YOUR INIQUITIES.*

The same Doctrine they Preach to the High Priest and Rulers, *Acts* V. 30. *The God of our Fathers raised up Jesus, whom ye slew and hanged on a Tree. Him hath God Exalted with his right hand, to be a Prince and a Saviour for to give REPENTANCE to Israel, and Forgiveness of Sins; And we are witnesses of these things, and so is also the Holy Ghost, whom God hath given to them that obey him.*

Acts XVII. 30. *Paul* tells the *Athenians*, That now under the Gospel, *God commandeth all Men every where to REPENT.*

Acts XX. 20. St. *Paul* in his last Conference with the Elders of *Ephesus*, professes to have taught them the whole Doctrine necessary to Salvation. *I have*, says he, *kept back nothing that was profitable unto you; But have shewed you, and have taught you publickly, and from house to house; Testifying both to the Jews and to the Greeks*: And then gives an | account what his [236] Preaching had been, *viz. REPENTANCE towards God, and Faith towards our Lord Jesus the Messiah.* This was the Sum and Substance of the Gospel which St. *Paul* Preached; and was all that he knew necessary to Salvation; *viz. Repentance, and believing Jesus to be the Messiah.* And so takes his last farewel of them, whom he should never see again, *v.* 32. in these words. *And now Brethren, I commend you to God, and to the word of his Grace, which*

184   THE REASONABLENESS OF CHRISTIANITY

is able to build you up, and to give you an inheritance among all them that are sanctified. There is an Inheritance conveyed by the Word and Covenant of Grace; but it is only to those who are *Sanctified.*

Acts XXIV. 24. *When Felix sent for Paul,* that he and his Wife *Drusilla* might hear him, *concerning the Faith in Christ*; Paul reasoned of *Righteousness*, or Justice, and *Temperance*; the Duties we owe to others, and to our selves; and of the Judgment to come; Till he made *Felix* to tremble. Whereby it appears, that *Temperance and Justice* were Fundamental parts of the Religion that *Paul* professed, and [237] were |contained in the Faith which he Preached. And if we find the Duties of the Moral Law not pressed by him every where; We must remember, That most of his Sermons left upon Record, were Preached in their Synagogues to the Jews, who acknowledged their Obedience due to all the Precepts of the Law: And would have taken it amiss to have been suspected, not to have been more Zealous for the Law than he. And therefore it was with reason that his Discourses were directed chiefly to what they yet wanted, and were averse to; the knowledge and imbracing of Jesus their promised *Messiah*. But what his Preaching generally was, if we will believe him himself, we may see *Acts* XXVI. Where giving an Account to King *Agrippa* of his Life and Doctrine, he tells him, *v.* 20. *I shewed unto them of Damascus, and at Jerusalem, and throughout all the Coasts of Judea, and then to the Gentiles, that they should repent and turn to God, and do works meet for Repentance.*

Thus we see, by the Preaching of our Saviour and his Apostles, that he [238] required of those who believed him to | be the *Messiah*, and received him for their Lord and Deliverer, that they should live by his Laws: And that (though in consideration of their becoming his Subjects, by Faith in him, whereby they believed and took him to be the *Messiah*, their former Sins should be forgiven) Yet he would own none to be his, nor receive them as true denizons of the New *Jerusalem*, into the inheritance of Eternal Life; but leave them to the Condemnation of the Unrighteous; who renounced not their former Miscarriages, and lived in a sincere Obedience to his Commands. What he expects from his Followers, he has sufficiently declared as a Legislator. And that they may not be deceived, by mistaking the Doctrine of Faith, Grace, Free-Grace, and the Pardon and Forgiveness of Sins and Salvation by him, (which was the great End of his Coming) He more than once declares to them; For what omissions and miscarriages he shall Judge and Condemn to Death, even those who have owned him, and done Miracles in his Name; when he [239] comes at last to render to every one according to what he hath | DONE in

AS DELIVERED IN THE SCRIPTURES 185

the Flesh; Sitting upon his Great and Glorious Tribunal, at the end of the World.

The first place where we find our Saviour to have mentioned the day of Judgment, is *John* V. 28, 29. in these words; *The hour is coming, in which all that are in their Graves shall hear his* [i. e. the Son of God's] *Voice, and shall come forth; They that have DONE GOOD unto the Resurrection of Life; And they that have DONE EVIL, unto the Resurrection of Damnation.* That which puts the distinction, if we will believe our Saviour, is the having *done good or evil.* And he gives a reason of the necessity of his Judging or Condemning those *who have done Evil,* in the following words; *v.* 30. *I can of my own self do nothing. As I hear I judge; And my Judgment is just: Because I seek not my own Will, but the Will of my Father who hath sent me.* He could not judge of himself; He had but a delegated Power of Judging from the Father, whose Will he obeyed in it, and who was of purer Eyes than to admit any unjust Person into the Kingdom of Heaven. |

Mat. VII. 22, 23. Speaking again of that day, he tells what his Sentence will be, *depart from me ye WORKERS of Iniquity.* Faith in the Penitent and Sincerely Obedient, supplies the defect of their Performances; and so by Grace they are made Just. But we may observe; None are Sentenced or Punished for Unbelief; but only for their Misdeeds. *They are Workers of Iniquity* on whom the Sentence is Pronounced.

Mat. XIII. 41. *At the end of the World, the Son of Man shall send forth his Angels; And they shall gather out of his Kingdom all Scandals, and them which DO INIQUITY; And cast them into a Furnace of Fire; There shall be wailing and gnashing of Teeth.* And again, *v.* 49. *The Angels shall sever the WICKED from among the JUST; and shall cast them into the Furnace of Fire.*

Mat. XVI. 27. *For the Son of Man shall come in the Glory of his Father, with his Angels: And then he shall Reward every Man according to his WORKS.*

Luke XIII. 26. *Then shall ye begin to say; We have eaten and drunk in thy Presence, and thou hast taught in our Streets. But he shall say, I tell you, I | know you not; Depart from me ye WORKERS of Iniquity.*

Mat. XXV. 31–46. *When the Son of Man shall come in his Glory; and before him shall be gathered all Nations; He shall set the Sheep on his right hand, and the Goats on his Left: Then shall the King say to them on his Right hand, Come ye blessed of my Father, inherit the Kingdom prepared for you, from the Foundation of the World; For, I was an hungred, and ye gave me Meat; I was thirsty, and ye gave me drink; I was a stranger, and ye took me in; Naked, and ye cloathed me; I was sick, and ye visited me; I was in Prison, and*

186   THE REASONABLENESS OF CHRISTIANITY

ye came unto me. Then shall the Righteous Answer him, saying, Lord, When saw we thee an hungred, and fed thee? etc. And the King shall answer, and say unto them; Verily, I say unto you, In as much as ye have done it unto one of the least of these my Brethren, ye have done it unto me. Then shall he say unto them
5 *on the left hand, Depart from me, ye Cursed, into everlasting Fire, prepared for the Devil and his Angels. For I was an hungred, and ye gave me no meat; I was*
[242] *thirsty, and ye gave me no drink; | I was a stranger, and ye took me not in; Naked, and ye cloathed me not; Sick and in prison, and ye visited me not. In so much that ye did it not to one of these, ye did it not to me. And these shall go into*
10 *Everlasting Punishment: But the Righteous into Life Eternal.*

These, I think, are all the places where our Saviour mentions the last Judgment; or describes his way of Proceeding in that Great Day: Wherein, as we have observed, it is remarkable, that every where the Sentence follows, doing or not doing; without any mention of believing,
15 or not believing. Not that any to whom the Gospel hath been Preached, shall be Saved, without believing *Jesus* to be the *Messiah*: For all being Sinners, and Transgressors of the Law, and so unjust; are all liable to Condemnation; unless they believe, and so through Grace are justified by God for this Faith, which shall be accounted to them for
20 Righteousness. But the rest wanting this Cover, this allowance for their Transgressions, must answer for all their Actions: And being found Transgressors of the Law, shall by the Letter, and Sanction of that Law, |
[243] be Condemned, for not having paid a full Obedience to that Law: And not for want of Faith. That is not the Guilt, on which the Punishment is
25 laid; though it be the want of Faith, which lays open their Guilt uncovered; And exposes them to the Sentence of the Law, against all that are Unrighteous.

XIII The common Objection here, is; If all Sinners shall be Condemned, but such as have a gracious allowance made them; And so are justified by
30 God, for believing *Jesus* to be the *Messiah*, and so taking him for their King, whom they are resolved to obey, to the utmost of their Power; What shall become of all Mankind, who lived before our Saviour's time; Who never heard of his Name; And consequently could not believe in him? To this, the Answer is so obvious and natural, that one would
35 wonder, how any reasonable Man should think it worth the urging. No body was, or can be, required to believe what was never proposed to him, to believe. Before the Fulness of time, which God from the Council of his own Wisdom had appointed to send his Son in, he had at several
[244] times, and in diffe|rent Manners, promised to the People of *Israel*, an
40 extraordinary Person to come; Who, raised from amongst themselves,

AS DELIVERED IN THE SCRIPTURES 187

should be their Ruler and Deliverer. The time; And other Circumstances of his Birth, Life, and Person; he had in sundry Prophesies so particularly described, and so plainly foretold, that He was well known, and expected by the Jews; under the Name of the *Messiah*, or Anointed, given him in some of these Prophesies. All then that was required before his appearing in the World, was to believe what God had revealed; And to rely with a full assurance on God for the performance of his Promise; And to believe, that in due time he would send them the *Messiah*; this anointed King; this promised Saviour, and Deliverer; according to his Word.

This Faith in the promises of God; This relying and acquiescing in this Word and Faithfulness; The Almighty takes well at our hands, as a great mark of homage, paid by us poor frail Creatures, to his *Goodness* and *Truth*, as well as to his *Power* and *Wisdom*; And accepts it as an acknowledgment of his peculiar Providence, and | Benignity to us. And [245] therefore our Saviour tells us, *John* XII. 44. *He that believes on me, believes not on me; But on him that sent me.* The works of Nature shew his Wisdom and Power; But 'tis his peculiar Care of Mankind, most eminently discovered in his Promises to them, that shews his Bounty and Goodness; And consequently engages their Hearts in Love and Affection to him. This oblation of an Heart, fixed with dependance on and affection to him, is the most acceptable Tribute we can pay him; the foundation of true Devotion; and Life of all Religion. What a value he puts on this depending on his Word, and resting satisfied in his Promises, We have an Example in *Abraham*; whose Faith *Was counted to him for Righteousness*; As we have before remarked out of *Rom.* IV. And his relying firmly on the Promise of God, without any doubt of its performance, gave him the Name of the Father of the Faithful; And gained him so much favour with the Almighty, that he was called the *Friend of God*: The Highest and most Glorious Title can be bestowed | on [246] a Creature. The thing promised was no more, but a Son by his Wife *Sarah*; and a numerous Posterity by him, which should possess the Land of *Canaan*. These were but Temporal Blessings; And (except the Birth of a Son) very remote; Such as he should never live to see, nor in his own Person have the benefit of. But because he questioned not the Performance of it; But rested fully satisfied in the Goodness, Truth, and Faithfulness of God who had promised; It was counted to him for Righteousness. Let us see how St. *Paul* expresses it; *Rom.* IV. 18–22. *Who, against hope, believed in hope, that he might become the Father of many Nations; According to that which was spoken, so shall thy Seed be. And being not weak in his Faith, he considered not his own Body now dead, when he was*

188 THE REASONABLENESS OF CHRISTIANITY

above an hundred years old; Neither yet the deadness of Sarah's *Womb. He staggered not at the Promise of God through unbelief, but was strong in Faith, giving Glory to God; And being fully perswaded, that what he had promised, he was able to perform. And* THEREFORE, *it was imputed to him for* |

[247] *Righteousness.* St. *Paul* having here Emphatically described the strength
6 and firmness of *Abraham*'s Faith, informs us, that he thereby *gave glory to God*; And therefore it was *accounted to him for Righteousness.* This is the way that God deals with poor frail Mortals. He is graciously pleased to take it well of them; And give it the place of Righteousness, and a kind of
10 merit in his sight; If they believe his Promises, and have a steadfast relying on his veracity and goodness. St. *Paul, Heb.* XI. 6. tells us; *Without Faith it is impossible to please God*: But at the same time tells us what Faith that is. *For,* says he, *He that cometh to God, must believe that he is; And that he is a rewarder of them that diligently seek him.* He must be
15 perswaded of God's Mercy and good Will to those, who seek to obey him; And rest assured of his rewarding those who rely on him, for whatever, either by the light of Nature, or particular Promises, he has revealed to them of his tender Mercies; and taught them to expect from his Bounty. This description of *Faith* (that we might not mistake what he

[248] means | by that *Faith*, without which we cannot please God, and which
21 recommended the Saints of Old) St. *Paul* places in the middle of the List of those who were Eminent for the *Faith*; And whom he sets as Patterns to the converted *Hebrews*, under Persecution; to encourage them to persist in their confidence of Deliverance by the Coming of *Jesus Christ*;
25 And in their belief of the Promises they now had under the Gospel. By those examples he exhorts them, not to *draw back* from the Hope that was set before them; Nor Apostatize from the Profession of the Christian Religion. This is plain from *v.* 35–38. of the precedent Chapter: *Cast not away therefore your confidence, which hath great recompence of Reward. For ye*
30 *have great need of persisting, or Perseverance;* (for so the *Greek* word signifies here, which our Translation renders *Patience. Vid. Luke* VIII. 15.) *That after ye have done the Will of God, ye might receive the Promise. For yet a little while, and he that shall come will come, and will not tarry. Now the just shall live by Faith. But if any man draw back, my soul shall*
35 *have no pleasure in him.* |

[249] The Examples of *Faith*, which St. *Paul* enumerates and proposes in the following words, *Chap.* XI. plainly shew, that the *Faith* whereby those Believers of old pleased God, was nothing but a steadfast relyance on the Goodness and Faithfulness of God, for those good things, which either
40 the light of Nature, or particular Promises, had given them grounds to

AS DELIVERED IN THE SCRIPTURES 189

hope for. Of what avail this *Faith* was with God, we may see, *v.* 4. *By Faith* Abel *offered unto God a more excellent Sacrifice than* Cain; *by which he obtained witness that he was Righteous*. Verse 5. *By Faith* Enoch *was translated, that he should not see Death: For before his translation he had this Testimony, that he pleased God*. Verse 7. Noah, *being warned of God of things not seen as yet*; being wary, *by Faith prepared an Ark, to the saving of his House; By the which he condemned the World, and became Heir of the Righteousness which is by Faith*. And what it was that God so graciously accepted and rewarded, we are told, *v.* 11. *Through Faith also* Sarah *her self received strength to conceive seed, and was delivered of a Child; when | she was past age*. How she came to obtain this Grace from God, the Apostle tells us; *Because she judged him Faithful who had promised*. Those therefore who pleased God, and were accepted by him before the Coming of *Christ*, did it only by believing the Promises, and relying on the Goodness of God, as far as he had revealed it to them. For the Apostle, in the following words, tells us, *v.* 13. *These all died in Faith, not having received* (the accomplishment of) *the Promises; but having seen them afar off: And were perswaded of them, and embraced them*. This was all that was required of them; to be perswaded of, and embrace the Promises which they had. They could be *perswaded of* no more than was proposed to them; *Embrace* no more than was revealed; according to the Promises they had received, and the Dispensations they were under. And if the Faith of things *seen afar off*; If their trusting in God for the Promises he then gave them; If a belief of the *Messiah* to come; were sufficient to render those who lived in the Ages before *Christ*, Acceptable to God, and Righ|teous before him; I desire those who tell us, that God will not, (nay, some go so far as to say) cannot accept any who do not believe every Article of their particular Creeds and Systems, to consider, why God, out of his Infinite Mercy, cannot as well Justifie Man now for believing *Jesus of Nazareth* to be the promised *Messiah*, the King and Deliverer; as those heretofore, who believed only that God would, according to his Promise, in due time send the *Messiah*, to be a King and Deliverer.

IV There is another Difficulty often to be met with, which seems to have something of more weight in it: And that is, that though the *Faith* of those before *Christ*; (believing that God would send the *Messiah*, to be a Prince, and a Saviour to his People, as he had promised;) And the *Faith* of those since his time, (believing *Jesus* to be that *Messiah*, promised and sent by God) shall be accounted to them for Righteousness, Yet what shall become of all the rest of Mankind; who having never heard of the

190   THE REASONABLENESS OF CHRISTIANITY

[252] Promise or News of a Saviour, not a word of a *Messiah* to | be sent, or that
was come, have had no thought or belief concerning him?

To this I Answer; That God will require of every man, *According to
what a man hath, and not according to what he hath not.* He will not expect
5   the Improvement of Ten Talents, where he gave but One; Nor require
any one should believe a Promise, of which he has never heard. The
Apostle's Reasoning, *Rom.* X. 14. is very just: *How shall they believe in
him, of whom they have not heard?* But though there be many, who being
strangers to the Common-wealth of *Israel*, were also strangers to the
10   Oracles of God committed to that People; Many, to whom the Promise
of the *Messiah* never came, and so were never in a capacity to believe or
reject that Revelation; Yet God had, by the Light of Reason, revealed to
all Mankind, who would make use of that Light, that he was Good and
Merciful. The same spark of the Divine Nature and Knowledge in Man,
15   which making him a Man, shewed him the Law he was under as a Man;
Shewed him also the way of Attoning the merciful, kind, compassionate
[253] Author | and Father of him and his Being, when he had transgressed that
Law. He that made use of this Candle of the Lord, so far as to find what
was his Duty; could not miss to find also the way to Reconciliation and
20   Forgiveness, when he had failed of his Duty: Though if he used not his
Reason this way; If he put out, or neglected this Light; he might,
perhaps, see neither.

The Law is the eternal, immutable Standard of Right. And a part of
that Law is, that a man should forgive, not only his Children, but his
25   Enemies; upon their Repentance, asking Pardon, and Amendment. And
therefore he could not doubt that the Author of this Law, and God of
Patience and Consolation, who is rich in Mercy, would forgive his frail
Off-spring; if they acknowledged their Faults, disapproved the Iniquity
of their Transgressions, beg'd his Pardon, and resolved in earnest for the
30   future to conform their Actions to this Rule, which they owned to be
Just and Right. This way of Reconciliation, this hope of Attonement, the
Light of Nature revealed to them. And the Revelation of the Gospel
[254] ha|ving said nothing to the contrary, leaves them to stand and fall to their
own Father and Master, whose Goodness and Mercy is over all his
35   Works.

I know some are forward to urge that place of the *Acts, Chap.* IV. as
contrary to this. The words, *v.* 10. and 12. stand thus: *Be it known unto
you all, and to all the People of* Israel, *that by the Name of Jesus Christ of*
Nazareth, *whom ye crucified, whom God raised from the dead, even by him*
40   *doth this man,* [*i. e.* The lame man restored by *Peter*] *stand here before you*

AS DELIVERED IN THE SCRIPTURES 191

whole. This is the stone which is set at nought by you builders, which is become the head of the Corner. Neither is there Salvation in any other: For there is none other name under Heaven given among men, in which we must be saved. Which, in short, is: that *Jesus* is the only true *Messiah*; Neither is there any other Person but he given to be a Mediator between God and Man, in whose Name we may ask and hope for Salvation.

It will here possibly be asked, *Quorsum perditio hæc?* What need was there of a Saviour? What Advantage have we by *Jesus Christ?* |

It is enough to justifie the fitness of any thing to be done, by resolving it into the *Wisdom of God*, who has done it; though our short views and narrow understandings may utterly incapacitate us to see that wisdom, and to judge rightly of it. We know little of this visible, and nothing at all of the state of that Intellectual World; wherein are infinite numbers and degrees of Spirits out of the reach of our ken or guess; And therefore know not what Transactions there were between God and our Saviour, in reference to his Kingdom. We know not what need there was to set up a Head and a Chieftain, in opposition to *The Prince of this World, the Prince of the Power of the Air,* etc. Whereof there are more than obscure intimations in Scripture. And we shall take too much upon us, if we shall call God's Wisdom or Providence to Account, and pertly condemn for needless, all that our weak, and perhaps biassed *Understandings,* cannot Account for.

Though this general Answer be Reply enough to the forementioned Demand, and such as a Rational Man, or fair searcher after Truth, will acquiesce | in; Yet in this particular case, the Wisdom and Goodness of God has shewn it self so visibly to common Apprehensions, that it hath furnished us abundantly wherewithal to satisfie the Curious and Inquisitive; who will not take a Blessing, unless they be instructed what need they had of it, and why it was bestowed upon them. The great and many Advantages we receive by the coming of *Jesus* the *Messiah,* will shew that it was not without need, that he was sent into the World.

The Evidence of our Saviour's *Mission* from Heaven is so great, in the multitude of Miracles he did before all sorts of People; that what he delivered cannot but be received as the Oracles of God, and unquestionable Verity. For the Miracles he did were so ordered by the Divine Providence and Wisdom, that they never were, nor could be denied by any of the Enemies or Opposers of Christianity.

Though the Works of Nature, in every part of them, sufficiently Evidence a Deity; Yet the World made so little use of their Reason, that they saw him not; Where even by the | impressions of himself he was

192   THE REASONABLENESS OF CHRISTIANITY

easie to be found. Sense and Lust blinded their minds in some; And a
careless Inadvertency in others; And fearful Apprehensions in most (who
either believed there were, or could not but suspect there might be,
Superior unknown Beings) gave them up into the hands of their Priests,
5 to fill their Heads with false Notions of the Deity, and their Worship
with foolish Rites, as they pleased: And what Dread or Craft once began,
Devotion soon made Sacred, and Religion immutable. In this state of
Darkness and Ignorance of the true God, Vice and Superstition held the
World. Nor could any help be had or hoped for from *Reason*; which
10 could not be heard, and was judged to have nothing to do in the case:
The Priests every where, to secure their Empire, having excluded *Reason*
from having any thing to do in Religion. And in the croud of wrong
Notions, and invented Rites, the World had almost lost the sight of the
One only True God. The Rational and thinking part of Mankind, 'tis
[258] true, when they sought after him, found the One, | Supream, Invisible
16 God: But if they acknowledged and worshipped him, it was only in their
own minds. They kept this Truth locked up in their own breasts as a
Secret, nor ever durst venture it amongst the People; much less amongst
the Priests, those wary Guardians of their own Creeds and Profitable
20 Inventions. Hence we see that *Reason*, speaking never so clearly to the
Wise and Virtuous, had never Authority enough to prevail on the
Multitude; and to perswade the Societies of Men, that there was but One
God, that alone was to be owned and worshipped. The Belief and
Worship of One God, was the National Religion of the *Israelites* alone:
25 And if we will consider it, it was introduced and supported amongst that
People by *Revelation*. They were in *Goshen*, and had Light; whilst the rest
of the World were in almost *Egyptian* Darkness, *without God in the World*.
There was no part of Mankind, who had quicker Parts, or improved
them more; that had a greater light of Reason, or followed it farther in all
[259] sorts of Speculations, than the *Athenians*: And yet | we find but one
31 *Socrates* amongst them, that opposed and laughed at their Polytheism,
and wrong Opinions of the Deity; And we see how they rewarded him
for it. Whatsoever *Plato*, and the soberest of the Philosophers thought of
the Nature and Being of the One God, they were fain, in their outward
35 Professions and Worship, to go with the Herd, and keep to the Religion
established by Law; Which what it was, and how it had disposed the
minds of these knowing, and quick-sighted *Grecians*, St. *Paul* tells us,
Acts XVII. 22–29. *Ye men of Athens*, says he, *I perceive that in all things ye
are too superstitious. For as I passed by, and beheld your Devotions, I found an*
40 *Altar with this Inscription, TO THE UNKNOWN GOD. Whom therefore*

AS DELIVERED IN THE SCRIPTURES 193

ye ignorantly worship, him declare I unto you. God that made the World, and all things therein, seeing that he is Lord of Heaven and Earth, dwelleth not in Temples made with hands: Neither is worshipped with mens hands, as though he needed any thing, seeing he giveth unto all life, and breath, and all things; And hath made of one Blood all the | Nations of Men, for to dwell on the face of the Earth; And hath determined the times before appointed, and the bounds of their Habitations; That they should seek the Lord, if haply they might feel him out, and find him, though he be not far from every one of us. Here he tells the *Athenians*, that they, and the rest of the World (given up to Superstition) whatever Light there was in the Works of Creation and Providence, to lead them to the True God, yet they few of them found him. He was every where near them, yet they were but like People groping and feeling for something in the dark, and did not see him with a full clear day-light; *But thought the Godhead like to Gold, and Silver, and Stone, graven by Art and man's device.*

In this state of Darkness and Error, in reference to the *True God*, our Saviour found the World. But the clear Revelation he brought with him, dissipated this Darkness; made *the One Invisible True God* known to the World: And that with such Evidence and Energy, that *Polytheism* and *Idolatry* hath no where been able to withstand | it: But where ever the Preaching of the Truth he delivered, and the Light of the Gospel hath come, those Mists have been dispelled. And in effect we see that since our Saviour's time, the *Belief of One God* has prevailed and spread it self over the face of the Earth. For even to the Light that the *Messiah* brought into the World with him, we must ascribe the owning, and Profession of *One God*, which the *Mahometan* Religion had derived and borrowed from it. So that in this sense it is certainly and manifestly true of our Saviour, what St. *John* says of him; 1 *John* III. 8. *For this purpose the Son of God was manifested, that he might destroy the works of the Devil.* This Light the World needed, and this Light it received from him: That there is but *One God*, and he *Eternal, Invisible*; Not like to any visible Objects, nor to be represented by them.

If it be asked, whether the Revelation to the *Patriarchs* by *Moses*, did not teach this, and why that was not enough? The Answer is obvious; that however clearly the Knowledge of One Invisible God, maker of Heaven and | Earth, was revealed to them; Yet that Revelation was shut up in a little corner of the World; amongst a People by that very Law, which they received with it, excluded from a Commerce and Communication with the rest of mankind. The Gentile World in our Saviour's time, and several Ages before, could have no Attestation of the

194   THE REASONABLENESS OF CHRISTIANITY

Miracles, on which the *Hebrews* built their Faith, but from the *Jews* themselves; A People not known to the greatest part of mankind; Contemned and thought vilely of by those Nations that did know them; And therefore very unfit and unable to propagate the Doctrine of *One* 5 *God* in the World, and diffuse it through the Nations of the Earth, by the strength and force of that Ancient Revelation, upon which they had received it. But our Saviour, when he came, threw down this Wall of Partition; And did not confine his Miracles or Message to the Land of *Canaan*, or the Worshippers at *Jerusalem*. But he himself preached at 10 *Samaria*, and did miracles in the Borders of *Tyre* and *Sydon*, and before [263] multitudes of People gathered from | all Quarters. And after his Resurrection, sent his Apostles amongst the Nations, accompanied with Miracles; which were done in all Parts so frequently, and before so many Witnesses of all sorts, in broad day-light, that, as I have before observed, 15 the Enemies of Christianity have never dared to deny them; No, not *Julian* himself: Who neither wanted Skill nor Power to enquire into the Truth; Nor would have failed to have proclaimed and exposed it, if he could have detected any falshood in the History of the Gospel; or found the least ground to question the Matter of Fact published of Christ, and 20 his Apostles. The Number and Evidence of the Miracles done by our Saviour and his Followers, by the power and force of Truth, bore down this mighty and accomplished Emperour, and all his Parts, in his own Dominions. He durst not deny so plain Matter of Fact; Which being granted, the truth of our Saviour's Doctrine and Mission unavoidably 25 follows; notwithstanding whatsoever Artful Suggestions his Wit could invent, or Malice should offer, to the contrary. |

[264]   2. Next to the Knowledge of one God; Maker of all things; A clear *knowledge of their Duty* was wanting to Mankind. This part of Knowledge, though cultivated with some care, by some of the Heathen Philosophers; 30 Yet got little footing among the People. All Men indeed, under pain of displeasing the Gods, were to frequent the Temples: Every one went to their Sacrifices and Services: But the Priests made it not their business to teach them *Virtue*. If they were diligent in their Observations and Ceremonies; Punctual in their Feasts and Solemnities, and the tricks of 35 Religion; The holy Tribe assured them, the Gods were pleased; and they looked no farther. Few went to the Schools of the Philosophers, to be instructed in their Duties; And to know what was Good and Evil in the Actions. The Priests sold the better Pennyworths, and therefore had all the Custom. Lustrations and Processions were much easier than a clean 40 Conscience, and a steady course of Virtue; And an expiatory Sacrifice,

AS DELIVERED IN THE SCRIPTURES 195

that attoned for the want of it, was much more conveni|ent, than a strict [265]
and holy Life. No wonder then, that Religion was every where
distinguished from, and preferred to *Virtue*; And that it was dangerous
Heresy and Prophaneness to think the contrary. So much *Virtue* as was
necessary to hold Societies together; and to contribute to the quiet of 5
Governments, the Civil Laws of Commonwealths taught, and forced
upon Men that lived under Magistrates. But these Laws, being for the
most part made by such who had no other aims but their own Power,
reached no farther than those things, that would serve to tie Men
together in subjection; Or at most, were directly to conduce to the 10
Prosperity and Temporal Happiness of any People. But *Natural Religion*
in its full extent, was no where, that I know, taken care of by the force of
Natural Reason. It should seem by the little that has hitherto been done
in it, That 'tis too hard a task for unassisted Reason, to establish Morality
in all its parts upon its true foundations; with a clear and convincing 15
light. And 'tis at least a surer and shorter way, to the Apprehensions of |
the vulgar, and mass of Mankind, that one manifestly sent from God, and [266]
coming with visible Authority from him, should as a King and Law-
maker tell them their Duties; and require their Obedience; Than leave it
to the long, and sometimes intricate deductions of Reason, to be made 20
out to them. Such trains of reasonings the greatest part of Mankind have
neither leisure to weigh; nor, for want of Education and Use, skill to
judge of. We see how unsuccessful in this, the attempts of Philosophers
were before our Saviour's time. How short their several Systems came of
the perfection of a true and compleat *Morality* is very visible. And if, since 25
that, the Christian Philosophers have much outdone them; yet we may
observe, that the first knowledge of the truths they have added, are
owing to Revelation: Though as soon as they are heard and considered,
they are found to be agreeable to Reason; and such as can by no means be
contradicted. Every one may observe a great many truths which he 30
receives at first from others, and readily assents to, as consonant to
reason; which he would have | found it hard, and perhaps beyond his [267]
strength to have discovered himself. Native and Original truth, is not so
easily wrought out of the Mine, as we who have it delivered, ready dug
and fashon'd into our hands, are apt to imagine. And how often at Fifty 35
or Threescore years old are thinking Men told, what they wonder how
they could miss thinking of? Which yet their own Contemplations did
not, and possibly never would have helped them to. Experience shews
that the knowledge of Morality, by meer natural light, (how agreeable
soever it be to it) makes but slow progress, and little advance in the 40

196   THE REASONABLENESS OF CHRISTIANITY

World. And the reason of it is not hard to be found in Men's Necessities, Passions, Vices, and mistaken Interests; which turn their thoughts another way. And the designing Leaders, as well as following Herd, find it not to their purpose to imploy much of their Meditations this way. Or
5 whatever else was the cause, 'tis plain in fact, that humane reason unassisted, failed Men in its great and Proper business of *Morality*. It
[268] never from unquestionable Principles, by clear deductions, made out | an entire Body of the *Law of Nature*. And he that shall collect all the Moral Rules of the Philosophers, and compare them with those contained in
10 the New Testament, will find them to come short of the *Morality* delivered by our Saviour, and taught by his Apostles; A College made up for the most part of ignorant, but inspired Fishermen.

   Though yet, if any one should think, that out of the saying of the Wise Heathens, before our Saviour's time, there might be a Collection made
15 of all those Rules of *Morality*, which are to be found in the Christian Religion; Yet this would not at all hinder, but that the World nevertheless stood as much in need of our Saviour, and the *Morality* delivered by him. Let it be granted (though not true) that all the *Moral Precepts* of the Gospel were known by some Body or other, amongst
20 Mankind, before. But where or how, or of what use, is not considered. Suppose they may be picked up here and there; Some from *Solon* and *Bias* in *Greece*; Others from *Tully* in *Italy*: And to compleat the Work, let
[269] *Confutius*, as far as *China*, be consulted; And *Anacarsis* | the *Scythian* contribute his share. What will all this do, to give the World a *compleat*
25 *morality*, that may be to Mankind, the unquestionable Rule of Life and Manners? I will not here urge the impossibility of collecting from men, so far distant from one another, in time, and place, and languages. I will suppose there was a *Stobeus* in those times, who had gathered the *Moral sayings*, from all the Sages of the World. What would this amount to,
30 towards being a steady Rule; A certain transcript of a Law that we are under? Did the saying of *Aristippus*, or *Confutius*, give it an Authority? Was *Zeno* a Lawgiver to Mankind? If not, what he or any other Philosopher delivered, was but a saying of his. Mankind might hearken to it, or reject it, as they pleased; Or as it suited their interest, passions,
35 principles or humours. They were under no Obligation: The Opinion of this or that Philosopher, was of no Authority. And if it were, you must take all he said under the same Character. All his dictates must go for
[270] Law, certain and true; Or none of them. And then, If | you will take any of the Moral sayings of *Epicurus* (many whereof *Seneca* quotes, with
40 esteem and approbation) for Precepts of the *Law of Nature*; You must

AS DELIVERED IN THE SCRIPTURES 197

take all the rest of his Doctrine for such too; Or else his Authority ceases: And so no more is to be received from him, or any of the Sages of old, for parts of the *Law of Nature*, as carrying with it an obligation to be obeyed, but what they prove to be so. But such a Body of *Ethicks*, proved to be the Law of Nature, from principles of Reason, and reaching all the Duties of Life; I think no body will say the World had before our Saviour's time. 'Tis not enough, that there were up and down scattered sayings of wise Men, conformable to right Reason. The Law of Nature, was the Law of Convenience too: And 'tis no wonder, that those Men of Parts, and studious of Virtue; (Who had occasion to think on any particular part of it) should by meditation light on the right, even from the observable Convenience and beauty of it; Without making out its obligation from the true Principles of the Law of Nature, and | foundations of *Morality*. But these incoherent apophthegms of Philosophers, and wise Men; however excellent in themselves, and well intended by them; could never make a Morality, whereof the World could be convinced, could never rise up to the force of a Law that Mankind could with certainty depend on. Whatsoever should thus be universally useful, as a standard to which Men should conform their Manners, must have its Authority either from Reason or Revelation. 'Tis not every Writer of Morals, or Compiler of it from others, that can thereby be erected into a Law-giver to Mankind; and a dictator of Rules, which are therefore valid, because they are to be found in his Books; under the Authority of this or that Philosopher. He that any one will pretend to set up in this kind, and have his Rules pass for authentique directions; must shew, that either he builds his Doctrine upon Principles of Reason, self-evident in themselves; and deduces all the parts of it from thence, by clear and evident demonstration: Or must shew his Commission from Heaven; That he comes with Authority from God, to deliver his | Will and Commands to the World. In the former way, no body that I know before our Saviour's time, ever did; or went about to give us a *Morality*. 'Tis true there is a *Law of Nature*. But who is there that ever did, or undertook to give it us all entire, as a Law; No more, nor no less, than what was contained in, and had the obligation of that Law? Who, ever made out all the parts of it; Put them together; And shewed the World their obligation? Where was there any such Code, that Mankind might have recourse to, as their unerring Rule, before our Saviour's time? If there was not, 'tis plain, there was need of one to give us such a *Morality*; Such a Law, which might be the sure guide of those who had a desire to go right; And if they had a mind, need not mistake

198 THE REASONABLENESS OF CHRISTIANITY

their Duty; But might be certain when they had performed, when failed in it. Such a *Law of Morality*, Jesus Christ hath given us in the New Testament; But by the latter of these ways, by Revelation. We have from him a full and sufficient Rule for our direction; And conformable to that

[273] of Reason. But | the truth and obligation of its Precepts have their force,

6 and are put past doubt to us, by the evidence of his Mission. He was sent by God: His Miracles shew it; And the Authority of God in his Precepts cannot be questioned. Here *Morality* has a sure Standard, that Revelation vouches, and Reason cannot gainsay, nor question; but both together

10 witness to come from God the great Law-maker. And such an one as this out of the New Testament, I think the World never had, nor can any one say is any where else to be found. Let me ask any one, who is forward to think that the Doctrine of *Morality* was full and clear in the World, at our Saviour's Birth; Whither would he have directed *Brutus* and *Cassius*,

15 (both Men of Parts and Virtue, the one whereof believed, and the other disbelieved a future Being) to be satisfied in the Rules and Obligations of all the parts of their Duties; If they should have asked him where they might find the Law, they were to live by, and by which they should be charged or acquitted, as guilty or innocent? If to the sayings of the Wise,

[274] and | the Declarations of Philosophers; He sends them into a wild Wood

21 of uncertainty, to an endless maze; from which they should never get out: If to the Religions of the World, yet worse: And if to their own Reason, he refers them to that which had some light and certainty; but yet had hitherto failed all Mankind in a perfect Rule; And we see,

25 resolved not the doubts that had arisen amongst the Studious and Thinking Philosophers; Nor had yet been able to convince the Civilized parts of the World, that they had not given, nor could without a Crime, take away the Lives of their Children, by Exposing them.

If any one shall think to excuse humane Nature, by laying blame on
30 Men's *negligence*, that they did not carry Morality to an higher pitch; and make it out entire in every part, with that clearness of demonstration which some think it capable of; He helps not the matter. Be the cause what it will, our Saviour found Mankind under a Corruption of Manners and Principles, which Ages after Ages had prevailed, and must be

[275] confessed | was not in a way or tendency to be mended. The Rules of

36 Morality were in different Countries and Sects, different. And natural Reason no where had, nor was like to Cure the Defects and Errors in them. Those just measures of Right and Wrong, which necessity had any where introduced, the Civil Laws prescribed, or Philosophy recom-
40 mended, stood not on their true Foundations. They were looked on as

AS DELIVERED IN THE SCRIPTURES 199

bonds of Society, and Conveniences of common Life, and laudable Practises. But where was it that their Obligation was throughly known and allowed, and they received as Precepts of a Law; Of the highest Law, the Law of Nature? That could not be, without a clear knowledge and acknowledgment of the Law-maker, and the great Rewards and Punishments, for those that would or would not obey him. But the Religion of the Heathens, as was before observed; little concerned it self in their Morals. The Priests that delivered the Oracles of Heaven, and pretended to speak from the Gods, Spoke little of Virtue and a good Life. And on the other side, | the Philosophers who spoke from Reason, made not much mention of the Deity in their *Ethicks*. They depended on Reason and her Oracles; which contain nothing but Truth. But yet some parts of that Truth lye too deep for our Natural Powers easily to reach, and make plain and visible to mankind, without some Light from above to direct them.

When Truths are once known to us, though by Tradition, we are apt to be favourable to our own Parts; And ascribe to our own Understandings the Discovery of what, in reality, we borrowed from others; Or, at least, finding we can prove what at first we learnt from others, we are forward to conclude it an obvious Truth, which, if we had sought, we could not have missed. Nothing seems hard to our Understandings, that is once known; And because what we see we see with our own Eyes, we are apt to over-look or forget the help we had from others, who shewed it us, and first made us see it, as if we were not at all beholden to them for those truths, which they opened the way and lead us into. For Knowledge being only of Truths that are perceived to be so, we are partial enough to our own Faculties to conclude that they of their own strength would have attained those Discoveries without any assistance from others. Knowledge is light in the mind, which we see and perceive: And whilst it is cer|tain that they be our own eyes that see and perceive it, who shall perswade us that ours were not made and given us to find truth as well as theirs who had no other advantage but the luck to be before us? Thus the whole stock of Human Knowledge is claimed by every one, as his private Possession, as soon as he (profiting by others Discoveries) has got it into his own mind; And so it is: But not properly by his own single Industry, nor of his own Acquisition. He studies, 'tis true, and takes pains to make a progress in what others have delivered; But their pains were of another sort, who first brought those Truths to light, which he afterwards derives from them. He that Travels the Roads now, applauds his own strength and legs, that have carried him so far in such a scantling

200 THE REASONABLENESS OF CHRISTIANITY

of time; And ascribes all to his own Vigor, little considering how much he owes to their pains, who cleared the Woods, drained the Bogs, built the Bridges, and made the Ways passable; without which he might have toiled much with little progress.

5   A great many things which we have been bred up in the belief of from [278] our Cra|dles, (and are Notions grown Familiar, and as it were Natural to us, under the Gospel,) we take for unquestionable obvious Truths, and easily demonstrable; without considering how long we might have been in doubt or ignorance of them, had Revelation been silent. And many are 10 beholden to Revelation, who do not acknowledge it.

   'Tis no diminishing to Revelation, that Reason gives its Suffrage too to the Truths Revelation has discovered. But 'tis our mistake to think, that because Reason confirms them to us, we had the first certain knowledge of them from thence, and in that clear Evidence we now possess them. 15 The contrary is manifest, in the *defective Morality of the Gentiles* before our Saviour's time; and the want of Reformation in the Principles and Measures of it, as well as Practice. Philosophy seemed to have spent its strength, and done its utmost; Or if it should have gone farther, as we see it did not, and from undenyable Principles given us *Ethicks* in a Science 20 like Mathematicks in every part demonstrable, this yet would not have [279] been so effectual to man in this imperfect | state, nor proper for the Cure. The greatest part of mankind want leisure or capacity for Demonstration; nor can they carry a train of Proofs; which in that way they must always depend upon for Conviction, and cannot be required to assent to 25 till they see the Demonstration. Wherever they stick, the Teachers are always put upon Proof, and must clear the Doubt by a Thread of coherent deductions from the first Principle, how long, or how intricate soever that be. And you may as soon hope to have all the Day-Labourers and Tradesmen, the Spinsters and Dairy Maids perfect Mathematicians, 30 as to have them perfect in *Ethicks* this way. Hearing plain Commands, is the sure and only course to bring them to Obedience and Practice. The greatest part cannot know, and therefore they must believe. And I ask, whether one coming from Heaven in the Power of God, in full and clear Evidence and Demonstration of Miracles, giving plain and direct Rules 35 of *Morality* and Obedience, be not likelier to enlighten the bulk of Mankind, and set them right in their Duties, and bring them to do | [280] them, than by Reasoning with them from general Notions and Principles of Humane Reason? And were all the Duties of Humane Life clearly demonstrated; yet I conclude, when well considered, that Method of 40 teaching men their Duties, would be thought proper only for a few, who

AS DELIVERED IN THE SCRIPTURES 201

had much Leisure, improved Understandings, and were used to abstract Reasonings. But the Instruction of the People were best still to be left to the Precepts and Principles of the Gospel. The healing of the Sick, the restoring sight to the Blind by a word, the raising, and being raised from the Dead, are matters of Fact, which they can without difficulty conceive; 5 And that he who does such things, must do them by the assistance of a Divine Power. These things lye level to the ordinariest Apprehension; He that can distinguish between sick and well, Lame and sound, dead and alive, is capable of this Doctrine. To one who is once perswaded that Jesus Christ was sent by God to be a King, and a Saviour of those who do 10 believe in him; All his Commands become Principles: There needs no other Proof | for the truth of what he says, but that he said it. And then [281] there needs no more but to read the inspired Books, to be instructed: All the Duties of Morality lye there clear, and plain, and easy to be understood. And here I appeal, whether this be not the surest, the safest, 15 and most effectual way of teaching: Especially if we add this farther consideration; That as it suits the lowest Capacities of Reasonable Creatures, so it reaches and satisfies, Nay, enlightens the highest. The most elevated Understandings cannot but submit to the Authority of this Doctrine as Divine; Which coming from the mouths of a company of 20 illiterate men, hath not only the attestation of Miracles, but reason to confirm it; Since they delivered no Precepts but such, as though Reason of itself had not clearly made out, Yet it could not but assent to when thus discovered; And think itself indebted for the Discovery. The Credit and Authority our Saviour and his Apostles had over the minds of Men, 25 by the Miracles they did; Tempted them not to mix (as we find in that of all the | Sects of Philosophers, and other Religions) any Conceits; any [282] wrong Rules; any thing tending to their own by-interest, or that of a Party; in their Morality. No tang of prepossession or phansy; No footsteps of Pride or Vanity; No touch of Ostentation or Ambition, 30 appears to have a hand in it. It is all pure, all sincere; Nothing too much, nothing wanting: But such a compleat Rule of Life, as the wisest Men must acknowledge, tends entirely to the good of Mankind: And that all would be happy, if all would practise it.

3. The outward forms of *Worshipping the Deity*, wanted a Reforma- 35 tion. Stately Buildings, costly Ornaments, peculiar and uncouth Habits, And a numerous huddle of pompous, phantastical, cumbersome Ceremonies, every where attended Divine Worship. This, as it had the peculiar Name, so it was thought the principal part, if not the whole of Religion. Nor could this possibly be amended whilst the Jewish Ritual 40

THE REASONABLENESS OF CHRISTIANITY

stood; And there was so much of it mixed with the Worship of the True God. To this also our Saviour, with the knowledge of the infinite in|visible supream Spirit, brought a Remedy; in a plain, spiritual, suitable Worship. *Jesus* says to the Woman of *Samaria, The hour cometh, when ye shall neither in this Mountain, nor yet at* Jerusalem, *worship the Father. But the True Worshippers, shall worship the Father, both in Spirit and in Truth; For the Father seeketh such to worship.* To be Worshipped in Spirit and in Truth; With application of Mind and sincerity of Heart, was what God henceforth only required. Magnificent Temples, and confinement to certain Places, were now no longer necessary for his Worship; Which by a Pure Heart might be performed any where. The splendor and distinction of Habits, and pomp of Ceremonies, and all outside Performances, might now be spared. God who was a Spirit, and made known to be so, required none of those; but the Spirit only: And that in publick Assemblies, (where some Actions must lie open to the view of the World) All that could appear and be seen, should be done decently, and in order, and to Edification. Decency, Order, Edification, were to regulate all their | publick Acts of Worship; And beyond what these required, the outward appearance, (which was of little value in the Eyes of God) was not to go. Having shut out indecency and confusion out of their Assemblies, they need not be solicitous about useless Ceremonies. Praises and Prayer, humbly offered up to the Deity, was the Worship he now demanded; And in these every one was to look after his own Heart, And know that it was that alone which God had regard to, and accepted.

4. Another great advantage received by our Saviour, is the great incouragement he brought to a virtuous and pious Life: Great enough to surmount the difficulties and obstacles that lie in the way to it; And reward the pains and hardships of those, who stuck firm to their Duties, and suffered for the Testimony of a good Conscience. The Portion of the Righteous has been in all Ages taken notice of, to be pretty scanty in this World. Virtue and Prosperity, do not often accompany one another; And therefore Virtue seldom had many Followers. And 'tis no wonder She prevailed not much in a State, | where the Inconveniencies that attended her were visible, and at hand; And the Rewards doubtful, and at a distance. Mankind, who are and must be allowed to pursue their Happiness; Nay, cannot be hindred; Could not but think themselves excused from a strict observation of Rules, which appeared so little to consist with their chief End, Happiness; Whilst they kept them from the enjoyments of the Life; And they had little evidence and security of another. 'Tis true, they might have argued the other way, and concluded;

AS DELIVERED IN THE SCRIPTURES 203

That, Because the Good were most of them ill treated here, There was another place where they should meet with better usage: But 'tis plain, they did not. Their thoughts of another life were at best obscure: And their expectations uncertain. Of *Manes*, and Ghosts, and the shades of departed Men, There was some talk; But little certain, and less minded. They had the Names of *Styx* and *Acheron*; Of Elisian fields, and seats of the Blessed: But they had them generally from their Poets, mixed with their Fables. And so they looked more like the Inventions of | Wit, and [286] Ornaments of Poetry, than the serious perswasions of the grave and the sober. They came to them bundled up amongst their tales; And for tales they took them. And that which rendred them more suspected, and less useful to virtue, was, that the Philosophers seldom set their Rules on Men's Minds and Practises, by consideration of another Life. The chief of their Arguments were from the excellency of Virtue: And the highest they generally went, was the exalting of humane Nature, Whose Perfection lay in virtue. And if the Priest at any time talked of the Ghosts below, and a Life after this, it was only to keep Men to their Superstitious and Idolatrous Rites; Whereby the use of this Doctrine was lost to the credulous Multitude; And its belief to the quicker sighted, who suspected it presently of Priest-craft. Before our Saviour's time, the Doctrine of a future State, though it were not wholly hid, yet it was not clearly known in the World. 'Twas an imperfect view of Reason; Or, perhaps the decay'd remains of an ancient Tradition; which rather seemed to float | on Mens Phansies, than sink deep into their Hearts. It [287] was something, they knew not what, between being and not being. Something in Man they imagined might scape the Grave: But a perfect compleat Life of an Eternal duration, after this; was what entred little into their thoughts, and less into their perswasions. And they were so far from being clear herein, that we see no Nation of the World publickly professed it, and built upon it: No Religion taught it: And 'twas no where made an Article of Faith, and Principle of Religion till Jesus Christ came; Of whom it is truly said, that he at his appearing *brought life and immortality to light*. And that not only in the clear Revelation of it; And in instances shewn of Men raised from the Dead; But he has given us an unquestionable assurance and pledge of it, in his own Resurrection and Ascension into Heaven. How hath this one truth changed the Nature of things in the World, and given the advantage to Piety over all that could tempt or deter Men from it? The Philosophers indeed shewed the beauty of Virtue: | They set her off so as drew Mens Eyes and approbation to [288] her: But leaving her unendowed, very few were willing to espouse her.

204   THE REASONABLENESS OF CHRISTIANITY

The generality could not refuse her their esteem and commendation; But still turned their Backs on her and forsook her, as a match not for their turn. But now there being put into the Scales, on her side, *An exceeding and immortal weight of Glory*; Interest is come about to her; And Virtue
5 now is visibly the most enriching purchase, and by much the best bargain. That she is the perfection and excellency of our Nature; That she is her self a Reward, and will recommend our Names to future Ages, is not all that can now be said for her. 'Tis not strange that the learned Heathens satisfied not many with such airy commendations. It has
10 another relish and efficacy, to perswade Men that if they live well here, they shall be happy hereafter. Open their Eyes upon the endless unspeakable joys of another Life; And their Hearts will find something solid and powerful to move them. The view of Heaven and Hell, will cast
[289] a slight upon the short pleasures and | pains of this present state; and give
15 attractions and encouragments to Virtue, which reason, and interest, and the Care of our selves, cannot but allow and prefer. Upon this foundation, and upon this only, Morality stands firm, and may defy all competition. This makes it more than a name; A substantial Good, worth all our aims and endeavours; And thus the Gospel of Jesus Christ
20 has delivered it to us.

5. To these I must add one advantage more we have by Jesus Christ, and that is the promise of assistance. If we do what we can, he will give us his Spirit to help us to do what, and how we should. 'Twill be idle for us, who know not how our own Spirits move and act us, to ask in what
25 manner the Spirit of God shall work upon us. The Wisdom that accompanies that Spirit, knows better than we how we are made, and how to work upon us. If a wise Man knows how to prevail on his Child, to bring him to what he desires; Can we suspect, that the Spirit and Wisdom of God should fail in it; though we perceive or comprehend not
[290] the ways of his Operation? Christ has promi|sed it, who is faithful and
31 just; And we cannot doubt of the Performance. 'Tis not requisite on this occasion, for the inhancing of this benefit, to enlarge on the frailty of our Minds, and weakness of our Constitutions; How liable to mistakes, how apt to go astray, and how easily to be turned out of the paths of Virtue. If
35 any one needs go beyond himself, and the testimony of his own Conscience in this point; If he feels not his own errors and passions always tempting, and often prevailing, against the strict Rules of his Duty; He need but look abroad into any Age of the World to be convinced. To a Man under the difficulties of his Nature, beset with
40 Temptations, and hedged in with prevailing Customs; 'tis no small

AS DELIVERED IN THE SCRIPTURES 205

encouragement to set himself seriously on the courses of Virtue, and practise of true Religion, That he is from a sure hand, and an almighty arm, promised assistance to support and carry him through.

XV There remains yet something to be said to those who will be ready to Object, If the belief of Jesus of *Nazareth* to be the *Messiah*, together with those | concomitant Articles of his Resurrection, Rule, and coming again to Judge the World, be all the Faith required as necessary to Justification, to what purpose were the Epistles written; I say, if the belief of those many Doctrines contained in them, be not also necessary to Salvation? And if what is there delivered, a Christian may believe or disbelieve, and yet nevertheless be a Member of Christ's Church, and one of the Faithful?

To this I Answer, That the Epistles were written upon several occasions: And he that will read them as he ought, must observe what 'tis in them is principally aimed at; find what is the Argument in hand, and how managed; if he will understand them right, and profit by them. The observing of this will best help us to the true meaning and mind of the Writer: For that is the Truth which is to be received and believed; And not scattered Sentences in Scripture-Language, accommodated to our Notions and Prejudices. We must look into the drift of the Discourse, observe the coherence and connexion of the Parts, and see how it is consistent with it self, and other parts of Scripture; if we will con|ceive it right. We must not cull out, as best suits our System, here and there a Period or a Verse; as if they were all distinct and independent Aphorisms; and make these the Fundamental Articles of the Christian Faith, and necessary to Salvation, unless God has made them so. There be many Truths in the Bible, which a good Christian may be wholly ignorant of, and so not believe; which, perhaps, some lay great stress on, and call Fundamental Articles, because they are the distinguishing Points of their Communion. The Epistles, most of them, carry on a Thread of Argument, which in the stile they are writ, cannot every where be observed without great Attention. And to consider the Texts, as they stand and bear a part in that, is to view them in their due light, and the way to get the true sense of them. They were writ to those who were in the Faith, and true Christians already: And so could not be designed to teach them the Fundamental Articles and Points necessary to Salvation. The Epistle to the *Romans* was writ to all *that were at* Rome, *beloved of God, called to be Saints, whose* | *Faith was spoken of through the World*, Chap. I. 7, 8. To whom St. *Paul's* first Epistle to the *Corinthians* was, he shews, *Chap.* I. 2, 4, *etc. Unto the Church of God which is at* Corinth, *to them that*

206   THE REASONABLENESS OF CHRISTIANITY

are sanctified in Christ Jesus, called to be Saints; with all them that in every place call upon the Name of Jesus Christ our Lord, both theirs and ours. I thank my God always on your behalf, for the grace of God which is given you by Jesus Christ; That in every thing ye are enriched by him in all utterance,
5 *and in all knowledge: Even as the Testimony of Christ was confirmed in you. So that ye come behind in no gift; waiting for the coming of the Lord Jesus Christ.* And so likewise the second was, *To the Church of God at* Corinth, *with all the Saints in* Achaia, *Chap.* I. 1. His next is to the *Churches of* Galatia. That to the *Ephesians* was, *To the Saints* that were *at* Ephesus,
10 *and to the faithful in Christ Jesus.* So likewise, *To the Saints and faithful Brethren in Christ at* Colosse, *who had Faith in Christ Jesus, and love to the Saints. To the Church of the* Thessalonians. *To Timothy* his *Son in the*
[294] *Faith. To Titus* his *own Son after the* | *common Faith. To* Philemon *his dearly beloved, and fellow-labourer.* And the Author to the *Hebrews* calls
15 those he writes to, *Holy Brethren, partakers of the Heavenly Calling, Chap.* III. 1. From whence it is evident, that all those whom St. *Paul* writ to, were *Brethren, Saints, Faithful* in the *Church,* and so *Christians* already; And therefore wanted not the Fundamental Articles of the Christian Religion; without a belief of which they could not be saved: Nor can it
20 be supposed, that the sending of such Fundamentals was the reason of the Apostle's Writing to any of them. To such also St. *Peter* writes, as is plain from the first Chapter of each of his Epistles. Nor is it hard to observe the like in St. *James* and St. *John*'s Epistles. And St. *Jude* directs his thus: *To them that are sanctified by God the Father, and preserved in Jesus*
25 *Christ, and called.* The Epistles therefore being all written to those who were already Believers and Christians, the occasion and end of writing them, could not be to Instruct them in that which was necessary to make
[295] them Christians. This 'tis plain they knew and believed already; or | else they could not have been Christians and Believers. And they were writ
30 upon Particular Occasions; and without those Occasions had not been writ; and so cannot be thought necessary to Salvation: Though they resolving doubts, and reforming mistakes, are of great Advantage to our Knowledge and Practice. I do not deny, but the great Doctrines of the Christian Faith are dropt here and there, and scattered up and down in
35 most of them. But 'tis not in the Epistles we are to learn what are the Fundamental Articles of Faith, where they are promiscuously, and without distinction mixed with other Truths in Discourses that were (though for Edification indeed, yet) only occasional. We shall find and discern those great and necessary Points best in the Preaching of our
40 Saviour and the Apostles, to those who were yet strangers, and ignorant

AS DELIVERED IN THE SCRIPTURES 207

of the Faith, to bring them in, and convert them to it. And what that was, we have seen already out of the History of the Evangelists, and the *Acts*; where they are plainly laid down, so that no body can mistake them. The Epistles to particular Chur|ches, besides the main Argument of each of [296] them, (which was some present Concernment of that particular Church to which they severally were address'd) do in many places explain the Fundamentals of the Christian Religion; and that wisely; by proper Accommodations to the Apprehensions of those they were writ to, the better to make them imbibe the Christian Doctrine, and the more easily to comprehend the Method, Reasons, and Grounds of the great work of Salvation. Thus we see in the Epistle to the *Romans*, Adoption (a Custom well known amongst those of *Rome*) is much made use of, to explain to them the Grace and Favour of God, in giving them Eternal Life; to help them to conceive how they became the Children of God, and to assure them of a share in the Kingdom of Heaven, as Heirs to an Inheritance. Whereas the setting out, and confirming the Christian Faith to the *Hebrews*, in the Epistle to them, is by Allusions and Arguments, from the Ceremonies, Sacrifices, and Oeconomy of the Jews, and References to the Records of the Old Testament. And as for the General | Epistles, they, [297] we may see, regard the state, and exigencies, and some peculiarities of those times. These Holy Writers, inspired from above, writ nothing but Truth; and in most places very weighty Truths to us now; for the expounding, clearing, and confirming of the Christian Doctrine, and establishing those in it who had embraced it. But yet every Sentence of theirs must not be taken up, and looked on as a Fundamental Article necessary to Salvation; without an explicit belief whereof, no body could be a Member of Christ's Church here, nor be admitted into his Eternal Kingdom hereafter. If all, or most of the Truths declared in the Epistles, were to be received and believed as Fundamental Articles, what then became of those Christians who were fallen asleep? (as St. *Paul* witnesses in his First to the *Corinthians*, many were) before these things in the Epistles were revealed to them? Most of the Epistles not being written till above Twenty Years after our Saviour's Ascension, and some after Thirty.

But farther, therefore, to those who will be ready to say, May those Truths | delivered in the Epistles, which are not contained in the [298] Preaching of our Saviour and his Apostles, and are therefore by this Account not necessary to Salvation, be believed, or disbelieved without any danger? May a Christian safely question or doubt of them?

To this I Answer, That the Law of Faith, being a Covenant of Free

208 THE REASONABLENESS OF CHRISTIANITY

Grace, God alone can appoint what shall be necessarily believed by every one whom he will Justifie. What is the Faith which he will accept and account for Righteousness, depends wholly on his good Pleasure. For 'tis of Grace, and not of Right, that this Faith is accepted. And therefore he alone can set the Measures of it: And what he has so appointed and declared, is alone necessary. No body can add to these Fundamental Articles of Faith; nor make any other necessary, but what God himself hath made and declared to be so. And what these are, which God requires of those who will enter into, and receive the Benefits of the New Covenant, has already been shewn. An explicit belief of these, is absolutely required of all those to whom the Gospel of Jesus | Christ is preached, and Salvation through his Name proposed.

The other parts of Divine Revelation are Objects of Faith, and are so to be received. They are Truths whereof no one can be rejected; none that is once known to be such, may or ought to be disbelieved. For to acknowledge any Proposition to be of Divine Revelation and Authority, and yet to deny or disbelieve it, is to offend against this Fundamental Article and Ground of Faith, that God is true. But yet a great many of the Truths revealed in the Gospel, every one does, and must confess, a man may be ignorant of; nay, disbelieve, without danger to his Salvation: As is evident in those, who allowing the Authority, differ in the Interpretation and meaning of several Texts of Scripture, not thought Fundamental: In all which 'tis plain the contending Parties, on one side or tother, are ignorant of, nay, disbelieve the Truths delivered in Holy Writ; unless Contrarieties and Contradictions can be contained in the same words, and Divine Revelation can mean contrary to it self. |

Though all divine Revelation requires the obedience of Faith; yet every truth of inspired Scriptures is not one of those, that by the Law of Faith is required to be explicitly believed to Justification. What those are, we have seen by what our Saviour and his Apostles proposed to, and required in those whom they Converted to the Faith. Those are fundamentals; which 'tis not enough not to disbelieve: Every one is required actually to assent to them. But any other Proposition contained in the Scripture, which God has not thus made a necessary part of the Law of Faith, (without an actual assent to which he will not allow any one to be a Believer) a Man may be ignorant of, without hazarding his Salvation by a defect in his Faith. He believes all that God has made necessary for him to believe, and assent to: And as for the rest of Divine Truths, there is nothing more required of him, but that he receive all the parts of Divine Revelation, with a docility and disposition prepared to imbrace, and

AS DELIVERED IN THE SCRIPTURES 209

assent to all Truths coming from God; And submit his mind to whatsoever shall appear to him to | bear that Character. Where he, upon [301] fair endeavours, understands it not; How can he avoid being ignorant? And where he cannot put several Texts, and make them consist together; What Remedy? He must either interpret one by the other, or suspend his 5 Opinion. He that thinks that more is, or can be required, of poor frail Man in matters of Faith, will do well to consider what absurdities he will run into. God out of the infiniteness of his Mercy, has dealt with Man as a compassionate and tender Father. He gave him Reason, and with it a Law: That could not be otherwise than what Reason should dictate; 10 Unless we should think, that a reasonable Creature, should have an unreasonable Law. But considering the frailty of Man, apt to run into corruption and misery, he promised a Deliverer, whom in his good time he sent; And then declared to all Mankind, that whoever would believe him to be the Saviour promised, and take him now raised from the dead, 15 and constituted the Lord and Judge of all Men, to be their King and Ruler, should be saved. This is a plain intelligible Proposition; | And the [302] all-merciful God seems herein to have consulted the poor of this World, and the bulk of Mankind. These are Articles that the labouring and illiterate Man may comprehend. This is a Religion suited to vulgar 20 Capacities; And the state of Mankind in this World, destined to labour and travel. The Writers and Wranglers in Religion fill it with niceties, and dress it up with notions; which they make necessary and fundamental parts of it; As if there were no way into the Church, but through the Academy or Lyceum. The greatest part of Mankind have not leisure for 25 Learning and Logick, and superfine distinctions of the Schools. Where the hand is used to the Plough, and the Spade, the head is seldom elevated to sublime Notions, or exercised in mysterious reasonings. 'Tis well if Men of that rank (to say nothing of the other Sex) can comprehend plain propositions, and a short reasoning about things 30 familiar to their Minds, and nearly allied to their daily experience. Go beyond this, and you amaze the greatest part of Mankind: And may as well talk *Arabick* to a poor day Labourer, as | the Notions and Language [303] that the Books and Disputes of Religion are filled with; and as soon you will be understood. The Dissenting Congregations are supposed by 35 their Teachers to be more accurately instructed in matters of Faith, and better to understand the Christian Religion, than the vulgar Con- formists, who are charged with great ignorance; How truly I will not here determine. But I ask them to tell me seriously, whether half their People have leisure to study. Nay, Whether one in ten of those who 40

210 THE REASONABLENESS OF CHRISTIANITY

come to their Meetings in the Country, if they had time to study them, do or can understand, the Controversies at this time so warmly managed amongst them, about Justification, the subject of this present Treatise? I have talked with some of their Teachers, who confess themselves not to understand the difference in debate between them. And yet the points they stand on, are reckoned of so great weight, so material, so fundamental in Religion, that they divide Communion and separate upon them. Had God intended that none but the Learned Scribe, the [304] disputer or wise of this World, | should be Christians, or be Saved, thus Religion should have been prepared for them; filled with speculations and niceties, obscure terms, and abstract notions. But Men of that expectation, Men furnished with such acquisitions, the Apostle tells us, 1 *Cor.* I. are rather shut out from the simplicity of the Gospel; to make way for those poor, ignorant, illiterate, Who heard and believed promises of a Deliverer; and believed Jesus to be him; Who could conceive a Man dead and made alive again, and believe that he should at the end of the World, come again and pass Sentence on all Men, according to their deeds. That the poor had the Gospel Preached to them, Christ makes a mark as well as business of his Mission. *Mat.* XI. 5. And if the poor had the Gospel Preached to them, it was, without doubt, such a Gospel, as the poor could understand, plain and intelligible: And so it was, as we have seen, in the Preachings of Christ and his Apostles.

FINIS.

A Vindication of the Reasonableness
of Christianity, &c.

My Book had not been long out, before it fell under the Correction of the Author of a Treatise, Entituled, *Some Thoughts concerning the several Causes and Occasions of Atheism, especially in the present Age*. No contemptible Adversary I'le assure you; since, as it seems, he has got the Faculty to heigthen every thing that displeases him into the Capital Crime of Atheism; And breaths against those who come in his way a Pestilential Air, whereby every the least Distemper is turned into the Plague, and becomes Mortal. For whoever does not just say after Mr. *Ed's.* cannot 'tis evident escape being an Atheist, or a promoter of Atheism. I cannot but approve of any ones Zeal to Guard and Secure that great and Fundamental Article of all Religion and Morality, That there is a God: But Atheism being a Crime, which for its Madness as well as Guilt, ought to shut a Man out of all Sober and Civil Society, should be very warily charged on any one by deductions and Consequences which he himself does not own, or at least do not manifestly and unavoidably flow from what he asserts. This Caution, Charity, I think, obliges us to: And our Author would possibly think himself hardly dealt with, if, for neglecting some of those Rules he himself gives, *p.* 31. & 34. against Atheism, he should be pronounced a promoter of it: As rational a Charge, I imagine, as some of those he makes; And as fitly put together, as the *Treatise of the Reasonableness of Christianity*, &c. brought in among the causes of Atheism. However, I shall not much complain of him, since he joyns me, *p.* 104. with no worse Company than two Eminently Pious and Learned* Prelates of our Church, whom he makes favourers of the same *Conceit*, as he calls it. But what has that *Conceit* to do with Atheism? Very much. That *Conceit* is of Kin to *Socianism*, and *Socinianism* to *Atheism*. Let us hear Mr. *Ed's.* himself. He says, *p.* 113. I am *all over Socinianized*: and therefore my Book fit to be placed among the Causes of Atheism. For in the 64. and following Pages, he endeavours to shew, That *a Socinian is an Atheist, or lest that should seem harsh, one that favours the Cause of Atheism, p.* 75. for so he has been pleased to mollifie, now it is published as a Treatise, what was much more harsh, and much more

---

* Bp. Taylor, and Bp. Croft

212   THE REASONABLENESS OF CHRISTIANITY

confident in it, when it was Preached as a Sermon. In this abatement he seems a little to comply with his own Advice against his fourth Cause of Atheism; which we have in these words, *pag.* 34. *Wherefore that we may effectually prevent this folly in our selves, let us banish Presumption,* 5 *Confidence, and Self-conceit; let us extirpate all Pride and Arrogance: Let us not List our selves in the Number of Capricious Opiniators.*

I shall leave the *Socinians* themselves to answer his Charge against them, and shall Examine his Proof of my being a *Socinian*. It stands thus, *pag.* 112. *When he* [the Author of the Reasonableness of Christianity, 10 &c.] *proceeds to mention the Advantages and Benefits of Christ's coming into the World, and appearing in the Flesh, he hath not one Syllable of his satisfying for us, or by his Death purchasing Life or Salvation, or any thing that sounds like it. This and several other things shew that he is all over Socinianized.* Which in effect is, that because I have not set down all that this Author 15 perhaps would have done, therefore I am a *Socinian*. But what if I should say, I set down as much as my Argument required, and yet am no *Socinian?* Would he from my silence and omission give me the Lye, and say, I am one? Surmizes that may be over-turned by a single denial, are poor Arguments, and such as some Men would be ashamed of: At least if 20 they are to be permitted to Men of this Gentleman's Skill and Zeal, who knows how to make good use of Conjectures, Suspicions, and Uncharitable Censures in the Cause of God; yet even there too (if the Cause of God can need such Arts) they require a good Memory to keep them from recoiling upon the Author. He might have taken notice of 25 these words in my Book, *pag.* 10. 'From this estate of Death Jesus CHRIST RESTORES all Mankind to Life.' And a little lower, 'The Life which Jesus Christ restores to all Men.' And *p.* 205. 'He that hath incurred Death for his own Transgression, cannot LAY DOWN HIS LIFE FOR ANOTHER, as our Saviour professes he did.' This methinks 30 SOUNDS SOMETHING LIKE *Christ's purchasing Life for us by his Death.* But this Reverend Gentleman has an Answer ready; It was not in the place he would have had it in: It was not where I *mention* the Advantages and Benefits of Christ's coming. And therefore, I not having one Syllable of Christ's Purchasing Life and Salvation for us by his 35 Death, or any thing that sounds like it; this, and several other things that might be offered, shew that I am *all over Socinianized*. A very clear and ingenuous Proof, and let him enjoy it.

But what will become of me, that I have not mentioned *Satisfaction?*

Possibly this Reverend Gentleman would have had Charity enough for 40 a known Writer of the Brotherhood, to have found it by an *Inuendo* in

A VINDICATION 213

those words above quoted, of laying down his Life for another. But every thing is to be strained here the other way. For the Author of the *Reasonableness of Christianity*, &c. is of necessity to be represented as a *Socinian*; or else his Book may be read, and the Truths in it, which Mr. *Ed's.* likes not, be received, and People put upon examining. Thus one, as 5 full of Happy Conjectures and Suspicions as this Gentleman, might be apt to Argue. But what if the Author designed his Treatise, as the Title shews, chiefly for those who were not yet throughly or firmly Christians; proposing to work on those who either wholly disbelieved or doubted of the truth of the Christian Religion? Would any one blame his Prudence, 10 if he mentioned only those Advantages which all Christians are agreed in? Might he not remember and observe that Command of the Apostle, *Rom.* 14. 1. *Him that is weak in the Faith receive ye, but not to doubtful disputations*, without being a *Socinian*? Did he amiss, that he offered to the belief of those who stood off, that, and only that which our Saviour 15 and his Apostles preached for the reducing the unconverted World? And would any one think he in earnest went about to perswade Men to be Christians, who should use that as an Argument to recommend the Gospel, which he has observed Men to lay hold on as an Objection against it? To urge such Points of Controversie as necessary Articles of 20 Faith, when we see our Saviour and the Apostles in their Preaching urged them not as necessary to be believed, to make Men Christains, is (by our own Authority) to add Prejudices to Prejudices, and to block up our own way to those Men whom we would have access to, and prevail upon. But some Men had rather you should write Booty, and cross your own 25 design of removing mens Prejudices to Christianity, than leave out one tittle of what they put into their Systems. To such I say; Convince but Men of the Mission of Jesus Christ; make them but see the Truth, Simplicity, and Reasonableness of what he himself Taught, and required to be believed by his Followers; and you need not doubt, but, being once 30 fully perswaded of his Doctrine, and the Advantages which all Christians agree are received by him, such Converts will not lay by the Scriptures; but by a constant Reading and Study of them, get all the Light they can from this Divine Revelation; and nourish themselves up in the words of Faith, and of good Doctrin, as St. *Paul* speaks to *Timothy*. But some Men 35 will not bear it, that any one should speak of Religion, but according to the Model that they themselves have made of it. Nay, though he proposes it upon the very Terms, and in the very Words which our Saviour and his Apostles preached it in, yet he shall not escape Censures, and the severest Insinuations. To deviate in the least, or to omit any thing 40

214   THE REASONABLENESS OF CHRISTIANITY

contained in their Articles, is Heresie under the most invidious Names in fashion, and 'tis well if he escapes being a down-right Atheist. Whether this be the way for Teachers to make themselves hearkened to, as Men in earnest in Religion, and really concerned for the Salvation of mens Souls, 5 I leave them to consider. What success it has had towards perswading Men of the Truth of Christianity, their own complaints of the prevalency of Atheism on the one hand, and the Number of Deists on the other, sufficiently shew.

Another thing laid down to my Charge, *p.* 105. & 107. is my 10 *forgetting, or rather wilful omitting some plain and obvious Passages*, and some *Famous Testimonies in the Evangelists*; namely, *Mat.* 28. 19. *Go teach all Nations, baptizing them in the Name of the Father, and of the Son, and of the Holy Ghost.* And *John* 1. 1. *In the beginning was the Word, and the Word was with God, and the Word was God.* And verse 14. *And the Word was* 15 *made Flesh*. Mine it seems in this Book, are all sins of Omission. And yet when it came out, the buz, and flutter, and noise which was made, and the Reports which were raised, would have perswaded the World that it subverted all Morality, and was designed against the Christian Religion. I must confess Discourses of this kind, which I met with spread up and 20 down, at first amazed me; knowing the sincerity of those thoughts which perswaded me to publish it, (not without some hope of doing some Service to decaying Piety, and mistaken and slandered Christianity.) I satisfied my self against those Heats with this assurance, that if there was any thing in my Book, against what any one called Religion, it was not 25 against the Religion contained in the Gospel. And for that I appeal to all Mankind.

But to return to Mr. *Ed's*. in particular, I must take leave to tell him, that if omitting *plain and obvious Passages, and famous Testimonies in the Evangelists*, be a fault in me, I wonder why he, among so many of this 30 kind that I am guilty of, mentions so few. For I must acknowledge I have omitted more, nay, many more, that are *plain and obvious Passages, and famous Testimonies in the Evangelists*, than those he takes notice of. But if I have left out none of those *Passages or Testimonies* which contain what our Saviour and his Apostles preached, and required assent to, to make men 35 Believers, I shall think my Omissions (let them be what they will) no faults in the present case. What ever Doctrines Mr. *Edwards* would have to be believed, if they are such as our Saviour and his Apostles required to be believed to make a Man a Christian, he will be sure to find them in those Preachings and *Famous Testimonies* of our Saviour and his Apostles 40 that I have quoted. And if they are not there, he may rest satisfied, that

A VINDICATION 215

they were not proposed by our Saviour and his Apostles, as necessary to be believed, to make Men Christ's Disciples.

If the Omission of other Texts in the Evangelists (which are all true also, and no one of them to be disbelieved) be a fault, it might have been expected that Mr. *Edwards* should have accused me for leaving out *Mat.* 1. 18. to 23. and *Mat.* 17. 24. 35. 50. 60. for these are *plain and obvious Passages, and famous Testimonies in the Evangelists*; and such whereon these Articles of the Apostles Creed, *viz. Born of the Virgin* Mary, *suffered under* Pontius Pilate, *was crucified, dead, and buried*, are founded. These being Articles of the Apostles Creed, are look'd upon as *Fundamental Doctrines*: And one would wonder why Mr. *Edwards* so quietly passes by their Omission; did it not appear that he was so intent on fixing his Imputation of *Socinianism* upon me, that rather than miss that, he was content to drop the other Articles of his Creed. For I must observe to him, that if he had blamed me for the Omission of the places last quoted out of St. *Matthew* (as he had as much reason as for any other) it would plainly have appeared how idle and ill-grounded his charging *Socinianism* on me was. But at any rate he was to give the Book an ill Name. Not because it was *Socinian*. For he has no more reason to charge it with *Socinianism* for the Omissions he mentions, than the Apostles Creed. 'Tis therefore well for the Compliers of that Creed, that they lived not in Mr. *Edwards*'s days: For he would no doubt have found them *all over Socinianized*, for omitting the Texts he quotes, and the Doctrines he collects out of *Joh.* 1. & *Joh.* 14 p. 107, 108. *Socinianism* then is not the fault of the Book, whatever else it be. For I repeat it again, there is not one word of *Socinianism* in it. I that am not so good at Conjectures as Mr. *Edwards*, shall leave it to him to say; or to those who can bear the plainness and simplicity of the Gospel, to guess, what its fault is.

Some men are shrewd guessers, and others would be thought to be so: But he must be carried far by his forward Inclination, who does not take notice, that the World is apt to think him a Diviner, for any thing rather than for the sake of Truth, who sets up his own Suspicions against the direct Evidence of things; and pretends to know other mens Thoughts and Reasons better than they themselves. I had said, that the Epistles being writ to those who were already Believers, could not be supposed to be writ to them to teach them Fundamentals, without which they could not be Believers.

And the Reason I gave why I had not gone through the Writings in the Epistles, to Collect the Fundamental Articles of Faith, as I had through the Preachings of our Saviour and his Apostles, was, Because those

216   THE REASONABLENESS OF CHRISTIANITY

Fundamental Articles were in those Epistles promiscuously, and without distinction, mixed with other Truths. And therefore we shall find and discern those great and necessary Points best in the Preachings, of our Saviour and the Apostles, to those who were yet ignorant of the Faith, and unconverted. This, as far as I know my own thoughts, was the reason why I did (as Mr. *Edwards* complains, *p.* 109.) *not proceed to the Epistles, and not give an Account of them, as I had done of the Gospels and Acts.* This I imagined I had in the close of my Book so fully and clearly expressed, particularly *p.* 125. that I supposed no body, how willing soever, could have mistaken me. But this Gentleman is so much better acquainted with me than I am with my self; sees so deeply into my Heart, and knows so perfectly everything that passes there; that he with assurance tells the World, *p.* 109. *That I purposely omitted the Epistolary Writings of the Apostles, because they are fraught with other Fundamental Doctrines besides that one which I mention.* And then he goes on to enumerate those Fundamental Articles, p. 110, 111, viz. *The Corruption and Degeneracy of Humane Nature, with the true Original of it (the Defection of our first Parents) the Propagation of Sin and Mortality, our Restoration and Reconciliation by Christ's Blood, the Eminency and Excellency of his Priesthood, the Efficacy of his Death, the full Satisfaction made thereby to Divine Justice, and his being made an All sufficient Sacrifice for Sin. Christ's Righteousness, our Justification by it, Election, Adoption, Sanctification, Saving Faith, The Nature of the Gospel, The New Covenant, The Riches of God's Mercy in the way of Salvation by Jesus Christ, The certainty of the Resurrection of Humane Bodies, and of the future Glory.*

Give me leave now to ask you seriously whether these, which you have here set down under the Title of *Fundamental Doctrines*, are such (when reduced to Propositions) that every one of them is required to be believed to make a Man a Christian, and such, as without the actual belief thereof, he cannot be saved. If they are not so every one of them, you may call them *Fundamental Doctrines* as much as you please, they are not of those Doctrines of Faith I was speaking of, which are only such as are required to be actually believed to make a Man a Christian. If you say, some of them are such necessary Points of Faith, and others not, you by this specious List of well-sounding, but unexplained terms arbitrarily collected, only make good what I have said, *viz.* That the necessary Articles of Faith are in the Epistles promiscuously delivered with other Truths, and therefore they cannot be distinguished but by some other mark than being barely found in the Epistles. If you say, that they are all of them necessary Articles of Faith, I shall then desire you to reduce them

A VINDICATION 217

to so many plain Doctrines, and then prove them to be every one of them required to be believed by every Christian Man to make him a member of the Christian Church. For to begin with the first, 'tis not enough to tell us, as you do, that *the Corruption and Degeneracy of Humane Nature, with the true Original of it, (the Defection of our first Parents) the Propagation of Sin and Mortality, is one of the great Heads of Christian Divinity.* But you are to tell us what are the Propositions we are required to believe concerning this matter: For nothing can be an Article of Faith, but some Proposition; and then it will remain to be proved, that these Articles are necessary to be believed to Salvation. The Apostles Creed was taken, in the first Ages of the Church, to contain all things necessary to Salvation; I mean, necessary to be believed: But you have now better thought on it, and are pleased to enlarge it, and we, no doubt, are bound to submit to your Orthodoxy.

The List of Materials for his Creed (for the Articles are not yet formed) Mr. *Ed's.* closes, *p.* 111. with these words: *These are the Matters of Faith contained in the Epistles, and they are Essential and Integral parts of the Gospel it self.* What, just these? Neither more nor less? If you are sure of it, pray let us have them speedily, for the Reconciling of Differences in the Christian Church, which has been so cruelly torn about the Articles of the Christian Faith, to the great Reproach of Christian Charity, and Scandal of our true Religion.

Mr. *Ed's.* having thus, with two learned Terms of *Essential and Integral* Parts, sufficiently proved the Matter in Question, *viz.* That all those, he has set down, are Articles of Faith necessary to be believed to make a Man a Christian, he grows warm at my omission of them. This I cannot complain of as unnatural: The Spirit of Creed-making always arising from an heat of Zeal for our own Opinions, and warm Endeavours, by all ways possible to decry and bear down those who differ in a tittle from us. What then could I expect more gentle and candid, than what Mr. *Ed's.* has subjoyned in these words? *And therefore it is no wonder, that our Author, being sensible of this (viz.* That the Points he has named were *Essential and Integral parts of the Gospel) would not vouchsafe to give us an Abstract of those inspired Writings* [*the Epistles*] *but passes them by with some Contempt.* Sir, when your Angry Fit is over, and the abatement of your Passion has given way to the return of your Sincerity, I shall beg you to read this passage in 297 *pag.* of my Book. 'These Holy Writers (*viz.* the Penmen of the Epistles) INSPIRED from above, writ nothing but Truth, and in most places very weighty Truths to us now, for the expounding, clearing, and confirming of the Christian Doctrine; and

218 THE REASONABLENESS OF CHRISTIANITY

establishing those in it who had embraced it.' And again, *pag.* 299. 'The other parts of DIVINE REVELATION are Objects of Faith, and are so to be received. They are Truths, of which none that is once known to be such, *i.e.* revealed, may or ought to be disbelieved.' And if this does not
5 satisfie you that I have as high a Veneration for the Epistles, as you or any one can have, I require you to publish to the World those passages which shew my *Contempt* of them. In the mean time I shall desire my Reader to examine what I have writ concerning the Epistles, which is all contained between *p.* 290 and 301 of my Book; And then to Judge, whether I have
10 made bold with the Epistles in what I have said of them, or this Gentleman made bold with Truth in what he has writ of me. Humane Frailty will not, I see, easily quit its hold; What it loses in one part, it will be ready to regain in another; and not be hindred from taking Reprizals, even on the most Priviledged sort of Men. Mr. *Ed's.* who is entrenched in
15 Orthodoxy, and so is as safe in Matters of Faith almost as Infallibility it self, is yet as apt to Err as others in Matter of Fact.

But he has not yet done with me about the Epistles: All his fine Draught of my slighting that part of the Scripture will be lost, unless the last strokes compleat it into *Socinianism.* In his following words you have
20 the Conclusion of the whole Matter. His words are these. *And more especially, if I may Conjecture,* (by all means, Sir; Conjecturing is your proper Talent; you have hitherto done nothing else; And I will say that for you, you have a lucky Hand at it.) *He doth this (i.e. pass by the Epistles with Contempt) because he knew that there are so many and frequent, and*
25 *those so illustrious and eminent Attestations to the doctrine of the ever to be adored Trinity, in these Epistles.* Truly, Sir, if you will permit me to know what I know, as well as you do allow your self to conjecture what you please, you are out for this once. The Reason why I went not through the Epistles, as I did the Gospels and the *Acts,* was that very Reason I printed,
30 and that will be found so sufficient a one to all considerate Readers, that I believe they will think you need not strain your Conjectures for another. And if you think it be so easie to distinguish Fundamentals from not Fundamentals in the Epistles, I desire you to try your Skill again, in giving the World a perfect Collection of Propositions out of the Epistles,
35 that contain all that is required, and no more than what is absolutely required to be believed by all Christians, without which Faith they cannot be of Christ's Church. For I tell you, notwithstanding the shew you have made, you have not yet done it, nor will you affirm that you have.
40 His next Page, *viz.* 112. is made up of the same, which he calls, Not

A VINDICATION 219

Uncharitable Conjectures, *I expound*, he says, *John* 14. 9 &c. *after the Antitrinitarian Mode*: And I make Christ *and Adam to be Sons of God, in the same sense, and by their Birth, as the Racovians generally do*. I know not but it may be true, that the *Antitrinitarians and Racovians* understand those places as I do: But 'tis more than I know that they do so. I took not my sense of those Texts from those Writers, but from the Scripture it self, giving Light to its own meaning, by one place compared with another: What in this way appears to me its true meaning, I shall not decline, because I am told, that it is so understood by the *Racovians*, whom I never yet read; nor embrace the contrary, though *the generality of Divines* I more converse with, should declare for it. If the sense wherein I understand those Texts be a mistake, I shall be beholding to you if you will set me right. But they are not Popular Authorities, or Frightful Names, whereby I judge of Truth or Falshood. You will now no doubt applaud your Conjectures; The Point is gained, and I am openly a *Socinian*, since I will not disown that I think the *Son of God* was a Phrase that among the *Jews* in our Saviour's time was used for the *Messiah*, though the *Socinians* understand it in the same sense; And therefore I must certainly be of their Perswasion in every thing else. I admire the acuteness, force, and fairness of your Reasoning, and so I leave you to Triumph in your *Conjectures*. Only I must desire you to take notice, that that Ornament of our Church, and every way Eminent Prelate, the late Arch-Bishop of *Canterbury*, understood that Phrase in the same sense that I do, without being a *Socinian*. You may read what he says concerning *Nathanael*, in his first *Serm. of Sincerity*, published this year. His words are these, *p. 4. And being satisfied that he* [our Saviour] *was the Messiah, he presently owned him for such, calling him SON OF GOD, and king of Israel*.

Though this Gentleman know my Thoughts as perfectly as if he had for several years past lain in my Bosom, yet he is mightily at a loss about my Person: As if it at all concerned the Truth contained in my Book, what Hand it came from. However the Gentleman is mightily perplexed about the Author. Why, Sir? What if it were writ by a Scribler of *Bartholomew* Fair Drolls, with all that flourish of Declamatory Rhetorick, and all that smartness of Wit and Jest about *Capt. Tom, Unitarians, Units, and Cyphers*, &c. Which are to be found between 115 and 123 Pages of a Book that came out during the merry time of Rope-Dancing, and Puppet-Plays? What is Truth, would, I hope, nevertheless be Truth in it, however odly sprused up by such an Author: Though perhaps 'tis likely some would be apt to say, such Merriment became not the Gravity of my

220 THE REASONABLENESS OF CHRISTIANITY

Subject, and that I writ not in the stile of a Graduate in Divinity. I confess, (as Mr. *Ed's*. rightly says) my fault lyes on the other side, in a want of *Vivacity and Elevation*: And I cannot wonder that one of his Character and Palate, should find out and complain of my *flatness*, which
5 has so over-charged my Book with plain and direct Texts of Scripture in a matter capable of no other Proofs. But yet I must acknowledge his excess of Civility to me; He shews me more kindness than I could expect or wish, since he prefers what I say to him my self, to what is offered to him from the Word of God; and makes me this Complement, that I begin to
10 mend, about the Close; *i. e.* when I leave off quoting of Scripture: And the dull work was done, of *going through the History of the Evangelists and Acts*, which he computes, *p.* 105. to take up three quarters of my Book. Does not all this deserve at least that I should in return take some care of his Credit? Which I know not how better to do, than by entreating him,
15 that when he takes next in hand such a Subject as this is, wherein the Salvation of Souls is concerned, he would treat it a little more seriously, and with a little more Candor; lest Men should find in his Writings another cause of Atheism, which in this Treatise he has not thought fit, to mention. *Ostentation of Wit* in general he has made a *Cause of Atheism*.
20 *p.* 28. But the World will tell him, That frothy light Discourses concerning the Serious Matters of Religion; and *Ostentation* of trifling and misbecoming *Wit* in those who come as Ambassadors from God, under the Title of Successors of the Apostles, in the great Comission of the Gospel, is not of the least Causes of Atheism.
25 Some Men have so peculiar a way of Arguing, that one may see it influences them in the repeating another Man's Reasoning, and seldom fails to make it their own. In the next Paragraph I find these words: *What makes him contend for one single Article, with the exclusion of all the rest? He pretends it is this, That all Men ought to understand their Religion*. This, I
30 confess, is a Reasoning I did not think of; nor would it hardly, I fear, have been used but by one, who had first took up his Opinion from the Recommendation of Fashion or Interest, and then sought Topicks to make it good. Perhaps the deference due to your Character excused you from the trouble of quoting the Page where I *pretend*, as you say; and it is
35 so little like my way of Reasoning, that I shall not look for it in a Book where I remember nothing of it, and where, without your Direction, I fear the Reader will scarce find it. Though I have not *that vivacity of Thought, that elevation of Mind*, which Mr. *Ed's*. demands, yet common sense would have kept me from contending that there is but one Article,
40 because all Men ought to understand their Religion. Numbers of

A VINDICATION

221

Propositions may be harder to be remembered, but 'tis the abstruseness of the Notions, or obscurity, inconsistency, or doubtfulness of the Terms or Expressions that makes them hard to be understood: And one single Proposition may more perplex the Understanding than twenty other. But where did you find *I contended for one single Article, so as to exclude all* 5 *the rest*? You might have remembred, that I say, *p.* 44. That the Article of the One only true God, was also necessary to be believed. This might have satisfied you, that I did not so *contend for one* Article of Faith, as to be *at defiance* with more than one. However you insist on the word *one* with great vigour, from *p.* 108. to 121. And you did well, you had else 10 lost all the force of that killing stroke, reserved for the Close, in that sharp Jest of *Unitarians*, and a clinch of two more of great moment.

Having found by a careful perusal of the Preachings of our Saviour and his Apostles, that the Religion they proposed, consisted in that short, plain, easie, and intelligible Summary which I set down, *p.* 301. in these 15 words: 'Believing Jesus to be the Saviour promised, and taking him now raised from the Dead, and constituted the Lord and Judge of Men, to be their King and Ruler.' I could not forbear magnifying the Wisdom and Goodness of God (which infinitely exceeds the thoughts of ignorant, vain, and narrow-minded Man) in these following words. 'The All- 20 Merciful God seems herein to have consulted the Poor of this World, and the Bulk of Mankind: THESE ARE ARTICLES that the Labouring and Illiterate Man may comprehend.' Having thus plainly mentioned more than one Article, I might have taken it amiss, that Mr. *Ed's.* should be at so much pains as he is, to blame me for *contending for one* Article; 25 because I thought more than *one* could not be understood; had he not had many fine things to say in his declamation upon *one* Article, which affords him so much Matter, that less than seven pages could not hold it. Only here and there, as Men of Oratory often do, he mistakes the business, as *p.* 115. where he says, *I urge, that there must be nothing in* 30 *Christianity that is not plain and exactly levelled to all mens Mother Wit.* I desire to know where I said so, or that *the very manner of every thing in Christianity must be clear and intelligible, every thing must be presently comprehended by the weakest Noddle, or else it's no part of Religion, especially of Christianity*; As he has it, *p.* 119. I am sure it is not in *pag.* 255. 289. 292. 35 of my Book: These, therefore to convince him that I am of another Opinion, I shall desire some body to read to Mr. *Edwards*: For he himself reads my Book with such Spectacles, as make him find Meanings and Words in it, neither of which I put there. He should have remembred, that I speak not of all the Doctrines of Christianity, nor all that is 40

222 THE REASONABLENESS OF CHRISTIANITY

published to the World in it; but of those Truths only, which are absolutely required to be believed to make any one a Christian. And these I find are so plain and easie, that I see no Reason why every body, with me, should not Magnifie the Goodness and Condescension of the
5 Almighty; who having out of his free Grace proposed a new Law of Faith to sinful and lost Man, hath by that Law required no harder terms, nothing as absolutely necessary to be believed, but what is suited to Vulgar Capacities, and the Comprehension of Illiterate Men.

You are a little out again, *p.* 118. where you Ironically say, as if it were
10 my sense, *Let us have but one Article, though it be with defiance to all the rest.* Jesting apart, Sir. This is a serious Truth, That what our Saviour and his Apostles preached, and admitted Men into the Church for believing, is all that is absolutely required to make a Man a Christian. But this is without any *Defiance of all the rest*, taught in the Word of God. This excludes not
15 the belief of any one of those many other Truths contained in the Scriptures of the Old and New Testaments, which it is the Duty of every Christian to study, and thereby build himself up on our most Holy Faith; receiving with stedfast Belief, and ready Obedience all those things which the Spirit of Truth hath therein revealed. But that *all the rest* of the
20 inspired Writings, or, if you please, *Articles, are of equal necessity* to be believed to make a Man a Christian, with what was preached by our Saviour and his Apostles; that I deny. A Man, as I have shewn, may be a Christian and a Believer without actually believing them; Because those whom our Saviour and his Apostles, by their Preaching and Discourses,
25 converted to the Faith, were made Christians and Believers barely upon the receiving what they preached to them.

I hope it is no derogation to the Christian Religion, to say, that the Fundamentals of it, *i. e.* all that is necessary to be believed in it by all Men, is easie to be understood by all Men. This I thought my self authorized to
30 say by the very easie, and very intelligible Articles insisted on by our Saviour and his Apostles, which contain nothing but what could be understood by the *bulk of Mankind*; a Term which, I know not why, Mr. *Ed's.* p. 117. is offended at, and thereupon is, after his fashion, sharp upon me about Captain *Tom* and his *Myrmidons*, for whom he tells me I
35 am *going to make a Religion.* The making of Religions and Creeds I leave to others. I only set down the Christian Religion, as I find our Saviour and his Apostles preached it, and preached it to, and left it for the *ignorant and unlearned Multitude.* For I hope you do not think, how contemptibly soever you speak of *the Venerable Mob*, as you are pleased to
40 dignifie them, *p.* 117. that the Bulk of Mankind, or in your Phrase, the

A VINDICATION

223

Rabble, are not concerned in Religion, or ought not to understand it, in order to their Salvation. Nor are you, I hope, acquainted with any, who are of that *Muscovite* Divine's Mind, who to one, that was talking to him about Religion, and the other World, replyed, That for the *Czar* indeed, and *Bojars*, they might be permitted to raise their hopes to Heaven; But that for such Poor Wretches as he, they were not to think of Salvation.

I remember the *Pharisees* treated the Common People with Contempt, and said, *Have any of the Rulers, or of the Pharisees believed in him? But this People, who knoweth not the Law, are cursed.* But yet these, who in the Censure of the *Pharisees* were cursed, were some of the *Poor*, or if you please to have it so, the *Mobb*, to whom the *Gospel was preached* by our Saviour, as he tells *John's* Disciples, *Matth.* XI. 5.

Pardon me, Sir, that I have here laid these Examples and Considerations before you; a little to prevail with you, not to let loose such a Torrent of Wit and Eloquence against the *Bulk of Mankind* another time; and that for a meer Fancy of your own: For I do not see how they here came in your way; but that you were resolved to set up something to have a fling at, and shew your Parts, in what you call your *Different** strain though besides the purpose. I know no body was going to *ask the Mob what you must believe?* And as for me, I suppose you will take my word for it, that I think no *Mob*, (no, not your *Venerable Mob*) is to be asked, what I am to believe; Nor that *Articles of Faith* are to be *received by the Vote of Club-men*, or any other sort of Men you will name instead of them.

In the following words, *pag.* 115. you ask, *Whether a Man may not understand those Articles of Faith which you mentioned out of the Gospels and Epistles, if they be explained to him, as well as that one I speak of?* 'Tis as the Articles are, and as they are explained. There are Articles that have been some Hundreds of Years explaining; Which, there are many, and those not of the most illiterate, who profess, they do not yet understand. And to instance in no other but *He descended into Hell*, the learned are not yet agreed in the sense of it, tho' great pains has been taken to explain it.

Next, I ask, who are to explain your Articles? The Papists will explain some of them one way, and the Reformed another. The Remonstrants and Anti-Remonstrants give them different senses. And probably the *Trinitarians* and *Unitarians* will profess, that they understand not each others explications. And at last, I think it may be doubted whether any Articles, which need mens Explications, can be so clearly and certainly

* Preface

224   THE REASONABLENESS OF CHRISTIANITY

understood, as one which is made so very plain by the Scripture it self, as not to need any Explication at all. Such is this, That Jesus is the *Messiah*. For though you learnedly tell us, that *Messiah* is a Hebrew word, and no better understood by the Vulgar than *Arabick*; Yet I guess it is so fully explained in the New Testament, and in those places I have quoted out of it, that no body, who can understand any ordinary Sentence in the Scripture, can be at a loss about it: And 'tis plain it needs no other Explication than what our Saviour and the Apostles gave it in their Preaching; for as they preached it men received it, and that sufficed to make them Believers.

To conclude, when I heard that this Learned Gentleman, who had a Name for his study of the Scriptures, and Writings on them, had done me the Honour to consider my Treatise, I promised my self, that his Degree, Calling, and Fame in the World, would have secured to me something of weight in his Remarques, which might have convinced me of my Mistakes; and if he had found any in it, justified my quitting of them. But having examined what in his concerns my Book, I, to my wonder, find, that he has only taken pains to give it an ill Name; without so much as attempting to refute any one Position in it, how much soever he is pleased to make a noise against several Propositions; which he might be free with, because they are his own: And I have no reason to take it amiss, if he has shewn his Zeal and Skill against them. He has been so favourable to what is mine, as not to use any one Argument against any Passage in my Book. This, which I take for a Publick Testimony of his Approbation, I shall return him my Thanks for, when I know whether I owe it to his Mistake, Conviction, or Kindness. But if he writ only for his Bookseller's sake, he alone ought to thank him.

After the foregoing Papers were sent to the Press, The *Witnesses to Christianity*, of the Reverend and Learned Dr. *Patrick*, now Lord Bishop of *Ely*, fell into my hands. I regretted the not having seen it before I writ my Treatise of the *Reasonableness of Christianity*, &c. I should then possibly, by the Light given me by so good a Guide, and so great a Man, with more confidence directly have fallen into the knowledge of Christianity; which in the way I sought it, in its source, required the comparing of Texts with Texts, and the more than once reading over the Evangelists and *Acts*, besides other parts of Scripture. But I had the ill luck not to see that Treatise till so few hours since, that I have had time only to read as far as the end of the Introduction, or first Chapter: And there Mr. *Ed's*. may find, that this Pious Bishop (whose Writings shew he Studies, as well as his Life that he believes the Scriptures) owns what Mr.

A VINDICATION 225

Ed's. is pleased to call *a plausible Conceit*, which, he says, *I give over and over again in these formal words,* viz. *That nothing is required to be believed by any Christian Man but this, That Jesus is the Messiah.*

The Liberty Mr. *Ed's.* takes in other places deserves not it should be taken upon his word, *that these formal words* are to be found *over and over again* in my Book, unless he had quoted the Pages. But I will set him down the *formal words* which are to be found in this Reverend Prelate's Book, *p.* 14. *To be the Son of God, and to be Christ, being but different expressions of the same thing.* And *p.* 10. *It is the very same thing to believe that Jesus is the Christ, and to believe that Jesus is the Son of God; Express it how you please. This ALONE is the Faith which can regenerate a Man, and put a Divine Spirit into him; that is, makes him a Conquerour over the World, as Jesus was.* I have quoted only these few words; but Mr. *Ed's.* if he pleases, or any body else, may, in this first Chapter, satisfie himself more fully, that the Design of it is to shew, that in our saviour's time, *Son of God* was a known and received Name or Appellation of the *Messiah*, and so used in the Holy Writers. And that the Faith that was to make Men Christians, was only the believing that *Jesus is the Messiah.* 'Tis to the truth of the Proposition that he *examines his Witnesses*, as he speaks, *pag.* 21. And this, if I mistake not, in his Epist. Dedicatory he calls *Christianity, Fol. A.* 3. where he calls them *Witnesses to Christianity.* But these two Propositions, *viz.* That *SON of God* in the Gospel stands for *Messiah*; And that the Faith which alone makes Men Christians, is the believing *Jesus to be the Messiah*; displeases Mr. *Ed's.* so much in my Book, that he thinks himself Authorized from them to charge me with *Socinianism*, and want of Sincerity. How he will be pleased to treat this Reverend Prelate whilest he is alive (for the Dead may with good Manners be made bold with) must be left to his decisive Authority. This I am sure, which way soever he determine, he must for the future either afford me more good Company, or fairer Quarter.

FINIS.

7

FALL AND REDEMPTION

92
Peccatum originale

Queries concerning the Imputation of Adams sin to his Posterity

1 Whether it may be truely said that God imputes the first sin of Adam to his Posterity.

If you say I may then enquire

2 In what sense, it is truly said? Whether God imputes that sin to you as 'tis then properly & fformally or only as 'tis taken *Effectively*? Or in plainer sense whether God reputes them to have committed that Sin in Adam, or only Subjects them for the sake of that sin committed by him alone to the same Evills which he incurred by comitting it?

1. If you say God reputes them to have committed that sin in Adam then I enquire

3 Whether Gods reputing them to have committed that sin in Adam be grounded upon their real participation with Adam in that Sin or only upon the ffree determination of his own will

1° If you say upon their real participation with Adam in that Sin then I enquire two things viz

4 ffirst how they can be said really to participate with Adam in that sin who did not concurr to it by any act of theirs nor were in being when 'twas committed?

5 Secondly whether they do not as really participate with Adam in all the Sins committed by him after his ffall & with their immediate Parents & with all their foreffathers after Adam in all their Sins as with him in that Sin?

If you say they do so then I enquire

6 Whether they do not also as really participate with Adam in all his acts of ffaith & Repentence after his ffall & so in all the like Acts of all others their Pious foreffathers. These being as truely the Acts of Adam & of those their foreffathers (tho' not performed without the assistance of grace) or any of their Sins.

Q. If you say Gods reputing the Posterity of Adam to have Committed that sin in him is grounded only upon the ffree determination of the Divine will then I enquire also two things: viz

7 ffirst how it consists with Gods truth or Veracity to repute to the

230 FALL AND REDEMPTION

Posterity of Adam to have committed that Sin in him who did not concur to it by any Act of theirs, nor were in being when it was committed?

8 Secondly Whether God could not with the safety of his Attributes have created man at ffirst subject to all the Evills which follow upon his reputing the Posterity of Adam to have committed that Sin in him as well as Subject them to those evils by Arbitrarily reputing them to have committed that Sin in him

Q. If you say God does not repute the Posterity of Adam to have committed that Sin in him but only Subject them for the sake of that Sin committed by him alone to the same Evills which he incurred by committing it then I enquire 3 things viz

9 ffirst what those evills are that Adam incurred by committing that Sin?

10 Secondly whether in consideration of that Sin committed by Adam alone God does subject his Posterity to <u>all</u> the evills he incurred by committing it or to <u>some</u> only?

11 Thirdly whether those evils to which God does Subject Adams Posterity in consideration of that his Sins be such as make it more Eligible for them not to be than to be

1. If you say those evils be such as make it now Eligible for them not to be than to be then I enquire

12 Whether God might not as well have created man at ffirst subject to the same evills as Subject the Posterity of Adam to them for the sake of the Sin which he does not repute to them to have committed in Adam?

2. If you say those evils be not such as make it not more eligible for men not to be than to be then I have nothing further to enquire

Proast

93
Homo ante et post lapsum

Man was made mortal put into a possession of the whole world, where in the full use of the creatures there was scarce room for any irregular desires but instinct & reason caried him the same way & being neither capable of coviteousnesse or ambition when he had already the free use of all things he could scarce sin. God therefor gave him a probationary law whereby he was restraind from one only fruit, good wholsom & tempting in it self. The punishment annexed to this law was a natural death. For though he was made mortal yet the tree of life should after haveing observd this probationary law to a sufficient testimony of his obedience have clothed him upon with immortality without dieing. But he sind & the sentence of death was immediately executed. for he was thrust out from the tree of life Gen III. 22 & soe being excluded from that which could cure any distemper could come from too free an use of the creatures & renew his age he began to die from that time being separated from this source of life. Soe that now he & in him all his posterity were under a necessity of dyeing & there sin enterd into the world & death by sin. But here again God puts him under a new covenant of grace & there by into a state of eternal life but not without dyeing. This was the punishment of that 1st sin to Adam & Eve. viz death & the consequence but not punishment of it to all their posterity for they never haveing had any hopes or expectation given them of immortalitie, to be borne mortal as man was first made cannot be called a punishment By this sin Adam & Eve came to know good & Evil. i e the difference between good & evill for without sin man should not have known evil. upon their offence they were affraid of god, this gave them frightfull Ideas and apprehensions of him & that lessened their love which turnd their minds to the creature this root of all evill in them made impressions & soe infected their children, & when private possessions & labour which now the curse on the earth had made necessary, by degrees made a distinction of conditions, it gave roome for coviteousnesse pride & ambition, which by fashen & example spread the corruption which has soe prevailed over man kind JL

Resurrectio et quae sequuntur

St Paul treating expressly of the Resurrection 1 Cor XV tells us

1 That all men by the benefit of Christ shall be restord to life 21. 22

2 That the order of the resurrection is this. 1° Christ rises. 2° Those that are his at his 2d comeing 23

5   3 That the saints shall then have spiritual & immortal bodys. 42 And they shall then bear the Image of the heavenly Adam. i e be immortal as they befor bore the image of the Earthly. i e were mortal 44–49. Tis plain St Paul in the word we 49 & 51. 57. 58 speaks not of the dead in general, but of the saints who were to put on incorruption 54 & over whom

10 Death was never to have any more power because they were cleard of all sin 56. He that will read this chapter carefully may observe that St Paul in it speaking of the order of the resurrection mentions first Christs, then that of Beleivers 23 which he gives an account of to the end of that Chapter & discourse And soe never comes to the resurrection of the

15 wicked which was to be the third & last in order. Soe that from ver. 23 to the end of the Chapter is a discription only of the resurrection of the just though he cals it by the general name of the resurrection of the dead 42 which is plain from almost every verse of it from 41 to the end. 1° That which he here speaks of as raised is raised in glory 43 But the wicked are

20 not raised in glory. 2° He says we shall bear the image of the heavenly Adam. ver. 49 which cannot belong to the wicked. we shall all be changed that by puting on incorruptibility & immortality death may be swallowed up of victory which god giveth us through our Lord Jesus Christ 51. 52. 53. 54 57 which cannot likewise belong to the damned &

25 therefor we & us must be understood to be spoken of in the name of the dead that are Christs who are to be raised before the rest at his comeing. 3° He says 52 that when the Dead are raised they that are alive shall be changed in the twinkleing of an eye. Now that these dead are onely the dead in Christ which shall rise first & shall be caught up in the clouds to

30 meet the lord in the air is plain from 1 Thess IV. 16. 17. 4° He teaches 54 that by this corruptibles puting on incorruption is brought to pass the saying that Death is swallowed up of victory But I think noe body will say that the wicked have victory over death. yet that according to the Apostle here belongs to all those whose corruptible bodys have put on

35 incorruption which must therefor be only those that rise the second in

RESURRECTIO ET QUAE SEQUUNTUR 233

order & therefor their Resurrection alone is that which is here mentiond
and describd. 5° a farther proof whereof is given 56. 57. In that their sins
being taken away the sting whereby death kils is taken away. And
therefor St Paul says god has given us the victory, which must be the
same we which should bear the image of the heavenly Adam ver. 49 & 5
the same we which should all be changed. 51. 52 All which places can
therefor belong in none but those who are Christs which shall be raised
by themselves the second in order before the rest of the dead. Tis very
remarkable what St Paul says in this 51 ver.: We shall not all sleep but we
shall all be changed in the twinkleing of an eye the reason he gives for it 10
ver. 53. Because this corruptible thing must put on incorruption & this
mortal thing put on immortality. how? by putting off flesh & bloud by
an instantaneous change because as he tells them ver. 50 Flesh & bloud
cannot inherit the kingdom of god. And therefor to fit beleivers for that
kingdom those who are live at the sound of the trumpet shall be changed 15
in the twinkleing of an eye 51 & those that are in their graves changed
likewise at the instant of their being raised & soe all the whole collection
of the saints be put into a state of incorruptibility. 52. Takeing the
resurrection here spoken of to be the resurrection of all the dead in
general St Pauls reasoning in this place is very hard to be understood but 20
upon the supposition that he here describes the resurrection of the just
only, those who are mentiond 23 to rise next in order after Christ it is
very easy plain and natural and stands thus. Men alive are flesh & bloud,
the dead in the graves are but the remains of corruptd flesh & bloud. But
flesh & bloud can not inherit the kingdom of god, neither can corruption 25
inherit incorruption i e immortality.

Therefor to make those who are Christs capable to enter into his
eternal Kingdome of life as well those of them who are alive as those of
them who are raised from the dead shall in the twinkleing of an eye be all
changed & their corruptible shall put on incorrpution & their mortal 30
shall put on immortality & thus god gives them the victory over death
through their Lord Jesus Christ. This is in short St Pauls argueing here &
the account he gives of the resurrection of the blessed but how the
wicked which were afterwards to come to life were to be raised & what
was to become of them he here says noe thing as not being to his 35
purpose, which was to assure the Corinthians by the resurrection of
Christ of happy resurrection to beleivers & thereby to incourage them to
continue in the faith which had such a reward. That this was his design as
may be seen by the beginning of his discourse 12–21 & by the
conclusion ver. 58 in these words therefor my beloved brethren be ye 40

234   FALL AND REDEMPTION

stedfast unmoveable alway abounding in the work of the Lord for as much as ye know that your Labour is not in vain in the Lord which words plainly shew that what he had been speakeing of in the immmediately preceding verses viz their being changd & the puting on
5 of incorruption & immortality & their haveing thereby the victory through Jesus Christ was what belongd soly to the saints as a reward to those who remained stedfast & abounded in the work of the Lord. The like use of the like though shorter discourse of the resurrection, wherein he describes only that of the blessed he makes to the Thessalonians 1
10 Thess IV. 13–18 which he concludes thus: Wherefor comfort one an other with these words. Nor is it in this place alone that St Paul cals the resurrection of the Just by the general name of the resurrection of the dead, he does the same Phil. III. 11 where he speaks of his sufferings & endeavours if by any means he might attain to the resurrection of the
15 Dead, whereby he cannot mean the resurrection of the dead in General, which since it will overtake all men there needs noe endeavours to attain Our Saviour likewise speaks of the resurrection of the just in the Same general termes of the resurrection Mat XXII. 30 & the resurrection from the dead Luk. XX. 35 by which is meant only the resurrection of the just
20 as is plain from the context

How long after this the wicked shall rise shall be enquired hereafter I shall only at present take notice only I think it is plain it shall be before our Saviour delivers up the Kingdom to his father, for then is the end. the whole dispensation of god to the race of Adam will be at an end 1 Cor
25 XV. 24. yet these two things are plainly declard in Scripture concerning them

1 That they shall be cast into hell fire to be tormented this is soe express & soe often mentioned in Scripture that there can be noe doubt about it Math. XXV 41. 46 XIII. 42. 50. XVIII. 8.
30 2 That they shall not live forever This is soe plain in Scripture & is soe every where inculcated that the wages of sin is death & the reward of the righteous is everlasting life The constant language of the Scripture in the whole current of the new testament as well as old is life to the just, to beleivers, to the obedient; & death to the wicked & unbeleivers that one
35 would wonder how the readers could be mistaken when death is threatend soe constantly & declared every where to be the ultimate punishment & last estate to which the wicked must all come. To salve this they have invented a very odd signification of the word death which they would have stand for eternal life in torment They who will put soe
40 strange & contrary a signification upon a word in an hundred places

RESURRECTIO ET QUAE SEQUUNTUR 235

where if it had not its true litteral sense one would wonder if it should be soe often usd & that in opposition to life which in those places is used literaly, ought to have good proofs for giveing it a sense in those places of Scripture directly contrary to what it ordinarily has in other parts of Scripture & every where else. But leaveing this interpretation of the word Death to shift for it self as it can in the minds of reasonable men There are places of Scripture which plainly shew the different state of the just & the wicked to be ultimately life & death where in there is noe room for that evasion. I shall name one or two of them.

Our Saviour tells the Saduces Luke XX 35. 36 that they who are accounted worthy to attain that world & the resurrection from the dead neither marry nor are given in mariage NEITHER CAN THEY DIE ANY MORE; for they are equal unto the angels and are the children of god being the children of the resurrection. where Christ plainly declares of the children of god alone who have been accounted worthy to obtein the resurrection. i e the resurrection before the others that they are like the angels & can die noe more. which exception of the saints from dieing any more after their resurrection is a confirmation that the rest of man kinde may & shall die again. Accordingly St John Rev XX. 5. 6 says of this which he cals the first resurrection Blessed & holy is he who hath part in the first resurrection, on such the second death hath noe power

I crave leave to observe here that as St Paul speakeing of the Resurrection of the dead 1 Cor XV. 42 in general termes yet means only the first resurrection or the resurrection of the just Soe our Saviour does here where by Resurrection he plainly means only the first resurrection or the resurrection of the blessed & not the resurrection of all man kind, as is plain not only by makeing them the children of god who are the children of the resurrection, but by saying those who are accounted worthy to obtain the resurrection which destinction of worthyness can belong only to those who are Christs & cannot promiscuously take in all man kind.

An other text that declares the death & final end of the wicked is Gal VI. 7. 8 Be not deceived god is not mocked for whatsoever a man soweth that shall he also reap. For he that soweth to his flesh shall of the flesh reap corruption; but he that soweth to the spirit shall of the spirit reap life everlasting In other places where life everlasting & death are opposed say interpreters by everlasting life is meant everlasting perfect happyness joynd to life; by death is meant eternall sufferings & torments without death But here corruption & life everlasting are opposed. now φθορά

236 FALL AND REDEMPTION

corruption signifies the dissolution & final destruction of a thing whereby it ceases to be; but corruption can by noe body be pretended to signifye the endless sense of pain & torment in a being subsisting & continued on to eternity. Corruption is the spoiling any thing the
5 divesting it of the being it had accordingly St Paul uses incorruption 1 Cor. XV for an indefesable estate of immortality

That which gives some colour to their understanding by death an endless life in torment is the everlasting fire threatend by our saviour to the wicked Mat. XVIII.8 XXV 41.46 But not to trouble you with the
10 various significations of duration of the word Everlasting in Scripture & what else has been answerd by orthodox divines to shew that those texts did not necessarily imply eternal or endless torments espetialy by ArchBishop Tillotson. It may suffice to say that everlasting in a true scripture sense may be said of that which endures as long as the subject it
15 affects endures. Soe everlasting priesthood XL Exod 15 was a priesthood that lasted as long as the people lasted in an estate capable of the Mosaical worship. Psal. XXIV 7 Everlasting doors i e that should last as long as the temple which they belong to: Isay XXXV. 10 Everlasting joy i e that should continue as long as they lived. A like expression is that of hell fire
20 Mark IX. 43 44 that never shal be quenchd where their worm dieth not & the fire is not quenchd. an expression taken from Isai: LXVI. 24 which though we translate. hell is in the original Gehenna or the Vally of Hinnon where was kept a constant fire to burn up the carkasses of beasts & other filth of the citty of Jerusalem where though the fire never was
25 quenchd yet it does not follow nor is it said that the bodys that were burnt in it were never consumed only that the worms that gnawd & the fire that burnt them was constant & never ceased till they were destroyd. Soe though the fire was not put out yet the chaff was burnt up & consumed. Mat III. 12 & the tares. XIII. 30 in both which places & the
30 paralel, Luk. III. 17 the Greek word is κατακαίω. i e to consume by burning though in our bibles it be translated burn up but in one of them viz Mat III. 12

Takeing it then for evident that the wicked shall die & be extinguished at last how long they shall be continued in that unexpressable torment is
35 not that I know any where expressed, but that it shall be excessively terrible by its duration as well as sharpness the current of the Scripture seems to manifest. onely if one may conjecture it seems to be before our Saviours delivering up the Kingdome to his father. The account given of it by St Paul 1 Cor XV. 23–26 At Christs 2d comeing the Just rise by
40 them selves. Then Christ shall set up his kingdom wherein he shall

RESURRECTIO ET QUAE SEQUUNTUR 237

subdue all rule & all authority & power that opposes him for he must reigne till he hath put all enemies under his feet The last enemie that shall be destroyd is death, then he shall deliver up the Kingdome to God his father & then cometh the end i e a full conclusion of gods whole dispensation to Adam & his posterity, after which there shall be noe death noe change, the Scene will then be closed & every one remain in the same estate forever

One thing upon this occasion may be worth our enquiry. i e whither the wicked shall not rise with such bodys of flesh & bloud as they had before, for that all that is said of the change of bodys 1 Cor XV. & 1 Thess. IV has been already shewn to be spoken only of the saints, the like whereof may be observed in other places of Scripture where bodys changed into a better state are mentioned, as 2 Cor V. 1–4, it is alway spoken of the bodys of the saints. Nor doe I remember any mention of the change of the bodys where the resurrection of the wicked can be supposed to be comprehended But it is only spoken of thus. All that are in the graves shall hear his voice & shall come forth, they that have done good unto the resurrection of life, & they that have done evil unto the resurrection of damnation John V.28.29. We must all appear before the judgment seat of god that every one may receive the things done in his body according to that he hath done whether it be good or bad 2 Cor V.10. And soe like wise Raise the dead Act. 26.8 2 Cor I.9 Quicken the dead Rom. IV. 17 But of the change of their bodys of their being made spiritual or of their putting on incorruption or immortality I doe not remember any thing said. They shall be raised that is said over & over, But how they are raised or with what bodys they shall come the Scripture as far as I have observed is perfectly silent

We have seen what the Scriptur says of the state of the wicked after the Resurrection & what is the final catastrophie they are doomd to, Let us now see what the Scripture discovers to us of the state of the just after the Resurrection

That whatsoever was earthy corruptible mortal about them shall at the instant of the sound of the trumpet that is to call them at Christs comeing be changed into spiritual incorruptible immortall we have already seen

On the Priesthood of Christ:
Analysis of Hebrews

The text is an unglued insert placed in Locke's interleaved polyglot New Testament at page 249. (LL 2864; shelf mark, BOD Locke 9. 107). The title is supplied by the editor.

It is easy to Imagin that the convert Jews of Jerusalem & Judaea to whom this Epistle seems to be writ were more exposed to persecution than the Convert Gentiles. Because their own nation lookeing upon them as Apostates from their divine religion & revolted from their commonwealth & joyning in worship & conversation with unclean Gentiles were more animated against them than other Christians. Soe that these Christians haveing the common calamities of Jews every where else, had none of the protection or ease which others of their own nation had in Judaea it self but probably sufferd more there as Christians than the followers of Christ did else where. vid. 1 Thess: II. 14–16

To support them in this sad state & to confirme them in the faith of Christ & in a steady perseverance this Epistle seems cheifly to be writ. To this purpose

I–II. 6 1. He exhorts them to hold fast the faith & not let it slip from them which I take to be the meaning of Ch. II. 1. because it was deliverd by the son of god & soe exceeded the doctrine deliverd at Mount Sinay by the ministration of angels since the angels were but ministring Spirits but the Son of god was to have a kingdome an everlasting Kingdome, but that this kingdom was not subjected to the Angels. II. 5. And therefor if the law deliverd by Angels was to be obeyd much more the doctrine of a fuller salvation deliverd by Jesus Christ that was confirmd with soe many miracles. This argument seems to reach from I to II. 5

II 7–18 2. In the next place he seems to answer an objection.

ON THE PRIESTHOOD OF CHRIST 239

How can Jesus be above the angels when he was ~~but~~ a
man & a man is a little lower than the Angels? To which
he answers directly II. 9 Because it was necessary that he
should suffer & die the reasons whereof he prosecutes in
what follows to 18

III. 1–V. 14   3. He presses them to perseverance III. 6. 12–14. 18.
19. IV. 2. 11. 14 by shewing that Jesus was counted
worthy of more glory than Moses in that being an high
priest he is enterd into the rest into which they who
persevere in beleiving shall enter to him. who is by the
appointment of god an high priest forever after the order
of Milchisidec. which he rebukes them for not haveing
sufficiently studyed. And I think may be understood to
mean that the danger of their falling away was that they
advanced not enough in the Study of the Messiah as he
was prefigured in the types & prophesies of the old
testament; but though they were not very attentive to
those things & soe were but babes i e weake in the faith. V
11–14, yet he tels them VI. 1 he will for bear any repeated
discourse of the principles of Christianity τὸν λόγον τῆς
ἀρχῆς τοῦ χριστοῦ. for soe those words seem planly to
signifie if we compare them with V. 11 in which two
verses he seems to oppose λόγον περὶ Μελχισεδέκ & λόγον
περὶ ἀρχῆς χριστοῦ what was to be said concerning the
principles of Christianity & what he had to say
concerning Melchisidec. which he cals going to perfection, which he resolves to doe, VI. 1 in these words <u>let us</u>
i e me, for he speaks in his own person though he uses the
plural number all through this matter as appears V. 11.
VI 1 & 3 where he again professes his resolution to goe
on to the explication of Christs being an High priest after
the order of Melchisidec the better to establish &
strengthen them in the faith Because if they once
apostatizd after baptisme, it was impossible to restore

VI. 4–8   them VI. 4–8 & this he effectualy does (after his
VI. 9–12   declareing his hopes that they will not apostatize VI. 9–12
& a new argument from Abrahams faith to strengthen and
VI. 13–19   comfort them VI. 13–19) from VI. 19 to X. 20 & there
VI. 19–X. 20   upon pursues the main designe of his Epistle which is to
make them stedfast in the faith & dissuade them from

240 FALL AND REDEMPTION

Apostasizing to Judaisme by shewing that under the gospel the covenant is much better than that under the law. And from thence draws a strong argument for their persevering in the faith & not drawing back which is the maine designe of the Epistle

X. 21–39

XI. 1–XII. 3 Another argument to perswade them to perseverance is from the examples of many who were accepted for their judging him faithfull who had promised & soe persisting in their faith though they received not the promise

XII. 4–11 In the next place he perswades them to persist not with standing their afflictions because chastisement is a marke of gods love

XII. 12–17 He exhorts them to strengthen those that were weake in the faith amongst them & prevent their turning away from the Gospel to hinder apostates from ariseing amongst them such as Esau who sold his birthright & with it the promise, who might trouble them & turne them from persevering.

XII. 18–29 He exhorts them to hold fast grace. i e stick to the Gospel & not return to Judaisme, because the law by Moses was a terrible dispensation which was to be removed, but by Jesus they should receive a Kingdom which should never be moved.

XIII Exhortation to particular dutys not without mindeing them of the different advantages of the Gospel dispensation above that of the Levitical

[NB: on the recto of the last leaf of this insert are the following notes.]

Heb.

~~Perfect. an unchangeable state of happynesse, wherein there was noe more donne by or for the person to establish him in it. This I take to be the meaning of the word perfect in this Epistle wherein it is often used as. V. 9. VII. 19. X. 1~~

~~Perfect i e. perfectly attoned for once for all for whom there needed noe farther attonement VII. 19. X. 1. 14~~

perfect VIII. 19. X. 1. what perfect here means see X. 1–4, 14. 17. 18. & IX. 9. The spirits of Just men made perfect XII. 23 i e men whose sins are perfectly remitted

ON THE PRIESTHOOD OF CHRIST 241

soe that there needs noe more offering for their sins vid.
the places above quoted

What the perfection he speaks of VI. 1 is may be seen
VII. 11 i e being under a better priesthood than the
Levitical which could make noe thing perfect VII. 19 by 5
whose one sacrifice we might enter into eternal rest or as
tis expressed VII. 25–28 by such an high priest who
needs not dayly offer up sacrifice but by once offering up
himself saveth them to perpetuity : for soe might vs. 25 to
be translated & not to the uttermost those that come to 10
god by him

XIII. 13   Let us go &c Let us leave the observances & sacrifices
of the law, & beleive on Jesus who was sacrificed for sin
out of the citty

9   Doctrines. i e the doctrines of the law of Moses which 15
were various whereas Jesus Christ i. e. the doctrine of the
Gospel is short & plain the same to day & forever the
traditions of the Jews changed. strange. i e to the doctrine
of the Gospel Grace. i e the doctrine of Grace in the
Gospel, & not with meats. i e the Levitical or traditional 20
doctrines of meats, by which those have not been profited
who walked in the observances of them. For their sins
were not taken away by the sacrifice & other offerings
burnt in the Temple or in the camp i e in the Jewish
communion. but sins are taken away by Jesus who 25
answering the types of sin offerings Lev. XVI. 27 sufferd
without the gate

Christianae Religionis synopsis or
Christianae Religionis brevis delineatio

[i]

Man created after the Image of god i e Immortal I Gen. 26. 27 III. 19

Death   Had a positive law given him with the penalty of death annexed to the transgression of it. & by eating of the forbidden fruit became mortal Gen II. 17

He being mortal begat children in his own likeness i e Mortal Gen V. 3. Rom V 12–14

Sin is not charged with death but by the positive law to Adam in the day thou eatest thereof thou shalt die & yet death reigned from Adam to Moses over those who had not sined against that positive law which denounced death to the transgressor a proof that by the sin of Adam death enterd & he & his posterity became mortal

Mankind in the old world became very corrupt & sinfull their imaginations were onely evil Gen VI. 5–7 and the Gentile world after the flood became vain in their imaginations Rom I. 20–32

Law   When man kinde was in this forlorne state of mortality & corruption. God gave a law to the Jews by a perfect obedience to which life & immortality was to be recoverd Rom X. 5. Lev. XVIII. 5 Ezek XX. 11

But they all came short of obedience & so attained not the righteousnesse of the law Rom V. 9–21 Rom IX 31–32

Faith   Therefore there is noe rightousness but of grace through faith in Jesus Christ this is called the righteousness of god Rom X. 3 & the righteousness of faith Rom IX 30. & is opposed to the righteousness by the deed of the law III 20–22. X. 3

CHRISTIANAE RELIGIONIS SYNOPSIS 243

Obedience
Sincere   Being in this state of Justification We are to obey to the
uttermost the law of righteousness Rom VI. 1–VIII. 14

ii

The State of Man in Innocency   5
         Immortal
         Under a positive law whose penalty was mortality

Mortality   how it came in by one mans sin
Adam   being made mortal by his transgression all his posterity
begat in the image of their father became mortal though 10
they transgressed not that law to which mortality was
annexed.

Heathen world corrupt
God   made him self known to man kind by the works of the
Creation nevertheless the Gentile world apostatized to 15
Idolatry & were given up to unnatural lust & all sorts of
iniquity. Gen VI. 5 Rom I 21.32 Eph IV. 17–19. II. 11.
12 1 Thess IV. 5. Col I. 21. Gal IV. 8. Eph II 1–3. 1
Cor XII. 2. Col II. 13 Eph V. 5.6 Col III 5–7

Law   God gave the law to the Jews conteining the law of 20
nature to which were annexed many civil institituions &
religious ceremonys with a reward of life annexed to a
perfect obedience but without perfect obedience (which
in the new testament is called their own righteousness or
righteousness by the works of the law) there was noe 25
recovery of immortality this way but they were with the
rest of man kinde exposed to death they being all mortal
from Adam Besides this obvious visible sense of the
revelation given by Moses & the other prophets under
the law (which is all therefore called the law) there was 30
another more mystical hydden sense where by life is
promised to those who endeavouring sincerly to obey
the moral or eternal Law of right and wrong should
beleive in Christ the former of these is called the <u>letter</u>
the latter the <u>spirit</u>. Rom. II. 29. VII. 6. 2 Cor III. 6. 7. 35
17. And according to this <u>Spirit</u> or Spiritual sense of the
law the Ceremonial part of the Mosaical law is

244 FALL AND REDEMPTION

interpreted in the New Testament as typically containing the Spiritual sense (As circumcision Rom II 29. Phil III. 3. Coll. II. 11 et passim) more particularly all through the Hebrews

5 Righteousness Is the fulling of the law, this is called righteousness by the deeds of the law or a mans owne righteousnesse. There is an other righteousness where by men without a complete obedience are justified by free grace through faith in Christ. This is called gods righteousness Rom I.
10 17 & passim & is soe called 1° Because this righteousness is of grace is the guift of god, he of grace recons it where it is not Rom III. 21–25 2° it is called gods righteousness because it shews him to be just or righteouse, who has promised to Justifie those who
15 should beleive in Jesus Christ vers. 26

APPENDIX

A list of theological places in
An Essay concerning Human Understanding

The following is a list of places in the *Essay* where religious or theological themes are addressed or mentioned. Brief extracts of text and some comment make this more than a bare list. The places are listed in sequence according to Book (I, II, III, IV), Chapter (i, ii, iii, etc.), and section (1, 2, 3, etc.).

Title Page: Motto from Ecclesiastes 11: 5 9 (only in editions 4 & 5): 'As thou knowest not what is the way of the Spirit, nor how the bones do grow in the Womb of her that is with Child: even so thou knowest not the works of God, who maketh all things'.

I. i. 4–6 is a short discourse offering reasons for contentment and praise of God despite the limitation of our understanding, and an admonition against discontent and despair: God has given us (i.e. mankind) a 'Portion and Degree of Knowledge' that elevates our species high above all other terrestrial creatures; God has given us sufficient intellectual capability to discover the means to satisfy the needs of this life, and to busy our heads and to employ our hands 'with Variety, Delight, and Satisfaction'; God has given us sufficient light to illuminate the passage to eternal life in a world to come, i.e. to achieve a knowledge of God and of our moral duty. Our main business in life is to regulate our conduct, including the conduct of the understanding. See also II. ii. 3.

I. ii. 1: Incidental comment related to the case against innate principles: Just as 'it would be impertinent to suppose, the *Ideas* of Colours innate in a Creature, to whom God hath given Sight . . . No less unreasonable would it be to attribute several Truths, to the impressions of Nature, and innate Characters, when we may observe in our selves Faculties, fit to attain as easie and certain Knowledge of them, as if they were Originally imprinted on the Mind.' Compare this reference to God with the several

246 APPENDIX

references to 'Nature' throughout this chapter as the presumed provider of innate cognitions, in particular in §§ 10, 11, 14, 21, 22, 25, 27.

I. iii. 3: 'Nature [or God], I confess, has put into Man a desire of Happiness, and an aversion to Misery: These indeed are innate practical Principles which (as practical Principles ought) do continue constantly to operate and influence all our Actions, without ceasing . . . but these are Inclinations of the Appetite to good, not impressions of truth on the Understanding.'

I. iii is devoted entirely to refuting the claim that there are innate practical principles. Interwoven in the argument are assertions that when put together constitute a theory of moral religion. § 1: practical principles are as true as speculative ones, and although less evident, they are capable of demonstration. § 5: Christian, Hobbist, and Pagan reasons for keeping compacts compared; compare this section with II. xxviii. 6–10. § 6: the 'true ground of Morality' is the 'Will and Law of God' and divine enforcement of this through rewards and punishments; God has contrived to make evident the 'inseparable connexion' between '*Virtue* and publick Happiness'. § 12: the basic elements of a moral theory consist of '*Ideas* of God, of Law, of Obligation, of Punishment, of a Life after this'. § 13: the denial of innate principles does not entail that all laws are positive or that discovery of the law of nature requires 'the help of positive Revelation'. §§ 15–19: An examination of Lord Herbert's theory of moral religion.

I. iv. 4, 5: Preview of Locke's theory of personal identity and its religious application.

I. iv. 7–17: Theistic affirmations embedded in a long argument against innateness: § 7: 'That *God is to be worshipped,* is, without doubt as great a Truth as any can enter into the Mind of Man, and deserves the first place amongst all practical Principles.' § 8: 'If any *Idea* can be imagin'd *innate,* the *Idea of God* may, of all others, for many Reasons, be thought so . . .' (the same admission repeated in §§ 13, 17). § 9: 'the visible marks of extraordinary Wisdom and Power, appear so plainly in all the Works of the Creation, that a rational Creature, who will but seriously reflect on them, cannot miss the discovery of a *Deity*'. § 10: 'the suitableness' of the idea of God as 'a superior, powerful, wise, invisible Being' to 'the Principles of common Reason, and the Interest Men will always have to mention it often, must necessarily spread it far and wide; and continue it down to all Generations'. § 11: an enquiry 'into the Constitution and

THEOLOGICAL PLACES IN LOCKE'S *ESSAY*   247

Causes of things' easily leads 'to the Notion of a God' and its continuous propagation. § 12: 'But the Goodness of God hath not been wanting to Men without such Original impressions of Knowledge, or *Ideas* stamped on the Mind: since he hath furnished Man with those Faculties, which will serve for the sufficient discovery of all things requisite to the end of such a Being'. §§ 15–16: Because 'the truest and best Notions Men had of God' occur among the wise and are lacking among the uneducated and the young, even in lands where monotheism is affirmed, it follows that these ideas were 'acquired by thought and meditation, and a right use of . . . Faculties' and, therefore, are not innate.

I. iv. 19–22: Theistic affirmations embedded in arguments against innateness. § 19: 'Everyone that hath a true *Idea* of *God,* and *Worship,* will assent to this Proposition, That God is to be worshipped, when expressed, in a Language he understands . . .'. § 21: 'I that am fully perswaded, that the infinitely Wise GOD made all Things in perfect Wisdom . . .'. § 22: 'for though there be no Truth, which a Man may more evidently make out to himself, than the Existence of a God. . .'

II. i. 10: Incidental remark in connection with the question whether the soul always thinks: always to think and to be in action 'perhaps, is the Privilege of the Infinite Author and Preserver of things, *who never slumbers nor sleeps*'. Also in this section, Locke alludes to the question of the pre-existence of the human soul, a topic listed in the 'Adversaria Theologica 94'.

II. i. 15: Natural theological argument against the hypothesis that the mind always thinks.

II. ii. 3: The theme of this section is the limitation of human understanding and its confinement to a small part of an immense creation. (See also I. i. 3–6 and II. xv.) Here Locke invites his reader to consider the likelihood that God has created intelligent beings vastly superior to us. 'Such Variety and Excellency, being suitable to the Wisdom and Power of the Maker.' (See also II. xv. 11; II. xxiii. 13.)

II. vii. 3–6: a brief discourse on the wisdom of God in providing us with feelings of pleasure and pain and the divine sentiments that they should awaken in us.

II. xiii. 18: Because we lack a clear and distinct idea of substance, the use of the term to denote God, Spirits, and Body is of no philosophical value but may be a cause of perplexity and error. This observation is made in

248 APPENDIX

the context of Locke's case against the Cartesian identification of body and extension. (See also II. xvii. 30.)

II. xiii. 21, 21bis, 22, 26: The attributes of God considered in the light of certain paradoxes relating to the being of space, its infinity (§ 21), the possibility of a vacuum (§§ 21bis, 22), the immensity of God (§ 26).

II. xv: The topic of this chapter, 'Of Duration and Expansion, considered together', gives occasion for several theological reflections. §§ 2, 3, 4, 8: the eternity and immensity of God. § 7: the Julian calendar permits dating of events before the creation of the world, in particular, the creation and fall of angels. § 12: a concluding discourse comparing finite beings with God: there is no proportion between God's infinite duration (and other infinite attributes) with the temporality of mankind and with the capacities of other finite intelligences.

II. xvii. 1: Although it is beyond doubt that 'the Great GOD . . . is incomprehensibly Infinite', the limits of human understanding permit attribution of infinity to God 'primarily in respect of his Duration and Ubiquity', and 'more figuratively to his Power, Wisdom, and Goodness, and other Attributes, which are properly inexhaustible and incomprehensible'.

II. xvii. 5: A fragment of a theistic proof (See *Essay* IV. x): 'He that considers something now existing, must necessarily come to something eternal.' (See also II. xvii. 20.)

II. xvii. 20: The thesis defended in this section is that we have no positive idea of infinity, either of duration or of expansion. Locke observes that those who assert that we have a positive idea of eternity but not one of infinite space, are mistakenly led to this conclusion by the belief, which is 'past doubt', that 'GOD has existed from all Eternity'. (See also II. xxix. 16.)

II. xxi: This chapter, which was largely rewritten for the 2nd edition (1694), and II. xxvii, which was new in the 2nd edition of the *Essay*, together present the anthropological basis of Locke's theory of moral religion. §§ 5–71 present a long discussion of the faculties of the will and of liberty, the nature of motivation, and pursuits of happiness. §§ 2, 49–50: the distinction between active and passive power is applied to three sorts of being: material bodies, finite spirits, and God. § 34: 'our All-wise Maker . . . has put into Man the *uneasiness* of hunger and thirst, and other

THEOLOGICAL PLACES IN LOCKE'S *ESSAY* 249

natural desires . . . for the preservation of themselves, and the continuation of their Species'.

II. xxiii. 12, 13: These two sections constitute a digression into natural theology. The theme is the fitness of our 'Senses, Faculties, and Organs' to our situation in the universe and the wisdom of God displayed in their design. § 13 contains Locke's 'extravagant conjecture' concerning shape-shifting spirits able to alter their organs and powers of perception to suit their varying purposes.

II. xxiii: Some thoughts concerning God as spiritual substance. § 21: 'Motion cannot be attributed to GOD, not because he is immaterial, but because he is an Infinite Spirit.' § 28: 'Pure Spirit, *viz.* God, is only active; pure Matter is only passive; those Beings that are both active and passive we may judge to partake of both.' §§ 32–7: all our ideas of substances, 'even of God himself', are constituted of simple ideas of sensation and reflection. Moreover, with the exception of infinity, we attribute no idea to God that 'is not also a part of our complex *Idea* of other Spirits' (§ 36).

II. xxv. 8: To exemplify the claim that ideas of relation are clearer and more distinct than the ideas of the substances to which they relate, Locke remarks that he can 'much easier conceive what a Friend is, than what GOD'. See also §§ 3, 4, and 6 for more mention of God and Christ in connection with the meaning of relative terms.

II. xxvi. 2: Definition of creation: 'the thing is wholly made new, so that no part thereof did ever exist before; as when a new Particle of Matter doth begin to exist, *in rerum natura*'.

II. xxvii: The discussion of personal identity (§§ 6–29) makes up the bulk of this chapter. In § 2 the spatial and temporal conditions of identity are stated with respect to the three kinds of being: God, finite intelligences (i.e. spirits), and bodies. Since God is 'without beginning, eternal, unalterable, and every where' there can be no doubt about his identity. The identity of finite beings relates to the time and place of their origin; each continues to be the same as long as it exists, hence the *'principium Individuationis'* is 'Existence it self', or the mere existence of a thing. But the varieties of things, atoms, or masses of matter, flora and fauna, and human beings have different conditions of identity; this applies also to human individuals. Different conditions of identity determine whether a human individual is the same man or the same person. The identity of a person is not identity of substance but of

250 APPENDIX

consciousness. This idea of a person is a moral concept and is basic to Locke's religious anthropology. See § 26: Person 'is a Forensick Term appropriating Actions and their Merit; and so belongs only to intelligent Agents capable of a Law, and Happiness and Misery'. The relation between these actions and law, and between law and the states of happiness and misery, is described in the next chapter.

II. xxviii: The topic of this chapter is ideas of relation. §§ 4–20 treat ideas of moral relation. Moral relation is conformity or disagreement between a voluntary or free human action and a rule or law. §§ 4, 20: The lawgiver enforces his law, by his will and power, by rewarding and punishing agents with good or evil, pleasure or pain, consistent with the conformity of their actions to law or lack of it. § 5: There are three sorts of enforcement and correspondingly three sorts of law: divine law, civil law, and a law of reputation or fashion. §§ 7, 13: The divine law is 'the only true touchstone of *moral Rectitude*'. It is promulgated by right by the creator, who 'has Goodness and Wisdom' to direct the actions of his creatures 'to that which is best'. § 8: By comparing their actions to this law, men judge 'whether as *Duties,* or *Sins,* they are like to procure them happiness, or misery, from the hands of the ALMIGHTY'. §§ 8, 14: This moral theory, together with his religious anthropology (II. xxi, xxvii) and his proof of the being and attributes of God, comprises Locke's idea of natural religion.

II. xxix. 16: We have no clear idea of eternity. (See also II. xxvii. 20.)

II. xxxi. 2: All our simple ideas are adequate, i.e. perfectly represent their Archetypes, 'Because, being nothing but the effects of certain Powers in Things, fitted and ordained by GOD, to produce such Sensations in us, they cannot but be correspondent, and adequate to those Powers'. This argument is repeated in § 12. A variation of it is presented in II. xxxii. 14, 16 to justify the claim that simple ideas are true.

II. xxxiii. 17: Two examples of the ill effects of association of ideas: joining figure and shape to the idea of God or the idea of infallibility to a person and filling the mind with such thoughts by education and custom produce minds that are liable to think absurdities concerning the deity or an implicit acceptance of a bare contradiction, viz. 'one Body in two Places at once' (NB the reference is to the Roman doctrine of the real presence of Christ in the Eucharist).

III. i is a discourse on the origin of language and serves as an introduction to Book III. It opens with a natural-theological preamble: 'God having

THEOLOGICAL PLACES IN LOCKE'S *ESSAY*   251

designed Man for a sociable Creature, made him not only with an inclination, and under a necessity to have fellowship with those of his own kind; but furnished him also with Language, which was to be the great Instrument, and common Tye of Society.' Thereafter in this chapter, Locke speaks of 'Nature' as the outfitter of mankind with language and with 'the Originals and Principles of all their Knowledge' (§ 5).

III. ii. 1: The opening sentence of this chapter should be compared to its counterpart in the preceding chapter. Here the opening reference is to 'Man'. The theme of this section is the cooperation between Nature or God and human artifice in the development of language.

III. iii. 13: Although 'Nature in the Production of Things, makes several of them alike', yet 'the *sorting* of them under Names, *is the workmanship of the Understanding*'. § 14: 'if the abstract *Idea* or Essence, to which the Name Man belonged, were of Nature's making', it would be impossible to doubt 'whether the *Foetus* born of a Woman were a *Man*'. (See also II. vi. 27.) § 19: 'All Things, that exist besides their Author [i.e. God or Nature], are all liable to Change'; their real Constitutions 'begin and perish with them'.

III. v. 8: The untranslatability of words of different languages is proof that ideas of mixed modes are inventions of the mind, 'Collections made and abstracted by the Mind' and not products of 'the steady Workmanship of Nature'. See also § 12 and III. ix. 22–3.

III. vi: On real and nominal essences. § 3: Knowledge of real essences is not attainable by man, but God and angels have it. § 9: 'The Workmanship of the All-wise, and Powerful God' so far 'exceeds the Capacity and Comprehension of the most inquisitive and intelligent Man' that it would be 'in vain [to] pretend to range Things into sorts, and dispose them into certain Classes, under Names, by their *real Essences* . . . A blind man may as soon sort Things by their Colours'. § 11: Our ideas of God and spirits are of nominal essences. How the idea of God is formed from simple ideas.

III. vi. 12: Natural-theological reasons to believe that there is a great chain of being: 'And when we consider the infinite power and wisdom of the Maker, we have reason to think, that it is suitable to the magnificent Harmony of the universe, and the great Design and infinite Goodness of the Architect, that the *Species* of Creatures should also, by gentle degrees, ascend upward from us toward his infinite Perfection, as we see they

252 APPENDIX

gradually descend from us downwards: Which if it be probable, we have reason then to be persuaded, that there are far more *Species* of Creatures above us, than there are beneath; we being in degrees of Perfection, much more remote from the infinite Being of GOD, than we are from the lowest state of Being, and that which approaches nearest to nothing. And yet of all those distinct *Species*, for the reasons above-said, we have no clear distinct ideas.' See also IV. iii. 17.

III. vi: 28–9: In making *Ideas* of the nominal essences of substances the mind follows nature. §§ 37, 38: Just as Nature makes things similar in their sensible qualities, it *probably* makes them alike in their internal constitution, but it is not by this real essence that mankind sorts them into species.

III. vi, 44–51: Adam is depicted in his role of giving names.

III. ix: § 9: The indeterminacy of interpretation of law and Scripture is a consequence of the untranslatability of the names of mixed modes. §§ 22, 23: The diversity of languages and the remoteness from us of certain ancient writings, whose meaning may nonetheless be 'of great concernment to us', requires that we be charitable to one another '*in our Interpretations or Misunderstandings*' of them. Scripture may be infallibly true, but any reader's interpretation of it is fallible. See also III. x. 12.

IV. i. 7: The proposition that God exists, cited as an example of the fourth sort of knowledge, viz. real existence, i.e. the agreement 'of [the idea of] *actual real Existence* agreeing to any *Idea*'.

IV. iii: The topic of this chapter is the limits of human knowledge of the sorts of being, which provides occasion for natural-theological reflection and theodicy, viz. that although human knowledge is narrow and disproportionate to the whole realm of being, material and spiritual, it is adequate, if we use our faculties correctly, to discover evidence confirming the wisdom, power, and goodness of God. § 6: Locke's admission that 'God can, if he pleases, superadd to Matter a Faculty of Thinking'. § 17: Our limited understanding of the powers and operations of spirits. (See also III. vi. 12.) § 18–20: The possibility of a demonstrative science of morality founded on our ideas of God and our selves, and the difficulties of achieving it, considered. (See also IV. iv. 7–10; IV. xi. 13; IV. xii. 8; IV. xiii. 3.) § 21: concerning knowledge of real existence: we have an intuitive knowledge of our own existence and demonstrative knowledge of the existence of God. § 23: The infinite

THEOLOGICAL PLACES IN LOCKE'S *ESSAY*   253

power, wisdom, and goodness of the creator assure us of the vastness of being that is beyond our faculties to comprehend and of the likelihood of creatures with more perfect faculties. § 27: A summary of our knowledge and ignorance concerning other minds and of the degrees of spiritual beings between God and ourselves. For the latter we are dependent upon revelation. § 28: A knowledge of the necessary causal connection between things is not discoverable from our ideas of them and hence, for us, must be attributed 'to nothing else, but the arbitrary Determination of that All-wise Agent, who has made them to be'. (See also IV. iv. 4; IV. xi. 1.)

IV. iv. 4: Simple ideas are not *fictions* of our Fancies, but the natural and regular productions of Things without us; and so carry with them all the conformity' which our maker intended or our state requires. § 10: Wherever a 'Moral Name', i.e. the name of a moral idea, e.g. justice or temperence, is defined by 'God or any other law-maker', that definition becomes 'the essence of that species to which the name belongs', i.e. its archetype. §§ 14–16: Appended to his account of our real knowledge of substances, or, rather, of our lack of such knowledge (§§ 11–13), Locke considers a querulous objection to the use of the term 'Changeling' to signify a creature between man and beast: 'If *Changelings* are something between Man and Beast, what will become of them in the other World?' He remarks that it is enough to know that they are in the hands of a 'faithful Creator' and 'bountiful Father' who is not bound by 'Names and Species of our Contrivance', i.e. by nominal essences. The paradox that a human issue might by nature be excluded from immortality is dispelled by denying its assumptions, viz. that whatever has the outward form of a man or is human-born must be designed for immortality.

IV. vii: Consideration of the utility of maxims or axioms, viz. certain self-evident propositions that are supposed to be the foundation of science. The main thesis of Locke's deflationary account is that maxims of this sort are not the means of fundamental or real knowledge but have value only in disputation. In § 11 he considers their use for theology and the same restriction is applied: maxims have value only 'to silence Wranglers', but the Christian religion is founded upon revelation. Revelation here is described as twofold: by the voice of reason and by the voice of God's spirit: 'When we find out an *Idea*, by whose Intervention we discover the connexion of two others [i.e. by inference], this is a Revelation from God to us, by the Voice of Reason. For we then come to know a Truth that we did not know before. When God declares any

254 APPENDIX

Truth to us, this is a Revelation to us by the Voice of his Spirit, and we are advanced in our Knowledge.' (See also IV. xix. 4.)

IV. viii: On trifling propositions; and the difference between trifling and instructive propositions: § 6: An illustration of the distinction: the proposition that every man has sense, motion, reason, and laughter is trivial; whereas the proposition that every being with these properties also has an idea of God would be instructive because 'having the notion of God' is not contained in our complex idea of a man. § 9: The distinction between trifling and instructive propositions applied to our knowledge of substances, viz. 'GOD, *Spirits*, or *Bodies*'.

IV. ix. 2: A summary of our knowledge of the existence of things and the means of cognition: 'I say, then, that we have the Knowledge of *our own Existence* by Intuition; of the *Existence of* GOD by Demonstration; and of other Things by Sensation.' Knowledge of self-existence is treated in the succeeding section in § 2 of the next chapter as a premiss in Locke's demonstration of God's existence. The existence of God and of other things is the subject of chapters x and xi respectively. (See also IV. xvii. 2.)

IV. x: The entire chapter is devoted to Locke's demonstration of the existence of God.

IV. xi. 1: The existence of God is necessarily connected by inference with the existence of any particular man. § 3: Locke's personal assurance of the existence of other things derives from God and the connection of ideas of such things with pleasure and pain: 'As to my self, I think GOD has given me assurance enough of the Existence of Things without me: since by their different application, I can produce in my self both Pleasure and Pain, which is one great Concernment of my present state.' (The other 'concernment' or interest is eternal bliss.) § 12: 'We have ground from revelation, and several other Reasons, to believe with assurance, that there are such Creatures [finite spirits, angels]: but our Senses not being able to discover them, we want the means of knowing their particular Existences.' § 13: Moral propositions may be universal and certain: 'So having the *Idea* of GOD and my self, of Fear and Obedience, I cannot but be sure that GOD is to be feared and obeyed by me: And this Proposition will be certain concerning *Man* in general, if I have made an abstract *Idea* of such a Species, where I am one particular.'

IV. xii. 4: A warning against using maxims accepted in other sciences as principles in morality and divinity is followed by a brief critique of

THEOLOGICAL PLACES IN LOCKE'S *ESSAY*   255

philosophical morality and theology in antiquity. § 11: Our certainty of the existence of God and ourselves, which is the basis of morality, is contrasted with our limited knowledge of nature. From this Locke infers that the proper business in life is morality, by which we prepare ourselves for life in the world to come, and practical arts, by which we achieve relative happiness in this world.

IV. xiii. 3: More on the foundation of morality: 'He that hath the *Idea* of an intelligent, but frail and weak Being, made by and depending on another, who is eternal, omnipotent, perfectly wise and good, will as certainly know that Man is to honour, fear, and obey GOD, as that the Sun shines when he sees it.'

IV. xiv. 2, 3: The faculty of judgement and its domain are contrasted with the faculty of knowledge: the little that we know (i.e. things set by God 'in broad day-light') are given 'as a Taste of what intellectual Creatures are capable of, to excite in us a Desire and Endeavour after a better state', which is our greatest interest or 'concernment'; on the other hand, to meet our present worldly needs ('the greatest part of our Concernment') we depend on probability. (Here, God has 'afforded us only the twilight'.) From this comparison we should infer that we are probationers and pilgrims in this world. Locke likens the faculties of the mind to 'talents' (cf. the parable of the talents, Matt. 25: 14–30) and remarks that even without the light of revelation, it is reasonable to believe that 'as Men employ those Talents, God has given them here, they shall accordingly receive their Rewards at the close of the day'.

IV. xvi. 13, 14: On revelation: miracles (supernatural events 'suitable to ends aim'd at by him, who has the power to change the course of Nature') and the bare testimony of God (who 'cannot deceive, nor be deceived') are not subject to the limitations of probability as determined by 'common Experience' and 'the ordinary Course of Things'. Miracles have a sort of self-evidence and confirm other truths; revelation itself consists of propositions that carry with them 'Assurance beyond Doubt, Evidence beyond Exception'. Yet it is up to reason to verify that something is a revelation and to clarify the meaning of its expressions, without which we 'expose our selves to all the Extravagancy of Enthusiasm, and all the Error of wrong Principles'. In determining the authenticity and meaning of revelation, reason regulates the degree of our assent to it.

V. xvii. 4: Reason is a natural faculty that does not require a formal method (viz. Aristotle's syllogistic logic) to be effective. 'God has not

256 APPENDIX

been so sparing to Men to make them barely two-legged Creatures, and left it to *Aristotle* to make them Rational'. In this section, Locke illustrates his method of inference by deriving freedom and self-determination from the prospect of divine punishment of mankind. § 10: The difficulty in thinking about what it is to be a free created agent arises from the imperfection of our ideas concerning the operations of our minds and of God. § 23: Distinction between things according to, above, or contrary to reason. The existence of God is according to reason; the existence of more than one god is contrary to reason; the resurrection of the dead is above reason. § 24: The opposition of faith and reason is considered and rejected. Locke affirms the harmony of the two: '*Faith* is nothing but a firm Assent of the Mind: which if it be regulated, as is our Duty, cannot be afforded to any thing, but upon good Reason; and so cannot be opposite to it.' This is followed by a description of three ways of using or abusing reason, the last of which concludes with a classic expression of what has come to be described as 'the ethics of belief': 'he that makes use of the Light and Faculties GOD has given him, and seeks sincerely to discover Truth, by those Helps and Abilities he has, may have this satisfaction in doing his Duty as a rational Creature, that though he should miss Truth, he will not miss the Reward of it'.

IV. xviii: The entire chapter treats faith and reason and their 'distinct Provinces'.

IV. xix: This chapter, on enthusiasm, first appeared in the 4th edition (1700) of the *Essay*.

IV. xx. 3: Affirmation of one of the central theses of the book: 'GOD has furnished Men with Faculties sufficient to direct them in the Way they should take, if they will but seriously employ them that Way, when their ordinary Vocations allow them the Leisure.' Sufficient leisure 'to think of his Soul, and inform himself in Matters of Religion' is lacking to no man. The alternative to this view is to accept that human belief is either subject to chance or determined by bare authority. §§ 6, 9, 10, 11 apply the causes of wrong assent to matters of religion.

IV. xxi: In the division of the sciences, God belongs to our knowledge of things (§ 2); ethics, viz. happiness and the rational means of attaining it, belongs to practical reasoning (§ 3).

Notes

1. Theology, its Sources, and the Pragmatics of Assent

3.2. **as they are now destinguished**] It is unclear to what system of the sciences Locke is alluding. According to the division of the sciences in *Essay* IV. xxi speculative theology would fall under the general heading of our knowledge of things.

4.34. **physick**] that is, medicine.

4.37. **Dogmatists, Methodists or Chymists**] Three prevailing schools of medicine. The two former originated in antiquity. The last is connected with alchemical practices, with Paracelsus, but also with Boyle and Sydenham, with whom Locke, himself a physician, worked closely.

5.2. **Hippocrates**] Hippocrates of Cos (*c.*450–*c.*370 BCE). The reference is to the Hippocratic corpus of writings.

5.25. **The Volumes of Interpreters . . . proofs of this**] They are evidence of the imperfection of words.

2. Morality and Religion

'Of Ethick in General'

9.27. **all their heathen ceremonies . . . pretended to revelation**] Cf. *A Discourse of Miracles*, below, 45.26–30, where Locke restricts revelation to the attestation of the religion of the one true God.

11.20. **L 2 c. 21**] *Essay* II. xxi. 42.

12.19. **certeine complex Ideas of Modes**] The reference is to mixed modes. See *Essay* II. xxii; III. v.

12.27. **Anacarsis**] Anacharsis, 6th cent. BCE. A Scythian prince who travelled in Greece and was noted for his wisdom. See Diogenes Laertius, I. 8; Cicero, *Tusc. Disp.* V. xxxii.

13.33. **Εὐτϱαπελία**] viz. ready wit or ribaldry.

'Sacerdos 98'

17.1. **Sacerdos**] i.e. Priest.

17.6. **the charge of it**] i.e. the cost of religious rites.

17.20. **noe thing but Revelation**] See above, note on 'Of Ethick in General' (9.27).

258   NOTES

17.25. **Tusc. Quest. l. 2. c. 4.**] *Tusc. Disp.* V. iv. 11: 'How few philosophers are found to be so constituted and to have principles and a rule of life so firmly settled as reason requires!' (trans. J. E. King, Loeb Classical Library (London and Cambridge, Mass., 1950), 157).

17.32–3. **two very plain & simple institutions**] viz. Baptism and the Lord's Supper.

18.10–14. **cum de religione . . . nulla ratione reddita credere**] 'When Religion's the point I don't examine what *Zeno, Cleanthes,* or *Chrysippus* hold, but what the great Pontiffs say, *Coruncanus, Scipio,* and *Scaevola*: . . . I can hear a Philosopher explain the Reasons of Religion, but I believe our Forefathers without any Reason at all.' Cicero's *De Natura Deorum,* III. ii. 5, 6 (trans. from the English edition of *Pensées diverses: Miscellaneous Reflections, Occasion'd by the Comet which appear'd in December 1680* (London, 1708), i, 253). The ellipsis is Locke's. In the body of his text, Bayle gives the full text of Cicero in translation and provides the Latin text, with a shorter ellipsis in a corresponding footnote. The missing lines are as follows: 'And would rather hear Augur Laelius discourse of Religion in his noble manner, than the top Philosopher of the Stoic sect. 'Twas never my Principle to think meanly of any Article of the *Roman* Peoples Religion; and it's my fix'd Persuasion, that our Republick and Religion growing up together, the one must of necessity be approv'd by the Gods, or the other had ne'er become so powerful.'

3. 'Adversaria Theologica 94'

23.22. **malos**] Perhaps Locke meant by bad spirits those worldly powers who, although evil, are nonetheless, according to St Paul, Romans 13: 1, ordained by God to do good work.

23.37. **Trinitas**] The entries entitled 'Trinitas' and 'Non Trinitas' are on facing pages.

24.12. **[father**] Locke's brackets.

24.16. **Bidle $\frac{1}{24}$**] The reference is to John Biddle, *A Confession of Faith* (London, 1648), 1. In his note-taking, Locke employed a method of citing a work by the author's name and a fraction; the numerator indicates the page cited, the denominator, the total number of pages in the work.

25.2. **Propitiatio Placamen**] The means of atonement.

25.3–4. **Ipsi deo nihil minus gratum . . . et colendam viam**] 'nothing would be less pleasing to god himself than that the pathway to his favour and to his worship should not be open to all alike' (Cicero, *De Legibus,* II. x. 25). The translation is from the Loeb Classical Library edn. (London and Cambridge, Mass., 1959 401). Cicero was complaining about the costliness of rites.

25.6. **Christus Deus Supremus**] This and the next entry are on facing pages.

25.9. ὢν . . . εἰς τοὺς αἰῶνας] 'who is over all, God blessed for ever' (AV).

25.21. **itd.**] abbreviation of 'itidem', viz. the same.

NOTES 259

25.30. **This distinction . . .**] viz. the distinction between the divine and human nature of Christ. For the orthodox interpretation of 1 Cor. 15: 28, see the Westminster Divines' *Annotations upon all the Books of the Old and New Testament* (London, 1657): 'As man in respect to his mystical body, the Son shall be Subject to his father . . .' See also Augustine, *De Trinitate*, I. 8.

26.17. **Christus merus homo**] This and the next entry are on facing pages.

27.3–6. **If the eternal son . . . Mat XXII. 46**] A perpendicular line, about ⅓ inch from the margin, is drawn through this paragraph.

27.11. **Spiritus Sanctus Deus**] This and the next entry are on facing pages.

27.28. **Bidle $\frac{12}{16}$**] The reference is to John Biddle, *A Letter to a certain Knight*, which is prefixed to *Twelve Arguments Drawn out of Scripture. Wherein the commonly received Opinions touching the Deity of the Holy Spirit is clearly and fully refuted* (n.p., 1647).

27.35. **Persona est suppositum intelligens**] a person is an intelligent subject. 'Suppositum' is a scholastic term that was used to signify both a grammatical and an ontological subject or hypostasis. See, Norman Kretzmann, *et al.*, *The Cambridge History of Later Medieval Philosophy* (Cambridge, 1982), 813.

28.26. **Anima humana Immaterialis**] This and the next entry are on facing pages.

28.27. **An in corpore . . . nescio**] 'Whether in the body or whether outside the body I don't know'.

28.34–6. **Si anima . . . post mortem resurgat. Hactenus Episcopius $\frac{354}{440}$**] 'If the soul is a compound body that perishes completely when the body is dissolved, then it is impossible that it should be raised after death as the same numerical man. Thus much Episcopius.' The citation is of Simon Episcopius, *Opera Theologica*, 2nd edn. (London, 1678), i. 354. Episcopius, in contrast to Locke, believed that the identity of a man, and no doubt a person, is a simple indissoluble soul. (See *Essay*, II. xxvii. 3, 6, 9.) The term 'crasis' is transliterated from the Greek κρᾶσις.

28.39. **2 ψυχή In many places of the new Testament**] Compare this section with Locke's manuscript entitled 'Spirit, Soul, and Body' (MS Locke c. 27, fos. 1312–37). It has been transcribed and printed in Wainwright, *Paraphrase and Notes*, II, Appendix V, pp. 675–8. The manuscript is undated.

30.8–9. **οὐ κατελείφθη . . . εἰς ἅδου**] his soul was not left in hell (AV).

30.26. **Credenda**] lit. what is to be believed. 'Credenda' are fundamental articles of faith, what one must believe in order to be saved. They are complemented by 'agenda', what must be done, viz. duties owed to God, etc.

30.27–8. **Animae Immaterialitas . . . Epis. $\frac{354}{440}$**] 'Immateriality of the soul. Otherwise it is not possible to believe the resurrection of the same man' (Episcopius, *Opera Theologica*, 354).

30.30. **Homo lapsus Liber**] Adam fell freely. This and the next entry are on facing pages.

30.31. **Liber est . . . vel non agere**] 'Whoever is able to act or not to act is free'. See *Essay*, II. xxi. 27 & ch. xxi *passim*. In the margin next to 'Liber' Locke has inscribed an 'X'.

260 NOTES

30.32. Ubicunque necessitas . . . Epis $\frac{357}{440}$] 'Wherever absolute necessity rules, there religion has no place' (Episcopius, *Opera Theologica*, 357).

30.33–6. In libero agente . . . aut suspendere] 'In the free agent power to act is simultaneous with power not to act, but the agent himself is able to determine to act or not to act as he chooses or when he determines himself to act or to refrain from acting and withhold or suspend his action.'

30.40. Adami ⟨Hominis⟩ Status ante Lapsum] 'the state of Adam [or] of man before the Fall'. 'Hominis' is written in the line above as an insertion presumably to replace 'Adami', which, however, is not crossed out.

31.1–9. Anima non rasa tabula . . . et inordinatius amandi] '[Before the Fall] the soul does not employ a tabula rasa, rather after the birth of every infant it is provided with what it needs to know in that state and with the capability to obtain further knowledge, either through reasoning or through experience or through revelation. With this knowledge there was also 1° ignorance of certain things. He did not know that he was naked. Thus far he did not know good and evil &c. 2° the power of erring and suffering seduction. The serpent beguiled Eve . . . 3° the power of loving his wife excessively and inordinately.' Cf. also 'Homo ante et post lapsum', above.

31.11. Lex operum] This and the next entry are on facing pages.

32.7. Satisfactio Christi] This and the next entry are on facing pages.

32.10–29. Jesus Christ suffered . . . Considerations $\frac{11}{68}$] The passage is from [Stephen Nye], *Considerations on the explications of the doctrine of the Trinity* (London, 1694), 11.

32.31. Electio] In the margin next to this entry there is inscribed a large and a small 'X'.

4. Inspiration, Revelation, Scripture, and Faith

'Immediate Inspiration. Dec. 87'

37.14. traditional revelation] See *Essay* IV. xviii. 3.

37.19. Paul's powerfull reasoning on the schools of Tyranny &c.] Acts. 19: 9 is a possible referent of this comment; '&c.', which is an interlinear insertion, indicates that Locke had more than one place in mind.

37.23. faith is of things not seen & . . . shall be swallowed up in vision] See above, p. xviii.

38.10. Aholiab &c.] See Exodus 31: 1–11. Aholiab and the rest were craftsmen chosen by God to construct the tabernacle and its furnishing, the ark, priestly garments, and all the equipment of worship. Locke cites this as an instance where Scripture ascribes to the Spirit of God things 'brought about by the ordinary course of providence & humane means', i.e. naturally.

38.22. if so &] Locke crossed out these words, but the context seems to require them.

38.23. Abraham did amisse to send Dives's brethren to Moses & the

NOTES

Prophets] The reference is to the parable of the rich man (Lat. *dives*) and Lazarus (Luke 16: 9–31).

38.31. **θέχουσι**] The word does not appear in Liddell–Scott–Jones, *Greek–English Lexicon*.

39.19. **church of roome**] Church of Rome. See also 'Infallibility'.

39.29. **command of being able to render a reason of ones faith**] See 1 Peter 3:15.

40.37–40. **from the time of Moses . . . schools & sons of the prophets**] Locke most likely based this claim on the work of Richard Simon, *Histoire critique du vieux Testament* (Rotterdam, 1685) (LL 2673). See Locke's notes on Simon, BOD MS Locke f. 32, fos. 1, 2, 11.

'Scriptura Sacra'

42.24. **Enthusiasts**] Those who believe that original revelation has not ended, but continues to occur through divine inspiration to individuals. For a general account, see Christopher Hill, *The World Turned Upside Down* (London, 1972). See also, *Essay*, IV. xix.

A Discourse of Miracles

45.3–5. **The heathen World . . . had no room for a divine Attestation of any one against the rest**] Cf. 'Of Ethick in General' 9.27, and 'Sacerdos' 17.20.

45.6. **owners of many Gods**] 'owner' here signifies someone who believes that many Gods exist and who chooses to worship one or all of them.

45.26. **by what has been**] by the past, or more specifically, by events recounted in the Bible.

45.29–30. **and that this is so in the nature of the thing, and cannot be otherwise . . . will be made to appear in the sequel to this Discourse**] In the sequel, that is, in the next part of the *Discourse*, Locke will argue using historical examples the necessary connection between miracles and monotheism.

46.11–12. *we know that thou art a teacher . . . except God be with him*] John 3: 2.

46.13–27. **For example . . . and he cannot question its Truth**] The sequence of miracles: Jesus calms the tempest, Matt. 8: 23–7; walks on the sea, Matt. 14: 22, 23; cures 'an inveterate Palsie' by a word, Matt. 17: 14–21; heals a man born blind, John 9: 1–41; raises the dead, John 11: 1–44; raises himself [sic Locke] from the dead, Matt. 28: 1–8.

48.1–4. **and therefore to this day . . . which is a standing Miracle**] a standing or constant miracle is a continuing state of affairs or progress of events in contrast to a single extraordinary event. It must, like all other miracles, be 'above the comprehension of the spectator'. The standing miracle Locke is referring to is the propagation of Christianity. In his 'observations' on Philip Nye's *Discourse concerning Natural and Revealed Religion*, which he reviewed in manuscript, Locke remarks that the elliptical revolution of the sun or the earth

262　　　　　　　　　　　　　　　　NOTES

is most probably a standing miracle 'for the motion of one of them in a crooked line contrary to the nature of motion as far as we conceive of it is acknowledged by all the world' (BOD MS Locke c. 27, fo. 93).

'An Essay for the Understanding of St Paul's Epistles'

53.40. **Chapters and Verses**] The division of the Bible into chapter and verse was a recent innovation. Chapter divisions were introduced in the thirteenth century, and were common to all printed Bibles. The earliest printed Bible with numbered verses, a Latin translation by Santi Pagnini, was published in 1528 by Du Ry of Lyons. It retained a continuous text. In 1551 Henri Estienne published a New Testament with the verses numbered and divided. See S. L. Greenslade, *The Cambridge History of the Bible: The West from the Reformation to the present Day* (Cambridge, 1963), 436 ff., 441 ff.

54.28. **Tully's** *Epistles*] Cicero, *Epistolae ad Atticum* and *Epistolae ad Familiares*, both of which were in Locke's library (LL 712, 713).

55.20–31. **Saying of the Learned and Judicious Mr.** *Selden* . . . **we should find it meant no such thing.'**] John Selden, *Table Talk*, 2nd edn. (London, 1696), 8–9 (LL 2609).

57.15. *Hammond* **and** *Beza*] Henry Hammond, *Paraphrasis et adnotationes in Novum Testamentum* (Amsterdam, 1698) (LL 1382); Theodore Beza, *Testamentum Novum Graece cum interpretatione veteri et Bezae* (Geneva, 1588) (LL 2861).

61.8–9. **This being the only safe Guide (under the Spirit of God, that dictated these Sacred Writings)**] The attribution of the authorship of St Paul's letters to the Holy Spirit by dictation seems inconsistent with his earlier remark that Paul was taught by God himself and received the Gospel from 'the Fountain and Father of Light himself' (60.21–2). What need for further illumination, when St Paul had not only this original infusion of revelation, but also an impressive 'Stock of Learning'? Cf. also 'Immediate Inspiration'?

5. The Nature and Authority of the Church

'Infallibility'

75.25–9. **For, whoever tries to explain the trinity of persons . . . casts not so much light than darkness on scripture**] One may take this as evidence that in 1661 Locke accepted some version of the doctrine of the Trinity, but probably not the Athanasian one. It is also evidence that as early as this time, Locke did not regard this doctrine as a fundamental article of faith.

72.7. **i e custom**] The parenthetical insertion is Locke's. The term custom (Lat. *consuetudo*) normally translated the Greek νόμος, a practice established by positive law, custom, or convention, in contrast to that which is φύσει, according to nature. Locke's interpretation, however, is not unprecedented. See John C. Biddle, 'John Locke's Essay on Infallibility', *Journal of Church and*

NOTES 263

State, 19 (1977), 325 n. 15, who finds the same interpretation in Calvin, Grotius, and Hammond.

72.7–8. **οὐδὲ αὐτὴ ἡ φύσις διδάσκει ὑμᾶς ὅτι ἀνὴρ μὲν ἐὰν κομᾷ ἀτιμία αὐτῷ ἐστι**] 1 Cor. 11: 14: 'Doth not even nature itself teach you, that, if a man have long hair, it is a shame unto him?' (AV).

72.10. **πάντα εὐσχημόνως καὶ κατὰ τάξιν γινέσθω**] 1 Cor. 14: 40: 'Let all things be done decently and in order' (AV).

'Critical Notes upon Edward Stillingfleet's Mischief *and* Unreasonableness of Separation'—*Extracts*

74.9. **in the same chapter**] 1 Cor. 14: 40.

74.26. **persuaded ⟨or⟩ convinced**] Both words are written in the margin of the manuscript for insertion in such a way that Locke intended to include one or the other but not both.

76.38. **Bishop G. or Dr. S. . . . Mr. B. or Dr. O . . . Cardinal H. or Mr P**] **Bishop G.**: probably Peter Gunning (1614–84), Bishop of Ely, who at the Savoy Conference (1661) was a strong opponent of schismatics; **Dr. S.**: Edward Stillingfleet (1635–99), author of *The Mischief of Separation* &c., who was at the time Dean of St Paul's, later Bishop of Worcester; **Mr. B.**: Richard Baxter (1615–91), nonconformist Presbyterian divine, who wrote *Richard Baxter's Answer to Edward Stillingfleet's Charge of Separation* (1680); **Dr. O:** John Owen (1616–83), puritan divine, was Dean of Christ Church and Vice-Chancellor of the University of Oxford during the interregnum, when Locke was a student there; he wrote *Answer to Dr. Stillingfleet on the Unreasonableness of Separation* (1680); **Cardinal H.**: Pierre Daniel Huet (1630–1721), French scholar, Bishop of Arranches; **Mr P.**: William Penn (1644–1718), Quaker and founder of Pennsylvania.

77.9. **jure divino**] by divine right. See Stillingfleet, *Irenicum*, 9 f.: 'I assert any particular form of Government agreed on by the governours of the church, consonant to the general rules of Scripture, to bee by Divine right, *i.e.* God by his own Laws hath given men a power and liberty to determine the particular forme of Church-Government among them.' In constituting the church in any realm, the governors must be guided by an immutable principle, viz. the preservation of the peace and unity of the church. On the other hand, the particular form of a church is mutable and relative to circumstances, but not voluntary with respect to the individual Christian.

77.11. **The D^r. presses the necessity of a national Church**] On pp. 288–91 of *The Unreasonableness of Separation*, to which this comment refers, Stillingfleet defends the institution of a national church. He argues, on historical grounds, that from his appointment of the Twelve to rule the Church it may be inferred that Jesus Christ did not intend to limit the constitution of the Church to a particular congregation and, therefore, that a national church is not inconsistent with Jesus' intentions when he founded the Church. A national church is the result of the gradual increase of Christianity in a particular

264 NOTES

country. Stillingfleet argued that its establishment was the best means to maintain religion, to preserve peace and unity, and to prevent heresy and dangerous confusion.

77.15. **serry**] The *OED* (1971) lists 'serry' as a verb, 'to order in close ranks', with the past participle 'serried' signifying close-ordered.

79.3. **volerys**] volery: bird cage, aviary.

'Ecclesia 82'

80.1. **Hookers description . . . amounts to this**] The extract from Hooker may be better understood and Locke's use of it fairly appraised when it is set in a slightly larger context. The following is from Bk. I, Ch. 15 of Hooker, *Of the Laws of Ecclesiastical Polity, Folger Edition*, i. 130–1:

Positive lawes are either permanent or else changeable, according as the matter it selfe is concerning which they were first made. Whether God or man be the maker of them, alteration they so far forth admit, as the matter doth exact. Lawes that concerne supernaturall duties, are all positive, and either concerne men supernaturallie as men, or else as parts of a supernaturall societie, which societie we call the Church. To concerne men as men supernaturallie is to concerne them as duties which belong of necessitie to all, and yet could not have bene knowne by any to belong unto them, unlesse God had opened them him selfe, in as much as they do not depend upon any naturall ground at all out of which they may be deduced, but are appointed of God to supplie the defect of those naturall wayes of salvation, by which we are not now able to attaine thereunto. The Church being a supernaturall societie, doth differ from naturall societies in this, that the persons unto whome we associate our selves, in the one are men simplye considered as men, but they to whome we be joyned in the other are God, Angels and holie men. Againe the Church being both a societie and a societie supernatural, although as it is a societie it have the selfe same originall grounds which other politique societies have, namely, the naturall inclination which all men have unto socieable life, and consent to some certaine bond of association, which bond is the law that appointeth what kind of order they shall be associated in: yet unto the church as it is a societie supernaturall this is peculiar, that part of the bond of their association which belong to the Church of God, must be a lawe supernaturall, which God himself hath revealed concerning that kind of worship which his people shall doe unto him. The substance of the service of God therefore, so far forth as it hath in it any thing more then the law of reason doth teach, may not be invented of men, as it is amongst the Heathens, but must be received from God himselfe, as always it hath bene in the Church, saving only when the Church hath bene forgetfull of her dutie.

NOTES   265

6. The Reasonableness of Christianity

The Reasonableness of Christianity

89.2. **Systems of Divinity**] By 'system' Locke here means a treatise that gives an orderly exposition of a sum of doctrine on a particular subject. Although he supposed that there were at least two such systems in the New Testament, viz. the Epistles to the Romans and to the Hebrews, he did not believe that they were the best sources for the understanding he was seeking in the *Reasonableness*. His reasons for this are given in the last section (XV) of the book. Doubtless his remark in the first sentence of the Preface was not directed at them. In a letter to Limborch dated 10 May 1695 (*Correspondence*, v. 1901) he mentions two systems that he read and found unsatisfying and inconsistent, viz. Calvin's *Institutio* and Turrettin's *Institutio theologiae elencticae*. He also mentions consulting Limborch's system, *Theologia Christiana*, which he praises. He writes, however, that he consulted these works after having developed the theme of the *Reasonableness* from Scripture alone. It is most probable, however, that this was not the first time he had read them.

91.9. **two Extreams**] viz. Calvinism and Deism.

91.11. **all *Adam*'s Posterity**] Locke seems to subscribe to the orthodox belief that Adam is the progenitor of the human race and to biblical chronology generally. He was, however, aware of the pre-Adamite theory of Isaac Lepeyrère that Adam was not the first man. Locke possessed copies of two of Lepeyrère's books on the subject: *Praeadamitae* (LL 2381) and *Systema Theologicum ex Prae-Adamitarum Hypothesi, Pars Prima*. (LL 2381). Both were published in 1655. Locke acquired them sometime after 1683. Lepeyrère's hypothesis is based upon an ingenious interpretation of Romans 5: 12–14, which presents one of the central themes of the *Reasonableness*, viz. the doctrine of the first and second Adam. According to Lepeyrère the law referred to in Romans 5: 12 is neither the law of Moses nor the law of nature, but the positive law given to Adam; and that although Adam was not the first man in time, he was he was the representative of mankind and the first natural man to receive a law. He claims that mankind was made mortal, and that the death which resulted from Adam's sin was not, therefore, natural death, but a legal death (*Preadamitae*, 10 f.). For a recent account of Lepeyrère's life and work, see Richard H. Popkin, *Isaac Le Peyrère (1596–1676). His Life, Work and Influence* (Leiden, 1987).

92.32. **Firmacum Maternum**] Julius Firmacus Maternus (d. *c.*350), a rhetorician, converted to Christianity. Author of *De errore profanarum religionum*. See *The Reasonableness of Christianity*, ed. Higgins-Biddle, p. 7, n. 3.

92.35. **Mr. Smith of Prophesie**] John Smith (1618–52), one of the Cambridge Platonists. Locke's note is a paraphrase from Smith's discourse *Of Prophecy*, from *Select Discourses*, 2nd edn. (London, 1673), 165–6. The quotation from Maimonides is from *Guide to the Perplexed*, i. 33.

93.38. **Animas esse Mortales**] Souls are mortal. The quotation is from Justin

266   NOTES

Martyr's *Dialogue with Trypho*. Locke cites Justin's *Opera* (Heidelberg, 1593).
See Higgins-Biddle, p. 9 n. 4, and p. 17 n. 2.

95.36. **the Eternal and established Law of Right and Wrong**] Although Locke
is not a moral realist, in the sense that he believed that standards of right and
wrong exist independently of the will of God, nevertheless, like the Cambridge
Platonists, he believed that there is an eternal and immutable law of God, one
that is not merely willed by God, but is an expression of the purity of the divine
nature. See below, 96.24, 174.10–24.

97.28. **the late Excellent Archibishop Tillotson**] John Tillotson (1630–92)
was Locke's contemporary, friend, and theological adviser. He was appointed
primate of the Church of England in 1691. The sermon referred to is entitled
Of the eternity of hell torments and is based on Matt. 35: 46. It was preached
before the Queen at Whitehall on 7 Mar. 1690.

98.35–9. **Οὐδὲ μὴν ἀθάνατον χρὴ λέγειν αὐτήν ... ὁ Θεὸς θέλῃ**] trans. from
Higgins-Biddle, p. 17 n. 1: 'Nor indeed should [the soul] be called immortal.
The soul leaves the body and the person does not exist; so also whenever the
soul should no longer live, the spirit of life departs from it and the soul no
longer exists, but simply returns to the place whence it was taken | The same
souls are in all beings, itidem p. 171 | Souls are not immortal; souls of the
pious appearing worthy of God do not yet die, but the unjust and wicked ones
are punished as long as God wants them to exist and be punished, itidem
p. 172'.

113.19. **By Miracles**] Cf. *A Discourse of Miracles*, above. Cf. also 153.26–34
below, where Locke anticipates the central thesis of the *Discourse* that miracles
are evidential only when they are used to confirm a revelation from the one
true God.

115.37. **This concealment of himself will seem strange**] See the preceding
paragraph 114.38–115.36. Locke introduces what must be one of the earliest
discussions of the Messianic Secret. He makes this paradox the leitmotiv in the
succeeding account of the providential course of the dispensation of the
Gospel during the first coming of the Messiah that continues through 155.5.
For two other Messianic advents, see the note below on 134.10–11.

117.29–30. **fifth of St. *John***] The 2nd edn. of the *Reasonableness* contains three
new passages. There is manuscript evidence that these additions were
authorial. See Higgins-Biddle, Appendix I, pp. 182–3. These additions are
not found in any later edn. except the 2nd edn. of Peter Coste's French
translation (1715). The first of these additions appears here in the 2nd edn.
(London, 1696), 66. For the second and third, see the notes on 132.36 and
141.1.
The addition inserted here is as follows:

They all imaginable ways attacked him, and he as readily eluded all their
Attempts by the wonderful Quickness and Conduct of an unparalled Wisdom.
Here at this Feast of Tabernacles, *The Scribes and Pharisees brought unto him a
Woman taken in Adultery, they say unto him, Master* Moses *in the Law*

NOTES

267

commanded us that such should be stoned, but what sayest thou? This they said tempting him, that they might accuse him, John VIII. 3–6. 'Tis plain they hoped that this Criminal Cause of a Woman just taken in the Fact, brought before him in the sight of the People, would draw him, if he would preserve the opinion of being the *Messiah* their King, to give Judgment in it, and by the Exercise of such an Authority expose him to the Roman Deputy. Some such Accusation they watched for: But they could never get any such Advantage against him. He marvellously defeated their Design, and without lessening himself, sent them away covered with Shame and Silence.

126.2–3. **I have observed the order of time in our Saviour's Preaching**] Locke's interest in the harmony of the Bible, i.e. the chronological ordering of events related in the biblical narrative and especially of the gospel history, dates back at least to the mid-1670s. It was supposed that working out the real sequence of the biblical history was a way of proving its truth. Among those who worked on this ecumenical project was the Catholic scholar Nicholas Toinard, whom Locke met during his travels in France (1675–9). Toinard presented Locke with the sheets of his monumental harmony of the gospel history (*Evangeliorum harmonia Graeco-Latina*) in 1679. Although it was not published until 1707, Locke had a complete set of printed sheets, which he had bound interleaved. The volume is deposited in the Locke Room of the Bodleian Library together with the remains of Locke's library (LL 2934). Higgins-Biddle's remark that Locke had only some of the sheets (p. 56, n. 1) is mistaken. A more detailed account of Locke's work on biblical chronology and its theological significance will be given in my *Locke's Vindications of the Reasonableness of Christianity and other Theological Writings* (Oxford, in preparation).

132.36. **he was the *Messiah*, *v*. 20.**] The second of the three additions appears at this point in the 2nd edn. as a new paragraph (pp. 105–6):

The probability of this, *viz.* That he had not yet told the Apostles themselves plainly that he was the *Messiah*, is confirmed by what our Saviour says to them, *John* XV. 15. *Henceforth I call you not Servants, for the Servant knoweth not what his Lord doeth. But I have called you Friends,* viz. in the foregoing Verse, *For all things that I have heard of my Father, I have made known unto you.* This was in his last Discourse with them after *Judas* was gone out; wherein he committed to them the great Secret by speaking of the Kingdom as his, as appears from *Luke* XXII, 30. and telling them several other particulars about it, whence he had it, what Kingdom it was, how to be administred, and what share they were to have in it, &c. From whence it is plain, that till just before he was laid hold on, the very moment he was parting with his Apostles, he had kept them as Servants in Ignorance; but now had discovered himself openly as to his Friends.

134.10–11. **the two solemn manifestations to the World of his Rule and Power**] Locke interprets Matt. 26. 27, 28 as referring to two additional advents of the Messiah, in both of which the Messiah would come in power. In

268 NOTES

vs. 28, he supposed that Jesus was prophesying about the destruction of Jerusalem as an act of divine vengeance. In vs. 27, Jesus refers to his coming at the Last Judgment when the world as we know it would end. See also below 137.11 ff. and 156.17 ff. However, it should be noted that in 'Resurrectio et quae sequuntur' Locke describes the coming of the Messiah at the end of history as his second coming. See above, 232.4 and 236.39.

141.1. *Messiah;*] The third addition to the 2nd edn. is inserted here:

Messiah: It was necessary for him to avoid provoking the Rulers by a frequent Manifestation of himself in their sight at *Jerusalem*. They were his known and most implacable Enemies; and being under the Eye, and in the immediate Power of the *Sanhedrim* at *Jerusalem*, he could not expect they should suffer him quietly, if he had a continued Course of Preaching and Miracles there from the beginning, spread his Doctrine, and drawn the People after him in the Metropolis of the Nation, the Seat of the *Roman* and *Jewish* Authority. But now . . .

166.23–4. an *Historical*, and not a Justifying or Saving Faith] On this distinction see Turretin, *Institutio*, XV. vii. 4, Eng. trans. ii. 559:

Faith is more properly distinguished into that which is a bare assent to revealed and known truth, possessed even by devils (called 'historical faith,' which is referred to in Jam. 2:19). Or into that which with assent . . . has come delight and joy, which is evanescent, called 'temporary [*prokairos*] faith' . . . Or into that which indicates an assent to some particular promise concerning a miraculous event . . . called the 'faith of miracles'. . . . Or finally into that which involves a fiducial apprehension of Christ and his benefits, called 'justifying and saving faith'.

In the next section, XV. viii, Turretin offers a more elaborate scheme, not all of which may be relevant here. His principal claim is that faith is an act of the will as well as of the intellect. Hence although saving faith includes assent to a proposition, which he labels 'historical faith', it also involves desiring and receiving Christ, trusting in him, rejoicing in him, and an assurance that one does indeed believe in this way.

It seems likely that Locke had Turretin in mind when he remarked that he would 'allow the makers of Systems . . . to invent and use what distinctions they please'. Nevertheless, while it is understandable that Locke would reject this broadening of the idea of faith to include these volitional features on epistemological grounds, it is puzzling that he rejects the criticism that mere assent is not saving, only later on to insist that it is indeed not saving unless accompanied by repentance. See 167.30 ff. and 169.23 f.

173.30–1. **God of his free Grace justifies sinful Man**] Locke's use of the term 'free Grace' here is curious. In Calvin and his successors, justification is a free gift, bestowed because of the merits neither of the recipients nor of Christ. Cf. *Institutio,* II. 17. 1; III. 13. 5; III. 22. 9. Calvin's point is that justification proceeds absolutely and without condition from the goodness and mercy of

NOTES

269

God. The context in which Locke uses the term here does not convey that sense. For a second occurrence of the term 'free Grace' see 207.40 f. Here Locke uses the term to characterize the divine right to determine the content of the faith that justifies, which in this respect is a positive faith.

188.38. **Believers of Old**] The context makes clear that Locke includes in this group not just biblical characters, viz. Abel, Noah, *et al.*, but also pagans, that is, both those who believed particular promises made to them by God and those who were guided to their belief by the light of nature.

205.25. **Fundamental Articles**] The term was used to denote those propositions that make up what one must believe to be saved. Locke's claim, which he would have to defend against John Edwards, was that there was only one such proposition for all Christians, and this is stated in the Gospel. However, he does admit others: viz. the existence and attributes of God (101.39 f.), that God is true (208.17), and the various historical matters that make up the complex proposition that Jesus is the Messiah.

206.31. **and so cannot be thought necessary to Salvation**] Locke's argument against relying on the epistles for the doctrine of the Gospel seems to be this: the doctrine of the epistles is contingent upon certain occasions which are themselves contingent, that is, they might not have happened. Doctrines that might not have been promulgated 'cannot be thought necessary to Salvation'. In contrast, then, to these doctrines, Locke must have believed that the doctrine of the Gospel enjoyed a different status: viz. that it was in the course of divine providence necessary and that it has a universality that is lacking in other doctrines of Scripture.

208.27. **the obedience of Faith**] See 208.40: 'a docility and disposition prepared to imbrace, and assent to all Truths coming from God; And [to] submit his mind to whatsoever shall appear to him to bear that Character'.

210.2. **the Controversies at this time so warmly managed amongst them, about Justification**] The controversy to which Locke alludes raged between the Presbyterians and Independents. It was occasioned by the republication of the sermons of Tobias Crisp (1600–43) by his son. Crisp argued that since the election of those to be redeemed is unconditional, and since the death of Christ covers the sins of the elect for all time, subsequent sins of the elect cannot defeat their salvation. For an account of the controversy and a summary of the issues see my *John Locke and Christianity* (Bristol, 1997), 120–53.

A Vindication of the Reasonableness of Christianity, &c.

211.2. *Some Thoughts concerning the several Causes and Occasions of Atheism*] London, 1695. Locke's page numbers refer to this edition.

211.6. **And breaths . . . a Pestilential Air**] This characterization may be intended to remind readers of the excessive zeal of Edwards's father, Thomas Edwards (1599–1647). In the preface to Part III of his book, *Gangraena* (London, 1646), the elder Edwards described its purpose in a style consistent with its title:

270 NOTES

In this following Book, as in a clear and true Glasse, every impartiall and ingenuous Reader may plainly behold the many Deformities and great Spots of the Sectaries of these times, Spots of all kinds, Plague spots, Feaver spots, Purpule spots, Leprosie spots, Scurvey spots, Spots upon them discovering much malignity, rage & frensie, great corruption and infection . . .

211.10–13. **I cannot but approve . . . Atheism being a Crime . . . ought to shut a Man out of all Sober and Civil Society**] These remarks represent Locke's considered opinion concerning the moral and political significance of atheism. On theism as the foundation of morality, see *Essay*, I. iv. 8. In this same section, while reflecting on signs of the spread of atheism 'in more civilized Countries' (that is, in Europe) Locke allows that 'Complaints of Atheism, made from the pulpit, are not without Reason.' On theism as the foundation of civil society and Locke's argument for ostracizing atheists, see *A Letter Concerning Toleration*, trans. William Popple, ed. J. Tully (Indianapolis, 1983), 51; also, *Some Considerations of the Consequences of the Lowering of Interest*, in *Locke on Money*, 2 vols., ed. Patrick Hyde Kelly (Oxford, 1991), i. 213. On atheism as madness, see *A Letter Concerning Toleration*, 38. Locke believed that atheism is irrational because

the visible marks of extraordinary Wisdom and Power, appear so plainly in all the Works of the Creation, that a rational Creature, who will but seriously reflect on them, cannot miss the discovery of a Deity. And the influence, that the discovery of such a Being must necessarily have on the Minds of all, that have but once heard of it, is so great, and carries such a weight of thought and Communication with it, that it seems stranger to me, that a whole Nation of Men should be any where found so brutish, as to want the Notion of a God; than they should be without any Notion of Numbers, or Fire. (*Essay*, I. iv. 9.)

Locke's acceptance that there may be atheist nations with atheist polities, in particular in Siam and China (*Essay*, I. iv. 8), seems inconsistent with this expostulation. For further discussion see Ian Harris, *The Mind of John Locke*, 189 ff. and John Yolton, *A Locke Dictionary*, 'atheism', 23 f. See also Michael Hunter, 'Aikenhead the Atheist', in *Science and the Shape of Orthodoxy* (Woodbridge, Suffolk, 1995), 308–32, for a discussion of the case of Thomas Aikenhead who was tried by a Scottish court for blasphemy and executed on 8 Jan. 1697. Locke took a great interest in the case and had a friend send him copies of documents of the trial. These papers survive in the Lovelace Collection, BOD MS Locke B4, fos. 86–106.

211.23–5. **two . . . Prelates of our Church, whom he makes favourers of the same *Conceit***] The two prelates are Jeremy Taylor (1613?–77) Bishop of Down and Connor in Ireland, and Herbert Croft (1603–91), Bishop of Hereford. In *Some Thoughts*, Edwards names neither, although he refers to them as prelates; he rather identifies them respectively as authors of *The Liberty of Prophesying* and *The Naked Truth*. The term 'conceit' (Middle English *conceite* from the Latin *conceptus*) can mean simply an idea or notion or concept. Here it

NOTES 271

means an idea that originates in the imagination, a fancy that is pathological or fashionable and false. The word appears separately three times in *Some Thoughts*. It first appears in Edwards's remark that atheists believe that the idea of God is 'a Melancholick Conceit . . . the mere Effect of Credulity and Ignorance' (p. 2).

211.32. **Bp. Taylor, and Bp. Croft**] In an alternative and later state of the 1st edn. of the *Vindication* and in all subsequent editions, this note reads 'Bp. Taylor, and the Author of *The Naked Truth*'. The change was doubtless made because Croft published *The Naked Truth* anonymously.

212.25. *pag.* 10] Here and throughout the *Vindication*, Locke cites the 1st edn. of the *Reasonableness*. In the Clarendon edn. and here, page numbers of the 1st edn. are printed in brackets in the margins.

212.36. **I am *all over Socinianized***] The verb 'Socinianize', in its active and passive forms, was in use by the middle of the seventeenth century in England (see *OED* (1971)). To be 'all over Socinianized' is to be thoroughly imbued with Socinian principles and doctrines, to be a Socinian, to write with a Socinian intent. The name 'Socinian' derives from the Italian Reformers, Lelio Sozini (1525–62) and Fausto Sozzini (1539–1604), who were uncle and nephew. Faustus denied the doctrines of the Trinity, the divinity of Christ, the immortality of the soul, and the satisfaction of Christ. He became a leader of the Unitarian community in Racow, Poland.

212.38. **Satisfaction**] Locke is referring to the Satisfaction theory of the atonement. The satisfaction at issue is the debt of punishment that is owed to divine justice for the sin of mankind, which is paid for by the death of Christ. Locke expresses mock fear that he did not mention Christ's satisfaction as one of the advantages of Christianity. He does not expressly reject it, and in the second *Vindication* (1st edn. 1697, pp. 465 f.) he remarks, perhaps in deference to Samuel Bold, who defended him and whom he was then defending against Edwards:

Mr. *Bold* says right, That [Satisfaction] is a Doctrine that is of mighty Importance for a Christian to be well acquainted with. And I will add to it, that it is very hard for a Christian who reads the Scripture with Attention, and an unprejudiced Mind, to deny the *Satisfaction* of *Christ*: But it being a term not used by the Holy ghost in the Scripture, and very variously explained by those that do use it, and very much stumbled at by those I was there speaking to . . . I left it, with the other disputed Doctrines of Christianity, to be looked into . . . by those who were Christians, and believed Jesus to be the Saviour promised and sent from God.

There is, however, a manuscript, in which Locke explicitly asserts the doctrine of Satisfaction. (MS Locke, c. 27, fo. 101; see Higgins-Biddle, pp. 198–200 for a transcription and comment.) The text is a comment on Romans 5: 12–14. Higgins-Biddle has observed that it coincides thematically with the discussion of Adam and Christ in the opening pages of the *Reasonableness*. He

NOTES

concludes from what appears to be an insertion mark in the margin that it was an unused draft. It is, however, undated, and without further evidence, the occasion and Locke's intention in writing it must remain uncertain. The passage comes as the third of three comments on St Paul's remark in Romans 5: 14 that Adam is a type of Christ, a part of which is quoted below.

As sin made Adam mortal. Soe sin was the cause of the death of Christ not his own but of others for whose sins he laid down his life. Soe that here the Justice of god was Satisfied for the law was noe righteousnesse noe life. Righteousnesse and life. Christ was neither descended from Adam and soe was not to die as one of his issue. Christ had noe sin and soe was not to die and therefor had a right to live. But laying downe his life when he was the son of god free from sin, It was a payment to god for those of the posteritie of Adam who were under death The justice of gods law being satisfied that he might impute righteousness to them that beleived.

One may ask why Locke decided not to include this draft in the *Reasonableness*, if that was its original destination? Perhaps he saw that the doctrine of Satisfaction no longer fitted his understanding of the respective roles of Adam and Christ. In the opening pages of the *Reasonableness* Locke denies that God imputed Adam's sin to his descendants. So, with respect to what Adam lost, only Christ's role as the restorer of immortality is relevant here. One of the advantages of this conjecture is that it applies only to Locke's decision not to use the draft in this context, leaving open the possibility that he might find a place for it in some other context or at least still entertain the doctrine of Satisfaction as part of the Gospel and so affirm its importance as he does in the second *Vindication*.

212.40. **a known Writer of the Brotherhood**] a clergyman.

213.25. **write Booty**] According to the *OED* (1971) Booty § 4, the expression signifies to despoil or victimize in concert with others.

214.15–19. **And yet when it came out . . . designed against the Christian Religion**] Locke is alluding to early criticism of the *Reasonableness* that alleged its purpose was to subvert morality by denying punishment in an afterlife. There is manuscript evidence showing that he began to prepare an answer to these charges. See MS Locke c. 29, fo. 99. It is likely that he dropped this defence in order to answer the charge brought against the *Reasonableness* by John Edwards.

219.3. *the Racovians*] Racovian is a synonym for Socinian. It is derived from *The Racovian Catechism*, a systematic statement of Unitarian opinions. This work derived its name from its place of origin, the city of Racow in Poland, where during the latter part of the sixteenth century there was a flourishing Unitarian community which maintained a well-respected Unitarian academy.

219.9. **the *Racovians*, whom I never yet read**] Locke's claim is at best evasive, if not downright false. His library included many Unitarian works by continental and English authors and he took notes on them, and although the precise dates

NOTES

273

of acquisition or reading cannot be fixed, it is likely that he began to acquire them while he was in exile in Holland. The 'Adversaria Theologica 94' contains quotations from the writings of John Biddle and Stephen Nye, both Unitarians. Locke could have denied that they were 'Racovians', since the term was used mostly to denote continental Unitarians and their doctrines, but this would have been disingenuous. On Unitarian books in Locke's library, see Harrison and Laslett, *The Library of John Locke*, 2nd edn. (Oxford, 1971), 23 and *passim*.

219.23. **the late Arch-Bishop of** *Canterbury*, **understood that Phrase in the same sense that I do**] 'that Phrase' is 'Son of God'; the late archbishop is Tillotson. On ll. 26–9 Locke quotes from a sermon preached by Tillotson before the King on 25 Feb. 1695, a copy of which he had in his library (LL 2918). Another sermon by Tillotson should also be consulted. This is entitled 'Jesus the Son of God, prov'd by his resurrection', where Tillotson also cites Nathaniel's confession. The sermon is no. CXX in the 1741 collection of Tillotson's *Sermons*. In this sermon Tillotson offers a fuller account of what he means by 'Son of God'. He observes that one must distinguish between the sonship of the Messiah in his divine nature, which is an eternal sonship, and his sonship 'according to the flesh', i.e. in his human nature. In this second respect, Tillotson states that the evidence that Jesus the Messiah is the son of God is twofold: the miraculous circumstances of his birth, and his resurrection. I do not know whether Locke read this sermon.

219.33. **a Scribler of** *Bartholomew* **Fair Drolls**] In *Some Thoughts* Edwards mentions drollery as one of the causes of atheism: 'And it is this Jocular Humour that in part betrays them to *Atheism,* for they take liberty to jest with their Maker. These witty and facetious Folks must needs play with Heaven, and laugh God out of his being' (p. 29). The connection of drollery and atheism is not original to Edwards. Cf. Joseph Glanvill, *A Whip for the droll, fidler to the atheist: being reflections on drollery and atheism* [Part II of *Saducismus triumphatus*] (London, 1682).

223.3. **that** *Muscovite* **Divine's Mind**] I have not been able to identify this reference.

223.34. **Reformed**] i.e. Calvinist.

223.34. **Remonstrants and Anti-Remonstrants**] The Remonstrants, the followers of Jacob Arminius, hence Arminians, who objected to Calvinist doctrines of predestination, limited atonement, and irresistible grace. The name derives from *The Remonstrance*, a statement of Arminian principles published in 1610. Their doctrines and their persons were condemned at the Synod of Dort (1619), where Calvinist doctrine was reasserted by the Anti- or Contra-Remonstrants. Among the leaders of the Remonstrants at that time was Simon Episcopius, the father-in-law of Philippus van Limborch, Locke's friend.

223.39. **Preface**] Locke is citing the Preface of *Some Thoughts*, where Edwards writes of the mixture of styles in his work that are the result of his having expanded a sermon into a discourse.

NOTES

224.28. Witnesses to Christianity] Simon Patrick, *The Witnesses to Christianity; or, the Certainty of Our Faith and Hope: in a Discourse on 1 John V. 7, 8*, 2 vols. (London, 1677). A second edition was published in 1703 under the title *Jesus and the Resurrection justified by witnesses in Heaven and Earth*. There is a copy of the first edition, from which Locke here quotes, in the remainder of Locke's Library now in the Locke Room of the Bodleian Library (LL 2235).

7. Fall and Redemption

'Peccatum originale 92'

229.6. properly & fformally or . . . Effectively] The distinction intended here applied to the manner of imputation of guilt. Guilt would be formally or properly assigned only if certain requisite procedures were first followed; otherwise, it would be effectively assigned, that is, individuals would suffer judicial evil without an appropriate judicial process.

230.4. with the safety of his Attributes] whether imputation as described in this article is consistent with the attributes of God.

'Homo ante et post lapsum 93'

231.1. Man was made mortal] Cf. 'Christianae Religionis synopsis' 242.1.

'On the Priesthood of Christ: Analysis of Hebrews'

239.10. the order of Milchisidec] i.e. Melchizedek, lit. 'king of righteousness'. Cf. Genesis 14: 18 and Psalm 110: 4.

239.20. τὸν λόγον τῆς ἀρχῆς τοῦ χριστοῦ] Locke's translation precedes: 'discourse of the principles of Christianity'; cf. AV: 'the principles of the doctrine of Christ'.

239.23. λόγον περὶ Μελχισεδέκ & λόγον περὶ ἀρχῆς χριστοῦ] The expression λόγον περὶ Μελχισεδέκ does not occur in Hebrews, but chs. 6 and 7 of Hebrews could be characterized as a discourse concerning Melchizedek. Hebrews 5: 11 is taken by Locke to forecast this discourse. Hence his remark that in two verses, Hebrews 5: 11 and 6: 1, the author of Hebrews 'opposes', that is, distinguishes, the discourse about Melchizedek and the discourse about the principles of Christianity.

240.33. Perfect. an unchangeable state of happynesse] This definition is crossed out, perhaps because, on reflection, Locke concluded that it doesn't fit the sense of 'perfect' in Hebrews. However, the same idea of perfection, although not the term, is represented in 'Resurrectio et quae sequuntur'.

Bibliography

Abbreviations of titles of works frequently cited are noted just before their bibliographical entry.

Bibliographies

ATTIG, JOHN C., *The Works of John Locke, A Comprehensive Bibliography from the Seventeenth Century to the Present* (Westport, Conn.: 1985; revised edn. in preparation).

CHRISTOPHERSEN, H. O., *Bibliographical Introduction to the Study of John Locke* (Oslo, 1930).

HALL, ROLAND, and WOOLHOUSE, ROGER, *80 Years of Locke Scholarship* (Edinburgh, 1983) (covers the period 1900–80; annual supplements in *The Locke Newsletter*, ed. Roland Hall).

LL = HARRISON, JOHN, and LASLETT, PETER, *The Library of John Locke,* 2nd edn. (Oxford, 1971).

LONG, P., *A Summary Catalogue of the Lovelace Collection of the Papers of John Locke in the Bodleian Library* (Oxford, 1959).

YOLTON, JEAN S., *John Locke, A Descriptive Bibliography* (Bristol, 1998).

YOLTON, JEAN S., and YOLTON, JOHN W., *John Locke, A Reference Guide* (Boston, 1985).

Primary Works

1. Selected works by John Locke in more or less chronological order

Two Tracts of Government, ed. Philip Abrams (Cambridge, 1967).

'Infallibility', Public Record Office: PRO 30/24/47/33; 'John Locke's Essay on Infallibility', ed. with an introduction and notes by John C. Biddle, *Journal of State and Church*, 19 (1997), 301–28.

Essays on the Law of Nature, ed. Wolfgang Von Leyden (Oxford, 1954).

Questions on the Law of Nature, ed. R. Horwitz, J. S. Clay, and D. Clay (Ithaca, 1990).

'Draft A', 'Draft B', in *Drafts for the Essay concerning Human Understanding, and other Philosophical Writings*, i, ed. P. H. Nidditch and G. A. J. Rogers (Oxford, 1990). (Contains Drafts A and B of *An Essay concerning Human Understanding.*)

'Ecclesia', BOD MS Locke d. 10, Lemmata Ethica, pp. 43–4.

BIBLIOGRAPHY

Locke's Travels in France, 1675–79 as related in his Journals, Correspondence & other Papers, ed. John Lough (Cambridge, 1953).

Discourses &c. translated from Nicole's Essays, trans. John Locke, ed. Thomas Hancock, M.D. (London, 1828 repr. Bristol, 1991).

'Critical Notes Upon Edward Stillingfleet's *Mischief* and *Unreasonableness of Separation*', BOD MS Locke c. 34.

Draft C of *An Essay concerning Human Understanding*, MS 998, The Pierpont Morgan Library.

'Of Ethick in General', BOD MS Locke c. 28, fos. 146–52

'Immediate Inspiration', BOD MS Locke c. 27, fos. 73–4.

Epistola de Tolerantia (Amsterdam, 1689); new edn. Raymond Klibansky (Oxford, 1968).

A Letter concerning Toleration, trans. from the Latin by William Popple (London, 1689; repr. with an introduction by John Tully, Indianapolis, 1989).

A Second Letter concerning Toleration (London, 1690).

A Third Letter concerning Toleration (London, 1691).

Part of a Fourth Letter concerning Toleration, in *The Posthumous Works of John Locke* (London, 1706).

Two Treatises of Government (London, 1690; critical edn. by Peter Laslett, Cambridge, 1967).

Essay = *An Essay concerning Human Understanding* (London, 1690; 2nd edn., 1694; 3rd edn., 1695; 4th edn., 1700; critical edn., ed. Peter Nidditch, Oxford, 1975).

'Ethica', BOD MS Locke c. 42, p. 224.

'Peccatum Originale', BOD MS Locke Film 77, pp. 294–5.

Some Thoughts concerning Education (London, 1693; critical edn. by J. W. and J. S. Yolton, Oxford, 1989).

'Homo ante et post lapsum 93', BOD MS Locke c. 28, fo. 113.

'Adversaria' = 'Adversaria Theologica 94', BOD MS Locke c. 43.

Some Considerations of the Consequences of the Lowering of Interest, in *Locke on Money*, ed. Patrick Hyde Kelly (Oxford, 1991).

Reasonableness = *The Reasonableness of Christianity as delivered in the Scriptures* (London, 1695); ed. with an introduction and notes by John C. Higgins-Biddle, Oxford, 1999. French trans. by Peter Coste, 1st edn., *Que la religion chretienne est tres-raisonnable*, Amsterdam, 1696, ed. with an introduction and notes by Hélène Bouchilloux, Oxford, 1999; 2nd edn. of French trans. by Peter Coste, *Le Christianisme raisonnable tel qu'il represente dans l'Ecriture Sainte* (Amsterdam, 1715).

A Vindication of the Reasonableness of Christianity &c. From Edwards's Reflections (London, 1695).

A Second Vindication of the Reasonableness of Christianity (London, 1697).

Vindications: Second partie du Christianisme raisonable [Extracts from the first and second *Vindications*, translated into French with introductions by Peter Coste] (Amsterdam, 1703).

BIBLIOGRAPHY 277

A Letter to the Right Reverend Edward Ld. Bishop of Worcester, concerning some Passages relating to Mr. Locke's Essay of Humane Understanding (London, 1697).

Mr. Locke's Reply to the Right Reverend the Lord Bishop of Worcester's Answer to his Letter (London, 1697).

Mr. Locke's Reply to the Right Reverend the Lord Bishop of Worcester's Answer to his Second Letter (London, 1699).

Some Thoughts concerning Reading and Study for a Gentleman, The Works of John Locke, 8th edn. (London, 1777), iv. 600–5; critically edited with notes by J. W. Yolton and J. S. Yolton, in *Some Thoughts concerning Education* (Oxford, 1989), Appendix III, pp. 319–27.

'Resurrectio et quae sequuntur', BOD MS c. 27, fos. 162–73; Wainwright, *Paraphrase & Notes*, ii. 679–84.

'Christianae religionis synopsis', BOD MS c. 27, fos. 213^r–214^v; Wainwright, *Paraphrase & Notes*, ii. 686–8.

'On the Priesthood of Christ: Analysis of Hebrews', insert in Locke's interleaved New Testament, LL 2864; shelf mark, BOD. Locke 9. 107.

'Error', BOD MS Locke Film 77 (1661 Notebook), pp. 320–1.

'Sacerdos' BOD MS Locke Film 77, p. 93.

Paraphrase and Notes = Paraphrase and Notes of the Epistles of St Paul, ed. A. W. Wainwright, 2 vols. (Oxford, 1987).

Of the Conduct of the Understanding, in *The Posthumous Works of John Locke* (London, 1706); critical text, introduction and notes by Paul Schuurman (Dissertation, University of Keele, 2000).

A Discourse of Miracles, in *The Posthumous Works of John Locke* (London, 1706). French trans. by Jean LeClerc, in *Œuvres diverses de Monsieur Jean Locke* (Rotterdam, 1710), ed. with notes by Hélène Bouchilloux (Oxford, 1999).

A New Method of a Common-Place-Book, The Posthumous Works of John Locke (London, 1706).

Correspondence = The Correspondence of John Locke, ed. E. S. de Beer, 8 vols. (Oxford, 1976–89).

The Works of John Locke, 8th edn., ed. Edmund Law (London, 1777).

2. Works by other authors

AMES, WILLIAM, *Medulla theologica* (Amsterdam, 1623); Eng. trans. *The Marrow of Theology*, trans. with an introduction by John Dykstra Eusden (Grand Rapids, 1997).

[ANONYMOUS,] *Animadversions on a late book entituled the Reasonableness of Christianity, as delivered in the Scriptures* (Oxford, 1697).

BAYLE, PIERRE, *Lettre à M. L. A. D. C., docteur de Sorbonne, Où il est prouvé par plusieurs raisons tirées de la philosophie, & de la theologie, qui les comits ne sont point le presage d'aucun malheur* (Cologne, 1682); Engl. trans., *Miscellaneous Reflections, Occasion'd by the Comet which appear'd in December 1680*, 2 vols. (London, 1708).

BIBLIOGRAPHY

Baxter, Richard, *Catholick Theologie: Plain, Pure Peaceable: For Pacification of the Dogmatical Word-Warriors* (London, 1675).

—— *Richard Baxter's Answer to Edward Stillingfleet's Charge of Separation* (London, 1680).

BEZA, THEODORE, *Testamentum Novum Graece cum interpretatione veteri et Bezae* (Geneva, 1588).

BIDLE [BIDDLE], JOHN, *A Confession of Faith* (London, 1648).

—— *Twelve Arguments Drawn out of Scripture. Wherein the commonly received Opinions touching the Deity of the Holy Spirit are clearly and fully refuted* (n.p., 1647).

BOLD, SAMUEL, *A Reply to Mr. Edwards Brief Reflections on Socinianism, &c.* (London, 1697).

—— *Some Passages in the Reasonableness of Christianity, &c. and its Vindication; with some Animadversions on Mr. Edward's Reflections on the Reasonableness of Christianity, and on his Book, entituled Socinianism Unmask'd* (London, 1697).

—— *Observations on the Animadversions (Lately Printed at Oxford) on a Late Book entituled, The Reasonableness of Christianity* (London, 1698).

—— *Some Considerations on the Principal Objections and Arguments which have been Publish'd against Mr. Locke's Essay of Human Understanding* (London, 1699).

—— *A Discourse concerning the Resurrection of the Same Body: with two letters concerning the necessary immateriality of created thinking substance* (London, 1705).

[BURNET, THOMAS,] *Remarks upon an Essay concerning Humane Understanding* (London, 1697).

—— *Second Remarks upon an Essay concerning Humane Understanding . . . Being a Vindication of the First Remarks, Against the Answer of Mr. Lock at the end of His Reply to the Lord Bishop of Worcester* (London, 1697).

—— *Third Remarks upon an Essay concerning Humane Understanding &c.* (London, 1699).

—— *Remarks upon an Essay concerning Humane Understanding* (New York, 1984) [Contains facsimile editions of Burnet's 1st, 2nd, and 3rd *Remarks*, together with Locke's *Reply* and Noah Porter's *Marginalia Locke-a-na*].

CALVIN, JOHN, *Institutio religionae christianae*, 5th edn. (Geneva, 1559); Eng. trans. *Institutes of the Christian Religion*, ed. John T. McNeill, trans. Ford Lewis Battles (Philadelphia, 1960).

—— *The Epistles of Paul the Apostle to the Romans and to the Thessalonians*, trans. Ross Mackenzie (Grand Rapids, 1961).

CHILLINGWORTH, WILLIAM, *The Religion of Protestants a Safe Way to Salvation* (Oxford, 1638).

—— *The Works of William Chillingworth M.A.*, 3 vols. (Oxford, 1838).

CARROLL, WILLIAM, *A dissertation upon the tenth chapter of the fourth book of Mr. Locke's Essay, concerning humane understanding. Wherein that author's endeavors to establish Spinoza's atheistical hypothesis . . . are discover'd and confuted. To which is subjoyn'd; a short account of the sense wherein the titles of, and the reasonings in the*

BIBLIOGRAPHY 279

following books, are to be understood, viz. the reasonableness of Christianity &c. (London, 1706).

COCKBURN, CATHERINE TROTTER, *A defence of the Essay of human understanding written by Mr. Lock . . . in answer to* [Thomas Burnet's] *Some remarks on that essay* (London, 1702); repr. in *The Works of Mrs. Catherine Cockburn . . . with an Account of the life of the author by Thomas Birch, in two volumes* (London, 1751).

—— *A Letter to Dr. Holdsworth . . . concerning the resurrection of the same body, in which the passages that concern Mr. Locke are chiefly considered* (London, 1726); repr. in *Works.*

—— *A Vindication of Mr. Locke's christian principles, from the injurious imputations of Dr. Holdsworth*, parts I and II, first published in *Works.*

[CROFT, HERBERT,] *The Naked Truth, or the True State of the Primitive Church* (London, 1675).

EDWARDS, JOHN, *Some Thoughts concerning the several causes of Atheism in the Present Age* (London, 1695).

—— *Socinianism Unmask'd: A discourse shewing the Unreasonableness of a Late Authors opinion concerning the necessity of only one Article of the Christian Faith* (London, 1696).

—— *A Brief Vindication of the Fundamental Articles of the Christian Faith* (London, 1697).

—— *The Socinian Creed; or, A Brief Account of the Professed Tenets and Doctrines of the foreign and English Socinians* (London, 1697).

EPISCOPIUS, SIMON, *Opera Theologica*, 2nd edn. (London, 1678).

FLEETWOOD, WILLIAM, *An Essay on Miracles* (London, 1701).

—— *A Compleat Collection of the Sermons, Tracts, and Pieces of all Kinds* (London, 1737).

GLANVILL, JOSEPH, *A Whip for the droll, fidler to the atheist: being reflections on drollery and atheism*, Part II of *Saducismus triumphatus* (London, 1682).

HAMMOND, HENRY, *Paraphrasis et adnotationes in Novum Testamentum* (Amsterdam, 1698).

HERBERT, EDWARD = LORD HERBERT OF CHERBURY, *De Veritate* (London, 1645), Eng. trans. by Meyrick. H. Carré (Bristol, 1937; repr. Bristol, 1992).

—— *De religione gentilium* (Amsterdam, 1663). Eng. trans. *Pagan Religion*, ed. John Anthony Butler (Ottawa, 1996).

HOADLY, BENJAMIN, *A Letter to Mr. Fleetwood &c.* (London, 1702).

HOLDSWORTH, WINCH, *A defence of the doctrine of the resurrection of the same body: in two parts* (London, 1727).

—— *A Sermon preached before the University of Oxford, at St. Mary's, on Easter-Monday, 1719: in which the cavils, false reasonings, and false interpretations of Scripture of Mr. Locke and others, against the resurrection of the same body, are examin'd and answered*, 2d edn. (London, 1728).

HOOKER, *Of the Lawes of Ecclesiastical Politie* (London, 1594–7, 1648); ed. with introduction by W. Speed Hill *et al.*, *The Folger Library Edition of the Works of Richard Hooker*, 4 vols. (Cambridge, Mass., 1977–82).

BIBLIOGRAPHY

[LeClerc, Jean,] *Five Letters concerning the Inspiration of the Holy Scriptures* (London, 1690).

Lee, Henry, *Anti-scepticism: or Notes upon each chapter of Mr. Lock's Essay concerning human understanding* (London, 1702).

Lepeyrère, Isaac, *Praeadamitae* (n.p., 1655).

—— *Systema Theologicum ex Prae-Adamitarum Hypothesi, Pars Prima* (n.p., 1655).

Limborch, Philippus van, *Theologia Christiana ad praxem pietatis ac Promotionem pacis Christianae unice directa* (Amsterdam, 1686; 2nd edn., Amsterdam, 1695). English translation, *A Compleat System, or Body of Divinity, both Speculative and Practical: founded on Scripture and Reason* (London, 1702).

Lowth, William, *A Vindication of the Divine Authority of the Old and New Testaments* (London, 1692).

Luther, Martin, *Lectures on Romans*, trans. and ed. Wilhelm Pauck (London, 1961).

[Masham, Damaris Cudworth,] *A Discourse concerning the Love of God* (London, 1696).

[Milner, John,] *An Account of Mr. Lock's Religion, out of his own Writings and in his own Words* (London, 1700).

Norris, John, *Cursory Reflections upon a book call'd, An Essay concerning Human Understanding* (London, 1690).

[Nye, Stephen,] *Considerations on the Explications of the Doctrine of the Trinity* (London, 1694).

—— *The exceptions of Mr. Edwards, in his causes of atheism, against the Reasonableness of Christianity . . . examin'd; and found unreasonable, unscriptural and injurious* (London, 1695).

Owen, John, *An Enquiry into the Original, Nature, Institution, Power, Order and Communion of Evangelical Churches: the First Part, with an answer to the Discourse of the Unreasonable of Separation written by Dr. Stillingfleet* (London, 1681).

Patrick, Simon, *The Witnesses to Christianity; or, the Certainty of Our Faith and Hope: in a Discourse on 1 John V. 7, 8*, 2 vols. (London, 1677).

[Proast, Jonas,] *The Argument of the Letter concerning Toleration briefly Consider'd and Answered* (Oxford, 1690).

—— *A third Letter concerning Toleration: In defense of the Argument &c.* (Oxford, 1691).

—— *A Second Letter to the Author of the Three Letters of Toleration, &c.* (Oxford, 1704).

—— *Racovian Catechism* [English translation of *Catechesis ecclesiarum Polonicarum*, 1659], trans. and ed. Thomas Rees (London, 1818).

Sargent, John, *The Method to Science* (London, 1696).

—— *Solid Philosophy Asserted, Against the Fancies of the Ideasts . . . with Reflexions on Mr Locks Essay concerning Human Understanding* (London, 1697).

Simon, Richard, *Histoire critique du vieux Testament* (Rotterdam, 1685).

Smith, John, *Select Discourses*, 2nd edn. (London, 1673).

BIBLIOGRAPHY 281

STILLINGFLEET, EDWARD, *Irenicum. A Weapon-Salve for the Churchs Wounds, or the Divine Right of Particular Forms of Church-Government* (London, 1662).

—— *The Mischief of Separation* (London, 1680).

—— *The Unreasonableness of Separation*, 2nd edn. (London, 1681).

—— *A Discourse in Vindication of the Doctrine of the Trinity* (London, 1697).

—— *The Bishop of Worcester's Answer to Mr. Locke's Letter, &c.* (London, 1697).

—— *The Bishop of Worcester's Answer to Mr. Locke's Second Letter, &c.* (London, 1698).

TAYLOR, JEREMY, ΘΕΟΛΟΓΙΑ 'ΕΚΛΕΚΤΙΚΗ. *A Discourse of The Liberty of Prophesying. Shewing the Unreasonableness of prescribing to other mens Faith, &c.* (London, 1647).

TILLOTSON, JOHN, *The Works . . . in twelve volumes* (London, 1753).

TURRETIN, FRANCIS, *Institutio theologiae elencticae* (Geneva, 1679); Eng. trans. George Musgrave Giger, ed. James T. Dennison, Jr., *Institutes or elenctic Theology*, 3 vols. (Phillipsburg, NJ, 1992).

TYRRELL, JAMES, *Bibliotheca politica: or An enquiry into the ancient constitution of the English government; both in respect to the just extent of regal power, and the rights and liberties of the subject* (London, 1694).

[WEST, RICHARD?,] *Animadversions on a Late Book entituled The Reasonableness of Christianity, As delivered in the Scriptures* (London, 1697).

WESTMINSTER DIVINES, *Annotations upon all the Books of the Old and New Testament*, 2 vols., 3rd edn. (London, 1657).

WHITBY, DANIEL, *A Paraphrase and Commentary on all the Epistles of the New Testament* (London, 1700).

WILKINS, JOHN, *Ecclesiastes: or a Discourse concerning the Gift of Preaching as it falls under the Rules of Art*, 8th edn. (London, 1704).

[WILLIS, RICHARD,] *The Occasional Paper: Number I* (London, 1697).

—— *The Occasional Paper, Number V, With a Post-Script relating to the author of The Reasonableness of Christianity* (London, 1697).

Secondary Works

AARSLEFF, HANS, *From Locke to Saussure* (Minneapolis, 1982).

ASHCRAFT, RICHARD, 'Faith and Knowledge in Locke's Philosophy', in John W. Yolton (ed.), *John Locke, Problems and Perspectives* (Cambridge, 1969).

AYERS, MICHAEL, *Locke*, 2 vols. (London, 1991).

BERMAN, DAVID, *A History of Atheism in Great Britain* (London, 1988).

BIDDLE, JOHN C. 'John Locke on Christianity: His Context and his Text' (Doctoral Dissertation, Stanford University, 1972).

BROWN, STUART, 'F. M. van Helmont: His Philosophical Connections and the Reception of his later Cabbalistic Philosophy', in M. A. Stewart (ed.), *Studies in Seventeenth Century European Philosophy* (Oxford, 1997), 97–116.

CHAPELL, VERE (ed.), *Locke* (Oxford, 1998).

BIBLIOGRAPHY

COLLINSON, PATRICK, *The Religion of Protestants* (Oxford, 1982).

COLMAN, JOHN, *John Locke's Moral Philosophy* (Edinburgh, 1983).

CRANSTON, MAURICE, *John Locke: A Biography* (New York, 1957).

DUNN, JOHN, *The Political Thought of John Locke* (Cambridge, 1969).

—— *Locke* (Oxford, 1984).

FORCE, JAMES E., and POPKIN, RICHARD H., *The Books of Nature and Scripture* (Dordrecht, 1994).

FOX-BOURNE, HENRY R., *The Life of John Locke*, 2 vols. (London; 1876 repr. Bristol, 1991).

GOLDIE, MARK, 'John Locke, Jonas Proast and Religious Toleration 1688–1692', in John Walsh, Colin Haydon, and Stephen Taylor (eds.), *The Church of England c. 1689–c. 1833: From Toleration to Tractarianism* (Cambridge, 1993), 143–71.

GREENSLADE, S. L., *The Cambridge History of the Bible: The West from the Reformation to the Present Day* (Cambridge, 1963).

HARRIS, IAN, *The Mind of John Locke, a Study of Political Theory in its Intellectual Setting* (Cambridge, 1994; rev. edn. 1998).

—— 'The Politics of Christianity', in G. A. J. Rogers (ed.), *Locke's Philosophy: Content and Context* (Oxford, 1994).

HILL, CHRISTOPHER, *The World Turned Upside Down* (London, 1972).

—— *The English Bible and the Seventeenth-Century Revolution* (London, 1993).

HUNTER MICHAEL, *Science and the Shape of Orthodoxy* (Woodbridge, Suffolk, 1995).

HUNTER, MICHAEL and WOOTON, DAVID (eds.), *Atheism from the Reformation to Enlightenment* (Oxford, 1992).

ISRAEL, JONATHAN, *Radical Enlightenment* (Oxford, 2001).

JAEGER, WERNER, *Early Christianity and Greek Paideia* (Cambridge, Mass., 1961).

KING, PETER, *The Life of John Locke, with extracts from his correspondence, journals and common-place books,* new edn. in 2 vols. (London, 1830; repr. Bristol, 1991).

KRETZMANN, NORMAN, *et al.*, *The Cambridge History of Later Medieval Philosophy* (Cambridge, 1982).

KROLL, RICHARD, ASHCRAFT, RICHARD, and ZAGORIN, PEREZ (eds.), *Philosophy, Science, and Religion in England, 1640–1700* (Cambridge, 1992).

MCLACHLAN, HERBERT, *The Religious Opinions of Milton, Locke and Newton* (Manchester, 1941).

MCLACHLAN, H. JOHN, *Socinianism in Seventeenth-Century England* (Oxford, 1951).

MARSHALL, JOHN, *John Locke: Resistance, Religion and Responsibility* (Cambridge, 1994).

MOMIGLIANO, ARNALDO, *Alien Wisdom, The Limits of Hellenization* (Cambridge, 1975).

BIBLIOGRAPHY 283

MOORE, JOHN T., 'Locke's Analysis of Language and the Assent to Scripture', *Journal of the History of Ideas*, 37/4 (1978), 707–4.

—— 'Locke on the Moral Need for Christianity', *Southwestern Journal of Philosophy*, 11/1 (1980), 61–8.

NUOVO, VICTOR, 'Locke's Theology, 1694–1704', in M. A. Stewart (ed.), *English Philosophy in the Age of Locke* (Oxford, 2000), 183–215.

—— 'Introduction' to John Locke, *The Reasonableness of Christianity* (Bristol, 1997), pp. v–xxx.

—— Review of *The Reasonableness of Christianity*, ed. John C. Higgins-Biddle, *The Locke Newsletter*, 30 (2000), 159–77.

—— (ed.), *John Locke and Christianity: Contemporary Responses to the Reasonableness of Christianity* (Bristol, 1997).

PASSMORE, JOHN, *Ralph Cudworth, An Interpretation* (Cambridge, 1951; repr. Bristol, 1990).

—— 'Locke and the Ethics of Belief', in Vere Chapell (ed.), *Locke* (Oxford, 1998).

POCOCK, J. G. A., *Politics, Language & Time* (Chicago, 1989).

POPKIN, RICHARD H., *Isaac Le Peyrère (1596–1676). His Life, Work and Influence* (Leiden, 1987).

PORTER, NOAH, *Marginalia Locke-a-na*, in Thomas Burnet, *Remarks Upon an Essay concerning Humane Understanding.*

RIVERS, ISABEL, *Reason, Grace, and Sentiment, A Study of the Language of Religion and Ethics in England 1660–1780*, 2 vols. (Cambridge, 1991, 2000).

ROGERS, G. A. J., *Locke's Enlightenment* (Hildesheim, 1998).

—— (ed.), *Locke's Philosophy: Content and Context* (Oxford, 1995).

SCHOULS, PETER A., 'John Locke: Optimist or Pessimist?', *British Journal for the History of Philosophy*, 2/2 (September, 1994), 51–74.

SELL, ALAN P. F., *John Locke and the Eighteenth-Century Divines* (Cardiff, 1997).

SPELLMAN, WILLIAM M., *John Locke and the Problem of Depravity* (Oxford, 1988).

—— *John Locke* (London, 1999).

SPURR, JOHN, *The Restoration Church of England* (New Haven, 1991).

STEWART, M. A., Review of Horvitz, Clay, and Clay, *Questions on the Law of Nature*, in *The Locke Newsletter*, 23 (1992), 145–65.

—— 'Stillingfleet and the Way of Ideas', in M. A. Stewart (ed.), *English Philosophy in the Age of Locke* (Oxford, 2000).

—— (ed.), *English Philosophy in the Age of Locke* (Oxford, 2000).

STRAUSS, LEO, *Natural Right and History* (Chicago, 1959).

TULLOCH, JOHN, *Rational Theology and Christian Philosophy in England in the Seventeenth Century*, 2 vols. (Edinburgh, 1874).

TULLY, JAMES, 'Locke', in J. H. Burns (ed.), *The Cambridge History of Political Thought 1450–1700* (Cambridge, 1991), 616–56.

TYACKE, NICHOLAS, *The Anti-Calvinists* (Oxford, 1987; 2nd edn. 1990).

—— (ed.), *The History of the University of Oxford, Vol. IV. Seventeenth-Century Oxford* (Oxford, 1997).

BIBLIOGRAPHY

VERNON, RICHARD, 'Locke's Antagonist, Jonas Proast', *The Locke Newsletter*, 24 (1993), 95.

WALLACE, DEWEY D., 'Socinianism, Justification by Faith, and the Sources of John Locke's *The Reasonableness of Christianity*', *Journal of the History of Ideas*, 45/1 (1984), 49–66.

WALSH, JOHN, HAYDON, COLIN, and TAYLOR, STEPHEN (eds.), *The Church of England c. 1689–c. 1833: From Toleration to Tractarianism* (Cambridge, 1993).

WOLTERSTORFF, NICHOLAS, *John Locke and the Ethics of Belief* (Cambridge, 1996).

YOLTON, JOHN W., *John Locke and the Way of Ideas* (Cambridge and Oxford, 1968).

—— *Locke and the Compass of Human Understanding* (Cambridge, 1970).

—— *Thinking Matter: Materialism in Eighteenth-Century Britain* (Minneapolis, 1983).

—— *Perceptual Acquaintance from Descartes to Reid* (Minneapolis, 1984).

—— *Locke and French Materialism* (Oxford, 1991).

—— *A Locke Dictionary* (Oxford, 1993).

—— (ed.), *John Locke, Problems and Perspectives* (Cambridge, 1969).

YOUNG, B. W., *Religion and Enlightenment in Eighteenth-Century England: Theological Debate from Locke to Burke* (Oxford, 1998).

Index

Abraham xlix, 31–2, 38, 101, 187–8, 239

Adam
  as Son of God liv, 169
  Fall of 91–2, 229, 231
  heavenly 233
  original sin of, and its consequences (death, imputation of guilt) lii–liv, 22, 91–6, 229–30, 231, 237, 243, 274
  original state of, liv, 30–1, 92–3, 231, 242, 243, 252

adversaria, meaning of term xxi n. 15, xxix

Aholiab 38, 260

Anacarsis (Anacharsis) 12

angels xxx, 50, 94, 238–9, 247, *see also* spirits
  cognitive power of xviii, xxx–xxxii
  fall of xxx

articles of faith, *see* fundamental articles

apostles
  Jesus selection of 152–4, 196
  miracles of 126, 160
  preaching of 104–11, 115, 128–9, 152, 160, 164, 166–7, 176, 183–4
  see also Holy Spirit

Apostles' Creed 217

Aristotelianism xvii, xxi–xxii

Aristotle 10–11, 12, 64, 256

Atheism li, 211, 220, 270
  ostentation of wit as cause of 220, 273

Augustinianism xviii, xix

baptism

Bayle, Pierre xxviii–xxix, 18, 258

Baxter, Richard, on the law of faith and the law of nature xlvi n. 82

Bible 54–6
  as infallible book xxiii
  harmony of 267
  see also Scripture(s)

Biddle (Bidle), John xxxii, 24–8, 258, 259, 273

Bold, Samuel xv n. 1, xlv, 271

Burnet, Thomas xv n. 2, xxviii n. 32

Calvin, John xlv, 32, 265, 268
  on the law of faith xlvi

candle of the lord *see* light of nature, natural religion

Chillingworth, William xxxix–xl

Christ, meaning of the term 103
  see also Jesus Christ, messiah

Christianity, *see* gospel

church xxxix–xlii
  as supernatural society 80
  as voluntary society 75, 80
  independent 78–9, *see also* Congregationalism
  national 77, 263–4
  true notion and end of 73–4
  see also Church of England, Church of Rome

Church of England xx, 77, *see also* Latitudinarianism

Church of Rome xxxix–xl, xlii, 76, 77

Cicero (Tully) xxxii, 54, 262
  De legibus 258

286 INDEX

Cicero (Tully) (*cont.*)
  De natura deorum 18, 258
  Tusculan Disputations 17, 258
Confucius 12
Congregationalism xlii
covenant(s) xlvi, lvi, 101, 182–4,
    208
  of grace (new covenant) 167, 169,
    182, 207, 231
credenda 30, 259, *see also*
    fundamental article(s)
Croft, Herbert 270, 271
custom 262

death
  consequence of Adam's sin 92–6,
    242
  meaning of the word 93, 97 n.
  of the wicked 235–6
  see also mortalism
Deism xxiv, xlviii
devils 115, 126
  faith of 167
disciples 132, 134, *see also* apostles
divine right (*jure divino*) 263

Edwards, John xv. n. 2, li–lii,
    211–25 *passim*, 269
Edwards, Thomas 268–9
election, doctrine of 32–3
Enlightenment lvii
Episcopius, Simon xvii, 28, 259–60
Epistles of St Paul
  as part of the English language 56
  Locke's rule of interpretation
    58–60
  style of 61
  see also New Testament Epistles
ethics, *see* morality

faith xlvii–xlviii, 101–3,
    historical 166, 268
  obedience of 269

see also fundamental article(s),
    justification by faith, law of faith
Firmicus Maternus, Julius 92n., 265
Fleetwood, William xxxvi–xxxvii, 50
fundamental article(s) (fundamentals)
    xlv, 81, 101–2, 203, 208,
    216–17, 221–4, 269
  in New Testament Epistles 205–7,
    215–17
  St John's preaching of 166
  St Paul's preaching of 165

God
  as *Deus Optimus Maximus* xxx, 21
  as sovereign lawmaker 14
  attributes of 248, 249
  free grace of 173, 184, 205–6,
    268–9
  image of 169–72
  justice of 94–5
  knowledge of existence of 252,
    254
  mercy of, to those who did not
    receive the gospel 190–1
  providence of 120, 191
  purity of his nature requires a strict
    law 96
  see also religion, revelation,
    theology, monotheism, Trinity
good, as pleasure 15, *see also*
    happiness
gospel 33, 82–3, 91–210 *passim*,
    241
  Jesus promulgation of 122–8,
    155–7
  see also fundamental articles,
    doctrine of redemption
great chain of being 251–2

happiness 9, 16, *see also* good
    and misery, innate practical
    principles 246
hell 236
Hoadly, Benjamin xxxvi

INDEX

Holy Spirit (Holy Ghost) 23, 27–8, 112, 204
  promised to Apostles 159–61
Hooker, Richard
  on the nature of the church xlii–xliv, 80, 264
  on the law of faith xlvi–xlvii
human knowledge
  adequate for the business of life 245, 256
  limitation of 252–3, 255
  see also mankind

ideas 250
  complex 10
  innate xxxiv, 38–9, 40, 245
immorality xlix, 9, 171
immortality 232, 236, loss of 92, *see also* resurrection, soul
imputation of guilt, *see* Adam
infallibility xxiii–xxxiv, xxix–xliv, 5
  and interpretation of Scripture 65–6, 69–72

Jesus Christ 22–3
  advantage of 191–205
  as bearer of divine revelation xxiv, 17, 91–210 *passim*
  as king 114, 117, 119, 148, 162, 172–3, 175, *see also* kingdom of God
  as messiah, *see* messiah
  as priest lvi, 175, 239, 241
  as prophet 175
  as second Adam lvi, 95
  as son of God 106–7, 111, 112, 129, 169–70, 238, 273
  concealment of identity (messianic secret) 115–55, 266, 268
  delivers up Kingdom 234, 236
  expiatory death of lvi 33, 172, *see also* Satisfaction
  humanity and divinity of xxxii, 25–7, 259

moral teaching of xlix, 17–18, 121, 176–83, 198, 202–4
  preaching of, *see* gospel
  resurrection of liv, 164–5, 232
  second coming 155–8, 184, 232, 236–7, 267–8, *see also* Last Judgment
  superior to angels lvi
  union with God 159
  virgin birth of 169
  see also gospel
John the Baptist 126, 131, 176
  testimony of concerning Jesus as messiah 112–13
justification by faith xlv, 101–3, 166–7, 173–5, 186–9, 210, 241, 242, 244, 268–9
Justin Martyr, *see* mortalism

kingdom of God 112, 115, 119, 121, 148, 162, 233, 234, 238

language, Locke's theory of 250–1
Last Judgment xix, xlix, 133–4, 175, 184–6, *see also* Jesus Christ
Latitudinarianism xx, xxi n. 14, xxxv
law of faith xxxi, xlvi, 31–2, 98–100, 174–5, 207–9
  see also Baxter, Richard; Calvin, John; Hooker, Richard; Westminster Assembly of Divines
law of nature 96, 190–9, 209 *see also* law of works; religion, natural
law of works (law of Moses) xxxi, 31, 98–101, 117, 168, 241, 243
  spiritual meaning of 243–4
Lepeyrère, Isaac
  pre-Adamite theory 265
light of nature xlix, 74, 190, 197
  see also morality; religion, natural
Limborch, Philippus van xv n. 1, xvii, xliv–xlv, 265

288 INDEX

Locke, John
on morality xxvii–xxix, xlix–l,
9–16, 246, 249–50, 253, 255,
266, see also law of nature,
morality
realism of xxiii, xxxviii
religion and theology in the
thought of xv–xxi
Writings of:
A discourse of Miracles xxxvi–xxxvii
A Letter concerning Toleration xv
n. 2, 270
*A Second Vindication of the
Reasonableness of Christianity* xlv
n. 2, li
*A Paraphrase and Notes to the
Epistles of St Paul* xxxi,
xxxvii–xxxviii, lv
*A Vindication of the Reasonableness
of Christianity* li–lii
'Adversaria Theologica 94'
xxix–xxxii
*An Essay concerning Human
Understanding* xxiv–xxvi, xxxiii,
245–56
*An Essay for the Understanding of St
Paul's Epistles* xxxvii–xxxix
'Christianae Religionis synopsis' lvi
'Critical Notes upon Edward
Stillingfleet's *Mischief* and
Unreasonableness of Separation'
xli–xlii
'Ecclesia' xlii–xliii
'Error' xliii–xliv
'Ethica' xxviii
Fourth Letter concerning Toleration
xv n. 2
'Homo ante et post lapsum' liv
'Immediate Inspiration' xxxiii–xxxv
'Infallibility' xxxix–xli
*New Method of a Common-Place
Book* xxxi
'Of Ethick in General' xxvii–xxviii

*Of the Conduct of the
Understanding* xxii–xxiii
'On the Priesthood of Christ' lv–lvi
'Peccatum originale' lii–liv
The Reasonableness of Christianity
xv n. 2, xxxi, xxxviii, xliv–l, xlviii
liv, lv, lvi, 211–25 *passim*
'Resurrectio et quae sequuntur'
liv–lv
'Sacerdos' xxviii–xxix
'Scriptura Sacra' xxxv–xxxvi
*Some Considerations of the
Consequences of the Lowering of
Interest* 270
'Spirit, Soul, and Body' 259
mankind 22
as rational creature 49, 96, 191,
255–6
fall of 30 see also Adam, human
knowledge
free agency of 30, 259–60
matter 21
Melchisidec (Melchizedek) 239,
274
messiah
expectation of 111–13, 120
faith in Jesus as xlv, xlvii, 102–4
kingdom of 114
prophecies concerning 111–12,
136, 139, 164
threefold declaration of Jesus as
113–15
see also Jesus Christ
miracles xxxvi–xxxvii, 44–50, 102–3,
113–14, 117, 142, 153, 191,
194, 238, 255
standing 48
monotheism 45, 192–94
morality 82–3
in pagan antiquity 17–18,
194–201
as divine law implanted in human
nature 74
see also Locke, John; law of nature

INDEX

mortalism, doctrine of xxxiii, 93, 94, 97n., 98, 265–6
Moses 38, 98–9, 117, 164, 193, 239
  law of, *see* law of works
  revelation to xxxiv, lv, 45, 49

New Testament Epistles 211–12
  causes of obscurity in 51–2
  see also fundamental article(s)
Nye, Philip 260, 262, 273

original sin, *see* Adam
orthodoxy, and heresy 81–3

paideia xviii
Paradise 93–4
Patrick, Simon 97n., 224–5, 274
personal identity 249–50, 259
Plato 192
Platonism, as cause of misreading the New Testament 64
pragmatics of assent xxvi
Proast, Jonas xv n. 2, lii–liii, 230
prophecy 40
  spirit of 27, 113

Racovians 219, 272–3, *see* Socinianism, Unitarianism
rational theologian, definition of xx
real presence, doctrine of 250
reasonableness, meaning of applied to Christianity xlv, xlvii–l, 169
redemption 33
  doctrine of 91, *see also* gospel
Reformation xlv, lvii
religion
  definition of xvi, 73
  Jesus' reform of 202–3
  natural xix, xxi, xxiv–xxv, xlix–l, 5–6, 74, 91, 191–5, 246–7, 247, 250–1
  see also Locke, John; theology
Remonstrants and Anti-Remonstrants 223, 273

repentance xlviii
  as absolute condition of new covenant 167–83
resurrection liv–lv
  of the saints 233–4
  of the wicked 234–5
  order of 232
revelation 23–50, 208–9, 253–4
  immediate 60, 63
  traditional 199–201, 260
  see also Jesus Christ, monotheism, Moses, Scripture(s)
Roman Catholic Church, *see* Church of Rome

St Paul xix, xxxvii–xxxix, 45
  on justification 99–101, 188–9
  on the resurrection liv, 232–3, 235–6
  on the schools of Tyranny 37, 260
  possessed the whole gospel by revelation 60, 63, 262
  style and temper of his thoughts 52–3, 63, 65
  see also apostles, Epistles of St Paul, fundamental article(s), law of faith, law of works
Satisfaction, doctrine of 32, 212–13, 271–2
  see also Jesus Christ, expiatory death of
Scripture(s)
  clarity of moral instruction 71–2
  interpretation of xxiv, xxxviii, xxxix–xli, 5–6, 51–66, 205, 252, *see also* infallibility
  inspiration of xxxvi
  mysteries of 71
  see also Bible
Selden, John 55, 262
Simon, Richard 261
sin 95, 97, *see also* Adam
  universality of 96
Smith, John, on prophecy 92n., 265

290 INDEX

Socinianism li–lii, 211–25 *passim*, 271
  akin to atheism 211
  see also Unitarianism
soul xxx, xxxii–xxxiii, 21
  cognitive state before the fall 260
  materiality or immateriality of 28–30, 259
  see also mortalism
spirits 21, 22, 254, 258, *see also* angels
Stillingfleet, Edward xv n. 2, xxxiii n. 43, xlii, 73–9, 263–4
Strauss, Leo xxv n. 23

Taylor, Jeremy xl n. 66, xli, 211, 270, 271

theology xxiii
  definition of xvi, 3
  sources of xxi–xxii
  see also Locke, John
Tillotson, John xviii, liii, 97n., 236, 266, 273
Trinity 23–4, 25–7, 219, 262
Turretin, Francis 265, 268

Unitarianism xxxii, *see also* Racovian

Westminster Assembly of Divines xlvi, 259
wicked, eternal torment of the 234, 235–8
Willis, Richard xv n. 2